Short Stories
for Students

Presenting Analysis, Context, and Criticism on Commonly Studied Short Stories

Volume 15

Carol Ullmann, Editor

GALE®

Detroit • New York • San Diego • San Francisco • Cleveland • New Haven, Conn. • Waterville, Maine • London • Munich

National Advisory Board

Short Stories
for Students

Short Stories for Students

Carol Ullmann

Project Editor
David Galens

Editorial
Anne Marie Hacht, Michelle Kazensky, Michael L. LaBlanc, Ira Mark Milne, Pam Revitzer, Jennifer Smith, Daniel Toronto

Research
Nicodemus Ford, Sarah Genik, Tamara Nott, Tracie A. Richardson

Permissions
Debra Freitas, Shalice Shah-Caldwell

Manufacturing
Stacy Melson

Imaging and Multimedia
Lezlie Light, Kelly A. Quin, Luke Rademacher

Product Design
Michelle DiMercurio, Pamela A. E. Galbreath, Michael Logusz

ISBN 0-7876-4267-3
ISSN 1092-7735

Printed in the United States of America
10 9 8 7 6 5 4 3 2 1

Table of Contents

Why Study Literature At All?

Short Stories for Students is designed to provide readers with information and discussion about a wide range of important contemporary and historical works of short fiction, and it does that job very well. However, I want to use this guest foreword to address a question that it does *not* take up. It is a fundamental question that is often ignored in high school and college English classes as well as research texts, and one that causes frustration among students at all levels, namely—why study literature at all? Isn't it enough to read a story, enjoy it, and go about one's business? My answer (to be expected from a literary professional, I suppose) is no. It is not enough. It is a start; but it is not enough. Here's why.

First, literature is the only part of the educational curriculum that deals directly with the actual world of lived experience. The philosopher Edmund Husserl used the apt German term *die Lebenswelt,* "the living world," to denote this realm. All the other content areas of the modern American educational system avoid the subjective, present reality of everyday life. Science (both the natural and the social varieties) objectifies, the fine arts create and/or perform, history reconstructs. Only literary study persists in posing those questions we all asked before our schooling taught us to give up on them. Only literature gives credibility to personal perceptions, feelings, dreams, and the "stream of consciousness" that is our inner voice. Literature wonders about infinity, wonders why God permits evil, wonders what will happen to us after we die. Literature admits that we get our hearts broken, that people sometimes cheat and get away with it, that the world is a strange and probably incomprehensible place. Literature, in other words, takes on all the big and small issues of what it means to be human. So my first answer is that of the humanist—we should read literature and study it and take it seriously because it enriches us as human beings. We develop our moral imagination, our capacity to sympathize with other people, and our ability to understand our existence through the experience of fiction.

My second answer is more practical. By studying literature we can learn how to explore and analyze texts. Fiction may be about *die Lebenswelt,* but it is a construct of words put together in a certain order by an artist using the medium of language. By examining and studying those constructions, we can learn about language as a medium. We can become more sophisticated about word associations and connotations, about the manipulation of symbols, and about style and atmosphere. We can grasp how ambiguous language is and how important context and texture is to meaning. In our first encounter with a work of literature, of course, we are not supposed to catch all of these things. We are spellbound, just as the writer wanted us to be. It is as serious students of the writer's art that we begin to see how the tricks are done.

Seeing the tricks, which is another way of saying "developing analytical and close reading skills," is important above and beyond its intrinsic literary educational value. These skills transfer to other fields and enhance critical thinking of any kind. Understanding how language is used to construct texts is powerful knowledge. It makes engineers better problem solvers, lawyers better advocates and courtroom practitioners, politicians better rhetoricians, marketing and advertising agents better sellers, and citizens more aware consumers as well as better participants in democracy. This last point is especially important, because rhetorical skill works both ways—when we learn how language is manipulated in the making of texts the result is that we become less susceptible when language is used to manipulate us.

My third reason is related to the second. When we begin to see literature as created artifacts of language, we become more sensitive to good writing in general. We get a stronger sense of the importance of individual words, even the sounds of words and word combinations. We begin to understand Mark Twain's delicious proverb—"The difference between the right word and the almost right word is the difference between lightning and a lightning bug." Getting beyond the "enjoyment only" stage of literature gets us closer to becoming makers of word art ourselves. I am not saying that studying fiction will turn every student into a Faulkner or a Shakespeare. But it will make us more adaptable and effective writers, even if our art form ends up being the office memo or the corporate annual report.

Studying short stories, then, can help students become better readers, better writers, and even better human beings. But I want to close with a warning. If your study and exploration of the craft, history, context, symbolism, or anything else about a story starts to rob it of the magic you felt when you first read it, it is time to stop. Take a break, study another subject, shoot some hoops, or go for a run. Love of reading is too important to be ruined by school. The early twentieth century writer Willa Cather, in her novel *My Antonia*, has her narrator Jack Burden tell a story that he and Antonia heard from two old Russian immigrants when they were teenagers. These immigrants, Pavel and Peter, told about an incident from their youth back in Russia that the narrator could recall in vivid detail thirty years later. It was a harrowing story of a wedding party starting home in sleds and being chased by starving wolves. Hundreds of wolves attacked the group's sleds one by one as they sped across the snow trying to reach their village. In a horrible revelation, the old Russians revealed that the groom eventually threw his own bride to the wolves to save himself. There was even a hint that one of the old immigrants might have been the groom mentioned in the story. Cather has her narrator conclude with his feelings about the story. "We did not tell Pavel's secret to anyone, but guarded it jealously—as if the wolves of the Ukraine had gathered that night long ago, and the wedding party had been sacrificed, just to give us a painful and peculiar pleasure." That feeling, that painful and peculiar pleasure, is the most important thing about literature. Study and research should enhance that feeling and never be allowed to overwhelm it.

Thomas E. Barden
Professor of English and
Director of Graduate English Studies
The University of Toledo

Introduction

Purpose of the Book

The purpose of *Short Stories for Students* (*SSfS*) is to provide readers with a guide to understanding, enjoying, and studying short stories by giving them easy access to information about the work. Part of Gale's "For Students" Literature line, *SSfS* is specifically designed to meet the curricular needs of high school and undergraduate college students and their teachers, as well as the interests of general readers and researchers considering specific short fiction. While each volume contains entries on "classic" stories frequently studied in classrooms, there are also entries containing hard-to-find information on contemporary stories, including works by multicultural, international, and women writers.

The information covered in each entry includes an introduction to the story and the story's author; a plot summary, to help readers unravel and understand the events in the work; descriptions of important characters, including explanation of a given character's role in the narrative as well as discussion about that character's relationship to other characters in the story; analysis of important themes in the story; and an explanation of important literary techniques and movements as they are demonstrated in the work.

In addition to this material, which helps the readers analyze the story itself, students are also provided with important information on the literary and historical background informing each work.

This includes a historical context essay, a box comparing the time or place the story was written to modern Western culture, a critical overview essay, and excerpts from critical essays on the story or author. A unique feature of *SSfS* is a specially commissioned critical essay on each story, targeted toward the student reader.

To further aid the student in studying and enjoying each story, information on media adaptations is provided (if available), as well as reading suggestions for works of fiction and nonfiction on similar themes and topics. Classroom aids include ideas for research papers and lists of critical sources that provide additional material on the work.

Selection Criteria

The titles for each volume of *SSfS* were selected by surveying numerous sources on teaching literature and analyzing course curricula for various school districts. Some of the sources surveyed include: literature anthologies, *Reading Lists for College-Bound Students: The Books Most Recommended by America's Top Colleges*; *Teaching the Short Story: A Guide to Using Stories from around the World*, by the National Council of Teachers of English (NCTE); and "A Study of High School Literature Anthologies," conducted by Arthur Applebee at the Center for the Learning and Teaching of Literature and sponsored by the National Endowment for the Arts and the Office of Educational Research and Improvement.

Input was also solicited from our advisory board, as well as educators from various areas. From these discussions, it was determined that each volume should have a mix of "classic" stories (those works commonly taught in literature classes) and contemporary stories for which information is often hard to find. Because of the interest in expanding the canon of literature, an emphasis was also placed on including works by international, multicultural, and women authors. Our advisory board members—educational professionals—helped pare down the list for each volume. Works not selected for the present volume were noted as possibilities for future volumes. As always, the editor welcomes suggestions for titles to be included in future volumes.

How Each Entry Is Organized

Each entry, or chapter, in *SSfS* focuses on one story. Each entry heading lists the title of the story, the author's name, and the date of the story's publication. The following elements are contained in each entry:

- **Introduction:** a brief overview of the story which provides information about its first appearance, its literary standing, any controversies surrounding the work, and major conflicts or themes within the work.

- **Author Biography:** this section includes basic facts about the author's life, and focuses on events and times in the author's life that may have inspired the story in question.

- **Plot Summary:** a description of the events in the story. Lengthy summaries are broken down with subheads.

- **Characters:** an alphabetical listing of the characters who appear in the story. Each character name is followed by a brief to an extensive description of the character's role in the story, as well as discussion of the character's actions, relationships, and possible motivation.

  Characters are listed alphabetically by last name. If a character is unnamed—for instance, the narrator in "The Eatonville Anthology"—the character is listed as "The Narrator" and alphabetized as "Narrator." If a character's first name is the only one given, the name will appear alphabetically by that name.

- **Themes:** a thorough overview of how the topics, themes, and issues are addressed within the story. Each theme discussed appears in a sepa-

rate subhead, and is easily accessed through the boldface entries in the Subject/Theme Index.

- **Style:** this section addresses important style elements of the story, such as setting, point of view, and narration; important literary devices used, such as imagery, foreshadowing, symbolism; and, if applicable, genres to which the work might have belonged, such as Gothicism or Romanticism. Literary terms are explained within the entry, but can also be found in the Glossary.

- **Historical Context:** this section outlines the social, political, and cultural climate *in which the author lived and the work was created.* This section may include descriptions of related historical events, pertinent aspects of daily life in the culture, and the artistic and literary sensibilities of the time in which the work was written. If the story is historical in nature, information regarding the time in which the story is set is also included. Long sections are broken down with helpful subheads.

- **Critical Overview:** this section provides background on the critical reputation of the author and the story, including bannings or any other public controversies surrounding the work. For older works, this section may include a history of how the story was first received and how perceptions of it may have changed over the years; for more recent works, direct quotes from early reviews may also be included.

- **Criticism:** an essay commissioned by *SSfS* which specifically deals with the story and is written specifically for the student audience, as well as excerpts from previously published criticism on the work (if available).

- **Sources:** an alphabetical list of critical material used in compiling the entry, with bibliographical information.

- **Further Reading:** an alphabetical list of other critical sources which may prove useful for the student. It includes bibliographical information and a brief annotation.

In addition, each entry contains the following highlighted sections, set apart from the main text as sidebars:

- **Media Adaptations:** if available, a list of film and television adaptations of the story, including source information. The list also includes stage adaptations, audio recordings, musical adaptations, etc.

- **Topics for Further Study:** a list of potential study questions or research topics dealing with the story. This section includes questions related to other disciplines the student may be studying, such as American history, world history, science, math, government, business, geography, economics, psychology, etc.

- **Compare and Contrast:** an ''at-a-glance'' comparison of the cultural and historical differences between the author's time and culture and late twentieth century or early twenty-first century Western culture. This box includes pertinent parallels between the major scientific, political, and cultural movements of the time or place the story was written, the time or place the story was set (if a historical work), and modern Western culture. Works written after 1990 may not have this box.

- **What Do I Read Next?:** a list of works that might complement the featured story or serve as a contrast to it. This includes works by the same author and others, works of fiction and nonfiction, and works from various genres, cultures, and eras.

Other Features

SSfS includes ''Why Study Literature At All?,'' a foreword by Thomas E. Barden, Professor of English and Director of Graduate English Studies at the University of Toledo. This essay provides a number of very fundamental reasons for studying literature and, therefore, reasons why a book such as *SSfS*, designed to facilitate the study of literture, is useful.

A Cumulative Author/Title Index lists the authors and titles covered in each volume of the *SSfS* series.

A Cumulative Nationality/Ethnicity Index breaks down the authors and titles covered in each volume of the *SSfS* series by nationality and ethnicity.

A Subject/Theme Index, specific to each volume, provides easy reference for users who may be studying a particular subject or theme rather than a single work. Significant subjects from events to broad themes are included, and the entries pointing to the specific theme discussions in each entry are indicated in **boldface**.

Each entry may include illustrations, including photo of the author, stills from film adaptations (if available), maps, and/or photos of key historical events.

Citing Short Stories for Students

When writing papers, students who quote directly from any volume of *SSfS* may use the following general forms to document their source. These examples are based on MLA style; teachers may request that students adhere to a different style, thus, the following examples may be adapted as needed.

When citing text from *SSfS* that is not attributed to a particular author (for example, the Themes, Style, Historical Context sections, etc.), the following format may be used:

''The Celebrated Jumping Frog of Calavaras County.'' *Short Stories for Students*. Ed. Kathleen Wilson. Vol. 1. Detroit: Gale, 1997. 19–20.

When quoting the specially commissioned essay from *SSfS* (usually the first essay under the Criticism subhead), the following format may be used:

Korb, Rena. Critical essay on ''Children of the Sea.'' *Short Stories for Students*. Ed. Kathleen Wilson. Vol. 1. Detroit: Gale, 1997. 42.

When quoting a journal or newspaper essay that is reprinted in a volume of *Short Stories for Students*, the following form may be used:

Schmidt, Paul. ''The Deadpan on Simon Wheeler.'' *Southwest Review* Vol. XLI, No. 3 (Summer, 1956), 270–77; excerpted and reprinted in *Short Stories for Students*, Vol. 1, ed. Kathleen Wilson. (Detroit: Gale, 1997), pp. 29–31.

When quoting material from a book that is reprinted in a volume of *SSfS,* the following form may be used:

Bell-Villada, Gene H. ''The Master of Short Forms,'' in *Garcia Marquez: The Man and His Work*. University of North Carolina Press, 1990 pp. 119–300; excerpted and reprinted in *Short Stories for Students*, Vol. 1, ed. Kathleen Wilson (Detroit: Gale, 1997), pp. 89–90.

We Welcome Your Suggestions

The editor of *Short Stories for Students* welcomes your comments and ideas. Readers who wish to suggest short stories to appear in future volumes, or who have other suggestions, are cordially invited to contact the editor. You may contact the editor via E-mail at: **ForStudentsEditors@gale.com.** Or write to the editor at:

Editor, *Short Stories for Students*
The Gale Group
27500 Drake Road
Farmington Hills, MI 48331–3535

Literary Chronology

1804: Nathaniel Hawthorne is born on Independence Day in Salem, Massachusetts.

1832: Nathaniel Hawthorne's "The Wives of the Dead" is published.

1864: Nathaniel Hawthorne dies in his sleep in May while visiting former president Franklin Pierce in Plymouth, New Hampshire.

1870: Saki is born Hector H. Munro on December 18 in Burma to a British army officer and his wife.

1885: Anzia Yezierska is born circa October 19 in Plinsk, a town on the Russian-Polish border.

1896: F. Scott Fitzgerald is born on September 24 in St. Paul, Minnesota.

1899: Vladimir Nabokov is born on April 23 in St. Petersburg, Russia, to an upper-class family.

1906: Samuel Beckett is born on April 13 in Foxrock, near Dublin, Ireland, to a middle-class Protestant family.

1908: Richard Wright is born on Rucker's Plantation on September 4 in Roxie, Mississippi.

1912: Saadat Hasan Manto is born on May 11 in Samrala, India.

1916: Saki (H. H. Munro) is killed by sniper fire on November 14.

1919: Saki's (H. H. Munro's) "The Interlopers" is published.

1922: Alain Robbe-Grillet is born on August 18 in Saint-Pierre-Quilbignon, France, a municipality that is now part of Brest in Brittany.

1922: F. Scott Fitzgerald's "Winter Dreams" is published.

1923: Anzia Yezierska's "America and I" is published.

1929: Paule Marshall is born on April 9 in Brooklyn, New York, the child of Barbadian immigrants.

1930: Grace Ogot is born in the Central Nyanza area of Kenya.

1934: Samuel Beckett's "Dante and the Lobster" is published.

1934: Harlan Ellison is born on May 27 in Cleveland, Ohio.

1935: Tomás Rivera is born on December 22 in Crystal City, Texas, the son of Mexican immigrants.

1938: Richard Wright's "Bright and Morning Star" is published.

1940: F. Scott Fitzgerald dies on December 21 of a heart attack, probably brought on by his alcoholism.

1943: Vladimir Nabokov's "That in Aleppo Once . . ." is published.

1946: Tim O'Brien is born on October 1 in Austin, Minnesota.

1955: Saadat Hasan Manto dies on January 18. The cause is diagnosed as cirrhosis of the liver.

1957: Beatriz Rivera is born on September 27 in Havana, Cuba, but, at the age of three, she immigrates to the United States.

1960: Richard Wright dies on November 28 in Paris, France. The official cause of death is given as a heart attack; however, some people suspect murder.

1962: Alain Robbe-Grillet's "The Replacement" is published.

1967: Harlan Ellison's "I Have No Mouth, and I Must Scream" is published.

1967: Paule Marshall's "To Da-duh, in Memoriam" is published.

1968: Grace Ogot's "The Green Leaves" is published.

1969: Samuel Beckett wins the Nobel Prize for literature.

1970: Anzia Yezierska dies on November 21 of a stroke in Ontario, California.

1977: Vladimir Nabokov dies of a lung ailment, with Vera (wife) and Dmitri (son) at his hospital bedside.

1984: Tomás Rivera dies on May 16 of a heart attack in Fontana, California.

1987: Saadat Hasan Manto's "The Dog of Tithwal" is published.

1987: Tim O'Brien's "How to Tell a True War Story" is published.

1989: Samuel Beckett, diagnosed with emphysema in 1986, dies of respiratory failure in December.

1989: Tomás Rivera's "The Harvest" is published.

1995: Beatriz Rivera's "African Passions" is published.

Acknowledgments

The editors wish to thank the copyright holders of the excerpted criticism included in this volume and the permissions managers of many book and magazine publishing companies for assisting us in securing reproduction rights. We are also grateful to the staffs of the Detroit Public Library, the Library of Congress, the University of Detroit Mercy Library, Wayne State University Purdy/Kresge Library Complex, and the University of Michigan Libraries for making their resources available to us. Following is a list of the copyright holders who have granted us permission to reproduce material in this volume of **Short Stories for Students (SSfS)**. Every effort has been made to trace copyright, but if omissions have been made, please let us know.

COPYRIGHTED MATERIALS IN *SSfS*, VOLUME 15, WERE REPRODUCED FROM THE FOLLOWING PERIODICALS:

African American Review, v. 34, Fall, 2000 for "Sugarcane as History in Paule Marshall's 'To Da-Duh, in Memoriam,'" by Martin Japtok. Copyright (c) 2000 *African American Review*. Reproduced by permission of the author.—*Extrapolation*, v. 32, Summer, 1991. (c) 1991 by The Kent State University Press. Reproduced by permission.—*Negro American Literature Forum*, v. 6, Winter, 1972. Reproduced by permission.—*Studies in Short Fiction*, v. 6, Summer, 1969; v. 20, Winter, 1983; v. 29 Summer, 1992. Copyright 1969, 1983,1992 by Newberry College. Reproduced by permission.

COPYRIGHTED MATERIALS IN *SSfS*, VOLUME 15, WERE REPRODUCED FROM THE FOLLOWING BOOKS:

Martin, Quentin E. From "Tamed or Idealized: Judy Jones's Dilemma in 'Winter Dreams,'" in *F. Scott Fitzgerald: New Perspectives*. Edited by Jackson R. Bryer, Alan Margolies, and Ruth Prigozy. The University of Georgia Press, 2000. (c) 2000 by the University of Georgia Perss. All rights reserved. Reproduced by permission.—Stevenson, Kay Gilliland. From "Belacqua in the Moon: Beckett's Revisions of 'Dante and Lobster,'" in *Critical Essays on Samuel Beckett*. Edited by Patrick A. McCarthy. G. K. Hall & Co., 1986. Copyright (c) 1986 by Patrick A. McCarthy. All rights reserved. Reproduced by permission.—Williams, Sherley Anne. From "Papa Dick and Sister-Woman: Reflections on Women in the Fiction of Richard Wright," in *American Novelists Revisited: Essays in Feminist Criticism*. Edited by Fritz Fleischmann. G. K. Hall & Co., 1982. Copyright (c) 1982 by Fritz Fleischmann. Reproduced by permission.

PHOTOGRAPHS AND ILLUSTRATIONS APPEARING IN *SSfS*, VOLUME 15, WERE RECEIVED FROM THE FOLLOWING SOURCES:

Beckett, Samuel, photograph. Archive Photos. Reproduced by permission.—"Dante and Virgil with the Condemned Souls in Eternal Ice," from Dante's "Divine Comedy," 15th century manuscript, painting. Archivo Iconographico, S.A./Corbis. Reproduced by permission.—Ellison, Harlan (seated on pool table), photograph by Chris Cuffaro. Reproduced by permission.—German troops riding down Champs Elysees from the Arc de Triomphe, after taking city of Paris, photograph. Hulton/Archive Photos. Reproduced by permission.—Hindu and Sikh women and children arriving at Bombay, on the British-India ocean liner "Owarka," photograph. Hulton/Archive Photos. Reproduced by permission.—Marshall, Paule, photograph. AP/Wide World Photos. Reproduced by permission.—Nabokov, Vladimir, photograph. AP/Wide World Photos. Reproduced by permission.—O'Brien, Tim, photograph (c) Jerry Bauer. Reproduced by permission.— "The Other Half; How It Lives and Dies in New York," magic lantern slide by Jacob Riis, family of Jewish tailors working in slum conditions, photograph. Hulton/Archive Photos. Reproduced by per-

mission.—Rivera, Tomás, photograph. Arte Público Press/University of Houston. Reproduced by permission.—Robbe-Grillet, Alain, photograph (c) Jerry Bauer. Reproduced by permission.—Santeria religious altar covered with figurines, photograph. (c) Robert van der Hilst/Corbis. Reproduced by permission.—A segregated outhouse at a Greyhound bus station in Louisville, Kentucky. Photograph by Esther Bubley. Corbis. Reproduced by permission.— Sugar cane cutters on sugar cane plantation taking break, in Barbados, photograph. Hulton/Archive Photos. Reproduced by permission.—United Farmworkers board members, Eliseo Median, Phillip Veracruz, Peter Velasco, Mack Lyons, Ceasar Chavez, Richard Chavez, unidentified aide to Cesar, and Dolores Huerta, all on a stage, photograph by Bob Titch. AP/Wide World Photo. Reproduced by permission.—Wright, Richard, photograph. Archive Photos. Reproduced by permission.

Contributors

Diane Andrews Henningfeld: Andrews Henningfeld is an associate professor at Adrian College in Adrian, Michigan, where she teaches literature and writing. She holds a Ph.D. in literature, and regularly writes book reviews, historical articles, and literary criticism for a wide variety of educational publishers. Entries on *How to Tell a True War Story* and *I Have No Mouth, and I Must Scream.* Original essays on *How to Tell a True War Story* and *I Have No Mouth, and I Must Scream.*

Bryan Aubrey: Aubrey holds a Ph.D. in English and has published many articles on twentieth-century literature. Entry on *The Harvest.* Original essay on *The Harvest.*

Greg Barnhisel: Barnhisel directs the writing center at the University of Southern California. Entry on *Dante and the Lobster.* Original essay on *Dante and the Lobster.*

Jennifer Bussey: Bussey holds a master's degree in interdisciplinary studies and a bachelor's degree in English Literature. She is an independent writer specializing in literature. Original essay on *That in Aleppo Once. . . .*

Kate Covintree: Covintree is a graduate of Randolph-Macon Women's College with a degree in English. Original essay on *America and I.*

Douglas Dupler: Dupler has published numerous essays and has taught college English. Original essay on *The Interlopers.*

Sandra Grady: Grady is a student in folklore and African studies. Original essay on *The Green Leaves.*

Joyce Hart: Hart has degrees in English literature and creative writing. Her published works are of literary themes. Entries on *African Passions* and *Bright and Morning Star.* Original essays on *African Passions* and *Bright and Morning Star.*

Catherine Dybiec Holm: Holm is a published writer and editor with a master's degree in natural resources. Original essay on *How to Tell a True War Story.*

Rena Korb: Korb has a master's degree in English literature and creative writing and has written for a wide variety of educational publishers. Entries on *America and I, The Interlopers,* and *To Da-duh, in Memoriam.* Original essays on *America and I, The Interlopers,* and *To Da-duh, in Memoriam.*

Laura Kryhoski: Kryhoski is currently employed as a freelance writer. Original essay on *African Passions.*

Daniel Moran: Moran is a teacher of English and American literature. Entry on *That in Aleppo*

Once.... Original essay on *That in Aleppo Once....*

Candyce Norvell: Norvell is an independent educational writer who specializes in English and literature. She holds degrees in linguistics and journalism. Entry on *The Dog of Tithwal*. Original essay on *The Dog of Tithwal*.

Wendy Perkins: Perkins is an instructor of English and American literature and film. Entries on *The Replacement* and *Winter Dreams*. Original essays on *The Replacement* and *Winter Dreams*.

Doreen Piano: Piano is a Ph.D. candidate in English at Bowling Green University in Ohio. Entry on *The Green Leaves*. Original essay on *The Green Leaves*.

Susan Sanderson: Sanderson holds a master of fine arts degree in fiction writing and is an independent writer. Original essays on *The Dog of Tithwal* and *The Harvest*.

Chris Semansky: Semansky is an instructor of literature and composition and publishes regularly in literary journals and magazines. Entry on *The Wives of the Dead*. Original essay on *The Wives of the Dead*.

African Passions

Beatriz Rivera

1995

Beatriz Rivera's short story "African Passions" first appeared in the *Bilingual Review* in 1995. In the same year, it was published by Arte Público Press in Rivera's first full-length book, a collection of short stories titled *African Passions and Other Stories*. The reaction to this collection, as well as to her subsequent books, has been very positive, with most critics praising Rivera for her sense of humor and intelligence, as well as for her memorable characters.

"African Passions" is a story about an ambitious and loving thirty-four-year-old woman, who, despite her lover's ambiguous nature, believes that she and he will one day be married and have children. The tale covers one day in the couple's life—a significant day, as by the end of the story they will have ended their fourteen-year-long relationship.

This is no ordinary story about relationships, however, unless a cat being pushed out of the window to its death by Afro-Cuban gods that are conjured up to guide the protagonist through a difficult challenge is considered a commonplace occurrence. Woven through this plot are themes of love, compassion, and the ability to laugh at those unexpected details that add both sorrow and a better understanding of what is really important in life. Rivera has created lovable characters, both real and fantastic, with the out-of-the-world gods sometimes appearing more bona fide than the human beings.

Author Biography

Beatriz Rivera was born on September 27, 1957, in Havana, Cuba, but at the age of three, she immigrated to the United States (soon after Castro's rise to power) with her parents, Mario Lorenzo and Aida (Rufin) Rivera. She lived with her family in Miami, Florida, until her high school years, when her parents sent her to Switzerland to complete her early education.

When it was time to go to college, Rivera chose to live in France, where she attended the Sorbonne, majoring in philosophy and eventually receiving her master's degree in 1979. Upon graduation, Rivera decided that she was not yet ready to return to the United States, so she found a job teaching English and Spanish in French schools. It was during this period that she also began writing her first novel.

Rivera lived in Paris for ten years, believing that she would never return to the United States. However, she reached a point in her life when she realized that as a writer she did not have a clear identity—she wasn't French, although she was living in France; she didn't really relate to being an American, although America was where she had spent much of her early years; and, although her ancestry was Cuban, she had left Cuba at such a young age that she didn't really associate herself with that country either. In the end, she decided to reestablish herself in the United States.

Upon her return to the United States, two of Rivera's short stories were published. "Paloma" appeared in *The Americas Review* and "Life Insurance" was published in *Chiricu*. Three years later, in 1995, both of these stories, along with the titled short story, were later collected in *African Passions and Other Stories*, Rivera's first book-length publication. Rivera followed this book with the novel *Midnight Sandwiches at the Mariposa Express* (1997) and the novel *Playing with Light* (2000).

Besides her creative writing endeavors, Rivera has also worked as a reporter for the *Jersey Journal* in Jersey City, New Jersey, and as a newspaper correspondent for the *Daily Freeman* in Kingston, New York. She has also taught at Fordham University and at Borough Manhattan Community College, both in New York City. In 1996, she enrolled in a Ph.D. program at CUNY Graduate Center in New York City, majoring in Spanish literature.

On June 21, 1988, she married Charles S. C. Barnes, with whom she has two children. She currently lives in the Hudson Valley region of New York.

Plot Summary

Rivera's "African Passions" opens with the protagonist Teresa making readers immediately aware of two important aspects of her life: the dishonesty of her live-in partner Armando, who is pretending to be sleeping, and Teresa's lack of self-confidence, as when she refers to herself as "an ugly brown bear," a description influenced by Armando's lack of attention to her.

Teresa tries to make Armando realize that his game of pretense is ineffectual, but Armando refuses to give in. Even though Armando continues to pretend to be asleep and thus not talk to her, Teresa continually asks him, "Do you still love me?" When her question arouses only more silence from Armando, Teresa half-jokingly contends that if Armando does not pay attention to her soon, she will "do something crazy."

Again, not receiving any reaction from Armando, Teresa calls on the "African Powers that surround our Savior" to help her find pleasure. "And," she adds, "I want it right away!" She then goes on to reveal that she really doesn't believe in Santería, an Afro-Cuban religious practice, but that she just likes to call on the African deities as "her private game, the way she liked to pray when she really wanted something."

After calling the gods, unbeknownst to the characters in the story, they materialize and begin taking matters into their own hands to answer Teresa's prayers and bring more pleasure into her life. The deities include an ever-hungry god and a fun-loving, sensual goddess, as well as several other funny characters. The gods watch as Teresa unsuccessfully tries to stir some affection from Armando. Armando, finally acknowledging that he is awake, suggests that Teresa go feed the cat, which she does. Before returning to bed, she also opens the window in the kitchen so her cat can enjoy the warm sun.

After feeding the cat, Teresa slips back into bed as the narrator fills in information about the couple. They have been together for fourteen years but have never married. They are both busy professionals who often find themselves living in separate cities, sharing only their weekends together, until recently, that is. As this narration continues, Teresa does not stop her efforts to snuggle up to Armando. Armando, on the other hand, refuses to be affectionate.

Teresa then reminisces about her cat. She found the cat out on the street the day that she and Armando began living together. At that time, Teresa was twenty years old and about to enter law school. She was also a paralegal in Armando's law firm. Armando was thirty at that time, and he and Teresa had often discussed their plans for the future in those earlier days, a future that included getting married and having babies. Armando was very attracted to Teresa back then, despite the fact that his parents did not approve of Teresa because she was a "lower-class Jersey City, New Jersey, Cuban girl." Although Armando had broken up with her in the past, he could not stand the fact that Teresa was seeing other men, so he made up to her and came back. However, fourteen years later, their relationship is again waning, and there are no signs of either the wedding or the babies. Instead, Armando has recently been distancing himself from Teresa.

The African gods, in the meantime, see things about Armando that Teresa refuses to recognize. One of the goddesses, Yemayá decides to give Armando a stomachache because of Armando's deceitfulness. When Armando feels uneasy, he asks Teresa to get him something from the medicine chest. He then tells Teresa that he needs to make a phone call and that she should not disturb him.

Teresa, who appears to love Armando blindly, does, however, become somewhat suspicious of his mannerisms when she inadvertently interrupts his phone call. She says to him, "every time I ask you a question you look so embarrassed!" But she dismisses the thought when one of the gods blows Teresa's suspicions away. Meantime, in the kitchen, the gods are watching the cat that is greedily eating all the leftover chicken. The gods are hungry, as well as angry that the cat is getting the best food, so they push the cat out of the window to its death. The cat, having existed in Teresa's life for the exact amount of time as her relationship with Armando, thus takes on the semblance of a metaphor for Teresa and Armando's relationship. In other words, the relationship is now dead, and the middle of the story takes up the quest of Teresa and Armando finding some place to bury it.

Armando's reaction to the death of the cat appears authentic to Teresa, but she is confused about the other signals that she is receiving from him. She states that "he looked sex-guilty even when he said they should take the car and find somewhere in the suburbs to bury that poor cat." They both want to give the cat a decent burial, but there are not many places in New York City where they could dig a hole in the earth. So they decide to drive out into the suburbs. At this news, the gods become very excited. They are anxious to go along for the ride.

Teresa and Armando study a map of the area, discussing the places nearby that offer some open land. They talk about going to a golf course, a college campus, and a few state parks. When they try each of them out, they are always interrupted in their attempts by a police officer or a guard who shoos them on their way.

To give Armando and Teresa time to talk, the African gods first slash one of the car's tires; then later they make the couple get stuck in a traffic jam. The first delay causes Armando to tell Teresa that he'll not be home next weekend. He is going to a golf seminar in Virginia, and his parents are going to meet him there. Teresa reminds him that he had originally told her that his parents were coming to visit them in New York next weekend. Armando tells Teresa that he thought she would not be interested in spending time with his parents, so he made a change in their plans.

During the second delay, Armando turns to Teresa and says, "I have something to tell you. You know how much I love you and how devoted I am to you. But I can't marry you." To this, Teresa responds that she's known that for a long time. Armando then continues by telling her that he has great ambition and that he's always had this dream of having his future father-in-law take him to an exclusive golf club. This is something that Teresa's father could never do, and therefore Armando has become engaged to a woman whose father will be taking him to this exclusive club next weekend. When Teresa reacts with sarcasm, Armando says, "Somehow, I knew you wouldn't take this well."

The gods are all sitting in the back seat of the car during the above discussion. Some of them are disgusted that Teresa is taking Armando's declaration so unemotionally. "This woman's got no blood in her veins," one of them says. "After what he told her! And she hasn't even cut him!" another god says. "This is like the end of a bullfight . . . and with a very polite bull." But when Armando further confesses that he also became engaged over the previous weekend, the god Shangó unsheathes his sword, and Yemayá starts "running all over the world looking for another man for Teresa."

Armando and Teresa find no place to bury the cat and return home with the dead animal. The last scene of the story finds Armando and Teresa in the elevator of their apartment building, with Armando holding the cold cat in his arms. Armando shoots a side-glance at Teresa when the goddess Oshún puts lust and jealousy into his body, making him think about Teresa being with another man. Teresa, meanwhile, wipes a tear from her face and says another prayer to the gods, asking them to help her "get over this man."

Characters

Armando

Armando is Teresa's boyfriend. He is forty–four years old and a junior partner in a law firm. He is ten years older than Teresa. In the first lines of the story, Armando is covertly described as a fake. He is pretending to be asleep. Shortly afterward, he also pretends to have to make a business telephone call when, it is suggested, he is probably calling another woman.

Although Armando and Teresa have been living together for fourteen years, Armando has never proposed marriage. Teresa believed that they would eventually get married, but Armando has always made excuses to avoid taking vows to make Teresa his wife. Armando is referred to as a "'country club' Cuban," a reference to his family having money.

In the beginning of their affair, Armando did not mind that his parents did not approve of Teresa. They thought of her as a "lower-class Jersey City, New Jersey, Cuban girl whose family owned a laundromat." However, by the day on which the story takes place, Armando has fallen in love with another woman and has asked this other woman to marry him. In breaking the news to Teresa, Armando says, "First I really want you to know how devoted I am to you, but you know I've always had my dreams and ambitions." Then he tells her not to take it personally, but his "axiom" for the day on which

he would become engaged was that his "future father-in-law would take me to a very exclusive golf club." He then goes on to remind Teresa that her father could never do this.

Armando is a shallow character without real emotions. He looks at Teresa lustfully but without understanding or appreciating any of her traits that run deeper than her skin. For Armando, ambition means rising up the economic ladder. He wants power and prestige that he believes will come to him only through money.

Babalú Ayé

Of the African gods that Teresa summons, Babalú Ayé is most arrogant. He is angry that she has summoned him last, and he also believes that Teresa is too arrogant. In his anger, he says bad things about Teresa and doesn't like her cat because Babalú's body is covered in wounds and the cat's tongue is too rough to lick him. He accuses Teresa of using her race to get into top colleges and into top law firms. When he gets angry with Teresa, he spills sesame seeds on the kitchen floor so that she will get gangrene. Babalú is one of the gods responsible for pushing Teresa's cat out of the window.

Eleggua

Eleggua is the African god who lives under the sugar bowl in Teresa's kitchen. He is said to be the one who has "opened roads" for Teresa. Eleggua is also a bit distracted by food, always sniffing it out, and he makes Teresa's cat do things toward his goal of getting Teresa to open the refrigerator so he can get at the food inside.

Obatalá

Obatalá is a "virile warrior" and lives in the marjoram. He slashes the tire of Armando's car, placing obstacles in Armando's way as he and Teresa try to bury the dead cat.

Ogún

Ogún is described as bloodthirsty and lives in the rosemary in Teresa's kitchen. Ogún is one of the gods responsible for pushing Teresa's cat out of the window.

Orula

Orula, another of the gods, lives in the pepper shaker, and he is clairvoyant. He is also the husband of Yemayá. Orula blows thoughts out of Teresa's mind when Teresa becomes suspicious of Armando's love for her. He does not want her to be prepared for what Armando will tell her later.

Oshún

Oshún loves Teresa's jewelry box. She is described as a "beautiful" and "fun-loving" goddess. Oshún likes to protect Teresa, and she also declares her sexual attraction to Armando. At one point, she says, "I love his genitals!" Oshún makes Teresa ask questions of Armando, helping Teresa understand that Armando does not love her. In the end, Oshún puts lust and jealousy into Armando, reminding him "that Teresa would probably find someone else soon."

Shangó

Shangó loves fire and lives in the bay leaves. Shangó is the god who is protective of Teresa and wants to burn Armando because Shangó knows that Armando only pretends to love Teresa. When Armando tells Teresa that he is engaged to another woman, Shangó "unsheathed his sword," symbolizing the death of Teresa's love for Armando.

Teresa

Teresa is the protagonist of the story. She is intelligent, as reflected in the fact that she has graduated from the "top colleges" and has found jobs with the "top law firms." She is thirty-four years old at the time of the story.

Teresa loves Armando, the man with whom she has been living for fourteen years, more than he loves her, but she loves him to a fault. Even though she is suspicious of his actions, she keeps herself in a frame of mind that does not allow those suspicions to enter her conscious thoughts. Therefore, she is hesitant to take action that would root out the story behind Armando's reluctance to marry her. She is also totally unsuspicious of Armando's unfaithfulness.

At the age of thirty-four, Teresa is thinking about having children. She has lied to her parents about her arrangement with Armando. Her parents believe that Teresa and Armando are married. Teresa told her parents that she and Armando secretly eloped several years ago. She seems content with Armando and their relationship, but she is growing a little wary of his lack of commitment and looks back at the beginning of their relationship, wondering why Armando has not kept his promise of having babies. Although she does not seem to suspect Armando's affair with another woman, she does keep asking him if he loves her.

Teresa is a complex character with beliefs that conflict with one another. Although she does not appear to question Armando's lack of compassion for her, she does use all her forces to try to make him pay more attention to her. Teresa also does not truly believe in the powers of the African gods that she conjures, and yet she calls upon them to make fate turn in her direction. She uses the gods to make decisions for her that she cannot make alone. The gods represent her subconscious will. She is a woman who lives outside of what she feels is her natural culture, and yet, the culture in which she does live does not quite feel her own. As the narration states, "She lived on the Upper East Side of Manhattan . . . it had been years since she'd belonged to the old neighborhood." However, when she "really wanted something," she reclaimed her ancestral culture by calling up the gods who were familiar to her.

Teresa may have moved away from the old neighborhood, but she remains fond of her parents, even though Armando puts them down for their lack of education and money. When Armando describes Teresa's father as a man who's been "working in that laundromat all his life," Teresa responds, "Oh, no, not all his life . . . before that he was a plasterer, but he could paint, too." She is using sarcasm here, putting Armando down for his highbrow attitude, but she is also standing up for her parents as well. Her parents are proud of her, and she cherishes them for that.

At the end of the story, Teresa once again conjures up the African gods, as she brushes away "a tear" (her only show of emotion) upon digesting the news that Armando is engaged to another woman. She asks the gods to "help me get over this man."

Yemayá

Yemayá is a goddess who lives in the cilantro. She is also the wife of Orula. When she gets angry with Armando, she makes him have a stomachache. Yemayá, after Armando tells Teresa that he is engaged to another woman, starts "running all over the world looking for another man for Teresa."

Topics for Further Study

- In Rivera's story ''African Passions,'' parental approval of their child's marriage partner is largely determined by economic status. Create a survey that asks specific questions about factors that are important to parents in approving a mate for their child. Hand out the survey to as many people as you can, then compile the data and write a report on the conclusions that you find. What were the most prevailing issues? Were they economically based? What role does religion or education play? Were there any concerns about same sex or bi-racial marriages? Were issues of culture raised? How often were abstract concepts such as love, beauty, peace of mind, or happiness considered?

- One of the challenges that face the characters in ''African Passions'' is finding a place to bury their pet cat. Research the laws in your state governing the burial of pets. What are the options available to pet owners? Include in your research the industry of pet cemeteries. Is there a pet cemetery in your area? Conclude your study with a personal annotation of what you would do if you had a pet that died. Would you bury the animal? If so, where? Or would you take the pet to an animal shelter or veterinarian's office?

- Aspects of Santería play a role in Rivera's story. Write a paper on the origins of this religion.

Gather information about the belief systems of the Yoruba people and combine this with historic facts concerning African slaves having to give up their native creeds once they arrived in the Western world. Conclude your paper with a detailed description of how Santería combines the African deities with the Roman Catholic faith.

- Fidel Castro's rise to power has caused great changes in Cuba. Write a paper on this communist leader, giving a full account of his political beliefs, a description of the people who most influenced him, and the changes that Cuba has incurred during his long tenure. Conclude your paper with your personal assessment of what Cuba's political future might be upon Castro's death.

- The character Armando in Rivera's story comes across as a rather shallow person. Although ''African Passions'' is written in the third person omniscient point of view, the story is biased toward Teresa. Pretend that you are Armando. Describe yourself. Explain why you are ending this fourteen-year-long relationship. Defend your reasons for marrying someone who matches your parents', as well as your own, economic status. In other words, give readers of this story the other side of the story. Create some redeeming qualities for Armando.

Themes

Passivity

One of the strongest characteristics of Rivera's protagonist, Teresa, is her passivity. Despite the fact that she intuitively acknowledges that her lover is avoiding her, lying to her, and refusing to pay any attention to her, she remains faithful to him. She waits on him, fetching medicine for his aching stomach and making him a cup of coffee while he makes a phone call that Teresa suspects is to another woman. She never directly confronts him on any issues. She also waits on him in another sense: the passage of time. For fourteen years she swallows his lame excuses for not marrying her, accepting the insults that he heaps onto her and her family's economic and social status without much more than the nodding of her head.

However, Teresa's passivity is somewhat misleading. Although she accepts Armando and his excuses on a conscious level, on a subconscious level, she conjures up the spiritual powers of her beliefs, in the form of African deities, to wreak havoc on her lover and expose his false-hearted intentions that she, herself, is not outwardly strong enough to face. Though she suspects that Armando does not love her, it is through the actions of the gods that Armando is forced to confess that he has been scheming to leave her. When Armando does declare that he has become engaged to another woman, even the gods are disgusted by Teresa's lack of emotional aggression, comparing her to a ''very polite bull'' in the middle of a bullfight.

Social Hierarchies

The first sense of hierarchy in Rivera's ''African Passions'' actually appears with the materialization of the African deities. When Babalú Ayé is summoned last in Teresa's prayer for pleasure, he becomes so indignant that he tries to put a curse on Teresa that will lead to her death. Later, this same awareness of a perceived pecking order becomes apparent when the gods push Teresa's cat out of the window because the cat was eating too much of the leftover chicken.

Rivera uses this more comical sense of hierarchy of the gods to heighten the awareness of the social hierarchy that pollutes Armando's search for a lover. Although Armando is attracted to Teresa, albeit more of a physical connection than an emotional one, he is more committed to his ambition to rise in the social ranks than he is to love. He constantly reminds Teresa that she comes from a more common stock than he because her parents' only claim to fame is their ownership of a New Jersey laundromat. Armando, in the meantime, dreams of belonging to exclusive golf clubs, of marrying into money and status. He is ambitious, he tells Teresa, believing that this explains his leaving her for another woman. He could never marry her, not because he doesn't love and adore her, or so he says, but because his parents would never approve of his marrying beneath his social class.

Teresa's parents also play into the system of social hierarchy as they tell Teresa how proud they are of her for ''having found an upper-crust Cuban, or a 'country club' Cuban.'' Whereas her father ''only got to see the inside of those clubs'' when he cleaned the toilets, he is glad that Teresa, by virtue of her supposed marriage, would belong to the country club set.

Grace

The theme of grace lies underneath the overall plot of Rivera's story. It is somewhat subtle but nonetheless very visible at the same time. From the opening paragraph, Rivera sets up the theme by presenting Armando as corrupted deceit and Teresa (coincidentally the name of a popular Roman Catholic saint) as loving innocence. It is through Teresa's innocence that she receives the grace of the gods that she summons, whereas, it is suggested, Armando will receive only the sword.

Teresa prays for pleasure, and the gods immediately respond. Although they kill her cat, this appears as a symbolic gesture meant to show Teresa that her love affair with Armando is dead. The rest of the story contains a series of actions that expose Armando's shallowness in comparison to Teresa's patience and understanding. As a consequence of Teresa's saintly virtues, she is, in the end, rewarded with an answer to her prayers, as the gods chase away the deadbeat Armando and then scour the world for a new lover, appropriate for Teresa's ability to love.

Spirituality

Although Rivera's narrator states that Teresa doesn't really believe in Santería but only uses it when she really wants something, some of the beliefs of Santería pervade this short story. Santería is a combination of beliefs, incorporating the spiritual practices of several African religions with the rituals and saints of the Roman Catholic religion. In ''African Passions,'' Teresa is now living ''on the Upper East Side of Manhattan where there are gourmet delis instead of live poultry markets and those religious stores called *Boánicas*,'' and thus she is very much removed from her Cuban cultural heritage. However, she has not forgotten her past, and when she is in need, she turns to the spiritual beliefs—her Santería, with its mostly benevolent gods—that have been handed down to her. The confidence that she lacks in herself presents itself in a more robust form in the gods that she conjures.

It is through her spiritual beliefs that Teresa is able to withstand the pain of a failed relationship, the humiliation of an unfaithful lover, and the trauma of losing her cat. She might not be strong in herself, but she is strong in her belief that if she prays, her supplications will be answered. When she feels herself faltering, she prays for guidance. Rivera makes spirituality playful, but this should not be taken as a sign of disrespect, for in the end it is due to her spirituality that not only will Teresa bear the breakup of her fourteen-year-long relationship but that the gods will direct her fate.

Style

Magic Realism

Rivera's ''African Passions'' is written in a style referred to as magic realism. This term was coined to define the way in which art forms, especially literature, display odd and dreamlike anomalies as if they were commonplace events. Thus, there is the mixture of what might be termed magical with what is deemed everyday reality. Rivera's use of magic realism comes about with the materialization of the African deities. Although the characters themselves are not aware of the presence of the gods, the depth as well as the fun of the story relies on the reader knowing that it is the gods who are controlling the fate of Teresa and Armando.

That gods can be jealous, hungry, sexually aroused, and petty (in other words, that they can have human qualities) is taken for granted. As a matter of fact, it is this display of their human side that makes the story so enjoyable. By using magic realism, Rivera adds more than just humor, however; she also adds depth by proclaiming her belief that there are underlying powers in everyday affairs. The tire of Armando's car does not become flattened by accident but rather because the gods want Armando to stop and think. The cat does not fall out of the window by chance but because the gods want Teresa to have a physical symbol of the death of her and Armando's relationship.

Point of View

''African Passions'' is told in third person omniscient point of view. This means that the reader is privileged to know not only what is going on in the story but also some of the thoughts of the characters. A third person narrator tells the story, filling in background information as well as hinting at the motivation behind the actions of the people involved.

In using third person omniscient point of view, Rivera gives the reader a look into Teresa's insecurities about herself. More importantly, this point of view also allows the reader to know that there are spiritual beings involved in the plot, whereas the characters themselves are not aware of their presence.

Symbolism

The cat in this story symbolizes the relationship of Teresa and Armando. Teresa found the cat in the streets on the same day that she and Armando moved into their apartment, which marked the beginning of their living together. Both characters appear to have feelings for the cat, although it is Teresa who feeds it and must retrieve the dead cat from the alley below when the gods push the cat out of the window.

By having Teresa appear as the caretaker of the cat, Rivera also demonstrates that it is Teresa who is the caretaker of Teresa and Armando's relationship. By having the gods push the cat out of the window to its death, Rivera symbolizes the death of Teresa and Armando's union, with the burial of the dead cat signifying the ritual burial of the same relationship. In the end, it is Armando who is left holding the dead cat's body. In other words, Rivera is suggesting, Armando is responsible for having killed the relationship.

Setting

The setting of Rivera's short story is New York City. It is New York as adopted by a woman from New Jersey. Because she was raised in New Jersey, as opposed to having been raised in New York, Armando makes fun of her. He puts her down. New York is considered more sophisticated, maybe even more aristocratic. New Jersey, in comparison, symbolizes to Armando the blue-collar worker and the lower class.

It is also New York City as adopted by Cuban immigrants who have had to adjust their lives to the busy northern streets. They have given up their homeland and have tried to acculturate themselves to the life that the American city dictates. It is also a cemented city, where there is no place to bury a cat. There is little nature left in New York City. What is left is regulated by park police. This cemented city stands in contrast to Cuba, which is known for its lush countryside.

Historical Context

Magic Realism in Latin American Literature

Although not restricted to Latin American literature, magic realism holds a strong court in the writings of Hispanic authors. Some of the more famous examples of such writing include Gabriel

García Márquez's *One Hundred Years of Solitude*, Laura Esquivel's *Like Water for Chocolate*, and Isabel Allende's *Love and Shadows*.

The term magic realism was first coined by German art critic Franz Roh in the late 1920s, but the phrase did not really catch on until Miguel Angel Asturias (from Guatemala) used the term to describe his writing when he received the Nobel Prize (1967) for his life's work in literature. Many of Rivera's stories take on the style of magic realism, such as the appearance of African gods in "African Passions."

Fidel Castro and Cuban Emigration

The United States occupied Cuba from 1899 to 1901 under a military governor, General John Brooke, who blocked Cubans from governmental service. Brooke also disbanded the Cuban army. He was eventually replaced, under supervised elections that gave Cuba its first elected president, Tomás Estrada Palma. The United States at this time envisioned a Cuba that would serve U. S. economic needs. In 1901, the Platt Amendment gave the United States the right to determine Cuba's economy, international and internal affairs, as well as the right to establish a military base at Guantánamo Bay.

Between 1901 and 1959, the United States set up several puppet administrators in Cuba, none of them very successful in appeasing the needs of the Cuban people with the dictates of the U.S. government. On January 1, 1959, Fidel Castro, a young lawyer invested in radical politics, who had at one time been a political prisoner, rose to power on the backs of poor peasants, urban workers, and young and idealistic Cubans. With Castro's victory, the Communist Party of Cuba assumed political control of the government, becoming the first socialist country in the Americas.

These were not easy years for Cuba. Castro represented change, but many of the changes were difficult. With the 1960s U.S. trade embargo imposed on Cuba, food and other material shortages became prevalent. Added to this was Castro's strong campaign against the ownership of private property. Private businesses were nationalized. These conditions led to the emigration of thousands of Cubans to the United States.

Santería

Santería is a religion of Caribbean origin. It combines the beliefs of Roman Catholicism with those brought over to the Western world by Africa slaves, mostly the Yoruba and Bantu people from Southern Nigeria, Senegal, and Guinea Coast. Historically, the African slaves were forced to suppress the religions of their homelands, as they were baptized into the Roman Catholic Church upon their arrival in the New World. To maintain their more familiar spiritual concepts, the slaves covertly wrapped the names of the new Catholic saints around the African deities they truly believed in. For instance, this resulted in having St. Lazarus take on the persona of Babalú Ayé, the patron of the sick; St. Barbara became representative of Shangó, the one who controls fire; and St. Anthony was the cover name for Eleggua, he who controls all the roads.

The religion was active in Cuba but was suppressed by Fidel Castro in the 1950s. However, a resurgence in the religion was witnessed in Cuba in the 1990s, and with the emigration of Cubans to the United States, there are growing communities of people practicing Santería in Florida, New York City, and Los Angeles. It has been reported that there are over 300,000 practitioners of Santería in New York alone. The religion is also very active in Brazil.

Although there is very little definite information known outside of the practicing circles of Santería, some general details can be offered. Secrecy is a very important element of the religion, with rituals, symbols, and practices not divulged until a practitioner is initiated into the group. There is no book of guidance associated with this religion as it is based on ancient practices handed down by oral tradition. A typical ritual is usually accompanied by the beating of African drums with a special rhythm assigned to each god and goddess. An integral, as well as a most controversial, element of the religion is ritual animal sacrifice, with chickens being most commonly used in sacrifice. A statement concerning this ritual from one Santerían group asserts that the animals are killed in a humane manner and later eaten.

Each of the Santerían gods has a special calling, somewhat similar to the myths about Greek gods. Eleggua, for instance, is the god who opens doors. He is also the guardian of the crossroads and the messenger to the all-knowing God. Eleggua corresponds to Mercury in Greek mythology. Oshún is considered the goddess of love, sexuality, beauty, and diplomacy, much like her Greek sister, Aphrodite. Shangó is the god of storms and lightning, just like the Greek Mars.

Critical Overview

Although Rivera has received critical praise for her writing, her introspection, and her development of strong characters, there is little mention expressly applied to her individual short story "African Passions." This story has not yet received a lot of attention outside of the Latino/a and Afro-Cuban reading community. *African Passions and Other Stories* was her first full-length published work, and although she has written two novels since then, she is still very much considered a newcomer in the literary world.

In general, however, Rivera has received some commentary on her eccentric characters, her sure-handed writing, and the energetic entanglements in her stories. Critics refer to her writing as inventive and provocative. Adrienne A. Bendel, writing for the *Denver Post*, states that Rivera "explores universal themes . . . spiced with the uniqueness of the Cuban-American experience." This reviewer also states that Rivera writes with "humor, irony, affection and zest."

Sybil S. Steinberg, writing for *Publishers Weekly*, refers to some of the characters that Rivera creates as "endearingly self-absorbed." In a specific review of *African Passions and Other Stories*, M. V. Ekstrom writes in *Choice*, "The stories touch on many aspects of Latin American history and cultural identity, yet the themes are universal." He then adds, "This is a fine collection."

Criticism

Joyce Hart

Hart has degrees in English literature and creative writing. Her published works are of literary themes. In this essay, Hart examines the way that Rivera uses the materialization of gods and goddesses to express the subconscious desires of her protagonist in his story.

It does not take Rivera long in her story "African Passions" to divulge the truth about her protagonist. Teresa is a woman of contrapuntal desires—a deep-seated passion to love and a self-defeating compulsion to remain passive. She cries outwardly for attention and affection, but her only action in the

direction of love is to serve her lover and to pray. It is when she prays that her emotional energies are most nearly aligned with her desires; and it is through these suppressed emotions that the ancient gods of Africa are brought forth to seek, in her name, the bridge between her desires and her submissiveness.

From the first paragraph, readers are told that Armando, Teresa's love partner, is a fraud. Teresa knows this as well, but she is forever forgiving. Teresa knows many things about Armando, but as soon as a truth enters her mind, she finds something else to distract her so she does not have to think too hard about the status of her relationship with this man. The relationship is on shaky ground, but Teresa continues to tiptoe around the facts, hoping that she is wrong, not wanting to wake up to the realization that the relationship is more than not going any place; the relationship is dead.

"Do you still love me?" she asks this man in her bed, who is pretending to be sleeping; but deep down, Teresa already knows the answer. She envisions a picture of herself from what she imagines to be Armando's view: "He was on the alert, as if she were an ugly brown bear ready to pounce if he didn't play dead." In this thought of hers is the essence of her definition of their relationship. She thinks of herself as ugly and threatening. She thinks of him as an actor. She excuses his pretense by telling herself that Armando is afraid of her, possibly afraid that she will take something from him: his status, his life, or maybe just his love. In truth, Teresa is really afraid that she does not deserve his love. However, something is missing in her life. This she knows, and she is looking for that something. She, like the god Eleggua, is hungry. "If you don't pay attention to me soon," she says to Armando, "I'll do something crazy!"

The crazy thing that she eventually does is conjure up the African gods with whom she has played games ever since she was a child. She prays to them, although she denies believing in them. Her game is to call the gods when she is frustrated and needs to acknowledge her emotions. She tells the gods what she wants and then waits to see if they answer her requests. She has needs but does not have the confidence to trust that she can find the means to satisfy them on her own. Teresa is passive about life because she is insecure, but her passivity does not satisfy her desires; it merely shoves them into a back closet until they are ready to explode. It

Santería religious altar

is this suppressed energy that imbues the psyche with the power to bring the gods forth. The gods thus represent Teresa's emotions.

Somewhere in her personal history, Teresa learned to believe that she was not worthy of the kind of love that she craves. Her poor self-image could be the result of her feeling as if she lives on the fringes of American society—in the society but not truly of it—due to her bicultural status. It also could have arisen from the pressures placed on her to excel economically, a sure sign of success in the eyes of her parents. Even though she has made remarkable accomplishments, Armando is present in her life to remind her that no matter what she does, she cannot erase her heritage, which, in Armando's eyes, is that of a daughter of lower-class parents. So Teresa turns to love, hoping that those warm, fuzzy feelings that are romantically linked to the concept of love will somehow fill in all the empty places in her soul.

Toward this goal, she turns to Armando. She's been turning to him for a long time, and she's always come up empty, especially lately. Teresa is locked into a mode. She can turn toward Armando, but she cannot turn away. Although she and Armando have talked of marriage, he has always put it off, telling her he couldn't marry her because his parents

did not approve of her. Then later, he says that he doesn't believe in marriage. Teresa is ever hopeful that Armando will change, at least she is hopeful on a rational level. On a subconscious level, however, Teresa is a bit more aware. There, in that secret place where she hides her emotions, she begs the gods to bring her pleasure, the thing she is missing in her life. Interestingly, readers should note that Teresa does not specify in her prayers that she wants this pleasure to come from Armando. She does not demand that the gods make Armando love her. Her prayer is a more generic: "I want pleasure! And I want it right away!"

The god Babalú Ayé is the first god to reveal some of Teresa's hidden feelings. Babalú Ayé is the god of healing. In the story, a side note enlightens readers that Babalú Ayé does not like cats because their tongues are too rough for his skin. Babalú Ayé's "body was covered with open wounds," an empathetic symbol of his healer status. He is aware of Teresa's emotional wounds caused by her insecurities and exposes her ambivalent feelings about having used her Hispanic culture to help her get into "top universities, top law firms, and top floors." Through Babalú Ayé it becomes apparent that Teresa is not totally confident in her intelligence and skills. There are lingering doubts inside of her as to whether

What Do I Read Next?

- Cristina García's debut novel *Dreaming in Cuban* (1992) follows the stories captured in the diary of the protagonist Pilar. Readers are privy to Pilar's internal thoughts as she and her family face the challenges of a family torn between two countries when Pilar's parents emigrate to New York to escape the Castro regime. The novel covers the emotional effects on her parents, herself, and her siblings, as well as on her relatives who remain in Cuba.

- *Playing with Light* (2000) is Rivera's second novel, in which her central theme explores the pitfalls of human vice and the redemptive power of literature. When Rebecca, the protagonist, tries to bring a group of her women friends together in a reading group, they experience strange time warps. This contemporary group of women reads a book set in the late nineteenth century about a group of women reading a book set in the future; and slowly the lives of the two groups of women begin to entwine. The theme of this book centers on the exploration of the circumscribed role of women in both centuries.

- Rivera's novel *Midnight Sandwiches at the Mariposa Express* (1997) is told through the voice of Cuban immigrant Trish Izquierdo, a New Jersey town councilwoman, who tries to instill civic pride in her town's mostly Hispanic population. Told with humor and wit, the story unfolds through wisps of gossip that filter through the Mariposa Express, a cafeteria that acts as the unofficial town hall. The book is filled with a large cast of endearing, self-absorbed characters, who come alive in Rivera's thought-provoking first novel.

- Julia Alvarez wrote *How the Garcia Girls Lost Their Accents* (1991) in order to tell the story about three sisters who were brought up in the United States by their immigrant Dominican Republic parents. In an attempt to ensure their children's success, the parents try their best to acculturate their daughters to their new country. However, in looking back at their lives, the sisters second-guess their parents' choices, because despite all their efforts, emotionally the women's lives have been a mess. Told with humor and psychological insight, this is a fun book to read.

- *The Voice of the Turtle: An Anthology of Cuban Stories* (1998), edited by Peter R. Bush, offers an excellent introduction to Cuban literature. Included in this collection are classic authors Reinaldo Arenas, Guillermo Cabrera Infante, Lydia Cabrera, and Calvert Casey, as well as modern Cuban writers Senel Paz, Zo Volds, and Jess Vega.

---

she could have accomplished as much on her own without using her minority classification. These fears feed her low self-esteem, which in turn keeps her in a dissatisfying relationship.

It is through the goddess Oshún that readers become aware of the fact that sexual passion is also suppressed in Teresa. Oshún is the goddess of love and sexuality. Sexuality is very important to Teresa, as this is how she defines love. She repeatedly tells Armando that she loves him as she snuggles close to him in bed and gently caresses his stomach and thighs and chest. There are several mentions of Teresa caressing Armando's thighs, whispering, "I love you. I adore you." When she thinks back to when she and Armando first began living together, she recalls, "he adored her, he couldn't take his hands off her." However, Teresa is not overtly sexual. She only displays gestures that hint she is aroused and would like to share a passionate moment with Armando. He, of course, is not interested and thus, much like all the rest of Teresa's desires, her sexuality must be suppressed. So Rivera has the "fun-loving" goddess Oshún speak for Teresa when Oshún openly declares: "I'll get his genitals! I love his genitals!'' Later, while Armando is making his secretive phone call (presumably to another woman), it is Oshún who makes the telephone receiver too hot for Armando to hold. ''I feel like burning him,'' Oshún says, voicing Teresa's suppressed anger. Teresa intuitively senses that Armando is cheating on her, as she notices that he had ''an embarrassed look on his face.'' Teresa refers to this as Armando's sex guilt. She confronts him briefly: ''Armando, every time I ask you a question you look so embarrassed!'' However, several seconds later, after Armando tells her to leave him alone, Teresa is back to telling Armando that she loves him.

Yemayá is the goddess who represents the archetype of mother. She is the goddess of the sea and the moon and is often invoked in fertility rituals. After Armando refuses to acknowledge Teresa's passionate gestures, as well as ignoring Teresa's desire all these years to have children, Yemayá gives Armando a stomachache, symbolic of menstrual cramps or preliminary birthing pains. Yemayá strikes back at Armando when Teresa is incapable of standing up to him. Yemayá is also the goddess who, at the end of the story, ''started running all over the world looking for another man for Teresa.''

Ogún, the god of iron and metals and a fierce warrior, also wants to lash out at Armando but in an even more drastic manner. When Ogún hears Armando talking on the phone to another woman, he responds, ''And I'll cut him.'' Minutes later, Armando cuts himself while shaving. Ogún is also partially involved in pushing Teresa's cat out of the window, but it is Eleggua who is the mastermind behind this endeavor.

Eleggua is the guardian of the crossroads, the god who opens the doors to all endeavors. He is also known as the trickster, a character common to many aboriginal faiths. The trickster figure is credited with creating calamities in order to teach lessons. He pushes Teresa's cat out the window, giving Teresa a symbolic manifestation of the death of her and Armando's relationship.

When Teresa walks into the bedroom to tell Armando that the cat is dead, she gets mixed signals from Armando. ''He seemed ashamed of himself.'' She wonders about his reaction, asking herself how she could be so confused. ''Didn't she know him by heart? . . . but he looked so guilty! And how can you look sex-guilty when you're on the phone talking business?'' However, when Teresa starts thinking more deeply about Armando's reaction, the god

> **" Teresa is passive about life because she is insecure, but her passivity does not satisfy her desires; it merely shoves them into a back closet until they are ready to explode."**

Orula, a clairvoyant who is associated with the future and fate, blows the thoughts away. He does not want her to be prepared for the day, probably an allusion to Teresa's tendency to forgive Armando. Orula wants Teresa to be so devastated, so caught off guard by Armando's announcement that he is engaged to another woman (at the end of the story) that she will finally ''get over this man.''

Obatalá is the next god to enter the dialogue. He is the god of peace and harmony. While Armando and Teresa are driving around New York to find a place to bury their cat, it is Obatalá who slashes the tire of the car. He wants to place Armando and Teresa in a stalled position, where they will have nothing to do but talk to one another. He is disturbed (much like Teresa) when Armando hints at being irritated. But even Obatalá, the god known for his coolness of thought, wisdom, and clarity, becomes irritated with Teresa's passivity. After Armando tells Teresa that he cannot ever marry her because she comes from such poor stock and that he has in fact met a man who would make a much better father-in-law than Teresa's father ever could, Obatalá, reacting to Teresa's complacency states: ''This woman's got no blood in her veins. After what he told her! And she hasn't even cut him!'' If Obatalá represents Teresa's coolheadedness, he also represents her disgust and frustration for having put up with Armando's disloyalty and criticism all these years. Having noticed, while the couple is driving around the city, that they have driven to Queens, a neighborhood that is removed by both distance and economic opportunity from Manhattan, where Armando and Teresa live, Obatalá declares that he is getting out of the car right there and staying there. The last thing he wants is to go back to Manhattan, back to the couple's old life. Suggested here is that

Teresa, too, has finally made this decision. Maybe she has finally realized that she wants something entirely different in her life.

The story continues, but Armando has not yet told Teresa everything. At last, he drops the most startling news. He tells Teresa that he is engaged to another woman. After this announcement, Shangó unsheathes his sword. Shangó is the god of storms and lightning. He is the god who brings a purifying moral terror to those at whom he lashes out. He often reduces his enemies to ashes. It is through Shangó that Teresa finally feels appeased. However, the gods are not finished with Armando.

Oshún, the goddess of love and sexuality, fills Armando with lust for Teresa so he will always be aware of what he has left behind. Also, by the end of the story, Babalú Ayé has finally gotten over his anger at Teresa, because she now summons him first (previously she had summoned him last). With Babalú happy, readers can assume that Teresa may now be healed. Also, Eleggua, the god who opens the doors to all endeavors, has finally satisfied his hunger, as he sits on top of a bucket of chicken wings that Teresa holds in her arms. It is at this moment that Teresa again summons the African gods to help her ''get over this man,'' ending the story with the hope that Teresa has learned her lessons and has finally unlocked her passions.

Source: Joyce Hart, Critical Essay on ''African Passions,'' in *Short Stories for Students,* The Gale Group, 2002.

Laura Kryhoski

Kryhoski is currently employed as a freelance writer. In this essay, Kryhoski considers the influence of Santería on Rivera's work.

''African Passions'' is the signature piece in a collection of stories by Beatriz Rivera. This story, like others in the collection, is about a woman preoccupied with the possible infidelities of her live-in lover. Rivera cleverly captures, with humor and great insight, the struggle her protagonist, or central character, Teresa, goes through to realize her lover is unfaithful and ill-suited for her. She accomplishes this by drawing on Santería, a practice closely linked to her own Cuban ethnicity. Without a basic understanding of Santería, it is difficult for the reader to appreciate Teresa's plight, as well as Rivera's message regarding the power of feminine intuition.

''African Powers that surround our savior: Eleggua, Ogún, Obatalá, Shangó, Yemayá, Oshún, Orula, Babalú Ayé. I want pleasure, and I want it right away!'' states Teresa at the beginning of the work. The ''African Powers'' she is drawing on are, as she reveals, related to the practice of a religion with Carribean roots that was influenced by Catholicism as it was spread through Central and South America. In Cuba, this religion evolved into what is known as the practice of Santería, or the Way of the Saints. The foundation of the religion rests on the belief that the world is not tangible or material but is simply a function of energy, of forces in continual process. By adding and removing energy, it is believed such movements can be changed. More specifically, Ashe is an energy or force moving towards completeness and divinity. An understanding of these principles of energy enables an individual to control his or her environment. Likewise, an understanding of Ashe enables an individual to control his or her true destiny.

The African Powers that Teresa calls on— namely, Eleggua, Ogún, Obatalá, Shangó, Yemayá, Oshún, Orula, Babalú Ayé–are collectively called Orisha, beings who represent the forces of nature and serve as guardian angels. How these powers relate to an individual is a function of consciousness. Santería advocates the notion that everyone's fundamental personality and character are attributable to an underlying pattern of energy. Returning to the story, specific energy patterns of Teresa's consciousness are represented by Orisha. The Orisha function as an extension of the true self, and by working with them and understanding them, it is believed one can learn lessons sufficient to live in harmony with nature, with creation as well as self. For Teresa, the Orisha are a vehicle for expression. They act in her defense, working behind the scenes, expressing themselves in various ways that Teresa would not consciously choose, and in this way they seem to represent the movement of her subconscious.

A consideration of those of the Orisha that Teresa calls on throughout the story illuminate this movement of Teresa's subconscious. Eleggua is identified as the owner of roads and opportunities. He confirms this, commenting on his role in Teresa's relationship by claiming he had ''opened all the roads for Teresa.'' As in Teresa's summons, Eleggua is always called upon first because he serves as the link between humans and other Orisha. He is not evil; rather, his tricks are to be received as opportunities for learning and growth. Upon examination of the text, Eleggua actually does support Orula, the seventh Orisha summoned, in his efforts to push the cat out the window. This action, however seemingly cruel and unjust, is not an evil act, but instead "opens all roads" for Teresa, leading her to the truth about her relationship with Armando. Eleggua's protectiveness also shines through in his response to others of the Orisha who criticize Teresa for her inability to stand up to Armando. He defends her, commanding the other Orisha to "cut it out," because Teresa is "a sweet girl."

Ogún, the god of war and iron and labor, in contrast to Eleggua, is frustrated by Teresa's flimsy backbone. When Obatalá says, "I'm staying here in Queens, guys," Ogún chimes in supportively, responding, "me too, I'm getting off." Obatalá is described as being the father of all humanity and Orisha. He created humanity and the world, and is deemed the owner of all heads/minds. Purity, peace and compassion are the primary elements comprising or making up his character. Ogún is outwardly frustrated with Teresa and her response to Armando's infidelities, claiming, "this woman's got no blood in her veins. After what he told her! And she hasn't even cut him!" This expression of frustration only comes after the reader has witnessed Obatalá's own efforts to escalate the conflict between Armando and Teresa. Obatalá is responsible for slashing Armando's tire—his intentions are to create a diversion big enough to drag out the day, thus giving Armando ample opportunity and time to confess his infidelity.

Shangó rules over lightening, thunder, drums, and dance. He is hot-blooded, strong willed, and loves all the pleasures of life, particularly drumming, dancing, song, women, and eating. In an amusing moment in the beginning of the story, he is quick to negotiate the terms of the relationship between Armando and Teresa. In an aside, another Orisha, Shangó bargains with Oshún, asking, "what about a once a week affair," between the couple, demonstrating his unwillingness to surrender the more pleasurable aspect of the relationship, i.e., his desire for sexual gratification. But Shangó has rage similar to lightening striking a tree, and in the end his temper gets the best of him. He reacts to Armando's call to another woman by making the phone receiver too hot for Armando to touch and, wishing Armando would burn himself, makes his coffee too hot as well. As Armando speaks of his engagement, revealing his betrayal to Teresa, Shangó is quick to unsheathe his sword.

The next two Orisha that Teresa summons are females: Yemayá and Oshún. Described as the mother of all, Yemayá rules over all seas and lakes.

> " Santería advocates the notion that everyone's fundamental personality and character are attributable to an underlying pattern of energy."

Her reign is built on association, those involving the environment of the womb, which, by extension, is related to the sea in terms of its watery, amniotic environment. She is described as being the root of all paths and manifestations, demonstrated also during Armando's confession at the end of the story. While Armando is revealing the truth to Teresa, Yemayá begins to run around the world, looking for another man for Teresa. Oshún also rules over the waters of the world, but those of the rivers and streams, known as the sweet waters, and she embodies or symbolizes love and fertility. She is also a playful seductress, characterized as "the beautiful, giggling, party-loving Oshún," demonstrated in a moment when the Orisha are ganging up on Armando. In this particular scene, she offers, "I'll get his genitals. I love his genitals." Later in the text, "party-loving Oshún" makes Teresa inquire about Armando's parents' upcoming visit. Finally, it is Oshún who delights at the notion of Armando's demise, having "just reminded him that Teresa would find someone else soon." It makes Oshún "laugh so hard to notice that she'd just put lust and jealousy into his body." She then exclaims, "I am having the time of my life!"

The last two Orisha to come to Teresa's aid are Orula and Babalú Ayé. Orula is described in the text as "the clairvoyant," and in addition to being able to predict the future, is in charge of destiny. In the case of Teresa's destiny, Orula pushes the cat out the window, a tragedy that sets off an entire chain of events leading to Armando's confession. In addition, Orula pushes all thoughts of possible infidelity out of Teresa's mind before Armando's announcement, betrayed in a reminder to herself (Orula): "Teresa was about to really start wondering what was going on when Orula, the clairvoyant, blew the thought away. 'Don't let her be prepared for this day!'" This comment suggests that the shock value of Armando's admission would perhaps prevent Teresa from succumbing to apathy and to instead take action, the desirable action being her termination of all relations with Armando. Babalú Ayé is the only Orisha to express any compassion for Armando, and naturally so, for it is in his nature. He is a known healer, full of compassion towards human suffering. In the confusion about where to bury the cat, Babalú Ayé assures Armando that his efforts are noble.

The Orisha are assigned to an individual and collectively act as parents would towards a child. Teresa's Orisha indeed demonstrate some protective qualities akin to parenting. In keeping with the nature of Orisha, it is important to note again that these "saints" or "spirits" are functioning as individual elements comprising her consciousness. The spiritual aspect of Santería involves Teresa's own realizations, that is, at the point at which she is aware of and in harmony with the activities of the Orisha, which comprise her personality. In this case, such harmony would be achieved in her rejection of Armando, inferred by her final statement, in which she summons the Orisha a final time, asking them to "help me get over this man." Awareness and actualization (the end result of realizing through action) are achieved, granting Teresa control over her environment and her true destiny.

Such religious beliefs driving the story are also easily related to elements of Jungian psychology. Robin Robertson, in *A Beginner's Guide to Jungian Psychology,* mentions Carl Jung's archetypes. In the text the term "archetype" is used to mean "formless patterns that underlay both instinctual behaviors and primordial images." They are a function of both images and behaviors collected as a result of personal experience, shaping basic ideas/concepts of mother and father, for example. These archetypes serve individuals just as Orisha might, by providing a frame of reference or mode of operation in which individuals effectively approach or deal with the world around them. As in Santería, Jung was interested primarily in those archetypes dealing with inner healing and growth, which he called individuation—the Shadow, the Animal/*Animus,* and the Self.

The importance of understanding Santería in relation to Beatriz Rivera's "African Passions" is of major importance in order to adequately understand the story. Teresa's discovery of Armando's infidelities does not constitute a moment of anguish for her. Instead, as the Orisha gather to her aid, this discovery clearly culminates in victory of spiritual proportions. The reader concludes that Teresa will be alright as she draws, in response to Armando, on her own inner strength, asking the Orisha to "help me get over this man." Teresa's spiritual shift is also evidenced in Babalú Ayé's closing comment, in which he joyfully exclaims, "she summoned me first, did you hear that?" One is left to conclude that all is right with the world.

Source: Laura Kryhoski, Critical Essay on "African Passions," in *Short Stories for Students,* The Gale Group, 2002.

Sources

Alvarez-Borland, Isabel, "Displacements and Autobiography in Cuban-American Fiction," in *World Literature Today,* Winter 1994.

Bendel, Adrienne A., "Humor Infuses Stories of Cuban-Americans," in *Denver Post,* March 19, 1995.

Ekstrom, M. V., Review of "African Passions," in *Choice,* October 1995.

Los Orichas (Los Santos), http://www.dropby.com/Santeria/, (July 16, 2001).

Miguel Angel Asturias, http://www.kirjasto.sci.fi/asturias.htm, (July 21, 2001).

Murphy, Joseph, *Santeria,* Indiana University Press, 1993.

Robertson, Robin, *Beginner's Guide to Jungian Psychology,* Nicholas-Hays, Inc., 1992.

Steinberg, Sybil S., Review of *Midnight Sandwiches at the Mariposa Express,* in *Publishers Weekly,* September 1, 1997.

Suarez, Virgil, "Cuban-American Literature of Exile: From Person to Persona," in *American Literature,* June 1999.

Further Reading

Behar, Ruther, ed., *Bridges to Cuba,* University of Michigan Press, 1996.
    This is a collection of art, poetry, personal essays, and fiction written by Cubans living both in Cuba and in the United States. The book captures the diverse experiences, thoughts, emotions, and conflicts caused by living in exile and by living in Cuba and undergoing the pain of being separated from family members.

Cabrera Infante, Guillermo, *Three Trapped Tigers,* Marlowe & Company, 1997.
    This is a fictional account of life in Havana before Castro. Through the skillful writing of Cabrera Infante, one of Cuba's classic novelists, readers are taken on a joyful literary and linguistic ride as four friends meet each night to tell stories. Through the use of puns,

tongue twisters, and palindromes (a word or sentence that reads the same backward and forward), these four characters parody classic European literature as they make their comical and clever way through the nightlife scene in Cuba.

Matibag, Eugenio, *Afro-Cuban Religious Experience: Cultural Reflections in Narrative,* University Press of Florida, 1996.

Through an interpretive reading of modern Cuban authors, this book examines ways in which the twentieth-century texts reveal the belief systems of Afro-Cubans. Explored are the cultural origins, the rituals, and the doctrines of the four major Afro-Cuban religions: Santería, Nanguismo, Palo Monte, and Voudou.

Perez, Louis A., *On Becoming Cuban: Identity, Nationality, and Culture,* University of North Carolina Press, 1999.

Perez traces the social and cultural impact of North American culture on Cuba during the period of 1860 through 1950, the pre-Castro era. This book offers an historical perspective on life in Cuba as well as a study of Cuban identity during this time frame.

Quirk, Robert E., *Fidel Castro,* W. W. Norton, 1995.

This biography traces Castro's evolution from marginalized student radical to communist dictator of Cuba. Castro, a student protester throughout his college years, eventually abandoned his law practice to devote himself full-time to his radical politics, culminating his efforts with the fall from power of Fulgencio Batista, a United States supported politician. The book covers the details leading up to Castro's leadership, including his friendship with Argentine revolutionary Che Guevara.

America and I

Anzia Yezierska

1923

Anzia Yezierska, known as the "Queen of the Ghetto" or "The Immigrant Cinderella," became a literary sensation in 1920 after the publication of her first volume of short stories, *Hungry Hearts*. Despite this instant celebrity, her career was erratic: her work had fallen out of popular favor by the 1930s, but she had a resurgence in 1950, with publication of the autobiographical *Red Ribbon on a White Horse*. Almost thirty years after Yezierska's death, Alice Kessler-Harris reintroduced her to the English-speaking public when she published *The Open Cage: An Anzia Yezierska Collection*.

"America and I," originally appearing in 1923 in *Children of Loneliness*, is one of three autobiographical articles in the book. While all of Yezierska's work takes as its most important theme the immigrant's creation of her place in America, in "America and I," she addresses these issues in a more direct manner. Her difficulties are multifold: not only must she learn to communicate with Americans, she must convince them that she has something worthy to say. Yezierska's experiences also take on a deeper, more universal meaning; in sharing the hard road to fulfillment of her creative goals, Yezierska chronicles the challenges that face all aspiring writers.

Author Biography

Yezierska was born circa October 19, 1885, in Plinsk, a town on the Russian-Polish border. Around 1892, the family immigrated to the United States, where they settled among other Eastern European Jewish immigrants in New York City's Lower East Side. Yezierska worked in a sweatshop and at other menial jobs during the day. In the evenings, she went to school to learn to read and write English.

At some point, she came to the attention of a group of German-Jewish women who helped immigrant girls obtain an education. With their help, she won a scholarship to study domestic science at Columbia University. She earned her certificate to teach in 1904 but found that she disliked this career.

After a brief marriage that was subsequently annulled, Yezierska married again and had a daughter in 1912. However, discovering that she was not suited to married life, she moved to California with her daughter in 1915. Unable to support the two of them, she sent her child back East and focused her attention on writing.

Her literary career was launched with the publication of the story ''Free Vacation House'' in *Forum* in December 1915. Two years later, she met the philosopher and social scientist John Dewey, who guided her intellectual development.

Recognition came to Yezierska in 1920, when her story ''The Fat of the Land'' was included in *The Best Short Stories of 1919*. A collection of short stories, *Hungry Hearts*, was also published that year, and Samuel Goldwyn, the movie producer, bought the rights to it. Yezierska became an instant celebrity. She moved to California for a second time, but realizing that she could not write away from home, she returned to New York within the year.

In the 1920s, Yezierska published several novels and short story collections. *Bread Givers* (1925), an autobiographical novel about an immigrant girl's struggles with her father, was her best fictional piece of the period, earning her critical acclaim. By the end of the decade, however, interest in Yezierska's work had waned.

From 1929 to 1930, Yezierska held a fellowship at the University of Wisconsin, which allowed her to continue writing despite her poor economic circumstance. However, the American readership remained uninterested, and Yezierska returned to New York in 1932, poor and in need of work. In the mid-1930s, she began to work with the Federal Writers Project, which was a New Deal program. She continued to write but did not publish anything until 1950, when her autobiographical novel *Red Ribbon on a White Horse* came out. This book was well received, and Yezierska wrote short stories and book reviews until her death. She died of a stroke in Ontario, California, on November 21, 1970. Yezierska was rediscovered in the 1970s. A new edition of the long-out-of-print *Bread Givers* came out in 1975 as well as several volumes of her collected fiction and essays.

Plot Summary

In ''America and I,'' Yezierska recalls her experiences finding work that expresses her creativity and thus the America of her dreams. She comes to the United States with hopes of building a new life, the kind of life that she and her ancestors were unable to achieve in Russia. She believes that in America, freed from the need to work constantly just to survive, she will have time to voice her creative self-expression.

She soon discovers she is mistaken. Unable to speak English and with no job skills or training, she is forced to work as a maid for an Americanized Russian family. Although they will not tell her how much she will be paid, she works hard for the family, grateful to have the chance to live with Americans and start to learn English. She also looks forward to receiving her first month's wages so she can buy new clothes and look like an American herself. The family, however, makes no move to pay her. When Yezierska asks them for her wages, they tell her that she should be paying them for the opportunities they are giving her; without knowing English, she is worthless. Yezierska leaves the family immediately, without a penny and having lost her trust for any Americanized immigrants.

Yezierska returns to the Lower East Side, where the Jewish immigrants live. She gets a job at a sweatshop sewing on buttons. She only makes enough money to live in a room that she shares with a dozen other immigrants. She is always hungry, but she likes this job better than working for the family because she has her evenings to herself. When the shop gets busier, however, Yezierska is asked to work longer hours. Eventually, she complains, which gets her fired.

This employment experience, however, allows her to get a job in a regular factory. She has more free time and better pay, but she still feels discontented because she does not speak English well enough. She begins to attend an English class at the factory and confides to the teacher her desire to work with her head and her thoughts, not her hands. The teacher tells her that learning the language will solve her problem, so after Yezierska has mastered reading and writing English, she approaches her teacher again. She follows the teacher's advice of joining a social club run by American women to help immigrant girls. The Women's Association holds a lecture about how to be a happy, efficient worker. However, Yezierska questions how she can be happy when she is not working at a job she loves. The next evening, she goes to see a counselor at a vocational center and tells the woman that she wants a job that will allow her to express her creativity. The counselor advises her to become a shirtwaist designer. Yezierska begins to think that the America of her dreams—the America of self-expression—does not exist.

Frustrated, Yezierska begins to read about American history and the country's first settlements. She realizes that as the Pilgrims had to create a new world, so must she. Unlike the Pilgrims, when confronted with adversity, she has always lost heart and faith in America. She has the epiphany that America is not a finished product but rather a world that is still being created. As a newcomer to America, she too can contribute to the country's development. She decides to write about the life that she and her fellow immigrants experience in America. In doing this, she finds a job she loves and the America she has been seeking. At the same time that she revels in her success, she cannot help but feel sympathy for all the other immigrants who have been unable to achieve their dreams in America.

Characters

Americanized Man

Yezierska's first job is with an Americanized family who originally came from the same town as she did. The man and his wife both chastise Yezierska for speaking to them of her wages and refuse to pay her.

Americanized Woman

Like her husband, the Americanized woman belittles Yezierska when she speaks to them of her wages. She tells Yezierska that working for them is like a summer vacation.

English Teacher

Yezierska takes a class at the factory where she works. She confides to her teacher her desire to work with her head, but the teacher treats her like a child and says she needs to learn English first. When Yezierska approaches the teacher again after she has learned to read and write English, the teacher advises her to join a social club run by American women to help young immigrants.

Sweatshop Owner

Yezierska's second job in America is working in a Lower East Side sweatshop. The old woman who runs the shop demands that the women work longer hours. When Yezierska eventually complains, she throws her out of the shop.

Vocational Counselor

Yezierska visits a vocational counselor so she can find out what kind of job will allow her to express the way she feels inside. The counselor, unable to understand what Yezierska wants, advises her to design shirtwaists instead of sewing them. She tells Yezierska that she must rise from job to job slowly and then she will earn more money. The counselor emphasizes the economic aspects of a job over personal fulfillment.

Anzia Yezierska

Yezierska narrates ''America and I.'' She first arrives in the United States filled with optimism about the fulfillment of her creative needs. In America, she will be valued for her thoughts and ideas, not for the work that her hands can perform. When she discovers that few such opportunities are available to her and that she will have to fight to be heard, she questions what America really is and what it means to her. Despite many disappointing experiences, she holds on to her determination to become a writer. Through self-analysis and perseverance, she is able to create a realistic definition of America and to find a place for herself within its culture. At the same time, she achieves her longed-for dream of doing the work she loves: writing.

Themes

Poverty

Yezierska describes the impoverished circumstances in which the immigrants in New York find themselves. People such as Yezierska came to America to escape such poverty; in Russia, they had to work all the time simply to survive. America, the land of opportunity, is supposed to be much different, but Yezierska finds this is not the case. She works long hours in a sweatshop but still earns only enough money to provide herself the barest of sustenance. When she loses that job, she has nothing to fall back on and is "driven out to cold and hunger" in the streets.

Yezierska experiences another, equally devastating sort of poverty: poverty of the soul. Unable to express her creativity, Yezierska feels something within her "like the hunger in the heart that never gets food." To Yezierska, feeding the soul is as important as feeding the body; a person who works solely for survival is a slave, whereas a creator is a human being. She craves a job that will allow her to share her inner thoughts and feelings. By becoming a writer, Yezierska is able to fulfill her physical and emotional needs and to work her way out of the impoverishment that continues to entrap so many of her fellow immigrants.

Immigration and Cultural Diversity

Throughout its history, the United States has drawn immigrants from around the world with its promise of freedom from religious, political, and economic persecution. From its earliest settlements in the late 1500s and early 1600s, people have come to America seeking a new life. The French and the Dutch first came to North America to earn money from trade. The Pilgrims came to present-day Massachusetts to find the freedom to practice their religion. Other early English settlers were drawn by the promise of obtaining their own land. For example, the state of Georgia was chartered in 1732 as a colony where poor English citizens, such as those who had been jailed for debt, could start a new life.

The generation of immigrants of which Yezierska was a part is no exception. Yezierska and people like her came to escape a country where they were discriminated against socially and economically because of their religion. These immigrants brought to America different ideas and traditions,

Topics for Further Study

- Find out more about Yezierska's life. Then read *Bread Givers* or *Red Ribbon on a White Horse* and analyze these works from a biographical perspective.

- Think about Yezierska's question "Where is America?" Write a personal response that you might share with Yezierska.

- How complete is Yezierska's portrayal of immigrant life? Explain your answer.

- Research political and societal conditions in Russia that caused so many Jews to immigrate to the United States.

- Find out more about the New York immigrant's life in the early 1900s.

- Yezierska has been criticized for her overwrought language and style. Analyze "America and I" from a stylistic point of view.

- Comment of the last paragraph of the story. Do you think Yezierska's prophecy has come through? Explain your answer.

which Yezierska was eager to share in her new country. In "America and I," she speaks of the "Russian soul" as an entity remarkably different from that of the soul of any other ethnicity. The essence that defines Yezierska arose from a background incomprehensible to the people she meets in New York, a background based on discrimination and drudgery, on fear of sudden violence, and on a system of erratic injustice. In Russia, Jewish people had no choice to become what they really wanted to be. In Yezierska, the "hidden sap of centuries would find release; colors that never saw light— songs that died unvoiced—romance that never had a chance to blossom in the black light of the Old World." Yezierska recognizes that the Americans do not understand her feelings; however, she comes to realize that by writing about the plight of the immigrant, she can share with them something of her culture. Through her writing, Yezierska helps to bridge that gap and helps to shape the ever-changing culture of America.

Charity

In the early 1900s, many charitable institutions had formed to help immigrants acclimate to their new lives and assimilate into American culture. In many instances, the cultural groups themselves formed organizations that would provide such services. In ''America and I,'' Yezierska receives aid from organizations created solely by Americans. She learns to read and write English through a class offered at the factory where she is employed. She attends a lecture sponsored by the Women's Association. She visits the Association's Vocational-Guidance Center. However, how much these charities benefit Yezierska is suspect. The Americans who try to help her find her path in America do not understand her hopes and dreams; all their advice is practical and geared toward sustaining a person's physical body, not a person's emotional well-being. When Yezierska tells the guidance counselor that she wants to let out her creative spirit, the counselor responds with a suggestion focusing on how Yezierska should design shirtwaists instead of sewing them, which will earn her more money. For a time, Yezierska feels that America owes her something. ''American gives free bread and rent to criminals in prison. They got grand houses with sunshine, fresh air, doctors and teachers, even for the crazy ones. Why don't they have free boarding-schools for immigrants—strong people—willing people?'' she asks the counselor. However, Yezierska comes to realize that she needs to rely on herself—not charitable associations, Americanized immigrants, or employers. Once she starts to do so, she is able to achieve her dreams and to find America in helping to create it.

Style

Autobiographical Essay

''America and I'' is one of three autobiographical pieces that Yezierska included in *Children of Loneliness*. All of these pieces explore the immigrant's preconceived notions about America, the inevitable disappointment, and finally the reconciliation of illusions and reality, which leads to the creation of a pragmatic, more helpful way of looking at life in this new country. In ''America and I,''

Yezierska finds her own version of America. She introduces herself—and the story—by announcing that she represents all those ''dumb, voiceless ones'' who cannot speak for themselves. Yezierska presents her own experiences of arrival in a new country: the search for work, the inability to communicate, the feelings of not being welcomed. She delves into the transformation that she underwent emotionally during this period, as she comes to realize that America is not the people she meets or simply a country that can fulfill anyone's dream but rather a constantly-changing concept, one that she can help create. As such, Yezierska's autobiographical piece takes on a more universal meaning; it speaks not only for Eastern European Jewish immigrants like herself but for any person who has moved away from home and wants to assimilate into that new culture, yet enhance it.

Point of View

As befits an autobiographical essay, Yezierska narrates ''America and I'' from the first person point of view. Yezierska shares with the reader all the thoughts and feelings she goes through during the course of the story. This point of view gives the reader a more personal connection with the author. For example, because Yezierska explains the hopes that she held for America before her arrival, the reader is able to understand the true depth of her disappointment and disillusionment.

However, because the first person point of view is a limited one, ''America and I'' does not present a cohesive, objective view of immigrant life. For example, in writing about the sweatshop where she works, Yezierska focuses on her own relationship with the owner and her response to the woman's attempts to manipulate the workers. Aside from the detail that the sweatshop is located in a dark basement, she does not provide a composite that would help the reader see the reality of the sweatshop, such as the unsafe, unhealthy working conditions that characterized such places.

Language and Imagery

As some critics pointed out upon the initial publication of *Children of Loneliness* in 1923, Yezierska's language tends to the exaggerated, even overwrought. The opening of ''America and I'' supports this contention to a very real degree; in one long sentence, Yezierska references the ''airless oppression of Russia,'' her own ''stifled spirit'' and darkness, and the Promised Land with its ability to turn such despair into the ''strings of a beautiful violin.'' However, the imagery upon which Yezierska relies suggests that such use of language stems from her own passionate response to coming to America and the power of her aspirations for her new life. When narrating her hopes for herself in America, she returns over and over again to images of flames, fire, and light; even sunlight is described as ''burning though my darkness.'' These words represent Yezierska's belief that America can transform her life and her own ardent longing for this to happen.

Historical Context

Immigrants in the 1900s

Between 1891 and 1910, around twelve million immigrants arrived in the United States. Unlike the wave of immigrants the United States had seen in the mid-1800s, the majority of these so-called new immigrants came from countries in southern or eastern Europe. Most of the Jewish families fled their homelands to escape religious or political persecution, whereas other immigrants sought improved economic opportunities.

Millions of immigrants first set foot on American soil on Ellis Island in New York Harbor. Hundreds of thousands then settled in New York City, where they often lived in slums and crowded, unhealthy apartments. Slum streets were often piled high with garbage and raw sewage, and the slums usually were located right next to polluted industrial areas.

The life of immigrants in the United States was filled with other hardships. They often were only able to obtain low-paying, unskilled jobs. Some worked as many as fifteen hours a day simply to support their families. Education was seen as the key to improving these circumstances, so many adult immigrants attended English classes at night; children often attended public schools. The children of immigrants often became Americanized more quickly than their parents, speaking English and adopting American habits.

Jewish Immigrants in New York City

Most Jews in New York City settled in the Lower East Side, which developed into a thriving community filled with Jewish stores and services. Immigrants could buy kosher meats and other Jewish delicacies, attend a Jewish theater that gave performances in Yiddish, and read a newspaper published in Yiddish. Many Jews faced discrimination; for example, some employers refused to hire Jews. Some Jewish immigrants responded by trying to assimilate into American culture. Among other measures, they adopted American clothing or worked on the Sabbath (Saturday). Other Jews, however, clung to the traditions of their former life, particularly their religious rituals and their habits of spending the majority of time studying the Torah, which is the first five books of the Old Testament.

Urban Reform in the 1910s and 1920s

As the cities became increasingly crowded, city officials found themselves unable to keep up with demands for housing and social services. As a result, thousands of families lived in unsafe, unsanitary conditions. The drive to reform the cities began in the early 1900s, and these problems were addressed in a number of ways. For example, New York passed a law in 1901 that greatly improved new tenement buildings. Other reformers led a campaign to provide children with safe places to play, and by 1920 cities had spent millions of dollars building playgrounds. A city-planning movement also grew with the goal of halting the spread of slums and beautifying the city. City planners controlled and regulated city growth, created safer building codes, and developed public parkland. Civil engineers improved city transportation and paved the streets. Sanitation engineers worked on solving the problems of water supply, waste disposal, and pollution.

Women in the 1920s

During the 1920s, the so-called New Woman appeared. No longer believing that marriage and family was the ultimate goal in her life, many women asserted their independence and challenged traditional ways of looking at their roles and behaviors. Some women became reformers or sought to gain entry into the work world. Many women simply enjoyed the personal freedoms changing social roles brought them, for example, exchanging restrictive Victorian garments for looser-fitting, more casual clothing and cutting their hair.

Critical Overview

Published in the 1923 collection *Children of Loneliness*, ''America and I'' is one of three autobiographical essays through which Yezierska relates aspects of the immigrant experience. This book

Compare
&
Contrast

- **1900s:** By the beginning of the decade, more than two million children in the United States work in factories. Reformers persuade state legislatures to pass laws regulating child labor. Some states prohibit the employment of young children. Other states limit the employment of older children to eight to ten hours a day or bar them from working at night or in dangerous conditions. Still other states require that children obtain literacy before they are sent to work.

  1920s: In the 1920s, children and adolescents generally enjoy more leisure time and less responsibility for family support. No major laws regarding child labor are passed, although reformers continue to be interested in the issue.

  Today: All states require that children attend school, generally from age six to sixteen, and laws prevent children under the age of fourteen from working, with the exception of specific jobs. Many students work part-time, however. Fourteen- and fifteen-year-olds may be employed outside of school hours no more than three hours a day and eighteen hours a week when school is in session. There are no federal laws restricting the work hours of sixteen- and seventeen-year-olds.

- **1900s:** In 1900, forty percent of Americans live in urban areas. Only three American cities have populations greater than one million. The majority of American cities have populations between 50,000 and 100,000.

  1920s: By 1920, for the first time in American history, more than half of all Americans live in urban areas.

  Today: In 1990, just over seventy-five percent of Americans live in urban areas.

- **1900s:** From 1900 to 1920, about 14.5 million people immigrate to the United States. The vast majority of immigrants come from Europe, particularly Austria-Hungary, Italy, and the former Soviet Union. The American population of people born in Europe stands at 8,882,000 in 1900.

  1920s: From 1920 to 1930, just over four million people immigrate to the United States. Of these, close to 2.5 million come from Europe, particularly from Italy and Germany. The American population of people born in Europe stands at 11,916,000 in 1920.

  Today: In the 1990s, just under seven million people immigrate to the United States. Of these, only about one million people are Europeans. The majority of immigrants come from Asia and Mexico. The American population of people born in Europe stands at 4,350,000 in 1990.

- **1900s:** By the turn of the century, reformers, primarily women, are attempting to achieve women's suffrage at a state level. However, they have few early successes, and by 1901 only four states have given women full voting rights. In 1914, however, some reform groups are attempting to win women's suffrage on a national level.

  1920s: The Nineteenth Amendment, which gives women the right to vote, is passed in 1919 and ratified the following year. The Equal Rights Amendment is first proposed to Congress in 1923 by Alice Paul, a leading member of the National Women's Party. Many people, including women, oppose this amendment because they fear it will make legislation protecting women workers unconstitutional, and the amendment fails to win political support.

  Today: More and more women are holding public office, with numbers rising continually throughout the 1980s and 1990s. In 1999, 1,664 women held offices in the state legislatures and sixty-five women served in Congress.

includes pieces that reiterate the author's major themes of the conflicts between the Old World and the New World, and the desire to be a crucial part of America.

Despite such fundamental similarities to 1920s *Hungry Hearts*, which helped drive Yezierska's early success, this volume drew less attention. Many Jewish critics reproved Yezierska for her rendering of immigrant speech patterns, which they felt made immigrants sound ignorant. Several mainstream critics commented on Yezierska's lack of self-control in her writing. "[H]er emotion tends to become emotionalism, to run away with her instead of being under firm control," wrote Dorothy Scarborough in the *Literary Review*. The critic for the *Springfield Republican* also commented that the work was at times "incoherent and reckless in its lack of restraint." Despite this characteristic, the critic believed that overall the volume "rings true." Similarly, the *New York Times* noted the book's frequent "slips into melodrama" but concluded that the book has "a value because of the vivid picture it gives of life on the east side, among the immigrants, their hopes and fears and way of looking at thing[s]."

Critics for the *Times Literary Supplement* (London) and the *Literary Digest International Book Review*, by contrast, had unreserved praise for *Children of Loneliness*. Wrote William Lyon Phelps in the *Literary Digest International Book Review*, "[L]ong before she had attained . . . mastery of the English language . . . there was in her work a core of fire." The writer for the *Times Literary Supplement* (London) posited different paths the immigrant in America might take: he may be absorbed, or undergo Americanization, thus losing his soul, or he may not be absorbed, in which case he will lose everything except his soul. However, there is one more alternative: "he may be absorbed and yet in rare cases save his soul actively and devote it to realizing his dream in the service of America. . . . This is what has happened to Anzia Yezierska." The writer further comments on how *Children of Loneliness* demonstrates the crucial lesson that Yezierska has learnt in America: "there is a thing more terrible than the hunger for bread—the hunger for people . . . [and] a burning desire for self-expression in art or literature"—a theme that particularly applies to "America and I."

The *New York Times* writer specifically singled out Yezierska's nonfiction pieces as "the most interesting portion of the volume." According to this critic, Yezierska's writing skill lies in her ability to portray the people and life that she knows— the life of the tenements. "Her gift is not creative," reads the review: "she is a reporter and an autobiographist rather than a fiction writer."

Criticism

Rena Korb

Korb has a master's degree in English literature and creative writing and has written for a wide variety of educational publishers. In the following essay, Korb explores the development of Yezierska's concept of America and her fulfillment of her creative goals.

In a *Literary Digest* issue from 1923, Yezierska shared her view of America as "a new world in the making, that anyone who has something real in him can find a way to contribute himself in this new world." At the same time, she noted, "But I saw I had to wait for my chance to give what I had to give, with the same life and death earnestness with which a man fights for his bread." That same year, her third published work, *Children of Loneliness* (a novella with ten short stories and three autobiographical pieces), came out. "America and I," one of those autobiographical pieces, describes the experiences that Yezierska went through that led to the development of this philosophy. This piece aptly fits Alice Kessler-Harris's description of Yezierska's mission, "to interpret her people to America," which she writes about in the introduction to *The Open Cage*, a 1979 reissue of some of Yezierska's work.

Yezierska relates her immigrant plight, from her first arrival in this "golden land of flowing opportunity" to her current success as a writer with the gift of introducing her people to their adopted culture. As an eager newcomer, Yezierska has grand dreams of what she will find in America; to Yezierska and the millions of immigrants like her, America stands in marked contrast to Russia. The Old World chokes its people with "airless oppression," but America brings sunlight to this darkness. In the Old World, Yezierska and her people have no opportunity for economic betterment, but in America they can escape "from the dead drudgery for bread." Yezierska's soul and spirit were "stifled" in the Old World, but in America, Yezierska can revel in her ability to give voice to her own forms of self-

Immigrant workers in the slums of New York in 1887

expression. "For the first time in America, I'd cease to be a slave of the belly," Yezierska recalls how she felt at the time. "I'd be a creator, a giver, a human being."

Yezierska sees her inability to communicate as the major obstacle standing in the way of her dreams. Although she is in America, she is pushed to the outskirts of American society because she has "No speech, no common language, no way to win a smile of understanding from them." Once she is able to speak the language, Yezierska is confident that the Americans would want to hear about "the richness" in her. When an "Americanized" immi-

grant family offers to hire her as a maid, she moves in with them, hoping this will allow her to "begin my life in the sunshine, after my long darkness." To Yezierska, this couple, "so well-dressed, so well-fed," seem symbolic of the transformative success that America can bring.

As the narrative style underscores, Yezierska glorifies everything American: the "music of the American language," American words, "new American things," "an American dress and hat." She is "so grateful to mingle with the American people" at the house where she works as a maid that she "never knew tiredness." While living there,

What Do I Read Next?

- Yezierska's *Bread Givers: A Struggle between a Father of the Old World and a Daughter of the New World* (1925) is the author's most fully realized fictional work. Based on events from her childhood, the novel explores the struggles that Sara goes through as she breaks free from her traditional Old World family to become an independent woman.

- *Red Ribbon on a White Horse* is Yezierska's fictionalized autobiography. Yezierska published this work, to great acclaim, in 1950, when she was nearly seventy years old.

- *Call It Sleep* (1934) is Henry Roth's highly praised novel about the experiences of Jewish immigrants in New York City. It focuses on a young boy, his difficult relationship with his father, and the squalid urban environment in which they live. Today, this novel is considered a classic of Jewish-American literature.

- Chaim Potok, the son of Polish immigrants, was raised in New York in the 1930s and 1940s. His first novel, *The Chosen* (1967) tells the story of the son of a Hasidic rabbi who is encouraged to study secular subjects. His next novel, *The Promise* (1969), follows the same characters into young adulthood.

- Betty Smith's *A Tree Grows in Brooklyn* (1943) chronicles the story of young Francie Nolan, growing up in a poor family in New York City in the early 1900s.

- Sholem Asch's *Salvation* (1934) is the story of a Polish Jewish community in the 1800s. This book vividly recreates the persecution of the Jews.

- *"A Scrap of Time"* and Other Stories (1987) collects Polish author Ida Fink's short fiction. These stories relate the experiences of Jews in Poland before and during the Holocaust.

- Cecyle S. Neidle's *America's Immigrant Women* (1976) discusses the contributions of women, including Yezierska's, to the development of the United States and its culture from the 1600s onward.

- Jacob A. Riis's *How the Other Half Lives* (1890), documenting slum life in the late 1800s, exposed the foul conditions under which New York's urban poor were forced to exist. His perennially popular work contributed to the social reform movements that improved city life.

- Abraham Cahan was a Jewish writer who came to the United States in 1882. His novel *The Rise of David Levinsky* (1917), one of the first books about the Jewish immigrant's experience, remains relevant for its vivid re-creation of life on New York's Lower East Side.

Yezierska comes to perceive herself as an American on the inside, for example "developing American eyes" with which to look at the world. All she needs—or so she thinks—is American clothing to cover up her immigrant heritage. With new clothes, "I'd show them I could look like an American in a day." She is still filled with optimism; she does not comprehend that merely possessing the outward trappings of an American will not make her one.

Through her experience with the family, however, Yezierska comes to learn a bitter lesson: being

"American" does not make something good. The family cheats her out of her wages, leaving Yezierska with nothing to show for a month's hard work other than a new distrust of so-called "Americans." However, Yezierska's narrative also shows her understanding that it is the man and woman who label themselves as such. They are not American-born, actually coming from Yezierska's own village in Russia. They only *want* to be American because of the economic opportunities it provides, such as the comfortable home and the nourishing food—as well as the chance to feel superior to other newer immi-

"The 'bridge of understanding' that Yezierska works to build with words can only expand and improve American-born and immigrant readers' ideas about the country they call home."

grants. This family so embraces their adopted country that they are even "ashamed to remember their mother tongue." Yezierska's reiteration of the word *"American"* implies that this family does not really represent America. Their self-portrayal of themselves as such is as fleeting as the "false friendship" they offered Yezierska. In turning her back on them, Yezierska is not turning her back on America at all.

Holding on to her belief in the concept of America and determining to search anew, Yezierska returns to the slums of New York, where her people have settled. She finds a job that she might have held in Russia—sewing buttons in a sweatshop—a job that affords her only the bare minimum of sustenance. The outward circumstances that face Yezierska make her wonder, "'Where is America? Is there an America?'" Yezierska begins to question what before had been her profound faith.

As time goes by, Yezierska moves her way up in the industrial world, going to work for a factory and maintaining a regular schedule with Sundays off. Still, she continues to hold fast to the belief that her America will be the place where can "work for love and not for a living." When she tries to take steps in this direction, however, the native Americans she meets seem intent on making her aware of the folly of this philosophy. In her efforts to better herself and to fulfill her creative dreams, Yezierska seeks out assistance, but the first person to whom she turns has no comprehension of the depth of her feelings. When she confides to her English teacher, "I want to do something with my head, my feelings," the woman advises her that she first worry about learning the language and then "patted me as if I was not yet grown up."

The teacher does tell her about the Women's Association, which Yezierska visits. This organization has the ostensible purpose of "trying to help the working-girl find herself," but instead it coordinates activities that promote the needs and success of employers. Yezierska attends a lecture "The Happy Worker and His Work," which is sponsored by the association. The lecturer extols efficiency in the factory worker at the same time he asserts, "It's economy for the boss to make the worker happy." Equating what makes the worker happy with her own vision of what would make her happy—expressing her thoughts and feelings through her writing—Yezierska believes these words apply to her. However, this lecture, filled with "educated language that was over my head," offers Yezierska nothing except for false hope.

Yezierska's next step toward achieving her goal is to go to the Vocational-Guidance Center, where she explains to the counselor that her job sewing shirtwaists makes her heart "waste away." She describes her major problem as "I think and think, and my thoughts can't come out." To this plaint, the counselor replies with an answer focused on economic achievement, not personal fulfillment: "Why don't you think out your thoughts in shirtwaists? You could learn to be a designer. Earn more money." The counselor cannot understand Yezierska's yearning to do more with herself than merely earn a living. More strikingly, as illustrated by her words "You have to *show* that you have something special for America before America has need of you," the counselor does not even believe that Yezierska yet has a right to aspire to more than being a menial worker. Her admonishment seems to tell Yezierska—and all immigrants—not to hold goals surrounding intellectual, philosophical, artistic, or creative pursuits, but instead to focus only on pragmatic ones. The counselor would feed the body while stifling the soul.

Frustrated, Yezierska comes to feel that "the America of my dreams never was and never could be." However, in letting go of her vision of America as a Utopia, Yezierska opens herself up to finding out what America really can be for her. By reading American history, she takes the important first step of rethinking her concept of America, and subsequently revamping it. America, she realizes, does not owe her the opportunities she seeks, but she must fight for them herself. Yezierska must emulate the Pilgrims who "made no demands on anybody, but on their own indomitable spirit of persistence." Yezierska also realizes that not only is she erring in "forever begging a crumb of sympathy," she is also doing so from the Americans—"strangers who could not understand."

Yezierska experiences her life-altering epiphany when she comes to realize that America is "a world still in the making." She can contribute to the ongoing creation of the country through the expression of her inner thoughts and feelings. In writing about the life of the immigrants, her achievement is two-fold: she finds the America of her dreams, but she also widens the perception of the country for the native born by "open[ing] up my life and the lives of my people to them." The "bridge of understanding" that Yezierska works to build with words can only expand and improve American-born and immigrant readers' ideas about the country they call home.

At the same time, particularly because she understands the role of *all* Americans in inventing the country, she feels sadness that so many immigrants "with my longing, my burning eagerness, to do and to be, [are] wasting their days in drudgery they hate." These people are losing out on the opportunity to fulfill their own dreams, and "America is losing all that richness of the soul." In these sentiments, Yezierska asserts her belief that people—even those who the American mainstream would ignore—have their unique gifts to offer and can thus shape the world in which they live.

"America and I" ends on the positive vision that Yezierska holds for the future of the country. She writes, "the America that is every day nearer coming to be, will be too wise, too open-hearted, too friendly-handed, to let the least lastcomer at their gates knock in vain with his gifts unwanted." Whether Yezierska's prophecy has come true is not for her to determine: it is for the individual, who may even decide to embrace self-expression as a further means of shaping the ever-unfolding world.

Source: Rena Korb, Critical Essay on "America and I," in *Short Stories for Students,* The Gale Group, 2002.

Kate Covintree

Covintree is a graduate of Randolph-Macon Women's College with a degree in English. In this essay, Covintree discusses the immigrant experience as expressed through Yezierska's short story.

First published in 1922, Anzia Yezierska's short story "America and I" touches on many of the issues and themes common in all her work, including the struggle of the immigrant to be a part of the promise of America. This is the story of a young female narrator who comes to America with a dream and a desire to make something of herself. She has many expectations of what she will be able to become when she arrives, but instead she is immediately introduced to the base reality of America and its treatment of the immigrant community. This is a story of the struggle of assimilation, of the challenges faced by an outsider trying to become part of the mainstream culture. In an ideal situation, aspects of both cultures begin to blend, and a variant of the main culture becomes primary. In this case, the narrator is in the minority group,—"one of the millions of immigrants"—of Jews from Eastern Europe, who are fighting to be heard in their new country and culture. Neither culture knows quite how to respond to the other.

Yezierska's narrator comes to America

[with a] soul pregnant with the unlived lives of generations clamoring for expression. What [her] mother and father and their mother and father never had a chance to give out in Russia, [she] would give out in America.

She believes that America is a place that will welcome her as an individual with ideas and passions that can make her and America flourish. She expects America to feed her soul, "I'd cease to be a slave of the belly. I'd be a creator, a giver, a human being!" What she finds, though, is that her expectations of the American dream fall short because she is an immigrant girl who enters a country without adequate money, clothing, training, or language skills. In addition, she longs to discover a way to make her dreams come true, a way to reinvent herself as a real American.

The narrator left Russia because she believed there was nothing for her there: she came to America with the desire to give of herself, without any knowledge of how to translate her passionate desire into something that would provide food and shelter and money. Her passions are not enough to sustain her, and she, like so many other immigrants, accepts a menial position as a maid for a family from the Old World who appear to have assimilated to this New World.

She takes this position with comfort, believing herself to be "in the hands of American friends, invited to share with them their home, their plenty, their happiness." With this job, she expects to learn the language and have money for clothes. She believes her vision of America is in sight. She works tirelessly for them, absorbing what she can about

> Yezierska's narrator has dreams that she does not want to trade, and she struggles to maintain them, to live in the new country based on her expectations, not the harsh reality she encounters."

her new country, only to discover they will not pay her for her work. Though providing room and board, these Old World connections do not help the narrator in fulfilling her American dream. In fact, they demean her and shame her for even believing that she is entitled to her own time and her own wages. For the narrator, this is a betrayal. "It went black for my eyes," she says. Her one American connection is soured, as are her feelings toward immigrants who become Americanized: "It was blotted out in my all trust in friendship from 'Americans.'"

This Americanized family becomes an example of one way immigrants choose to blend with their new culture, by almost dismissing their very origin. "[T]hey were so well fed, so successful in America, that they were ashamed to remember their mother tongue." As the husband and wife rise in wealth and stature, they have no qualms about taking advantage of a former neighbor by denying her wages and thereby a means to create a respectable place for herself in America. Perhaps this couple rose to their current status through such basic labor, or perhaps they had been a part of this new culture long enough that they felt entitled to make those who came after them struggle to survive. Whatever the reasons, Yezierska chooses not to explain them. She merely demonstrates, through this couple's callous nature towards the narrator, one reality of this New World.

This was a culture that did not and would not accept all the ways of the Old World, especially one immediately visible—dress. As Yezierska's narrator states from the beginning, she longs for new clothes so that she can appear American. The narrator believes, like many other immigrant Jews of the time, that American clothing held with it what

Christopher Okonkwo described in his article "Of Repression, Assertion, and the Speakerly Dress" as "transfigurative potential." With American clothes, the narrator could suddenly transform herself from an immigrant into an American. "Jews were compelled to discard that sartorial part of their ethnic identity in order to be accepted in America," according to Okonkwo. But of course, before Yezierska's narrator can buy these alternative clothes, she must work in the very shops that make them.

When she takes factory jobs, she begins to see the reality of the garment industry. Initially, the narrator believes these jobs allow her opportunity to pursue her own dreams and that even her defiance of their bribes is a sign of her assimilation to America. However, like the Americanized family before, she discovers her bosses have other motives. They bribe her with "tea [and] herring over black bread" and English classes only to keep her working in their factory. They are motivated by greed and will use whatever means to gain their profit. Yezierska's narrator cannot reconcile this motive for herself. Gaining the means to buy her American clothes does not quiet her longing to be American. Looking the part does not satisfy "the hunger in the heart that never gets food." She can sense her own soul seeping away. As Ron Ebest cites in his article "Anzia Yezierska and the Popular Debate Over the Jews": "The dead work with my hands was killing me. My work left only hard stones on my heart." It is as though she must trade her penniless dreaming for the financial reality of factory work which "stifles . . . expression." Yezierska's narrator has dreams that she does not want to trade, and she struggles to maintain them, to live in the new country based on her expectations, not the harsh reality she encounters.

The reality is Yezierska's America keeps the immigrant at a distance. This American culture is unwilling to accept or incorporate foreign ways. As Ebest goes on to say in his article: "Yezierska suggest[s] a casual relationship between American indifference [to the Jewish immigrants] and sweatshop labor." America abdicated any real responsibility for the narrator. The industry takes no interest in her passions nor her skills unless they can improve productivity. In the factory, with a regular American work schedule of eight-hour work days and five-day work weeks, the young woman at the Vocational-Guidance Center tells her: "You have to show that you have something special for America before America has need of you." What skills she has gained in the factories do not show she is something special. They show she is a typical immigrant who will get no special privileges. The guidance counselor explains the American dream as "earn[ing] your living at what you know and ris[ing] slowly from job to job." This is the reality she discovers, a lifetime of factory labor. It turns her dream into "a shadow . . . a chimera of lunatics and crazy immigrants."

When faced with this reality, Yezierska's narrator discovers a greater reality: no matter what clothes she wears or how well she speaks, she will always be an immigrant because America "could not understand what the Russian soul in me wanted." The narrator has followed all the channels she knows, and still she is forced to remain "one of the dumb . . . beating out their hearts at [America's] gates for a breath of understanding." This is the true struggle of assimilation for the immigrant, to find a way to make the dominant culture discover the true value and talents of the non-native so that he or she can be seen as an equal in the community, not just a slave laborer. The narrator wants to be heard, to "be a creator, a giver, a human being." Without language, the voice of the immigrant cannot speak and the New World appears deaf.

However, when the narrator learns English, commonality still cannot be achieved. Throughout the story, the narrator tries to share her dream of "living joy of fullest self expression." Each time she shares her dreams with America, she is rebuked, dismissed, and shamed into feeling grateful for her place in America. "You should be glad we keep you here." Even with common language, the narrator is silenced and must find her voice in some other way.

Yezierska emphasizes the New World's oppressive silence of the immigrant by never naming the narrator. In this way, this nameless character represents America's insensitivity to the immigrant. Americans can perhaps listen to the story of struggle but cannot relate it to a real person living in their own America. They can step back from the nameless stranger and remove themselves from the struggle. In the same respect, though, the narrator becomes the Everyman for all foreigners who bring their dreams to American shores. This story of longing and silence becomes their story. Persons who feel unable to find their place in American culture can hear their own voice in the cries of the narrator. As the narrator speaks, she tells of the "burning eagerness" waiting inside so many other voiceless immigrants.

It is in telling the story that Yezierska's narrator finally finds her voice and also fulfills her dream to be a part of America. This appears to take place for Yezierska's narrator after she researches American history and comes to the conclusion that Americans survived because of their own "indomitable spirit of persistence." She also concludes that all of her dreaming about being a part of America was really just her "begging for a crumb of sympathy." Suddenly she is enlightened and sees that she has a place in "the making of America like those Pilgrims who came in the *Mayflower*." The narrator finds her voice in sharing her immigrant story and finds that by doing so she is able to "build a bridge of understanding between the American-born and [her]self." Through writing, she discovers a means of joining her new American culture while still maintaining her immigrant heritage.

Her writing is her voice and her fulfillment of her American dream. "In only writing about the Ghetto I found America." She can use her own experience as an outsider clamoring to get in as a guide for other immigrants, and for America. With her story comes the exposure of the reality that "America is losing the richness of the soul." It is the narrator's hope that such exposure becomes an agent of change. This is her future vision of successful assimilation. Her hope for the immigrants is that they persevere long enough to share their gifts. For the Americans, she hopes they open their arms, ready to fully take in these immigrant treasures. In this new America, dreams of the future are not dashed and dismissed by the realities of the present.

Source: Kate Covintree, Critical Essay on "America and I," in *Short Stories for Students*, The Gale Group, 2002.

Sources

Ebest, Ron, "Anzia Yezierska and the Popular Debate Over the Jews," in *MELUS*, Vol. 25, No. 1, Spring 2000, pp. 105–27.

Kessler-Harris, Alice, Introduction to *The Open Cage, An Anzia Yezierska Collection* by Anzia Yezierska, Persea Books, 1979, p. viii.

Okonkwo, Christopher N., "Of Repression, Assertion, and the Speakerly Dress: Anzia Yezierska's Salome of the Tenements," in *MELUS*, Vol. 25, No. 1, Spring 2000, pp. 129–45.

Phelps, William Lyon, Review of *Children of Loneliness*, in *Literary Digest International Book Review*, December 1923, p. 21, quoted in Louise Levitas Henriksen, *Anzia Yezierska: A Writer's Life*, Rutgers University Press, 1988.

Review of *Children of Loneliness,* in *New York Times,* October 28, 1923, p. 9.

Review of *Children of Loneliness,* in *Springfield Republican,* Dec. 9, 1923, p. 7a.

Review of *Children of Loneliness,* in *Times Literary Supplement* (London), November 8, 1923, p. 748.

Scarborough, Dorothy, Review of *Children of Loneliness,* in *Literary Review,* Nov. 24, 1923, p. 279.

Yezierska, Anzia, Article, in *Literary Digest,* quoted in Alice Kessler-Harris, Introduction to *The Open Cage, An Anzia Yezierska Collection* by Anzia Yezierska, Persea Books, 1979, p. viii.

Further Reading

Blumenthal, Shirley, *Coming to America: Immigrants from Eastern Europe,* Delacorte Press, 1981.
Covering the period from 1874 through 1924, the author traces the path of the immigrants from impoverished peasants in Eastern Europe to factory, mills, and mines in America.

Glazer, Nathan, *American Judaism,* University of Chicago Press, 1989.
First published in 1957, this current edition of this definitive work on the nature of Judaism in post–World War II America offers an updated introduction covering shifts in American Judaism since the 1970s.

Howe, Irving, *World of Our Fathers,* Galahad Books, 2001.
This is a noted historian's massive sociocultural history of the Russian Jews who immigrated to the United States between 1881 and 1921.

Inglehart, Babette, ''Daughters of Loneliness: Anzia Yezierska and the Immigrant Woman Writer,'' in *Studies in American Jewish Literature,* Winter 1975, pp. 1–10.
This article discusses Yezierska's relation to her culture.

Meltzer, Milton, ed., *The Jewish Americans: A History in Their Own Words, 1650–1950,* Crowell, 1982.
This book synthesizes the experiences of Jewish Americans by presenting excerpts from such documents as letters, journals, diaries, autobiographies, and speeches.

Sachar, Howard, *A History of the Jews in America,* Knopf, 1992.
Sachar's comprehensive work examines significant American Jews, Jewish culture in America, and more from the country's earliest days of settlement up through contemporary times.

Schoen, Carol, *Anzia Yezierska,* Twayne Publishers, 1982.
Schoen presents an overview of Yezierska's literary career.

Bright and Morning Star

Richard Wright

1938

When Richard Wright wrote ''Bright and Morning Star,'' he was involved with the Communist Party. His first published stories (a category to which ''Bright and Morning Star'' belongs) centered on communist themes, such as organizing the working force and fighting for the rights of oppressed people. These first stories most often appeared in leftist periodicals.

At the time of publication of ''Bright and Morning Star,'' Wright was living in New York and was working as the Harlem editor for the communist newspaper the *Daily Worker*. ''Bright and Morning Star'' was first published in 1938 in *The Masses,* a radical, socialist monthly journal, and was not collected in the original publication of *Uncle Tom's Children*. Rather, it was in 1940, when *Uncle Tom's Children* was reprinted and expanded, that ''Bright and Morning Star'' was included in this collection.

Besides being influenced by the philosophy of the Community Party, Wright often made mention, especially during the beginning of his writing career, of Theodore Dreiser and Sinclair Lewis, writers who discussed topics such as the debilitating effects of the American class system and the struggles of working-class people, and whose writing styles impressed Wright. Wright admired their straightforward language and their goal to reproduce in their stories a reality that was as close to truth as possible, and he adopted the style to reflect on the absurdities of the oppression of black people.

However, it was not Wright's writing style that attracted his eventual wide readership. It was his subject matter, which he presented in shocking and realistic detail. When ''Bright and Morning Star'' was published in the revised edition of *Uncle Tom's Children,* Wright was well known because of the commercial success of his novel *Native Son.* He gained this fame just as the Harlem Renaissance (a name given to an era, vaguely assigned as the 1920s, of a flourishing of African-American arts) was fading. Wright's work, with its more realistic and angrier tone, is said to have signaled a new period in African-American literature. The new writing was more political than the body of works that had been produced during the Harlem Renaissance. Wright's books prefigured the beginning of the Black Arts Movement (1950s to 1970s), whose authors included Ralph Ellison (*The Invisible Man,* 1952) and James Baldwin (*Go Tell It on the Mountain,* 1953). The overall aim of this group's literature was to end racism, and the movement has been hailed as one of the more important forces behind the eventual Civil Rights movement. Many authors in this movement were said to have been greatly influenced by Wright's work.

Author Biography

Richard Nathaniel Wright was born on Rucker's Plantation on September 4, 1908, in Roxie, Mississippi. This was, writes Alfred Kazin in his article ''Too Honest for His Own Time,'' ''a terrible place for a poor black to be born.'' Wright's father, Nathan, an illiterate sharecropper, deserted his family when Wright was five years old. Ella (Wilson), Wright's mother, was a schoolteacher, but after her husband left, she had to take on jobs as a maid or cook. Wright was forced to move from state to state, as his mother pursued jobs and looked for financial support from other family members.

Because of his mother's disintegrating health, Wright spent the latter part of his youth under the supervision of his maternal grandmother, Margaret Bolden Wilson, a strict Seventh Day Adventist who believed that all nonreligious books were works of the devil. Wright, gifted with unusual intelligence, never understood why his mother and grandmother, as well as most of the black southern population around him, acted so subservient to white people, and he developed a rebellious attitude that included a love of learning about life outside of his daily parameters—specifically, life experiences referred

to in nonreligious books. He became a voracious reader, with H. L. Mencken, Theodore Dreiser, and Sinclair Lewis being among his first favorites.

Wright attended several different schools, but the last of his formal education ended with his graduation from the ninth grade, for which he was class valedictorian. One year prior to this graduation, the *Southern Register,* a local newspaper, published Wright's first work, an adventure story titled ''The Voodoo of Hell's Half-Acre.'' Whether it was this publication of his work or his rebellious nature that inspired him, Wright came to the conclusion that public education was not teaching him enough, and shortly after dropping out of school, he began a journey that would lead him to Chicago, where he would join the Federal Negro Theatre, the Illinois Writers' Project, and, eventually, the American Communist Party.

Most of Wright's early works were heavily influenced by the leftist politics of the Communist Party, and in 1937 he moved to New York to become the editor of the party's paper, the *Daily Worker.* One year later, a collection of Wright's short stories was published with the title *Uncle Tom's Children.* ''Bright and Morning Star'' (first published in *The Masses,* a monthly socialist journal of arts and politics) was not included in this collection until after Wright enjoyed a triumphal reception of his first published novel, *Native Son* (1940), and *Uncle Tom's Children* was reissued as an expanded edition.

Black Boy (1945), Wright's autobiographical story about his childhood, would mark the end of his most popular publications. He would continue publishing but not to the same wide publicity and sales that he had enjoyed earlier. He was, however, not idle during this time. Besides his continued writing projects, he was involved in the production of the film of *Native Son,* lectured in major European capitals, and made several guest appearances on radio and television. During the decade after World War II, when the foundations of European colonialism were in decline, Wright traveled to African and Asian countries, ''fascinated,'' as Robert Bone writes in his book *Richard Wright,* ''by this confrontation of a civilization and its former subject peoples.'' From these travels came Wright's summary of the colonial revolution in his book *White Man, Listen!* (1957).

Wright was married twice: first, in 1939, to Rose Dhima Meadman, a classical dancer; and second, in 1941, to Ellen Poplar, a Communist Party organizer. He had two daughters with Ellen: Julia (born in 1942) and Rachel (born in 1949). In 1947, Wright moved to Paris, France, where he remained until his death on November 28, 1960. Officially, Wright died of a heart attack; however, some people, including his daughter Julia, have contended that Wright was murdered. During the last year of his life, Wright suffered from amoebic dysentery, an ailment that he apparently acquired during his travels. While his wife and daughters visited London (a visit that Wright was denied by British government officials), he entered a medical clinic in Paris to recuperate. It was here that Wright was proclaimed dead. He was fifty-two years old. On the third of December, Wright's body was cremated, along with a copy of his *Black Boy*. His ashes remain at the Pere Lachaise Cemetery in Paris.

Richard Wright

Plot Summary

Part I

The first part of ''Bright and Morning Star'' begins with the protagonist, Sue, standing at the window, looking into the rain, wondering when her son Johnny-Boy will come home. He is late, and Sue is worried. She fears for her son because he is involved in organizing his community in order to gain power through the Communist Party. Her son Sug is already in jail for the same practices.

Sue is proud of her sons because they are strong enough to withhold secret information about the members of the Communist Party, even when pain is inflicted upon them by the sheriff and his men. Sue is a descendent of slaves, living in the South where Jim Crow laws prevail, under which blacks are systematically denied civil and political rights and their labor is exploited. Sue lives in poverty and stress. She is fearful of white people because of her own lack of power. Early in her life, Sue turned to Christianity to help ease the horrendous conditions under which she lived. She sought solace in religion, which promised her everlasting reward upon her death. All Sue had to do was make it through this life, avoiding all contamination from sin, and she would go to heaven. This meant that she had to be kind to her aggressors, submissive to their threats and abuses, and humble in her requests.

Sue's sons, on the other hand, take a different turn in their lives. They discover socialism as defined by the Community Party. They believe that

they must take their lives into their own hands and fight for what is rightfully theirs. Slowly, Sue has come to understand her sons' philosophy, although she still holds on to some of her religious beliefs. She also holds onto her fear and mistrust of white people, something that her sons attempt to resolve, because they believe that they need sympathetic white people to help them gain power.

While Sue is jointly involved in reminiscing and worrying about the late arrival of her son Johnny-Boy, she hears footsteps on her front porch. It is the young white girl Reva, who has a crush on Johnny-Boy and who also helps him in his attempts to organize the community. Sue and Reva have a brief conversation in which Reva tells Sue that one of the members of the secret group has told the sheriff about an upcoming meeting. Although Sue is troubled about Johnny-Boy, she does not tell Reva about her concern. She does not want Reva to worry. Sue only tells her that Johnny-Boy is a little late coming home and that maybe Reva should tell her father to get the word out on his own. Reva then leaves, and Sue ponders about the girl, wondering why she is so naive about becoming involved with her son. Interracial marriages or even physical contact between the sexes was not only illegal or forbidden in the South, it could be deadly.

Part II

As the second part opens, Sue hears footsteps in the mud outside her house. She recognizes them as the sounds of her son Johnny-Boy. He enters the house in silence, and Sue, as is her custom, doesn't look his way. The narrator explains that Sue and Johnny-Boy have a way of communicating in silence. Instead, Sue thinks about her husband and wonders how he might have affected the lives of her sons. She also thinks about Reva and Johnny-Boy, knowing that Reva loves him, but Sue is still worried about the dismal future of that relationship.

Johnny-Boy and Sue then engage in a brief conversation. Sue feeds him and dries his clothes before she tells him the news about the sheriff having found out about the secret meeting. She gives Johnny-Boy time to relax. When Sue does tell him, she begins a familiar argument with him, telling him that he shouldn't trust white people so much. Sue suspects that it is one of the white people in the group who has snitched to the sheriff. Johnny-Boy chastises her, telling her that white people and black people have to work together if black people are ever to succeed.

Before he leaves, Johnny-Boy hands his mother a wad of paper money that he has taken out of his pocket. He tells her to keep it should something happen to him. It is money that belongs to the Communist Party, and Johnny-Boy wants to make sure that it goes toward the party's success. Sue insists that Johnny-Boy keep the money. She tells him that she has been saving money to get her son Sug out of jail. She can use that money instead. When Johnny-Boy finally leaves, Sue senses that he will never return.

Part III

As Sue sleeps, a group of white men enter her home. She awakens to their voices. The men are rude and overtly racist. They make statements like, ''Gee, this place smells like niggers!'' and ''Niggers make good jam!'' They proceed to examine all the food Sue has in the kitchen, and when they are about to start eating it, the sheriff reminds them that they did not come there to eat the food, that they are looking for Johnny-Boy.

Sue rises from bed and approaches them, telling them to get out of her house. One of the men throws cooked greens into her face and asks, ''How they taste, ol [b——]?'' Caught up in the spirit of rebellion, Sue talks back to the men, trying to demonstrate that she is not afraid of them. They ask

her to tell them where her son is, but she refuses. She responds, ''Don yuh wished yuh knowed?'' This irritates the sheriff, and he slaps her. She continues to be noncompliant, and the sheriff slaps her again.

The narrator states that Sue was ''consumed with a bitter pride'' at this point. She did not care what they did to her; she would never tell them anything. The sheriff is eventually convinced that this woman will not reveal the whereabouts of her son or of the meeting, so he begins to leave. However, Sue, somewhat pumped up with that bitter pride, taunts the sheriff one more time. The sheriff has had enough. He walks back up the steps of her porch and beats Sue until she is unconscious.

Part IV

The fourth part opens with Sue by herself, lying in a dark hallway. She is just rousing herself back to consciousness. As she tries to gain some clarity of thought, she notices that something is standing before her. This something makes her nervous, but she does not know why. A few minutes later, she realizes that it is Booker, a white man who has recently joined the Communist Party. She is suspicious of him, but he eases his way into her thoughts, telling her that someone needs to warn the members that the sheriff is onto them. Booker, having just recently joined, does not know the names of the other members. As he helps her up and cleans her wounds, she slowly gives into his pleas and reveals the names of the members. When Booker leaves and Sue's thoughts become clearer, she fears that she might have made a horrible mistake.

Part V

As Sue sits in her house contemplating this awful thing she might have done, Reva comes back. She also nurses Sue's wounds and announces that her father has told her that Booker is the one who leaked the information about the meeting to the sheriff. Sue is terrified by this news. It confirms her worst suspicions. However, she does not want to tell Reva what she has done. Instead, she convinces Reva to go to bed. Once Reva is asleep, Sue pulls out an old gun, wraps it in a sheet, and goes looking for Booker, determined to kill him before he can tell the sheriff the names of all the members.

Part VI

The sheriff had warned Sue earlier that it did not matter if she did not tell them where Johnny-

Boy was, that he would find him anyway. When he did find him, if Johnny-Boy did not talk, Sue should plan to come to the sheriff with a sheet so she could wrap Johnny-Boy's body in it, for he would be dead. So when Sue shows up and faces the sheriff and his men with a sheet wrapped around her arms, they assume that she has come for her son's body. The men, however, tell her that Johnny-Boy is not yet dead. He is tied up and lying in the mud when she finds him. When the sheriff sees Sue, he comments that he must have slapped some sense into her after all, since she has come with the sheet as he told her to do.

In her presence, the group of men continue to ask Johnny-Boy to tell them the names of the people involved in the Communist Party and where they will be holding their next meeting. Johnny-Boy is silent. The men beat him, and at one point they place his legs over a log and break them with a crowbar. Then the sheriff pops Johnny-Boy's eardrums.

Sue watches all of this, waiting for Booker to appear. She hopes that she has time, after killing Booker, to put her son out of his misery. When Booker finally shows, Sue shoots him, but she then enters into a mental state that she refers to as having given up "her life before they took it from her." The sheriff's men then shoot both Sue and Johnny-Boy. Sue's last words are: "Yuh didnt git whut you wanted!"

Media Adaptations

- Wright's famous novel *Native Son* was produced as a play on Broadway in 1941. Wright wrote the script along with Paul Green. Orson Welles directed. The play starred Canada Lee.

- *Native Son* also was made into two motion pictures. Wright wrote the screenplay and played the lead role for the 1951 production, with Pierre Chenal directing. In 1986, Jerrold Freedman directed an updated version for Cinecom Pictures and American Playhouse (PBS).

- In 1995, a full-length documentary on Wright's life entitled *Richard Wright—Black Boy* and produced by Madison Davis Lacy, aired on Mississippi Educational Television and the Independent Television Service (ITVS). The program won a Southeast Regional Emmy.

- Both *Native Son* (read by James Earl Jones) and *Black Boy* (read by Brock Peters) are available from Caedmon Audio Cassette as tapes, or they can be downloaded at http://www.audible.com/ (last accessed February, 2002).

Characters

Booker

Booker is a white man who recently joined the Communist Party. He is such a new member that he does not know the name of the other people who belong to the party nor where they are planning their next meeting. Booker comes to Sue's house after she has been beaten by the sheriff. He helps Sue by giving her a cool, wet cloth to wipe her wounds. All the while he is assisting her, Booker questions Sue about the names of the other people who have joined the party.

After Booker leaves, Sue begins to doubt Booker's sincerity. Once Reva confirms that Booker is the turncoat, Sue hunts Booker down, and at the end of the story she shoots him in the head.

Johnny-Boy

Johnny-Boy is one of the two sons of Sue. The story opens with Sue waiting for Johnny-Boy, who is late in coming home. Johnny-Boy has taken up the slack in gaining membership in the local chapter of the Communist Party after the imprisonment of his brother, Sug.

Johnny-Boy is very quietly serious. He is driven by a mission: to liberate black people who have lived so many generations under the oppression imposed by white people. He does not necessarily like white people, but he does hold a ray of hope that if white people and black people can come together under the auspices of the Communist Party, then maybe blacks will be liberated. Toward this mission, Johnny-Boy risks his life and in the end sacrifices himself to the cause. He refuses, despite all the corporal punishment that is inflicted upon him, to name the secret members of the party. His actions reflect a vision that exceeds the personal. His life is not as important as the life of the party and its suggested rewards. His goal is freedom. If the only road to that freedom is death, he is willing to take it. However, he dies in a fashion that differs from the typical quiet black men of his past. Johnny-Boy has a vision of the future, and it is toward that goal that he gives up his life.

Reva

Reva is a young white woman. She is infatuated with Johnny-Boy, but the two never come into contact in the course of the story, symbolic of their ill-fated relationship. Reva is also a true believer, and she and her father help Johnny-Boy organize the Communist Party in their area.

Reva appears at Sue's doorstep in the middle of a rainstorm. She warns Sue that someone has told the sheriff about Johnny-Boy's activities. Sue, in turn, although she is concerned about Reva's having to go back into the storm, tells Reva that she must return to her father's home to tell him that Johnny-Boy is late coming home and might not be able to warn the other members of the Community Party.

Later in the story, Reva returns to Sue's house, to find that Sue has been beaten. She helps nurse Sue, wiping her wounds, making her drink coffee. Then Reva tells Sue that she knows who the "Judas" is. It is upon Reva's conveying this information that Sue knows that she has to find Booker and kill him.

Sheriff

The sheriff appears with a group of rowdy white men at Sue's home. He and the group of men with him walk into Sue's house without being invited and begin to eat her food. When the sheriff calls Sue "Anty," she tells him, "White man, don you *Anty* me!" The sheriff has come because he suspects that Johnny-Boy is involved in the organizing of the Communist Party. This threatens the sheriff's power, and he wants to ask Johnny-Boy the names of all the members. The sheriff promises that if Johnny-Boy talks, his life will be spared.

Sue does not trust the sheriff, but she does not back down from him. She talks back to him to the point that the sheriff loses his patience. He feels insulted by Sue's boldness and beats her before leaving her home. The sheriff tells Sue that if Johnny-Boy doesn't talk, she had better bring a white sheet with her to wrap Johnny-Boy's body in.

Later in the story, when Sue goes looking for Booker, she runs into the sheriff, who is in the process of torturing Johnny-Boy. The sheriff orders the breaking of Johnny-Boy's legs, and then he crushes Johnny-Boy's eardrums. After Sue shoots Booker, the sheriff comes over and beats her again. Then he orders that his men shoot both Sue and Johnny-Boy.

Sue

Sue holds the main focus of the story. She is the mother of Johnny-Boy and Sug. Although the story is told with a third person narrator, it is through Sue's world that the tale unfolds. Keneth Kinnamon, writing in *The Emergence of Richard Wright*, describes Sue as having a "governing passion" that is maternal. In other words, she does what she has to do in the name (and love) of her sons.

Although her sons are inflamed with the need to create change in the rural southern countryside in which they were born, where racism sequesters them in a world of mortal fear, Sue is willing to take the punishment that is forced onto her, believing that she will be rewarded upon her death. Sue has a very strong Christian faith, and the image of Jesus suffering on his cross allows her to swallow her own pain in silence. She will one day go to heaven, and those who have inflicted wounds on her will one day suffer.

However, because of her strong maternal passions, she is infected with her sons' zeal in the promise of the newly formed Communist Party in their rural setting. As her sons struggle with their clandestine activities in order to gain membership (both white and black) for the party and thus strength through the party, Sue is caught between her beliefs that she should suffer in silence, distrust all white people, and simultaneously support, nurture, and protect her grown children.

As Sue becomes more deeply involved in her sons' activities to fight oppression through a united, communistic front, she gains an inner strength that is quite different from the spiritual, and somewhat submissive, strength that she has found in Christianity. Abdul JanMohamed writes in his article

''Psychopolitical Function of Death in *Uncle Tom's Children*,'' that Sue ''is so sure of her strength that she fantasizes about her ability to prove her toughness.'' It is this factor that ultimately gets Sue into trouble. She almost romanticizes the act of confronting her dread, loathing, and fear of white people. She taunts the white sheriff until he beats her. This misfortune leaves her thoughts clouded, which ultimately forces her onto a path that can only end in death.

Sug

Sug is Sue's other son. Sug has been in jail for one year. He has been beaten, but so far he has not given away the names of the members of the Communist Party. Sug never appears in the story. Readers only learn about him through Sue's thoughts.

Themes

Racial Violence

Wright's story ''Bright and Morning Star'' begins with Sue standing at the window of her house, looking for her son, worried that he might have been caught by local officials and beaten. Sue's son is not doing anything illegal; he is merely trying to organize a group of oppressed people (mostly black people). Fearful of the power of African Americans, should they organize, white officials have terrorized black citizens, threatening physical abuse, torture, and ultimately death. One of Sue's sons has already been beaten and then thrown into jail because he would not tell the officials the names of everyone who had signed up to become members in the Communist Party.

Sue herself experiences racial violence when a group of white men enter her house without warrants or even without the customary politeness of knocking on her door. Once inside her house, they begin eating her food, and when she confronts them, they insult her. One white man throws Sue's food in her face and asks, ''How they taste, ol [b——]?'' When Sue talks back to the white men, one of them says, ''You need somebody t teach yuh how t be a good nigger!?'' A few minutes later, the sheriff, in an attempt to teach Sue to act according to his definition of how a black person should respond to a white person, punches her in the face, and when she falls down, he kicks her.

In the end, when Sue appears with a sheet in her arms to recover her son's body, the sheriff comments, ''Looks like them slaps we gave yuh learned yuh some sense, didnt they?'' When Sue refuses to ask her son to divulge the names, the sheriff orders his men to crush her son's legs with a crowbar. To confirm that the legs are broken, one of the men lifts one of the legs, which drops ''rearward from the kneecaps.'' ''Just lika broke sparrow wing,'' the man states. A few minutes later, the sheriff threatens to break the son's eardrums. One of his men confirms, ''he knows how t do it, too!'' Then another man states, ''He busted a Jew boy tha way once!?''

These passages are used to give a realistic portrayal of the conditions under which African Americans had to live. Because of the constant threat of racial violence, just as often coming from legal authorities as well as angry mobs, many blacks learned to submit to the degradation of unvarying humiliation at the hands of white people.

Martyrdom

Death is a theme that appears in most of Wright's works. In ''Bright and Morning Star,'' death is portrayed as a form of martyrdom. Sue is proud of her sons' silence. She knows that her sons will not ever divulge the names of the people who are involved in the Communist Party. At one point Sue claims, ''Po Sug! They sho musta beat the boy somethin awful! But, thank Gawd, he didnt talk! He ain no weaklin, Sug ain! Hes been lion-hearted all his life long.'' Sug is Sue's son, the one who has been in jail for a year.

Sue gets caught up in her sons' valiance, and when the sheriff threatens to beat her, she thinks, ''There was nothing on this earth . . . that they could not do to her but that she could take.'' A little later, the narrator comments that Sue was willing to sacrifice her sons, knowing that they were as good as dead once the sheriff had them, because she wanted the sheriff and all the white people to know that ''they could not get what they wanted by bluffing and killing.'' Then she thinks, exultingly, ''N yuh ain gonna *never* git it!''

Wright's use of the word ''exultingly'' is telling. The word has overtones of rejoicing and being

Topics for Further Study

- Wright's ''Bright and Morning Star'' takes place outside of Memphis, Tennessee, probably in the 1930s. Research the history of this city during this time frame to find stories about incidents of racial violence. Were there any crimes recorded against African Americans? What were they? How were the defendants treated? What was the racial breakdown of the population of prisoners in Tennessee at this time?

- Write a paper about the Communist Party in the United States. How active was the party in American politics? Were there any candidates in U. S. Senate races or the U. S. House of Representatives? What were the major causes of the party during the 1930s and 1940s? Were any of these causes taken up by other organized groups?

- Research the disenfranchised African-American voters in Florida during the 2000 presidential election. Then create a short story as Wright might have written it, using his style and tone of voice. The story does not have to match historical events, but make it relevant to modern times. Focus on one person's specific and personal frustrations with the voting that year.

- James Baldwin and Ralph Ellison were Wright's contemporaries. At one time, Ellison even considered Wright his mentor. Find out what happened to these relationships. How did they begin? When and how did they fall apart? What were the differences between these men? Be as objective as possible, showing both, or all three, sides of the arguments and their different political philosophies as well as their literary philosophies.

- In Chicago during the 1990s, several black men were released from jail after investigators discovered evidence that these men had been sentenced for crimes they did not commit. Research one of these cases and write about it. The story could be told as a journalistic article, a short story, a poem, or the lyrics to a song.

- Wright published a collection of haiku. Research the history of haiku, including the definition and format. Then write your own collection of ten haiku. The topics of the haiku do not all have to concern themselves with social issues, but try to include at least one that deals with racism.

triumphant. It exposes Sue's (and thus Wright's) sense of offering up her sons' lives in the fight toward freedom. Her sons will die, and their deaths will symbolize the strength needed for others to face their white oppressors without fear. Their deaths are not random or wasted. They have suffered and died for a cause. As Wright's last words in this story emphasize, these martyrs are 'the dead that never die.'

Communism

The philosophy of the Communist Party offered hope to Wright. It was through the Communist Party that he met other radical intellectuals. It was also through the Communist publications that his first stories were set in print. The party's promise of strength through unionizing workers was very ap-

pealing. Workers' rights and financial security were privileges that Wright had never experienced. The dream of socialism, which the Communist Party proffered, inspired Wright to conceive of a time when all people would experience equality. It was toward these ends that Wright's works would take on the theme of socialism, especially as portrayed in ''Bright and Morning Star,'' which put forth the concept that strength would be found if white people and black people could come together in a common cause.

Maternal Love

Although it might be argued that giving one's children up to a cause is a very different measure of maternal love, there is no doubt that Wright's protagonist, Sue, loves her children. Her life appears to be driven by her passion for them. She worries about their whereabouts. She considers their needs above her own. She even changes her philosophy of life to better align herself with her children's beliefs. By the end of the story, she has, in essence, become her sons, taking up their fervor, sacrificing her own life to protect their interests in the cause of organizing their people when their plight prohibits them from doing so. Her last words are ''Yuh didnt git whut yuh wanted,'' from which the reader can infer that she made sure that her sons did not die in vain.

Style

Colloquialism

The dialog in Wright's ''Bright and Morning Star'' is written in a colloquial form, emphasizing the pronunciation of words uttered both by a stereotypical Southern person as well as by a stereotypical African American living in the South. Wright uses this form not only to portray the tone of the South but also because he believed in a very realistic documentation of life. If people talked with an accent, muffling words, skipping over consonants, then that is what he would write. Examples of the dialog as written are the words ''yuh'' for *you,* ''astin'' for *asking,* ''ernuff'' for *enough.*

Within this colloquialism is also the use of non-standardized English grammar. Examples include ''Don yuh wish you knowed?'' (for *Don't you wish you knew?*); ''Yuh done did ernuff sass fer one night'' (for *You have done enough sass for one night*); and ''Whut she wans?'' (for *What does she want?*). This type of dialog, if done carefully, pulls the reader into the setting. In the case of ''Bright and Morning Star,'' Wright's use of colloquialism takes the reader into the rural South, a place that is somewhat exotic for many people. If he were to use this type of dialog throughout the story, it might be considered a bit heavy-handed. However, in most of the narration of the story, when Sue's thoughts are expressed, Wright uses standardized English, giving the reader a chance to flow with the story without having to translate the colloquialisms.

Suspense

Wright's stories are often criticized for their lack of fully fleshed out characters and complexity of plot. However, one characteristic of Wright's writing that most critics seem to agree on is his ability to create a tightly constructed psychological suspense in his narrative. Wright's story ''Bright and Morning Star'' is a perfect example of how masterful he is in creating a perfectly wrought tension in his writing. From the opening scene with Sue standing at the window waiting anxiously for her son Johnny-Boy to return home to the last few sentences of this story as Sue lies in the mud dying, the reader is held in check, wondering when the anticipated final blow will fall. Wright fills his story with fear, which affects his characters and his readers, in turn. And it is this fear that puts everyone on edge. Even if the ending of the story were known, or at least anticipated, Wright's direct and realistic depiction of pain and suffering make the reader first grimace and then wonder how much more his characters can and will endure. This question remains with the reader as the story unfolds and until the characters meet their doom.

Narration

Wright's story is narrated from a limited third person point of view. Readers are able to hear Sue's thoughts and see the action through Sue's eyes. They are not privy to the thoughts of any other character. Only through the dialog can the reader extrapolate the thoughts of the other people in the story. By using this point of view, Wright focuses all the attention on his protagonist, Sue. It is her story. She explains to the readers the motivations of her sons. Whether her interpretation is accurate will never be known.

The narration is so closely linked to the protagonist that there is no consideration given as to whether the narrator is not Sue. In other words, it is not a narrator who is watching the story; it is the narrator of Sue's thoughts. For instance, when the narrator states that Sue ''was consumed with a bitter pride,'' the reader does not question this statement. It is read as if Sue had come to this conclusion, and the reader is merely a witness to her realization.

Setting

The setting for this story is the rural South, probably during the 1920s or the 1930s when the Ku Klux Klan, Jim Crow laws, and frequent tortures and lynchings of African Americans were prominent. Although this story might have taken place in the North, as there certainly was racial violence there also, most people, at least in the United States, assume that it was in the South that this kind of activity took place. Due to the fact that Wright was raised in the South, he was more familiar with the social structure, the oppression, and the politics involved in living there. Trying to organize people and bringing white and black people together in order to do this were more dangerous endeavors in the South than in the North, thus giving his story a more dramatic edge.

Historical Context

The American Communist Party

The Communist Party, in the United States, was formed on September 1, 1919, in Chicago, Illinois. Having been inspired by the Russian Revolution (1917), unionists, intellectuals, and artists were attracted to the communist philosophy of helping oppressed people. During the 1930s, with most Americans feeling the effects of the Great Depression, the Communist Party's advocacy of unemployment insurance, social security, and the right of workers to organize, captivated the imaginations not only of the general public but also of many young and aspiring writers. The movement was strong enough that in 1932 William Z. Foster ran for president as a candidate of the Community Party.

Wright joined the party in 1932. Shortly after joining, he became the executive secretary of the Chicago branch of the John Reed Club, a left-wing cultural group sponsored by the Communist Party. The club afforded Wright the opportunity of meeting with other young, radical intellectuals and artists, helping him to define his own literary and social philosophy.

The themes of organizing workers and other oppressed groups of people in order to gain power against their aggressors mark much of Wright's early works. These themes were born with Wright's association with the Communist Party. Sometimes Wright's work, especially his journalistic work for

socialist papers, was so imbued with communist themes that it sounded, according to critic Robert Felgar writing in the Preface to his *Richard Wright,* "as if it were dictated by a computer programmed by Marx himself."

Jim Crow Laws

So-called Jim Crow laws are any laws that implement racial segregation. Named for an old minstrel routine (Jump Jim Crow), the term Jim Crow laws reflects the Supreme Court decision (*Plessy v. Fergusson,* 1896) that upheld the Louisiana law that required separate but equal railroad facilities for blacks and whites. From this decision, white people in power in the South took it upon themselves to create other separate but equal laws for everything from public transportation to public education; the emphasis in the implementation of these so-called laws was on the word *separate* with a total disregard for the word *equal*.

The Scottsboro Case

Representative of social attitudes of whites toward blacks during the 1930s (predominantly, but not exclusively, in the South) are the circumstances of the Scottsboro case. In March 1931, on a train traveling through Alabama, a group of white and black youths got into a fight. The white youths, having lost the fight and having been forced off the train by the black youths, reported the black youths to train officials. When the train stopped at the next station, nine black youths were rounded up and arrested.

Coincidentally, two white women were also arrested by the same officials for having crossed the state line for immoral purposes. In an attempt to dissuade the police from charging them, the women claimed that the black youths had raped them. Rape was, of course, a serious crime, but the rape of white women by black men was enough to cause whole southern communities to go on a lynching rampage. The black men were quickly jailed, accused, and all but one was sentenced to die in the electric chair.

The Communist Party, The National Association for the Advancement of Colored People (NAACP), and the American Civil Liberties Union all became interested in this case. They paid for lawyers who eventually appealed the convictions to the U.S. Supreme Court. In 1932, the Supreme

Compare & Contrast

- **1930s:** Mary McLeod Bethune becomes the first African-American woman to receive a major appointment from the U.S. government when she is appointed the director of Negro Affairs of the National Youth Administration.

  1950s: Jackie Robinson is named director of communications for NBC (National Broadcasting Company), becoming the first black executive of a major radio-TV network.

  1990s: Oprah Winfrey becomes the first black woman to own her own television and movie production company.

- **1930s:** Unemployment reaches as high as 25 percent of the total U.S. population as the effects of the Great Depression set in. A loaf of bread costs $.09.

  1950s: The U.S. economy prospers after World War II, and there is only a 2 percent unemployment rate. A loaf of bread costs $.14.

  1990s: The U.S. economy enjoys another prosperous decade as the stock market rises and the country has an overall unemployment rate of 4 percent. A loaf of bread costs anywhere between $1.50 and $4.00, depending on whether it contains conventional or organic ingredients.

- **1930s:** Jim Crow laws, fashioned on the mistaken interpretation of the ''separate but equal'' ruling of *Plessy v. Fergusson* (1896), are used to fortify strict segregation in the United States, especially in the South. Everything from movie theaters to drinking fountains is specifically des-

ignated as either available for use by whites or by blacks. Public schools are segregated.

1950s: The Supreme Court rules that segregated schools are unconstitutional in *Brown v. Board of Education of Topeka, Kansas,* setting the stage for a massive desegregation of all U.S. public schools.

1990s: Busing is still in effect in all U.S. states in a continuing effort to keep schools integrated. However, the system does not always work, leaving poorly funded inner-city schools to struggle with a lack of textbooks and computer access while wealthier suburban schools flourish. Since the majority of inner-city populations are black, African-American children tend to receive a poorer education than their white counterparts.

- **1930s:** Chief legal counsel of the National Association for the Advancement of Colored People (NAACP) Charles Houston lays the groundwork for a campaign throughout the South to end racial violence.

  1950s: Harry T. Moore, a leading NAACP organizer, and his wife are brutally murdered in Florida, setting off a decade of renewed white terrorism in the South. In Mississippi, Emmett Till is murdered for allegedly whistling at a white woman. His murderers are brought to trial and acquitted.

  1990s: Three white men in Texas chain James Byrd Jr., an African American, to the back of their pickup truck and drag him to his death. Two of the accused are given the death sentence. The third will spend his life in jail.

Court ruled that the defendants had been denied a fair trial. Subsequently, there was a second trial in 1933 in which one of the women recanted her story. However, the jury still found the defendants guilty.

There were many other appeals and many other trials, but in the end five of the original nine men

spent many years in jail, with the last of them being released on parole in 1950, nineteen years after having been tried for a crime he did not commit.

The Scottsboro case was considered a pivotal event in the Civil Rights movement. The NAACP gained quite a bit of publicity during the trials and gained strength as an organization. Formerly accused of aligning itself only with the bourgeois, the NAACP, through the Scottsboro case, redefined itself as the defender of all black Americans. The Scottsboro case also brought public attention to the poor ethics of the southern judicial system in reference to defending African Americans.

Marcus Garvey and Black Nationalism

Black nationalism is a term that has been applied to a movement among African Americans to fight against the dehumanizing conditions of slavery. Whereas socialism, in theory, would bring workers together to fight oppression, black nationalism proffered that black people should come together and create a separate society for themselves. Although the history of the movement is not well recorded, it is known that in 1916 the movement found a charismatic figurehead in the person of Marcus Garvey. Garvey formed a group he called the Universal Negro Improvement Association, which helped to develop black capitalist enterprises with a goal to build in Africa a black-governed nation. Garvey at one point claimed that there were about two million members in his organization, which would make this the largest mass movement of African Americans ever to occur.

Garvey, who was often referred to as Black Moses, often spoke of a ''new Negro'' who was proud of being black. He was successful in creating a chain of restaurants and grocery stores, laundries, a hotel, and a printing press. Unfortunately, he was better at managing crowds than he was at managing business. Eventually, mismanagement of his affairs plus his doctrine of racial purity and separatism brought strong criticism his way from other influential black leaders. His popularity weakened, and in 1922 he was indicted for mail fraud. Garvey, although eventually deported from the United States, rekindled a movement that would continue after his departure. He had given African Americans a sense of pride about themselves and their culture, which would spread throughout the black community and eventually inspire other organizations such as the Nation of Islam.

Literary Movements

The Harlem Renaissance movement, which flourished in the decade of the 1920s, marked the emergence of a new confidence among African-American artists. Some of the writers associated with this movement include Jean Toomer (*Cane,* 1923), Langston Hughes (*Not without Laughter,* 1930), and Zora Neale Hurston (*Their Eyes Were Watching God,* 1937). Many other artists of this period were published in Alain Locke's *The New Negro* (1925), a collection of stories, artwork, and essays by African Americans who voiced a new sense of independence as well as a new definition of black identity. Wright's works appeared as the Harlem Renaissance was fading, and although some of the writers in this movement were considered his peers, Wright wanted to move beyond the Harlem Renaissance goal of defining an African-American identity. He wanted action, and his work is said to have inspired a new movement in African-American literature that became more politically motivated. It was driven by the urge for freedom as only a true civil rights program could deliver.

Wright wrote during the transition between the old movement of the Harlem Renaissance and the new group of works that would be termed the Black Arts movement of the 1960s and 1970s. He would influence many other writers during this transitional period, although not all of them would agree with his political views. Two of the more famous writers were Ralph Ellison, who wrote *Invisible Man* (1952), and James Baldwin, who wrote *Go Tell It on the Mountain* (1953).

Critical Overview

In the Introduction to *Uncle Tom's Children,* Richard Yarborough makes reference to, as he calls it, ''an oft-quoted statement'' of Wright's concerning this publication as a whole. Yarborough writes that Wright himself criticized this collection harshly by stating, ''When the reviews of that book began to appear, I realized that I had made an awfully naïve mistake. I found that I had written a book which even bankers' daughters could read and weep over and feel good about.'' For Wright, this was not a mark of good literature but rather a failure of his to arouse action. As a matter of fact, Yarborough continues by explaining that Wright's words were actually a criticism of the American public and "their capacity to defuse the potency of harsh critique through the very act of commercial consumption and subsequent emotional release. In other words, mainstream America (in particular white Americans) loved this book, but that was far from Wright's intentions.

Despite Wright's disappointment, the reaction to *Uncle Tom's Children*, on the whole, was somewhat overwhelming, with Eleanor Roosevelt, wife of President Franklin D. Roosevelt, even taking the time to comment on it. Originally published in 1938, *Uncle Tom's Children* did not include the story "Bright and Morning Star." The short story first was published, in the same year, in *The Masses*, a monthly socialist journal of arts and politics. It was not until 1940, after Wright's popular success with the publication of *Native Son* that "Bright and Morning Star" was included in an expanded edition of the collection.

Abdul JanMohamed states that the stories in *Uncle Tom's Children*, especially as reflected in "Bright and Morning Star," "not only accurately maps the relationship between emotions and their underlying sociopolitical causes and effects but also traces the trajectory of the thematic development of his short stories. The fear, aroused by racist oppression and by the need to struggle with racism . . . is one of the most significant emotions in the very construction of the black psyche." It is a theme, JanMohamed writes, that Wright returns to over and over again in each of his succeeding works. JanMohamed continues: "The story in effect examines the strength of the political resolve that Wright feels is necessary to carry on a successful struggle against oppression." JanMohamed believes that Wright "memorializes all his heroes whose voluntary deaths permit the author to find a way out of the realm of social death and toward the realm of a fuller life." He believes that Wright attempted, almost compulsively, to find his own way out of that realm of social death (caused by racism) through his writing. JanMohamed concludes that "Bright and Morning Star" "bears the fruits of the entire anthology [*Uncle Tom's Children*]."

Keneth Kinnamon believed that the story was overtly communist, causing Wright to have to force issues and metaphors that sometimes did not work. Kinnamon concludes that, for him, "Bright and Morning Star," despite the fact that it received critical honors, was "not a good story." Edward

Margolies, commenting in his *The Art of Richard Wright*, might have agreed with Kinnamon. Margolies writes, "There is little the reader can do but sympathize with Wright's Negroes and loathe and despise the whites. There are no shadings, ambiguities, few psychological complexities." However, Margolies looks into this a little deeper and asks, "How then account for their [the stories'] success?" He then expresses the thought that Wright is, after all, a storyteller and that:

> his plots are replete with conflict, incident, and suspense. . . . He has an unerring 'feel' for dialogue, his narrations are controlled in terse, tense rhythms, and he manages to communicate mood, atmosphere, and character in finely worked passages of lyric intensity. But above all they are stories whose sweep and magnitude are suffused with their author's impassioned convictions about the dignity of man, and a profound pity for the degraded, the poor and the oppressed who, in the face of casual brutality, cling obstinately to their humanity.

Writing in 1991 for the *New York Times*, Alfred Kazin states that "Richard Wright was a most extraordinary writer." Kazin adds, "Wright was the novelist as thinker, not the thinker as novelist. . . . Truly, he was our native son, one of our best."

Criticism

Joyce Hart

Hart has degrees in English literature and creative writing. Her published works are of literary themes. In this essay, Hart studies Wright's use of rain (and water) as a metaphor and as an effect on the mood of his short story.

Wright's short story "Bright and Morning Star" is filled with rain. From the first line, in which the protagonist Sue is said to be standing "six inches from the moist windowpane" as she wonders, "would it ever stop raining," Wright uses rain as a metaphor of gloom and sorrow. Sue is worried about her son Johnny-Boy's return. Although Wright does not show Sue crying, the moisture on the window so close to her face represents her tears, while her concern that the sun may never return addresses her apprehension that she has little hope that her life will ever improve. Thus, in the story's first sentence, Wright has set the tone for the entire

This segregated outhouse represents the racially motivated Jim Crow laws

story, and this mood will prevail to the end, with the rain, as Sue feared, never ending.

Wright uses rain not only as a metaphor; he takes the image of rain and wraps it around other symbols such as in the opening paragraph when he mentions "a bright shaft of yellow that swung from the airplane beacon in far off Memphis." It is because the night is so clustered in dark clouds and the sky is so saturated with rain that this yellow beacon is unmistakably visible. The shaft of light, in contrast to its practical status of signaling a safe harbor, cuts "through the rainy dark" like a "gleaming sword" above Sue's head. The rain not only

emphasizes this image, it lends its sheets of water as symbolic material through which the beam cuts. If the rain were not present, the light would be diffused, its edges feathered, and therefore the image would be softened. With the presence of the rain, Wright has created a dark background through which the light takes on the menacing form of a weapon. With the "gleaming sword" hanging over Sue, Wright exposes Sue's fear as well as foreshadowing her death.

Sue is anxious about the well-being of her son. At first, readers might surmise that her anxiety is solely based on her concern that Johnny-Boy is

What Do I Read Next?

- *Sister Carrie* (1900) by Theodore Dreiser was instrumental in influencing Wright's writing style. It was Dreiser's first novel, and some critics call it his best. This book did not receive the level of popularity that *An American Tragedy* would later enjoy, and its distribution was even suppressed until 1912 because of its female character's defiance of conventional sexual morality. The book tells the story of a young, small-town girl who runs away to New York and both uses and is used by men on her way to becoming a successful actress. This novel is said to have been the first masterpiece of the American naturalistic movement and is credited with being the model for subsequent American writers of realism.

- *Kingsblood Royal* (1947) by Sinclair Lewis is a portrait of a successful white man who discovers that he is part black. Neil Kingsblood is a typical middle-class American with a comfortable life until he discovers his roots. This was a very shocking issue at the time of publication, and even though times have changed, the issues presented in this story are still being discussed today. Since Lewis's writing was a great influence on Wright, this is a good book to read.

- In 1953, James Baldwin wrote *Go Tell It on the Mountain,* a story that spans only one day and covers the spiritual and moral awakening of a young teenaged boy. The story reflects on the effects of poverty on an urban, African-American family during the Great Depression. A contemporary of Wright, Baldwin disagreed with Wright's ideology. This book is semi-autobiographical and offers a good contrast to Wright's style.

- Ralph Ellison, also a contemporary of Wright, wrote *Invisible Man* (1952). This first novel tells the story of a nameless narrator who grows up in the South but eventually finds his way to New York City. As he struggles with racism, both Southern and Northern style, the narrator searches for what he thinks is truth. However, he finds this concept very elusive. This work won the National Book Award for Ellison and remains an American classic.

- *Native Son* (1940) is Wright's first published novel. The main character, Bigger Thomas, a young man living in Chicago during the 1930s, tries to rise above poverty and racism but becomes entrapped in a sequence of horrific events. It is a book about the effects of poverty and what it means to be black in America. Most critics believe that this is Wright's most powerful work.

- *Black Boy* (1945) is Wright's autobiography of his early years in the rural South. It tells the story of a young boy growing up in an oppressive environment where Jim Crow laws and poverty make it all but impossible for an African-American male to exist. It is a criticism of racism as well as a coming-of-age story.

- Wright's *Twelve Million Black Voices, a Folk History of the Negro in the U.S.* was first published in 1941 and depicts the lives of black people during the 1940s, showing the harsh realities of living in crowded, run-down farmhouses in rural America and the challenges that families struggling in the inner city faced.

---

caught in the rainstorm. He has "been trampin in this slop all day wid no decent shoes on his feet." Readers might assume that Sue is merely worried that Johnny-Boy might catch a cold. However, this is not the level of apprehension that Wright wants,

so he raises tension by enlarging on Sue's thoughts as well as broadening the effects of the rainstorm. Not only is it raining, but it has been raining for too long. There is more rain than the ground can soak up. As Sue looks at the rain puddles that are forming

"Standing in the darkness, Sue is 'mired' in a place that is neither here nor there. She is not truly living because she is in a state of shock. Yet, she is not truly dead because she has not completed her fateful task."

in her yard, she observes that rain can be both good and bad. Rain can feed the earth and make plants flourish, but it can also "bog things down lika watah-soaked coffin." With this reflection, Sue again brings the element of death into the story. Wright, through Sue, is portraying rain as an image of sorrow that can help create a strong character in people, just as the rain can feed the earth. Grief can help people to learn to appreciate the benefits of life, but too much heartache and anguish can eventually kill the spirit.

Rain pervades this initial setting, as even the inside of Sue's house is saturated with moisture and images of water. There is the "filmy veil of sweat" on Sue's forehead, the "throaty bubble" from a pot of boiling water, and the "pile of damp clothes" that Sue must iron. As she irons, she reminisces about both of her sons as "a gust of wind dashed rain against the window." Sue's life appears inundated with sorrow. As she unconsciously completes her chores, her hands follow "a lifelong ritual of toil" while her mind follows the suffering she has endured in the loss of her husband, in the suffering of her son Sug, and finally in her worries about Johnny-Boy's late return. Sue's trials in life have left her in a state of constant fear, which Wright further describes as an "intense brooding" that she held so closely to her "that she could feel their grain, like letting cold water run over her hand from a faucet on a winter morning." Water also figures in Sue's attempts to help support her sons. She washes clothes for white people. She mentions walking across a wet field with a load of wet clothes upon her head. This load did not weigh her down until the day that she found out that Sug had been taken to jail and

beaten. Ever since, "things were becoming heavier. The tubs of water and the wet clothes were "becoming harder to lift."

The rain continues as Sue hears footsteps "sucking in the mud of the back yard." Sue is overpowered by the sound of these footsteps as she continues to anticipate her son's arrival. "With all the rain and fear" in the air, Sue's eyes fill with tears. Wright has created so much rain that the earth becomes soggy and grabs at the feet of those who are trying to make their passage home. This is a different type of weight than the water-laden clothes that Sue has carried on her head. With this image, the soaked earth makes footsteps heavy by "sucking" on the feet of those who pass by. It is hard to move, hard to progress when rain falls so heavily. Wright also incorporates more than sorrow into the rain. He now also links the rain with fear, and Sue has temporarily lost her ability to distract herself as she breaks down into tears.

Johnny-Boy finally makes it home. Sue feeds him and lets him "get dry" before she tells him that he has to go out into the rain again. She wants to give her son a moment of peace. As best as she can, she allows him to enjoy a short period of time when he still believes that hope is alive. In allowing him to dry off, Sue is temporarily lifting the weight of sorrow from his shoulders. Although she senses the fate that is soon to come down on him, she wants to give him the gift of motherly love. Then she says, without turning to look at him: "Yuh almos dry." This statement signifies to Johnny-Boy that "more was coming." In other words, having enjoyed his short respite, Johnny-Boy must once again return to the rain. When Johnny-Boy leaves, Sue watches the "rain take him." Then she goes to bed and listens to the rain, her feelings coursing "with the rhythm of the rain: Hes gone! Lawd, Ah *know* hes gone!"

In part 3 of the story, the sheriff and a group of his men come to Sue's house. During this whole section, there is no mention of rain. The dialog and action are hot and angry. Sorrow and fear have been put aside. In their place comes violence and blood. The rain remains absent when Booker, another white man associated with the sheriff, appears. Although fear is mentioned, it has become a white mountain of fear. It is different from the anxiety that Sue experiences when she thinks about her children. It is not the same fear as represented by rain. Not until Reva, a young white woman who is in love with Johnny-Boy, arrives on the scene is the rain made visible again.

As Sue ponders what she has to do to stop Booker from giving the sheriff the names of all the members of the Communist Party that Johnny-Boy has signed up, she notices that "the yellow beacon continued to flit past the window and the rain still drummed." She finds herself "mired . . . between two abandoned worlds, living, but dying without the strength of the grace that either gave." Then she feels something well up from deep inside of her and simultaneously senses that she is "naked against the night, the rain, the world." It is at that moment that she knows she must "wade the creek" and get to Booker before Booker reveals the names. The watery images that Wright uses at this point convey a variety of messages. With the yellow beacon and the rain still imposed, Wright reminds readers that that gleaming sword still hangs over Sue's head. Sue senses her own death. Standing in the darkness, Sue is "mired" in a place that is neither here nor there. She is not truly living because she is in a state of shock. Yet, she is not truly dead because she has not completed her fateful task. She accepts her fate, knowing that the things of this world are no longer significant. Naked, she will cross the creek, a symbol of crossing into the afterlife.

Walking toward the creek, Sue leans "her body against the wind and the driving rain." Although the wind and rain are pushing her back, she uses them to lean on, driving herself forward into it. When she reaches the creek, she studies it, looking for a low point. She steps into the water but does not feel it until the water rises halfway up her body. She gasps at the unexpected coldness, a coldness that soon will be repeated in the last lines of the story as she lies dying in the rain.

Sue arrives at the place where the sheriff is holding Johnny-Boy. Wright does not describe the scene in terms of rain. It is not mentioned that the men are wet from standing in the storm. Not until the sheriff takes Sue to see Johnny-Boy does Wright once again mention rain. "They led her to a muddy clearing. The rain streamed down through the ghostly glare of the flashlights." In a pool of black rainwater lies Sue's son.

Through the section of the story during which the sheriff and his men torture Johnny-Boy, Wright again does not mention rain. Only after Sue has killed Booker and after she has been pushed down into the mud does the rain reappear. "She lay without struggling, looking upward through the rain. . . . And she was suddenly at peace." It is then that Sue hears three shots fired, two at her son; the third shot she feels as a "streak of fire that tore its way through her chest [and] forced her to live again, intensely." Then she feels her flesh turning cold, "cold as the rain that fell from the invisible sky upon the doomed living and the dead that never dies." In death, Wright implies, Sue has found life. She has died a good death. The rain that once bothered her, that made her cold and bound her life in sorrow, is over. She has nothing more to fear. The rain, although it continues to fall, is meant for other people now.

Source: Joyce Hart, Critical Essay on "Bright and Morning Star," in *Short Stories for Students,* The Gale Group, 2002.

Sherley Anne Williams

In the following essay excerpt, Williams explores how Wright uses the "mammy" character of Aunt Sue to represent the capability of black women to achieve social change.

"Bright and Morning Star" is one of the most deft and moving renderings of a black woman's experience in the canon of American literature. Writing while he was still a staunch believer in communism as the hope of the world's oppressed. Wright was able to achieve in this story a synthesis of ideology and literary expression that he was only occasionally able to equal in later, longer works. The mute Lulu, the childish wanton Sarah in "Long Black Song," May, the stereotyped and scary wife of the hero in "Fire and Cloud": these characterizations of black women are somewhat redeemed in the character of Aunt Sue. Yet, paradoxically, Wright's loving characterization also reinforces the image of the black woman as a symbol of the reactionary aspects in Afro-American tradition implicit in the preceding three stories.

Aunt Sue is a blend of the mother of Afro-American ideal and the mammy of American experience. She takes in washing for a living, carrying the hundred-pound baskets on her head; her most characteristic pose—when she is not ironing—standing with her "gnarled black hands folded over her stomach," is one of familiar humbleness. This pose later helps her to hide a gun and so is akin to the minstrel mask and the vaudeville grin as one of the disguises forced upon black people and made "renegade" through sly acts of self-assertion. Sue is, to use the jargon of the day, a "single" parent (I have often wondered what a double or triple parent looks like), a widow who has raised her sons, Sug and Johnny Boy, to manhood alone. She has struggled against being engulfed in poverty and racism, aided

> "'Bright and Morning Star' is one of the most deft and moving renderings of a black woman's experience in the canon of American literature."

by her wits and, more importantly, an abiding faith in Jesus Christ as Lord of Heaven and Savior of the world. Personal service on whites, endurance, a necessary self-effacement, a truncated family structure—these factors so characterize our conception of the so-called matriarch that they have in the aggregate almost the quality of archetype. Certainly the character of Aunt Sue approaches the ideal. Yet Sue is also a dynamic character who in Wright's treatment rises above the social definition of *mammy.*

When Sug and Johnny Boy enter manhood and "walk forth demanding their lives," Sue has the strength to let them go. Her heart follows them as they become organizers, for she loves, as mother must, but she loves without smothering. Her love for her sons leads Sue to embrace the work of the Party; the wrongs and sufferings of black men "take the place of Him nailed to the Cross as the focus of her feelings," giving meaning to her life of toil as Christianity had before. In the party, Sue becomes aware of a kind of personal strength and pride that no one, least of all herself, thought a "black woman . . . could have:" the will to work against the racist power structure. We understand, of course, that Aunt Sue has willingly subsumed her own aspirations, her own personality under first one man, Jesus Christ, then another, the wronged heroic Black Man, that she would consider the wrongs done to her as a black woman negligible compared to what black men suffer. She believes that righting the wrongs of black men will automatically eliminate her own exploitation. This elementary conception of black liberation does not trouble us unduly; Wright subtly implies his own deeper understanding of the political situation of women when he explains why it is natural for Reva, a young white woman comrade, to trudge through a downpour to deliver an urgent message—"Being a woman, Reva was not suspect; she would have to go." He probably takes a devilish delight in portraying that

symbol of deadly femininity, the white woman, using her privileged position to strike at his white male oppressors.

Yet, despite the changes wrought in her attitude by the new light shed by the party, Sue never quite accepts its dictum that she "'not see white n [she] not see black.'" She cannot entirely discard the teachings of her experience: "'You can't trust ever white man yuh meet.'" Johnny Boy's position, "'Yuh can't judge folks by how yuh feel bout em n by how long yuh don knowed em,'" is, of course, the correct party line. And though in this instance, Sue proves correct (the informer is one of the newly recruited white party members), Sue's insistence upon "pitting her feelings against the hard necessity of his [Johnny Boy's] thinking" symbolizes the hold that the old life and the old ways still have over her.

A white man posing as a friend of the little band of party members tricks her into revealing the names of the local group, even as Johnny Boy is captured by the sheriff's posse. Carrying a sheet for his burial, Aunt Sue gains access to the place where Johnny Boy is held captive, the place to which the informer must return to lay his information before the sheriff. Sue is forced to watch while Johnny Boy is tortured. She considers killing him to spare him pain, but chooses to wait and kill the informer and so save the lives of all the other comrades. She succeeds in killing the informer and is herself killed. She dies with a defiant cry, "'You didn't git what you wanted!'" on her lips.

That defiant cry is ironic for these are the words of defiance that precipitated the crisis in the first place. They reinforce the quality of noble hubris that is an important part of her characterization. "'Ah just want them white folks t try t make me tell *who* is *in* the party n who *ain*! . . . Ahll show em something they never thought a black woman could have,'" she tells Johnny Boy early on in the story. And she is given a chance to show that something. The sheriff and his men come looking for Johnny Boy and refuse to leave when she orders them out of her house. Despite her uppitiness, the sheriff seeks to be conciliating: "'Now Anty . . .'" he begins, only to be brought up short by Sue's retort, "'White man don yuh *Anty* me!'" She rejects the bogus conciliation and the counterfeit respect the title implies; and rejects also the *place* in which that title puts her. In the ensuing exchange of words with the white men, she further demonstrates her pride and courage:

'''Twenty of yuh runnin over one ol woman! Now ain yuh white men glad yuh so brave?''' The sheriff slaps her, for she is not to him a woman, but a nigger woman, a beast of burden to be beaten when it proves recalcitrant. As Aunt Sue does: She refuses to tell them anything about Johnny Boy. Balked, the sheriff and his men start to leave. Sue, wanting to drive home her victory for she has shown that there is nothing they could do to her that she could not take, taunts them as they go out her door. '''Yuh didn't git wht yuh wanted! N yuh ain gonna nevah git it!''' This so enrages the sheriff that he beats her senseless.

While Sue is dazed from the assault, Booker, whom she suspects of being an informer, seduces her into telling the names of her comrades ('''Is yuh scared a me cause Ahm *white*?''' he demands indignantly; then, cleverly invoking her son's name, '''Johnny Boy ain like tha.''') Later, after Reva has confirmed her suspicions that Booker is the informer, Sue reflects, pinpointing her moment of transcendent strength as the moment of her blind fall. ''She put her finger upon the moment when she had shouted her defiance to the sheriff, when she had shouted to feel her strength . . . If she had not shouted at the sheriff, she would have been strong enough to resist Booker; she would have been able to tell the comrades herself,'' instead of entrusting the task to the traitor.

But hubris is only the superficial flaw. The ''fit of fear'' that had come upon her when she regained consciousness and discovered herself looking into a white face was ''a part of her life she thought she had done away with forever.'' But that part of her life, ''the days when she had not hoped for anything on this earth,'' had been evoked through her singing of the old sorrow songs, the spirituals that she '''can't seem to fergit,''' in the first part of the story. And in singing, she has opened herself to both the tragic expression of pride and that old-timey fear. She sang for the traditional reason, ''to ease the anxiety [about Johnny Boy's safety] that was swelling in her heart.'' She had thought that it meant no more than this when she sang now. But the events of the evening reveal that the songs are not, even now, an empty symbol. She has almost, without knowing it, called on Jesus; and He had not answered. This is the ''deeper horror'': the fight for black men's freedom had not truly replaced Christ in her heart. This realization mires her temporarily between two worlds, neither of which she seems able to abandon or live in.

In succumbing to the fit of fear induced by Booker's presence, Sue has in her own mind reverted to type, to the stereotypical image of the servile, cringing slave. And she is ashamed of herself and even more ''shamed whenever the thought of Reva's love crossed her mind.'' In the white girl's trust and acceptance of her, Sue has found her first feelings of humanity, and Reva's love draws her toward a reintegration and reaffirmation with the peoples of the earth. Reva's relationship to Aunt Sue is a re-reading of the conventional one between mammy and mistress. It represents the ideal solidarity possible between black and white workers and the sisterhood between women workers. Moreover, the black mother and the white girl are bound together by their love for Johnny Boy. Reva's love for Sue, her faith in the old black woman, represent for Sue the promise of the party made real in a genuine human relationship. That love is likened to the light from the airport beacon in far-off Memphis that in the story becomes a metaphor for the new day that communism will bring.

Sue's pride before the white girl causes her to shield Reva from any knowledge of the mistake she has made, and this is consistent with the literal, denotative level of the story. Sue has already lost one son, Sug, to ''the black man's struggle.'' He is in jail. Johnny Boy, she realizes during the sheriff's visit, is as good as gone; he will either be jailed, killed, or forced to flee because of his work with the party. Reva ''was all she had left.'' Thus, when the young white girl comes to her house, after the sheriff and Booker have left, she cannot bring herself to reveal the full extent of her weakness. Reva's confidence ('''An Sue! Yuh always been brave. Itll be awright!''') seems to mock her. It also goads her into thinking of a way to rectify her mistake. Ironically, this deception recalls the outline of the old mammy-mistress relationship, for one of the unacknowledged but understood tasks of the old family retainers—whether ''Aunty'' or ''Uncle''—was to guide their young charges through the shoals of adolescence, shielding them from as much unpleasantness as possible and ministering to their hurts when it was not possible to keep them from pain. This latent aspect of Sue's love for Reva is reinforced by the suggestion of Reva as a sleeping beauty at the end of Section V of the story. Reva has come to spend the night with Sue in case there is trouble. She stays, even though the trouble has already come. Sue, resolved upon a course of action, gets Johnny Boy's gun and a sheet. Reva is in the room ''sleeping; the darkness was filled with her quiet breathing . . . [Sue] stole to the bedside and watched Reva. Lawd, hep her!'' Sue then steals away on her deadly errand, leaving Reva asleep, Reva's trust in black people intact, her world unshaken.

Concomitant with re-reading the relationship between mammy and mistress is the explicit sanctioning of romantic love between black men and white women as a symbol of racial equality and economic justice. Long before Sue gives Johnny Boy up to physical death in the service of the party, she gives him up to Reva. ''The brightest glow her heart had ever known was when she had learned that Reva loved Johnny Boy''—this despite the fact that she knows the two of them '''couldna been together in this here south,''' to put it mildly. (We cannot help but remember the fate of Big Boy and his friends, the mob in ''Down by the Riverside''— '''Did he *bother* you Mrs. Heartfield? The Little girl? Did he *bother* you *then*?''') Yet Sue's approval of the match is used consistently to demonstrate that Sue has broken with her old outlook and embraced a new one, that she has broken with her old allies and found new ones. Sue never draws back from her approval of the match, whereas she early shows that she cannot accept all of the party tenets without reservation and her ''Lawd hep'''s are a kind of subconscious refrain through much of the story. Sue's last thought as she starts out with her winding sheet is of Reva: ''Lawd hep her! But maybe she was better off . . . she wont nevah know. Reva's trust would never be shaken.'' And as Sue starts across the fields holding the gun and the sheet against her stomach, '''Po Reva . . . po critter . . . Shes fast ersleep.'''

Reva is fast asleep to Johnny Boy's fate, to Sue's frailty, Sue's humanity, to the dark realities and hardships of black life. Despite the exigencies of life in the party, nothing has happened to disturb Reva's faith in human nature, the party, her belief in the perfectibility of the world. And it is as much to keep this white world intact as it is to redeem her own self-esteem that Aunt Sue sets out to hunt down the informer.

In ''Bright and Morning Star,'' Wright articulates a dream of rapprochement between the old and the new Negro, between the generations spawned in the bloody reprisals of Reconstruction and the generation nurtured on radical ideology in the new century, between black woman and white. He uses ''the most beloved and familiar character'' in American experience, the mammy, to inveigh against

adherence not only to the substance but to the form of the folk culture, to urge a complete break with the old-fogeyish past. The hope implicit in the story—if this old woman can change, any one can—is never realized in portrayals of younger black women. Indeed, an episode from *American Hunger* (1977), the posthumously published sequel to *Black Boy*, illustrates how completely Wright came to equate black women and black culture with the reactionary and regressive.

Source: Sherley Anne Williams, ''Papa Dick and Sister-Woman: Reflections on Women in the Fiction of Richard Wright,'' in *American Novelist Revisited: Essays in Feminist Criticism,* edited by Fritz Fleischmann, G. K. Hall & Co., 1982, pp. 394–415.

Carole W. Oleson

In the following essay, Oleson explores various symbols and their significance in ''Bright and Morning Star.''

Richard Wright manages to introduce most of his important symbols in the first five hundred words of his story, while catching up the reader in a mother's anxiety over the late return of her son. Rain forms the ever-present back-drop of the story and we are made aware of its monotonous presence in the first sentence. ''Rains good n bad,'' Aunt Sue mumbled, ''It kin make seed bus up thu the groun, er it kin bog things down lika watah-soaked coffin.'' Rain is literally and symbolically the pressure of adversity. Adversity has made her strong, keenly aware of life, resourceful. It has also bogged her down in inescapable poverty and political oppression which deprives her of her sons and of life itself.

The airplane beacon flashing through the wet darkness is like a flash of hope that keeps her going. *''Don give up hope.* Yeah; we gotta live in hope.'' The song of her childhood equating Jesus with the ''Bright n Mawnin Star'' links the title to the beacon, to song itself, and begins to form a cluster of shifting hopes that she has anchored her soul to over the years.

The ''rich black earth sprawling outside in the night,'' the clay which could not soak up such an interminable quantity of rain, is a perfect symbol for black people in America. To make the meaning inescapable, the earth is even personified in the image of a man sprawling, as if knocked down, and cast outside, away from light and warmth.

We reminisce with Aunt Sue as the song pulls her back to the vision of Christianity that sustained her in her youth. But the sense of security that it gives us is destroyed by the intrusion of the cold white mountain, explicitly identified as the white folks and their laws. The rain, the beacon, the earth may be natural, subconscious symbols to her, but the mountain image is fully conscious and unnatural, for there is no actual mountain there, as there are actually rain, earth, and beacon before her eyes. The white mountain clearly does not belong, is not in a sense real. It has physical reality only when her will permits it power over her. But at the beginning of the story, the white mountain is painfully real, jutting up from and dominating over the black earth.

She recalls the period of her life when the bright-and-morning-star Jesus became instead the bright-and-morning-star Communist Party. "The wrongs and sufferings of black men had taken the place of Him nailed to the Cross; the meager beginnings of the party had become another Resurrection." In another sense, however, the conversion was a reversion to the original perception. "Him nailed to the Cross" would have appealed to her as a symbol of the suffering of her people. She merely reverts from the symbol to the reality. The Resurrection had been a symbol of the hope for a new freedom for her people. The Party offers not a mystic other-word reward won by patience and long-suffering, but a practical plan for forcefully making another world out of the one we have.

After Reva's arrival the beacon is identified with Reva's love for Aunt Sue. "In Reva's trust and acceptance of her she had found her first feelings of humanity; Reva's love was her refuge from shame and degradation. If in the early days of her life the white mountain had driven her back from the earth, then in her last days Reva's love was drawing her toward it, like the beacon shows air-borne bodies the way through the rain clouds back to the earth. The warm yellow light of white persons' love can show the black person who is cut off from his black heritage the way back to self-respect and self-acceptance. But it comes as something of a shock that Aunt Sue with all of the strength developed through struggle and the strength of her hatred of the white oppressor should be unable to feel her own humanity, which was denied by the whites, until one of *them* recognizes her human worth. The beacon, white peoples' love, is a source of hope, but it is not absolutely necessary for salvation. The beacon is not present in the last scene of the story.

The earth symbol deepens beyond simple identification with black people to include their courage,

> The earth symbol deepens beyond simple identification with black people to include their courage, pride, and defiance."

pride, and defiance. "She stood on a narrow plot of ground from which she would die before she was pushed. And then it was, while standing there, feeling warm blood seeping down her throat, that she gave up Johnny-Boy, gave him up to the white folks . . . . She gave him up because she wanted them to know that they could not get what they wanted by bluffing and killing."

What the white man thinks is of utmost importance to her and it is her tragic flaw. The surprising superlative of the discovery of Reva's love for Johnny-Boy being the "brightest glow her heart had ever known" reinforces the weight of white folk's opinion first revealed by the importance of Reva's respect for her. Now the action of the story hinges on Aunt Sue's compulsion to make the white sheriff and his men *know* that they can not forcibly take anything from her, to make them "feel the intensity of her pride and freedom." Her shouted defiance brings her the blow and kicks that incapacitate her for the job she has to do and make it necessary for her to entrust it to Booker, the spy. She had maintained her human dignity throughout the encounter with the savages in her kitchen. She knew that she was proud and free, but self-knowledge was not enough for her. White man had to be made to know it, too. Concern for white man's opinion undid her. As she realized, too late:

> She had lost Sug to save others; she had let Johnny-Boy go to save others; and then in a moment of weakness that came from too much strength she had lost all. If she had not shouted to the sheriff, she would have been strong enough to have resisted Booker; she would have been able to tell the comrades herself.

Moreover, the defiant gesture was totally lost on them; they were much too obtuse to understand its significance.

The mountain image is closely associated with Booker when she is reacting to feeling and not to reason. Reason tells Aunt Sue to trust him, but when his fingers press into her arm, she felt "as though the white mountain was pushing her to the edge of a sheer height." Instinctive reaction proves true; he does force her to decisions of desperation.

As she gives Booker the names of Party members, she experience "a mounting horror of feeling herself being undone." As the rich black earth can be ravaged and find within itself the ability to restore itself, Aunt Sue, injured and heart-sick, finds the physical strength, the will and mental resourcefullness to outwit the sheriff's men. The star takes on new meaning, not the big generalized meanings of systems of belief—Christianity and Communism—but a very personal, specific meaning: "If she could only stop [Booker] some way! That was the answer, the point, the star that grew bright in the morning of new hope." All that she had learned from her life of dedication to visions became focused on this one last great task.

> The clearer she felt it the fuller did something well up from the depths of her for release; the more urgent did she feel the need to fling into her black sky another star, another hope, one more terrible vision to give her the strength to live and act.

She was "naked against the night, the rain, the world"; she had betrayed her vision. Then a plan came to her: "The sheet! thas it, the *sheet*! Her whole being leaped with will; the long years of her life bent toward a moment of focus, a point." Again, the plan to save the comrades is thought of in starlike terms. Now she does not need to make the white men aware of her defiance; she will "go lika nigger woman" for only humility will enable her to the traitor. "She stood straight and smiled grimly; she had in her heart the whole meaning of her life; her entire personality was poised on the brink of a total act."

Her life's meaning is focused on the point of a bright star—one act that will cost her her life but will giver her the life of one enemy—one act that will inspire others with hope, for she will help prove that individual courage can level the white mountain, one white rock at a time, can destroy the power white people have over black will in one sweep. The bright and morning star is the supreme courage (bright) and hope (morning) of one old workworn, careworn "nigger woman."

It was still important that she live up to Reva's trust; the beacon is flashing, feeding the light of her window where Reva lies sleeping as Aunt Sue sets out. She carries out her plan with her last reserve of physical and moral strength, towering above the morally degenerate posse of white citizens.

> "Kill the [b——]!"
> "Ah *thought* somethin wuz wrong bout her!"
> "Ah wuz fer given it t her from the firs!"
> "Thas whut yuh git for treatin a nigger nice!"

"Treating a nigger nice" means taunting her while torturing her son before her eyes. Fairness means allowing Booker's friend to be the one to shoot Aunt Sue. But Aunt Sue's greatness can never be appreciated by minds so small. They will never understand that they didn't take her life from her, that she gave it up of her own will before they could, just as she gave up Johnny Boy before they could take him from her. The white mountain was only in her mind; she had the power to take away the white man's power over her:

> She lay without struggling, looking upward through the rain at the white faces above her. And she was suddenly at peace; they were not a white mountain now; they were not pushing her any longer to the edge of life. Its awright . . . .

Source: Carole W. Oleson, "The Symbolic Richness of Richard Wright's 'Bright and Morning Star,'" in *Negro American Literature Forum,* Vol. 6, No. 4, Winter 1972, pp. 110–12.

Sources

Bakish, David, *Richard Wright,* Frederick Ungar Publishing Company, 1973.

Bone, Robert, *Richard Wright,* University of Minnesota Press, 1969.

Felgar, Robert, Preface, in *Richard Wright,* Twayne Publishers, 1980.

JanMohamed, Abdul, "Rehistoricizing Wright: The Psychopolitical Function of Death in *Uncle Tom's Children,*" in *Richard Wright,* edited by Harold Bloom, Modern Critical Views Series, Chelsea House Publishers, 1987, pp. 190–228.

Kazin, Alfred, "Too Honest for His Own Time," in *New York Times,* December 29, 1991.

Kinnamon, Keneth, "*Lawd Today* and *Uncle Tom's Children,*" in *The Emergence of Richard Wright,* University of Illinois Press, 1973, pp. 112, 116.

Margolies, Edward, "The Short Stories," in *The Art of Richard Wright,* Southern Illinois University Press, 1969, pp. 72–73.

McHenry, Elizabeth, "Literature, African American," at http://www.africana.com/Articles/tt_251.htm (last accessed February, 2002).

Smethurst, James, ''Black Arts Movement,'' at http://www.african.com/Articles/tt_438.htm (last accessed July 26, 2001).

Yarborough, Richard, ''Introduction,'' in *Uncle Tom's Children,* HarperPerennial, 1993, p. xxvii.

Further Reading

Carter, Dan T., *Scottsboro: A Tragedy of the American South,* Louisiana State University Press, 1979.
Carter carefully reconstructs the ill-fated path that led several young, black men to prison for a crime that they did not commit. This controversial case, which eventually made its way to the Supreme Court, reverberates with the details of a judicial system gone bad.

Gates, Henry Louis, and K. A. Appiah, eds., *Richard Wright: Critical Perspectives Past and Present,* Amistad Press, 1993.
Richard Wright has been credited with changing the mode of African-American writing, and this book offers readers a chance to see how he did it and what his critics thought about him. This book provides a great background study of his works.

Horne, Gerald, *Black Liberation/Red Scare: Ben Davis and the Communist Party,* University of Delaware Press, 1994.
Horne gives an in-depth analysis of the role played by the African-American communists in the struggle for equal rights. The book focuses on the role played by Ben Davis, who lived in Harlem and was twice elected to the New York City Council, and offers a different view of the forces behind the Civil Rights movement.

Walker, Margaret, *Richard Wright: Daemonic Genius: A Portrait of the Man, a Critical Look at His Work,* Amistad Press, 1988.
This is an unauthorized biography; Wright's widow took Walker to court to try to stop publication. Walker and Wright shared a friendship for several years, but it is said to have ended badly.

Watson, Steven, *The Harlem Renaissance: Hub of African-American Culture, 1920–1930,* Pantheon Books, 1995.
The Harlem Renaissance was a literary, creative, and intellectual movement that included the works of such authors as Zora Neale Hurston, Langston Hughes, Countee Cullen, and Jean Toomer and entertainers such as Duke Ellington, Josephine Baker, and Ethel Waters. This book covers that period with photographs and drawings, and Watson's colorful narration describes Harlem during this flowering of creative endeavors.

Dante and the Lobster

Samuel Beckett

1934

"Dante and the Lobster," published by London's Chatto and Windus in the 1934 collection *More Pricks than Kicks*, is in many ways the first important work of Samuel Beckett's illustrious, and ultimately Nobel prize-winning, career. An early version of the story was published in 1932, but in its final form "Dante and the Lobster" provides a fitting and enlightening introduction to Beckett's body of work. Most of his important themes are here: aimlessness, the desire not to act but rather to wait, and the ultimate meaninglessness and futility of existence.

These themes are in their infancy in this story, though, and the story is deeply indebted to Beckett's then-mentor, the Irish writer James Joyce. Where Beckett's later work is constricted and ruthlessly stripped-down, "Dante and the Lobster" takes place in a recognizable place (Dublin) and boasts a protagonist who has yet to descend to the levels of the tramps and decrepit chatterers of Beckett's postwar plays and prose works. Belacqua Shuah is a young man, like Beckett a student at Dublin's Trinity College. The work also depends heavily on allusion, both to literature and to religious (specifically Catholic) tradition. Belacqua's name, for instance, is taken from Dante and from the Bible. In his later works, Beckett drastically reduced the number of allusions and buried them inside the consciousnesses of his narrators rather than placing them on display as he does here. The story is a fascinating look at a young writer just beginning to find his voice and to emerge from under the immensely powerful influence of the greatest writer of the age.

Author Biography

Samuel Beckett was born on April 13, 1906, in Foxrock, near Dublin, Ireland, to a middle-class Protestant family. Beckett was an active and athletic boy, and he excelled at cricket. ''You might say,'' Beckett said, ''that I had a happy childhood . . . although I had little talent for happiness. But I was often lonely.'' He had a close and warm relationship with his father, Bill, but tension prevailed between Beckett and his mother, May. He attended the Portora Royal School in Enniskellen beginning in 1920, and upon graduation he matriculated at Dublin's prestigious Trinity College in 1923.

Beckett studied French and Italian at Trinity, and finally his bright academic potential began to be realized. By the end of his third year at Trinity, he won the Foundation scholarship, the most prestigious award given to undergraduates. While studying the French and Italian classics, he also became interested in contemporary literature, reading the avant-garde French poet Apollinaire and attending Dublin's Abbey Theatre. Impressed by Beckett's promise, Trinity selected Beckett for an exchange post as a tutor and researcher at the Ecole Normale Superieure in Paris.

Beckett arrived in Paris in 1928, and almost upon arriving, he became friends with another Irishman, Thomas MacGreevey, who introduced Beckett to the experimental literary circles of Paris. Beckett gravitated especially to James Joyce, another Irishman, who was generally recognized as the most important English-language writer alive. Joyce took Beckett on as a kind of assistant, and Beckett learned a great deal from Joyce. Most importantly, it was during this period that Beckett decided to start his own writing career: he wrote a short story (his first) and a poem and a critical study of Joyce, both of which achieved publication.

Beckett returned to Dublin in September 1930 to take up a post as a lecturer in modern languages at Trinity. After Paris, Dublin seemed provincial and conservative to the young academic, and Beckett's home life (specifically his difficult relationship with his mother and his father's death in 1933) exacerbated his unhappiness. He quit in 1932, and for the next few years he lived a wandering and unsettled

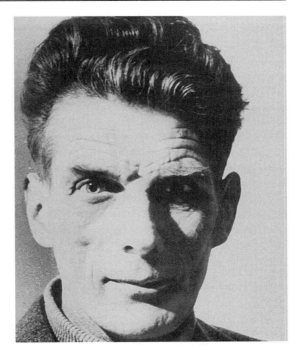

Samuel Beckett

life, going between Dublin, London, Paris, and Germany. During these years, though, Beckett continued writing, finishing two novels (*Dream of Fair to Middling Women*, which remained unpublished in his lifetime, and *Murphy*) and a collection of short stories (*More Pricks than Kicks*, from which ''Dante and the Lobster'' is taken). Finally, in 1937, Beckett returned to Paris—this time permanently.

Beckett resumed the life he had lived eight years earlier in Paris and immersed himself in writing. In 1940, the Nazis invaded the city, and Beckett fled to the south of France, where he and his companion Suzanne Deschevaux-Dumesnil joined the French Resistance. When their cell was betrayed, Beckett and Deschevaux-Dumesnil hid in the Vaucluse region, where they waited out the war and where Beckett finished his third novel, *Watt*. When the war ended, Beckett and Deschevaux-Dumesnil returned to their apartment in Paris.

With the end of the war, Beckett's writing underwent a dramatic change. Eliminating all traces of the influence of James Joyce, Beckett began writing about wanderers in unnamed landscapes, tramps, the aimless. He also began writing in French. From 1945 to 1955, Beckett produced most of the works that gave him fame: the trilogy of novels (*Molloy*, *Malone Dies*, and *The Unnamable*), the

Stories and Texts for Nothing, and his masterpiece plays *Waiting for Godot* and *Endgame*. Although his work was yet to find a large audience, a few readers and critics appreciated his novels, and one important director, Roger Blin, staged *Godot* and was a champion of Beckett's works for the rest of his life.

During the rest of his life, his writing continued to become even more compressed, stark, and unsparing. He wrote in many genres—stage plays, mimes, a film screenplay, radio plays, short prose pieces. He insisted that directors stage his plays exactly as he specified in the script and accepted no deviation. In 1960, he finally married Deschevaux-Dumesnil, but their relationship was never that of a traditional married couple. Rather, they seem to have been life partners more than lovers. In 1969, Beckett won the Nobel Prize for literature. From 1970 to his death in 1989, Beckett continued to produce short performance pieces that were ever more pared down to the barest elements: motion, light, sound, and, at times, language. He also continued to produce short prose pieces. Diagnosed with emphysema in 1986, Beckett died of respiratory failure in December 1989, following Suzanne Deschevaux-Dumesnil by eight months.

Plot Summary

The story opens with Belacqua Shuah, the protagonist, studying the "canti of the moon" of the *Paradiso* of Dante Alighieri. He is confused by the text and becomes bored with it. Frustrated, he slams the book shut and thinks about what he has to do with the rest of the day. "First lunch," he thinks, "then the lobster, then the Italian lesson." To prepare lunch, he spreads out a newspaper on the table and then goes over and lights the gas burner on the stove. He takes out the toaster and thinks about the proper way to make toast. Slicing some bread, he carefully and methodically toasts it. Coating the toast with mustard, hot pepper and salt, he prepares to eat it, then thinks better of it. He wraps the toast in newspaper and leaves his apartment.

Keeping his head down so as not to be bothered as he walks the streets of Dublin, Belacqua goes quickly to the cheese shop where, he knows, the proprietor has a slab of Gorgonzola waiting for him. But when Belacqua arrives at the cheese shop, he

refuses to take the cheese; it is not rotten enough for him. However, he relents, and cursing Angelo, he nonetheless takes the cheese and leaves without paying. Leaving the cheese shop, he reconsiders his schedule. He thinks that he can probably spend his money on beer and drink it while he waits for the fishmonger's shop to open in the afternoon.

As Belacqua nears the school where his lesson is to take place, he thinks back on the lunch that he has consumed and is immensely satisfied with it. Even though the cheese seemed like it would be mild, it ended up being quite strong. Reminiscing on the painful experience of chewing hard, toasted bread, he then begins musing about condemned murderers who might be executed in the near future. He picks up the lobster from the fishmonger, is confused by the man's description of it as "lepping fresh," and proceeds on to his Italian lesson. Immediately, he asks Signorina Ottolenghi, his teacher, about the canti of the moon. As they talk, the French teacher, Mlle. Glain, knocks on the door and wants to know what is in the package outside the door, since the cat was attacking the package and almost tore it "to flitters." When Belacqua and Signorina Ottolenghi begin their lesson again, Signorina Ottolenghi expresses exasperation that they never seem to make any progress.

After his lesson, Belacqua walks to his aunt's house for dinner. Seeing a dejected couple in a doorway, he thinks of the Bible and then of the condemned murderer McCabe and his last meal. When he arrives at his aunt's, he finds her in the garden. She embraces him, and they go into the basement kitchen, where she unwraps the package containing the lobster. He is stunned to discover that the lobster is alive, and his aunt laughs at him for that. When he asks what she intends to do with a live lobster, she says, "Boil the beast, what else?" He is horrified, thinking that it has survived so many perils only to be boiled alive. He reassures himself by thinking that it is a quick death, after all; the narrator, though, answers that "It is not."

Characters

The Aunt

Belacqua's aunt lives in Dublin. He goes and visits her, bringing her a lobster for their meal. She is a very down-to-earth and practical person, focused on the facts of everyday life. In many ways, she is the opposite of Belacqua.

Mademoiselle Glain

Mademoiselle Glain teaches French lessons next door to the room where Signorina Ottolenghi works. She has a cat that tries to eat Belacqua's lobster while Belacqua is taking his Italian lesson. Because of this, Belacqua decides he hates her, calling her a "base prying [b———]" and "a devout, virginal blue-stocking, honing after a penny's worth of scandal."

The Grocer

According to the narrator, the grocer is "a warm-hearted human man [who] felt sympathy and pity for this queer character who always looked ill and dejected." However, he is a "small tradesman" and is not motivated entirely by charity. Belacqua goes to the grocer's shop to buy a slab of Gorgonzola cheese for his sandwich. Belacqua thinks of the grocer as a "decent, obliging" person, but he also behaves badly toward him, quickly changing his mind about the grocer, calling him an "impudent dogsbody" [or low servant]. Although he curses the grocer for giving him a second-rate piece of cheese, he takes it anyway and leaves without paying. Because of his "small tradesman's sense of personal dignity," he is unwilling to make the effort to chase after Belacqua for the few pennies he steals from him.

McCabe

McCabe is a murderer who is to be put to death in the coming days. Belacqua sees his picture in the newspaper that he lays out on his table as the story opens, and thoughts of McCabe go through Belacqua's mind as he goes through his day. He symbolizes death, and since Belacqua has his mind on death throughout the day, death takes on the face of McCabe. He appears in many of the stories in *More Pricks than Kicks*, the collection in which "Dante and the Lobster" appears.

Adriana Ottolenghi

Signorina Adriana Ottolenghi is Belacqua's Italian tutor. He calls her "the Ottolenghi," a name similar to the names he gives to other women in other stories in *More Pricks than Kicks*—the Smeraldina, or the Alba, for instance. He has a "crush" on her (calling her "charming and remarkable") and looks forward to their meetings. The narrator says that he "had set her on a pedestal in her mind, apart from other women." She is "of a certain age," which means that she is no longer precisely young and marriageable, but neither is she old quite yet. The narrator says that she found "being young and beautiful and pure a bore," a trait which must certainly be alluring to the perverse Belacqua. During the class, he attempts to impress her with his knowledge of an Italian saying and by asking her questions about the particularly difficult passage in Dante's *Paradiso* that he was studying at the beginning of the story. At the start of the class, she compliments Belacqua on his progress in Italian, but by the end she mutters of how she regrets his lack of progress, saying that they are "where we were, as we were."

Belacqua Shuah

Belacqua Shuah is the main character both of "Dante and the Lobster" and of the collection *More Pricks than Kicks* as a whole. His primary characteristics are aimlessness and futility, characteristics that he takes from his namesake, Belacqua from Dante's *Purgatorio*. That Belacqua is condemned to remain in the Ante-Purgatory for a time equivalent to his entire life span and cannot enter Purgatory (where his sins will be purged and where he will be prepared for entry into Paradise) until that time has ended. Dante sees him slumped "with his arms around his knees, and between his knees he kept his head bent down" (*Purgatorio* VI.107–8). "What's the use in climbing?" he asks Dante when Dante questions him about his lack of motivation.

When we first see Belacqua Shuah, he is "stuck" or "bogged" in his reading, and the story follows him as he attempts to accomplish things. Some he does accomplish (he makes toast, after concerted effort, and obtains a slab of quite satisfactory cheese); others, he does not (the encounter with Signorina Ottolenghi does not go as well as he had hoped). It takes Belacqua an enormous amount of effort to accomplish the smallest things, and he seems always on the verge of getting stuck and not going on. He is also followed by images of death, thinking repeatedly of condemned murderers and finally realizing that the lobster he carried around all afternoon is in fact alive and that he will be present for its death. The lobster begins to represent him: "for hours, in the midst of its enemies, it had breathed secretly. It had survived the Frenchwoman's cat and his witless clutch." Like Belacqua, the lobster survives a hostile world only to be plunged into boiling water to meet its death. Futility, it seems, is at the very core of human (and crustacean) existence.

Themes

Dante

As suggested by the title, Dante is an important presence in ''Dante and the Lobster.'' The medieval Italian poet Dante Alighieri wrote an epic poem, the *Divine Comedy,* in 1307–1308. It is difficult to accurately assess the importance of Dante's accomplishment, but it is certainly not an overstatement to say that Dante brought classical literary traditions and Christian themes together more successfully than any other writer ever did, before or after, and that his poem showed writers that great literature could be written in local languages, not only in Latin or Greek.

The poem, written in 100 ''canti,'' or chapters, tells the story of Dante himself, who ''in the middle of life's journey'' finds himself lost and aimless. He comes upon the gates to Hell and is guided through the underworld by Virgil, the greatest Roman poet. After witnessing the torments and punishments suffered by sinners, Dante exits Hell and journeys through Purgatory (where sinners wait to have their sins purged so they can be allowed into Paradise) and ultimately to Paradise, where his beloved Beatrice explains to him the mysteries of God and the heavens. The poem attempted to systematize Christian belief and to apply mathematical structure to Christian cosmology. It also, on a very human level, reassured medieval readers that punishments would be meted out in strict proportion to the offense and detailed the nature of sin in an attempt to provide a model for Christian comportment.

Beckett was an Italian scholar at Trinity University and knew Dante well. He was especially captivated by the figure of Belacqua, a character from the fourth canto of the *Purgatorio* who embodies laziness and aimlessness. When Dante asks him why he does not climb up into the entrance to Purgatory, he responds, ''O brother, what's the use of climbing?'' Beckett was struck by this idea of

futility, of incomprehensible forces bent on thwarting all efforts, and of the response of apathy and aimlessness. The world is cruel and life is suffering, Beckett feels, so what's the use in striving? Belacqua in Dante and Belacqua in ''Dante and the Lobster'' both embody this philosophy.

Futility

As one who has adopted an almost dropout attitude toward the world, Belacqua is a character particularly attuned to feelings of futility. The story is full of images of being at an impasse or of the fear of being thwarted. In the first sentence, we learn that Belacqua is ''stuck in the first of the canti of the moon''—he is ''bogged,'' he cannot get through this ''impenetrable'' passage. And then, the narrator tells us, ''there is always something that one had to do next.'' The next thing for Belacqua is to prepare lunch. This comes off quite successfully, for he takes great precautions: locking the door, keeping his head down in the street, making sure that his cheese is rotten enough. After his success in the cheese shop, though, the narrator again focuses on what holds Belacqua back: he has a ''spavined gait, his feet were in ruins, he suffered with them almost continually.'' Signorina Ottolenghi compliments him on his ''rapid progress,'' but he is stalled in his conversation with her; she neither explains the canti of the moon to him nor does she translate the phrase ''*qui vive la pieta quando e ben morta*'' for him. Just before he leaves, Signorina Ottolenghi contradicts her earlier positive statement, telling Belacqua that they are still ''where we were, as we were.'' No progress has been made. Finally, the story ends with the image of the lobster, who has been alive even though thought dead all afternoon, finally being killed—slowly. The only progress we can make, Beckett asserts, is to death—and that slowly.

Style

Allusion

As would be expected from a story that alludes to Dante in its title and has a protagonist named after a Dantean character, ''Dante and the Lobster'' is rife with allusions. The allusions, in fact, give the

Topics for Further Study

- Research the life and times of the Italian poet Dante Alighieri. When did he live? Where? What was the political and the social life like in his times? What were his interests?

- In the 1930s, Europe's balance of power was precarious, and events such as the Spanish Civil War altered that balance. Research the years leading up to World War II in terms of competing national interests and power blocs.

- Beckett's friend and mentor James Joyce experienced censorship throughout his life, and Beckett also encountered publishers and governments that refused to allow his work to circulate because of its content. What were the United States laws about this in the 1930s? How does the Supreme Court determine whether a work is "obscene?" How have the laws changed in the last seventy years?

- European universities are organized very differently from the way American universities and colleges are organized. Examine the differences in teaching, classes, and living situations between an American state university and a school like Trinity University Dublin or Cambridge University.

---

story much of its meaning. *The Divine Comedy,* of course, is the primary text Beckett alludes to, but Christianity also appears prominently in the text in many explicit and implicit ways. The lobster, for instance, represents Christ and man in general in many ways (going through the travails of life only to be sacrificed), but smaller events and details in the story also carry Christian meaning: Belacqua "scoops up" his copy of Dante and holds it flat in his hands like a priest holding a Bible; the narrator refers to the "canti of the moon" as a "quodlibet," or a theological debate; the grocer, "instead of washing his hands like Pilate, flung out his hands in a wild crucified gesture of supplication." Christianity and Dante, Catholicism's most important poet, are the texts, or stories, that form the allusive backbone of "Dante and the Lobster."

Allusions are a very characteristic technique of the modernist writers. Although Beckett is not considered precisely a modernist, at the time "Dante and the Lobster" was written, Beckett was profoundly influenced by the most important of all modernists, James Joyce. Joyce's novels take place on many different symbolic levels, levels that can be disentangled and examined only by studying the allusions (to mythology, to Christianity, to literary history, to politics) embedded in the text. Many modernists felt that all of history simply repeated itself over and over again, and by using allusions these writers sought to underscore the similarities between stories and events that took place in different periods of history. As Beckett's writing evolved, he buried his allusions deeper into his text. In his later writings, he would not make such explicit allusions as he does here, although he continued to allude (albeit elusively) to such ideas as God in texts like *Waiting for Godot.*

Narration

The voice that narrates "Dante and the Lobster" is a third person narrator who can see inside the head of Belacqua and, at one point, inside the head of the grocer. For the most part, this is a traditional narrator, reliable, who plays no games with the reader and who subsumes any personality he or she has into Belacqua's personality. We hear Belacqua's thoughts, and the narrator reports them as if they were his or her own: "the first thing to do was to lock the door. Now nobody could come at him." However, at isolated points in the story, the narrator exhibits signs of a personality, of editorial judgments made about the characters and events of the story. The most notable instance of this is at the end of the story when the narrator notes that Belacqua, thinking about the imminent demise of his lobster, comforts himself that "it's a quick death, God help us all." The narrator, making almost the only direct assertion of the story, responds that "It is not." Because of this separation of the narrator and the main character at the very end of the story, the reader's impression of Belacqua changes. For the vast majority of the story, the narrator reports Belacqua's thoughts without commenting, and from this we have no reason to doubt Belacqua's authority. He is a reliable character, no matter what judgments we may make of his personality and character flaws. But this flat contradiction of Belacqua's idea makes Belacqua seem smaller, more foolish, sillier. It gives the reader a reason to judge Belacqua more harshly.

Historical Context

Samuel Beckett wrote this story in the early 1930s, at the very start of his writing career. Those years were a tumultuous time in Beckett's life (he was aimless and dissatisfied and did not settle down until he moved to Paris permanently in 1937), but it was a traumatic time in Europe. The Treaty of Versailles that ended World War I created a short-lived peace but set the stage for the power struggles that would culminate in World War II. Germany was impoverished because of the war and the reparations it had to pay to the victors; out of that humiliation rose Adolf Hitler and the Nazi Party. At the same time, Soviet Communism was hardening into a dogma, and the Soviet Union began pursuing its own national interests, which included encouraging left-wing movements throughout the world. The bourgeois republican nations of Europe (specifically France and England) found themselves caught between two aggressive radical forces and ideas: communism and fascism.

At first, fascism took the upper hand. Benito Mussolini took control of Italy in the early 1920s, and Hitler was elected to national office in Germany soon after. In the early 1930s, Spain became a kind of proving ground for the conflict between these two forces, and a civil war broke out between workers' groups (funded and supported by the So-

viet Union, but also provided with troops from the United States) and a fascist force headed by Francisco Franco. After a bloody conflict, the fascists triumphed. The democratic powers in Europe waited and hoped for the best as fascism grew in power and, eventually, allied itself to communism with the German-Soviet non-aggression pact.

The leading democratic powers in the world at this time were Great Britain, the United States, and France. Because France is on the continent of Europe, it has been historically decimated by fighting on its soil. France has a different kind of relationship to European power struggles; in addition, France has a different relation to the history of art and culture in Europe than does London or Madrid or Berlin. In the period between the two world wars, and to a lesser degree in the post-World War II period, Paris was the center of artistic experimentation in the Western world. In Paris, bohemianism was common. Artists of all kinds could find a sympathetic group of like-minded people who would support each other both morally and, at times, financially. In the 1920s, the "Lost Generation" of American writers and artists took advantage of the low cost of living in Paris and flocked there. Ernest Hemingway, Gertrude Stein, Robert McAlmon, Man Ray, Ezra Pound, and many others made Paris their home. The city appealed to American artists because it was the absolute opposite of the conservative, philistine, bourgeois culture that dominated almost everywhere in the United States. Paris also appealed to writers and artists from another repressed, religious country: Ireland.

Arguably, two of Ireland's most important exports to Paris of the early twentieth century were James Joyce and Samuel Beckett. Joyce came to Paris earlier than Beckett (in the early 1920s) but left Ireland before that, living in Switzerland and in the city of Trieste (today part of Italy) as well as in Paris. Like Beckett, Joyce was a promising young academic in Dublin, and, like Beckett, Joyce found the conservative Catholic environment of Ireland stifling to artistic creation. Most of his writings take place in Dublin, but it is a Dublin that the characters long to flee. These characters, of course, were simply versions of Joyce himself. Once he reached Paris, Joyce's immense talent was recognized immediately by his contemporaries, and during the years it took him to compose his masterpiece, *Ulysses,* he was supported financially by many friends and patrons. *Ulysses* was published in 1922

Compare & Contrast

- **1930s:** Like the United States, Europe in the 1930s suffers through the Great Depression. Millions of people are out of work, and as a result political parties on the extreme left and right (communist and fascist) gain popularity.

  Today: In the United States, the healthiest economy in decades begins slowing down. Many of the vast fortunes generated by the Internet "bubble" disappear quickly, and hundreds of thousands are "downsized" by companies that shrink or go out of business entirely.

- **1930s:** American president Herbert Hoover is voted out of office in 1932 largely because people are frustrated with his handling of the Great Depression, which began in 1929.

  Today: In an outcome marked by the most serious electoral dispute in American history, Texas governor George W. Bush loses the popular vote to Vice President Al Gore but, because of a favorable Supreme Court decision, wins the necessary votes in the electoral college and, therefore, the presidency.

- **1930s:** After being banned in the United States on grounds of obscenity since its publication, James Joyce's *Ulysses* is finally allowed to be imported into and sold in America in 1934. The court decision holding that the novel is not pornographic is spurred by the publication of Modern Library publisher Bennett Cerf's American edition.

  Today: The United States continues to struggle with changing ideas of permissibility. Controversies especially center on what can be aired on television: profane language, advertisements for birth control, and partial nudity all appear on television after being prohibited for decades.

- **1930s:** Europe moves inevitably toward war. In Germany, the ruling National Socialist (Nazi) party begins instituting laws restricting the freedom of Jewish citizens. British Prime Minister Neville Chamberlain meets in Munich with German leader Adolf Hitler and leaves reassured that Germany will not start a war. He is proven wrong on September 1, 1939.

  Today: Another dictator, Yugoslavian Slobodan Milosevic, is deposed by a democratic "revolution." In 2001, Milosevic is handed over to an international court of justice to stand trial for crimes against humanity (specifically, for ordering massacres and repression in the Yugoslav province of Kosovo and in the Bosnian city of Srebrenica).

---

to immediate acclaim, and Joyce spent much of the rest of his life composing a wildly experimental novel initially called *Work in Progress* and ultimately titled *Finnegans Wake.*

While he was working on *Finnegans Wake,* Joyce collected around him a circle of admirers. In 1928, Beckett met Joyce and quickly became a close associate, helping with the composition of the book and contributing an essay to a collection of studies of the (then unpublished) *Finnegans Wake* entitled *Our Exagmination Round His Factification for Incamination of Work in Progress.* Beckett, like Joyce, bothered by repressive Dublin and dubious about a career in academia, loved the bohemian life in Paris but soon had to return to Dublin. However, in 1937 he returned to Paris, this time for good. Beckett, unlike Joyce, relocated his consciousness to Paris. Whereas Joyce always wrote in English, immersed in the English literary tradition, and about Dublin, Beckett underwent a dramatic change in his writing during World War II and became an entirely different kind of writer. Whereas Joyce filled his works with particulars and details and local facts, Beckett voided his works of the particular after 1945. He also began writing in French. Whereas Joyce never returned to Ireland but also never left it mentally, in many ways Beckett (who occasionally returned to Dublin) became more French than the French, became almost the emblem of the Parisian intellectual.

Critical Overview

''Dante and the Lobster'' was originally published in the collection *More Pricks than Kicks*, one of Beckett's earliest published works. At the time of the book's publication, Beckett was almost completely unknown. He had published a poem, ''Whoroscope,'' and essays on Joyce and Proust, but this book marks Beckett's entry into what became his real career. Chatto and Windus, Beckett's London publishers, tried to interest American publishers in the collection but were unsuccessful, so the book appeared only in England.

The collection received reviews that were quite favorable, especially for a first book. Gerald Gould of the *Observer* remarked that the book was ''dry, harsh . . . not untouched by beauty, though betrayed by an artificial whimsicality and unnecessary obscurity.'' *Time and Tide*'s Richard Sunne and the London *Times Literary Supplement* dismissed the book as an imitation of Joyce, but another reviewer, Arthur Calder-Marshall of the *Spectator*, argued that the main influence was not Joyce but the humorist Ronald Firbank and that the humor of the book deserved praise. Edwin Muir of the *Listener* was impressed by the book's originality and called the style ''witty, extravagant, and excessive.''

These early stories were almost forgotten when Beckett embarked upon the most famous and accomplished phase of his career in 1945, and it was not until the 1970s that critics began again to look at these beginnings of a great writer's *oeuvre*. The stories, then, were almost exclusively read for the light they shed on Beckett's work as a whole. In a study of all of Beckett's short fiction, Robert Cochran points out that these stories show a ''heart'' and ''compassion'' that readers of Beckett's major works rarely saw. Most of the critical writing about Beckett has concentrated on his plays, while studies of his novels have been second in importance. Studies of his short fiction (which he continued to write until his death) are few. However, most of them discuss ''Dante and the Lobster,'' not for its own sake, but instead as a precursor to his later, more polished and self-contained work. One of the few critics to pay attention specifically to ''Dante and the Lobster'' is John Pilling, who writes that the story is ''one of the more impressive stories in a collection which varies in quality'' and that it is, nonetheless, ''by no means representative of *More Pricks than Kicks* as a whole'' (largely, according to Pilling, because in the story Belacqua's relations with the women are not amorous).

Criticism

Greg Barnhisel

Barnhisel directs the writing center at the University of Southern California. In this essay, Barnhisel discusses the Dantean and Joycean parallels of the story and how, in his later fiction, Beckett refined his work of these influences in order to arrive at a more individual voice.

In a story with Dante in the title and in which the protagonist bears a name taken from Dante, readers expect allusions to the greatest of medieval poets. In ''Dante and the Lobster,'' the work that in many ways commences Beckett's career as a writer, Beckett provides these allusions in significant numbers. However, it is too simple to read this story just as a response to or a rewriting of an episode from Dante. Also present, more powerfully, although much less explicitly, is the great literary figure of Beckett's life and the man who was Beckett's mentor during the years when he began writing: James Joyce. At the time he wrote ''Dante and the Lobster,'' Beckett had a close relationship with the elder Irish writer, serving as his assistant and, at one point, even going on a date with Joyce's daughter. If Dante was the presence Beckett wanted to have in his story, Joyce's is the presence that Beckett could not keep out.

The literary critic Harold Bloom sees literary history as a giant trans-historical Oedipal drama: ''Great poets'' fall under the dominating influence of a predecessor writer, then unintentionally ''misread'' that writer in an attempt to get past his influence, in effect ''slaying the father.'' ''Dante and the Lobster'' is Beckett's attempt to bring his two literary fathers together so as to forge his own space. Dante could be acknowledged in the text, for he was so distant in history that he was not a threat to Beckett's own identity as a writer. Joyce, however, as an Irish writer in exile in Paris, was initially a liberating and ultimately a crippling influence on Beckett. Harold Bloom might say that the absence of any explicit allusions to Joyce clearly proves Beckett's need to repress this influence, given the story's Joycean themes and main character.

But before discussing the Joycean resonances of "Dante and the Lobster," it is first necessary to examine the figure that Beckett proposes as the real influence: Dante. Specifically, from the time of his Italian studies at Trinity, Beckett found himself drawn to the hellish imagery of the *Inferno* and, perhaps even more, to the ambivalent darkness and promise of the *Purgatory*. According to Mary Bryden, Beckett's writing, "both early and late," is "imprinted with purgatorial characteristics which resonate within a Dantean context." In Dante, Purgatory is a locus of waiting and purgation where sinners, or other figures (from Greek and Roman times, for instance) who lived virtuous lives without knowing Christ, go to await admittance into Heaven. Salvation cannot be achieved though works performed in Purgatory, so the inhabitants of Purgatory must just wait for their time to expire or for enough members of the living to offer up prayers on their behalf.

Belacqua, the character in the *Purgatory* after whom Belacqua Shuah is named, embodies sloth and lassitude. At the end of the fourth book, while Dante is still in the Ante-Purgatory, Dante and his guide come upon a man "sitting with his arms around his knees" who looked "more languid than he would have been were laziness his sister." Belacqua tells Dante that his laziness and nonchalance come from the fact that he is condemned to just wait: he must wait before the entrance to Purgatory for a period of time equal to his own life on Earth unless some living people offer up prayers to shorten his time in Ante-Purgatory. Belacqua's sin was (appropriately enough) sloth: he never took the time or expended the energy to live as a good Christian while on earth.

Belacqua Shuah's primary characteristic is also laziness and a lack of forward motion. In the first paragraph of the story, the narrator describes him as "stuck" and "bogged." He takes a long time and a great deal of effort simply to get lunch; then, he dawdles on his way to the fishmonger and his Italian lesson. His intellect is also slow; he does not know that his lobster is alive the whole time he is carrying it around. The only mention of speed or quickness in the entire story is at the end. Reconciling himself to the fact that the lobster will be boiled to death, Belacqua thinks that "it's a quick death, God help

Illustration of Dante and Virgil in Dante's Divine Comedy

us all." The narrator then retorts, "It is not," undermining this one instance of anything being done quickly. Belacqua never gets anywhere, is always stuck in one place. "Where are we ever?" Signora Ottolenghi asks Belacqua. "Where we were, as we were."

The critic Rubin Rabinovitz extends Belacqua's sloth into his failure to do good deeds or even to be polite to others (this, of course, was the original Belacqua's downfall). Belacqua steals cheese from a shopkeeper (who allows him to do so out of pity); he does not thank Mlle. Glain when she saves his lobster from her cat, instead thinking that she is a "base prying [b——]." Signora Ottolenghi suggests, Rabinovitz points out, that Belacqua should study "Dante's rare moments of compassion in Hell," but, "thinking that she has only linguistic instruction in mind, Belacqua responds by quoting '*Qui vive la pieta quando e ben morta.*' Belacqua, carried away by the cleverness of the comment, never considers the unsettling ethical questions it raises." Rabinovitz points out that for Beckett, there are two types of compassion: one for undeserving victims (like the grocer and the lobster), and one for deserving victims (like Belacqua). The grocer and the lobster are described as being in "cruciform" posi-

What Do I Read Next?

- *Waiting for Godot,* first produced in 1953, is Beckett's masterwork. The play depicts two tramps who wait, through the course of the play, for a "Godot" who never arrives. Why they are waiting, or who Godot is, is never explained. The play is perhaps the ultimate statement of theatrical nihilism and modernist absurdity.

- After writing stories, Beckett moved on to write a very successful trilogy of novels. They are not easy reads, but *Molloy* (1951), *Malone Dies* (1951), and *The Unnamable* (1953) tell the stories of decrepit men who are on the edge of death, who demonstrate Beckett's certainty that the only irreducible characteristic of humans is their endless desire to go on, no matter what.

- James Joyce's short story collection *Dubliners* (1914) was initially reviled for its depressing tone and cynical portraits of Dublin and its citizens. Today, however, it is regarded as one of the most important collections of stories of the twentieth century.

- The great literary work of medieval Europe, Dante's *Divine Comedy* (1308), is an immensely entertaining, moving, and thought-provoking epic poem. Telling the story of Dante's journey through Hell, Purgatory, and Paradise, the *Divine Comedy* is a primary influence on Beckett's "Dante and the Lobster" and on Western literature as a whole.

---

tion, like the crucified Christ, while Belacqua himself is imagistically associated with the condemned murderer McCabe. (Throughout his life, Beckett was fascinated by the image of Christ crucified between the two thieves, one of which was saved; the difference between Belacqua and the grocer and lobster could represent the difference between the saved thief and the condemned thief.)

We are all condemned to suffering and death, the story tells us, whether we live a good life or whether we avoid our chances to do good. The critic Robert Cochran argues that this is the essential core of the story:

> From Dante's moon spots to the lobster in the pot, from the story's beginning to the story's end, the message is the same. The moon with its spots was Cain, 'seared with the first stigma of God's pity, that an outcast might not die quickly.' The lobster does not die quickly either.

The desire for and impossibility of achieving a quick and painless death pervades all of Beckett's work. In his most famous plays, *Waiting for Godot* and *Endgame,* the characters wait, saying to each other the same things they have said every day in memory and the things that they will continue to

repeat. Characters make comic attempts at suicide: the branch holding the noose breaks, autosuffocation fails, the limbs wither and freeze, but the compulsion to go on never ends. In the trilogy of novels he wrote immediately after the Second World War, the characters can do nothing but endlessly speak and grow ever more decrepit. Molloy fades away in a ditch, and the Unnamable ends the trilogy by saying, "I can't go on. I'll go on." In "Dante and the Lobster," Beckett first writes of this always-thwarted desire for a quick and painless end.

What makes this incarnation of Beckett's master-theme unique in "Dante and the Lobster" is the influence of Joyce, a writer who loved the world and all of the sensual pleasures it offered. "Dante and the Lobster"'s Belacqua bears many similarities with Joyce's sensitive young scholar-hero, Stephen Dedalus. Both, for instance, have improbably obvious allusive names (Belacqua Shuah's to Dante and the Bible, Stephen's to the St. Stephen myth and to the Greek mythological figure Daedalus). Both are young Dublin intellectuals who find no ultimate satisfaction in what they are doing. But where Stephen is an affectionate, if self-critical, portrait of Joyce himself as a younger man, Belacqua is ultimately a comic character with few redeeming qualities. Stephen, in *Portrait of the Artist as a Young Man,* must fly free of the nets of his home country's conservative culture, and in *Ulysses* Stephen seems in need of a father-figure to guide him away from narcissism. Rarified, hyperintellectual, and self-destructive Stephen Dedalus, once under the influence of the earthy and pleasant Leopold Bloom, could have become Joyce himself (but in *Ulysses* Stephen rejects Bloom's offer). Joyce could have lived easily in the world of metaphysics and quodlibets and literary history, but he was also just as comfortable in drinking bouts with French barflies, and *Ulysses* seems to suggest that he thinks the Stephen in him benefited from the influence of a Leopold Bloom at some point in his life.

Belacqua, though, is a self-contained entity. He is Stephen made significantly more petty, more inward, more selfish and contemptuous of the world around him. Belacqua, it seems, would never attract Bloom enough to merit an offer of stepfatherhood. A sneaky and rude character who is associated throughout *More Pricks than Kicks* with Cain and the murderer McCabe, Belacqua proceeds in the course of the book from a smug and simplistic dismissal of a lobster's death to his own comic and improbable demise.

For Beckett, Stephen must have been an indelible character, in many ways reminiscent of himself. How could Beckett write autobiographical short stories when another writer had already written the very stories Beckett wanted to write about himself? What character that he could create could serve as a better repository for his own traits than Stephen? His solution was to make Belacqua darkly comic and to condemn him more strongly than Joyce condemned Stephen. But in doing so, Beckett came upon the themes that would make his career: suffering, waiting for a death that never seems to come soon enough. Using the systematic afterlife Dante created, Beckett could confront the metaphysical questions that had obsessed him since his collegiate study of Descartes and Geulincx. Using the form and the characters used by Joyce, Beckett could dramatize his own worst characteristics. Later, though, in the postwar dramas and novels, the distinction between those who deserve compassion and those who do not becomes very blurry. Belacqua, the grocer, and Signora Ottolenghi meld into one another and become the eternal pairs—Hamm and Clov, Vladimir and Estragon, Molloy and Moran, Pozzo and Lucky—that are the center of Beckett's

> "'Dante and the Lobster' is Beckett's attempt to bring his two literary fathers together so as to forge his own space."

greatest works. Could these later duos have been initially inspired by ''Dante and the Lobster'''s duo of influences, Dante and Joyce?

Source: Greg Barnhisel, Critical Essay on ''Dante and the Lobster,'' in *Short Stories for Students,* The Gale Group, 2002.

Kay Gilliland Stevenson

In the following essay, Stevenson examines the original version of ''Dante and the Lobster'' and Beckett's revision, finding increased ''balance, or ambiguity'' in the character of Belacqua in the latter.

The first sentence of Samuel Beckett's ''Dante and the Lobster''—''It was morning and Belacqua was stuck in the first of the canti in the moon''—gives the reader pause. Or it should. Some ideal combination of information and ignorance is demanded by the story. Those experienced in Beckett's fiction may know too much, or assume they do, about his early collection of stories and therefore find it difficult to feel again the edge of wrongness in that opening sentence. Belacqua ''stuck in the first of the canti in the moon?'' How the hell did he get there? And in the morning, as well. In the context of Dante's *Commedia* the time is wrong, the place is wrong, and the action—or kind of inaction ''stuck'' establishes—is, if not quite wrong, certainly not quite right. It is precisely noon when Dante enters the sphere of the moon, where those inconstant in their vows glow and rejoice now in the grace which saved them. Belacqua does not belong in the canti of the moon, *Paradiso* II–V, at all; Dante met him far away, back in the fourth canto of *Purgatorio*, waiting with others late in repentence for a span of time equal to his earthly life before he can enter purgatory proper. He is waiting with striking stillness and lassitude—''more indolent than if sloth were his sister''—but this immobility has a completely different quality from that of ''stuck.'' That would be an odd verb even in relation to *Purgatorio* and it is absurd for *Paradiso*, explicitly absurd given that in the second of the canti in the moon Piccarda and other blessed shades smile at Dante's ignorance when he asks whether they don't desire a higher place; she corrects his assumption that they might feel stuck in this lowest sphere of paradise: "In His will is our peace. It is that sea to which all things move."

Though "impatient to get on to Piccarda," Belacqua slams shut his book when he hears midday strike. Here Belacqua of Dublin is distinguished from Belacqua of Florence, but with a minimum of circumstantial evidence. In later stories of *More Pricks Than Kicks* he acquires a surname, a "strong weakness for oxymoron," and various girlfriends. Knowing such details is far from necessary; indeed they can obscure the achievements of "Dante and the Lobster," the first story in the collection and one of the few which Beckett was willing to see reprinted for more than three decades. Students of Beckett too familiar with Belacqua Shuah may treat him with contempt. Raymond Federman, who considers all the stories of *More Pricks Than Kicks* together, describes Belacqua as if he were a consistent character and asserts that his "pedantry, arrogance, egocentricism, and morbidity reject the compassion aroused by Beckett's later heroes." He is, in "Dante and the Lobster," less easily summed up. Furthermore, a number of the changes Beckett made in revising the story between its first appearance in *This Quarter* (Winter 1932) and *More Pricks Than Kicks* (1934) work to increase the balance, or ambiguity, of Belacqua's presentation, and thus increase the tension between judgment and charity which is a major theme. Any single pronouncement about Belacqua would be as inappropriate as a single view of the moon, which presides over all three clearly marked sections of the story.

When Ruby Cohn briefly surveys the revisions made between the 1932 and 1934 printings, she concludes that "the main purpose of revision was to sharpen the comic." Despite admiration for Beckett's "early elegance," she finds the three incidents of the story inadequately unified and focused: "Each . . . is described in such meticulous and sardonic detail that the underlying theme, the difficulty of reconciling divine mercy with divine justice, frequently fades away." Concerned with comic techniques, she underestimates the seriousness of the story. I think that more needs to be said about the revisions, in relation to Belacqua, to the question of unity, and to the stylistic elegance which is a source of the comic and troubling effects. Both the instances she cites of comic incongruity arising from

"an image that is ludicrously out of key with what it describes" will repay further exploration: "In 'Dante and the Lobster,' there are several examples of incongruity which are sharpened in the revised version: 'to feel his fangs break through the splendid hard crust of toast into a yielding zone' becomes 'to feel his teeth meet in a bathos of pith and dough.' Similarly 'so that the whole presented an appearance of a diamond and square with common centre' is changed to 'so that the whole resembled the Japanese flag.'"

In the first of Cohn's examples, Beckett is naming explicitly a central rhetorical device for "Dante and the Lobster." From the title onward, equilibrium in the reader is troubled by juxtaposition of the grand and the commonplace. What have Dante and a lobster to do with each other, coupled in a coordinate phrase? Bathos is, again, wittily dominant in Beckett's play on the significance of the moon, as Belacqua moves from the blessed souls of *Paradiso* to a sandwich of green cheese. The bathetic and profound jostle in Belacqua's day: as his "three large obligations" of lunch, lobster, and Italian lesson parody Dante's trinitarian structures, as the story links the deaths of McCabe, Christ, and a lobster, and as his thoughts swing from banality ("We live and learn, that was a true saying") to theological questions ("Why not piety and pity, even down below? Why not mercy and Godliness together?").

The pattern of a Japanese flag, in Cohn's second example, contributes not simply to incongruity in general, but to the single most important image unifying Belacqua's progression through lunch, lesson, and lobster. After Beckett has changed the shape of Belacqua's loaf of bread from square to round, thus providing a new pattern on his toaster, Japan's rising sun is mirrored by the charred, seared moon on whose spots Beckett continues to muse. Beginning in the moon of *Paradiso,* "Dante and the Lobster" is as moonstruck as *A Midsummer Night's Dream,* and it triumphantly combines materials as diverse. Dante's moon underlies the high seriousness of the story, for in *Paradiso* the moon figures both the salvation of Piccarda and the wanderings of Cain (since Dante includes this folklore identification of the man in the moon by having Beatrice refute it). Lower comedy, and a different folklore about the moon, appear in Belacqua's exuberant, obsessive examination of the central ingredient in his lunch. It lacks any odor of sanctity: "He rubbed it. It was sweating. That was something. He stooped and smelt it. A faint fragrance of corruption. What good was that? He didn't want fragrance, he wasn't a bloody gourmet, he wanted a good stench. What he wanted was a good green stenching rotten lump of Gorgonzola cheese, alive, and by God he would have it.'' For the third section of the story, the moon makes a final, more puzzling appearance. ''Let us call it Winter,'' says Beckett, ''that dusk may fall now and a moon rise.'' Now this is a bit like the scarves in *Murphy*; it simply doesn't work out. Twice a year in the Northern Temperate Zone, thus in Dublin, sunset and moonrise coincide—for a few days around full moon at the autumnal equinox (''harvest moon'') and again at the next full moon (''hunter's moon''). Neither could be called ''Winter,'' and if there is definitely no autumnal fruition in the story, at least it is not the moon of Cain, tiller of the field. What Beckett provides here is typically Beckettian, in its wintry but not entirely dark setting, and in its fictive impossibility. It is also highly Dantean. At first I was inclined to think that Beckett was deliberately creating something entirely new. Reflection, however, produced—reflection. This winter moonrise is equal and opposite to the Dante's first sunrise. In the *Commedia,* the moon sets as the sun rises on Good Friday 1300. But scholars searching for a cluster of astronomical facts which will fit the descriptions find that ''there is no day in the year 1300 which meets all these conditions'' established by Dante for the sun and moon. Like Dante, Beckett creates an ideal rather than a naturalistic pattern.

In so moonstruck a story, it is natural that Belacqua should have some tinges of lunatic, lover, and poet. The virtuosity with which Beckett plays with his identity is not confined to the initial double-take, Belacqua of Florence and Belacqua of Dublin. In curious ways, at various points, he is associated with Dante and with the lobster, with Christ and with Cain.

Studying Beatrice's different explanation of spots on the moon, Belacqua is something of a model for the literary critic: ''Still he pored over the enigma, he would not concede himself conquered, he would understand at least the meanings of the words, the order in which they were spoken and the nature of the satisfaction that they conferred on the misinformed poet, so that when they were ended he was refreshed and could raise his heavy head, intending to return thanks and make formal retraction of his old opinion.'' In that sentence, ''he'' is at first firmly linked with Belacqua but becomes Dante by the end. The grammatical slippage does not occur in the *This Quarter* version; one of Beckett's revisions supplies the parallel series of verbs: ''he would not

> **The virtuosity with which Beckett plays with his identity is not confined to the initial double-take, Belacqua of Florence and Belacqua of Dublin. In curious ways, at various points, he is associated with Dante and with the lobster, with Christ and with Cain."**

concede . . . he would understand'' to ''could raise his heavy head.'' Moreover, in 1932 the next sentence, opening paragraph two, begins unequivocally'' Belacqua'' but in 1934 ''He.''

Dante's *Convivio,* from which Beckett had quoted shortly before, in his contribution to *Our Exagmination . . .* (1929), provides a link between verbal structures and the recurrent, changing moon. Dante associates the planetary spheres with the seven liberal arts, and the moon is the sphere of grammar. The kind of literary criticism with which Belacqua starts is that of the grammarian—the meanings of the words, the order in which they were spoken. What satisfactions follow? If one picks up a copy of *Paradiso* to check on the passage over which Belacqua is poring, finding there Dante raising his heavy head after Beatrice's explanation, and reads on to the appearance of Piccarda, one finds a gently ridiculous picture of Dante adjusting his view. When Piccarda appears, Dante takes her for a reflection, a mirror image, and he turns around, looking behind him. Reading ''Dante and the Lobster'' demands similar readjustments, recognition of mirroring relationships, the discovery of congruity in incongruous materials. Here is wit in Locke's sense, perception of likeness in unlike objects. Moreover, Beckett induces in the reader something like the habitual self-corrections, the scrupulous rejections of easy formulations, which he gives his most moving major characters.

A paragraph on moonspots (identical in the 1932 and 1934 versions) is sandwiched without transition between paragraphs describing Belacqua madly, methodically charring bread for his sandwich: "For the tiller of the field the thing was simple, he had it from his mother. The spots were Cain with his truss of thorns, dispossessed, cursed from the earth, fugitive and vagabond. The moon was that countenance fallen and branded, seared with the first stigma of God's pity, that an outcast might not die quickly. It was a mix-up in the mind of the tiller, but that did not matter. It had been good enough for his mother, it was good enough for him." Something odd is going on with the pronouns again. In "he had it from his mother," who is "he" and what is "it?" Is it the explanation of moonspots Belacqua had from his mother (the explanation which Beatrice rejects in the first of the canti in the moon), or is the mother not Belacqua's but Eve, and "it" the original sin Cain inherits from her? As the first of Beckett's footsore protagonists ("his feet were in ruins, he suffered with them almost continuously"), Belacqua has other links with wandering Cain. The description of his charred toast as "burnt . . . offering" could make him equally close to Cain or to Abel—as the name of condemned criminal McCabe makes him son of Abel or son of Cain.

He is curiously close to the lobster as well, partly because of marine metaphors. He "suddenly dived into a little family grocery" and goes "diving into the public, as usual"; he reflects that "all had gone swimmingly" with lunch and the collection of the lobster. In revising the first paragraph between 1932 and 1934, Beckett expands watery images. The phrase "complicated and up in the air" is abandoned; "straightforward" is replaced by "plain sailing." In 1932 Belacqua "was bogged, and could not get on." In 1934, "He was so bogged that he could move neither backward nor forward." A reader may recollect that one of the striking characteristics of lobsters is their swimming backward, and further reflect that Belacqua's movement in the story is in some sense a backwards version of Dante's pilgrimage, regressing from Paradise in the early paragraphs "down into the bowels of the earth, into the kitchen in the basement" for the final pages. There, in his shock at finding that lobsters are boiled alive, Belacqua mirrors "Dante's rare moments of compassion in Hell" with distant punning on the phrase he had quoted in his Italian lesson: "qui vive la pietà quando è ben morta," that is, "here pity lives when by rights it is dead."

The lobster is twice compared with Christ. Belacqua and his aunt contemplate it "cruciform on the oilcloth." Earlier, he identifies it for the French

teacher as a fish, with a play on the Greek anagram ΙΧΘΥΣ: "He did not know the French for lobster. Fish would do very well. Fish had been good enough for Jesus Christ, Son of God, Saviour. It was good enough for Mlle. Glain."

Belacqua's name, according to Hugh Kenner, is "compounded from Dante and gutter-Irish (Bollocky)." Amorous activity, prominent in other stories of *More Pricks Than Kicks*, plays little part in "Dante and the Lobster," except insofar as Belacqua's sentimental and flirtatious relationship to his Italian teacher, a middle-aged woman "who had found being young and beautiful and pure more of a bore than anything else," remotely parodies Dante's relationship to Beatrice. The qualities, and the quality, of "Dante and the Lobster" are apt to be obscured when *More Pricks Than Kicks* is discussed as a collection in which "In the main, Belacqua is involved in adventures with various ladies." While "Bollocky" possibilities are not developed, literal translations of the name into English and Irish underline the unity and the contradictions of the story. The epithet "Blissful Beatrice" in the opening paragraph encourages a reader to translate names directly. In English, Belacqua as "beautiful water" is ironically appropriate for the lobster's violent end. In Irish, the name changes to *fionn uisce* or Phoenix (the transformation by which Phoenix Park got its name), evoking one of the traditional symbols of Christ, as the phoenix which once in a thousand years bursts into flame and arises again from the ashes.

In both versions of the story, Belacqua's identity is fluid, as befits his name. In the second version, however, there occurs what might be called an improvement in his character. Some phrases are toned down: "a vicious piece of hooliganism" becomes "hooliganism pure and simple." Given the etymological precision with which other words are employed, the disappearance of "vicious" is particularly significant. When Belacqua "deployed an old Herald," the verb has the full sense of *displicare,* unfold, and a white slice of bread is literally a "candidate." Belacqua does not, of course, become fully virtuous by such a revision, but he becomes more ambiguous. A few sentences of no great importance, but generally unsympathetic, disappear completely: "His mind was tired, it could not be bothered carrying him beyond the lesson. . . . He did not feel like fake enthusiasm at the moment." In both versions, his lunch is "spiced" by the news that McCabe will hang at dawn. But in 1932, "If anything was wanted to crown that exquisite gastronomical experience, it was just such a piece of news,'' while in 1934 zest gives way to unspecified pungency: ''Belacqua, tearing at the sandwich and swilling the precious stout, pondered on McCabe in his cell.''

When Belacqua calculates his timetable for picking up the lobster, ''Assuming that his aunt had given her order in good time . . . so that her nephew should on no count be delayed'' becomes more roughly phrased: ''aunt'' becomes ''lousy old [b——] of an aunt,'' and ''nephew'' becomes ''blackguard boy.'' Curiously, however, the two derogatory phrases almost cancel each other; if Belacqua (or the narrator) is casually abusive about the aunt, he is also jocularly dismissive about the nephew. Furthermore, ''blackguard'' may be a small etymological joke: the equal and opposite of ''candidate''; the first definition for ''blackguard'' in the *OED* reads: ''The lowest menials of a royal or noble household, who had charge of pots and pans and other kitchen utensils, and rode in the wagons conveying these during journeys from one residence to another; the scullians and kitchen-slaves.'' One sentence added in 1934 is more ambiguous. After ''He had burnt his offering, he had not fully dressed it,'' Beckett inserts, ''Yes, he had put the horse behind the tumbrel.'' First, by turning a proverbial phrase around so that the cart is not (verbally) ahead of the horse, Beckett is neatly repeating and exemplifying the idea of lobster-like progress backwards. Secondly, however, the substitution of ''tumbrel'' for ''cart'' links Belacqua not with the lobster, innocent as Abel, but with executioners. There are many of these in the story: Cain, God as punisher of Cain, Ellis the hangman crossing from England to dispatch McCabe, and Belacqua's aunt matter-of-factly lifting the lobster into the pot.

Perhaps influenced by Joyce, Beckett radically simplified punctuation in the 1934 edition. One result is to make the distinction between Belacqua and the narrator, which is fine in both versions, even harder to draw. Beckett leaves such tags as ''He thought,'' but removes the quotation marks which in 1932 mark the ends of internal direct discourse: ''At the corner of the street a horse was down and a man sat on its head. I know, thought Belacqua, that that is considered the right thing to do. But why? A lamplighter flew by on his bike, tilting with his pole at the standards, jousting a little yellow light into the evening.'' The inquiring spirit of Belacqua, one of his attractive qualities, is clear. It is not, however, clear whether the metaphoric perception of the lamplighter as a knight belongs to him or to the narrator. In 1932 quotation marks signpost ''But why?'' as the end of Belacqua's conscious thought, but here as in other paragraphs the modulation between Belacqua's consciousness and the narrator's is subtle or disconcerting. Except for the third-person pronoun, a description of Belacqua's eagerness to ''avoid being accosted'' seems to be his own view of the situation, idiosyncratic but engagingly vigorous: ''To be stopped at this stage and have conversational nuisance committed all over him would be a disaster.'' Two sentences later, Beckett changes the 1932 phrasing ''hunger—obviously more of mind than of body'' to ''hunger, more of mind, I need scarcely say, than of body,'' and thus jostles a reader not only by the shift from vivid hyperbole to cliché but also by the insistent, intrusive *I*.

In 1934, the triangle of asterisks which set off the three sections of the story disappear, although a few centimeters of white space are left. Any reasonably alert reader can see without the help of the asterisks that, like the *Commedia,* the story is tripartite. Belacqua lists the major units—lunch, lesson, and lobster—and the second and third sections begin with the same phrase: ''Belacqua drew near to the school . . . Belacqua drew near to the house of his aunt.'' Given a reference to McCabe's last supper, the phrase thus emphasized by position and repetition suggests the liturgical ''Draw near with faith.'' For a reader steeped in Scripture, and alerted to echoes of the Bible by references to burnt offerings, Cain, Pilate, and Jonah, the phrase may recall Abraham's protesting at the destruction of Sodom: ''And Abraham drew near and said, Wilt thou also destroy the righteous with the wicked?'' It could also evoke Luke 15, a chapter in which Jesus tells three parables about God's mercy or his rejoicing over the saved, the parables of the lost sheep, the lost coin, and the prodigal son: ''Then drew near unto him all the publicans and sinners to hear him.'' God's awareness of even the fall of a sparrow (though Belacqua sweeps away crumbs ''as though there were no such thing as a sparrow in the wide world'') and the story of ''Jonah and the gourd and the pity of a jealous God on Nineveh'' on which Belacqua ponders are among the clear Biblical allusions. Belacqua refrains from mentioning one obvious Biblical story, even more watery than Jonah's: by omitting the Flood he keeps the balance of justice and mercy tilted, precariously, toward mercy.

Simplified punctuation in 1934 shows Beckett trusting a reader to catch the allusion to Keats near the end of the story. In 1932, a snatch of the ''Ode to a Nightingale,'' l. 54, is set off with quotation marks and followed by ellipsis marks: ''Take into the air my quiet breath . . ., '' thus sending one off to look at its richly ironic context. Within the stanza, ''easeful Death'' and ''To cease upon the midnight with no pain'' contrast with the lobster's boiling; in the larger pattern, wishful imagination is defeated by experience. The quotation appears in 1934 without any signal, except the shift from ''it'' to ''my,'' that Belacqua's train of thought about the lobster has been complicated: ''In the depths of the sea it had crept into the cruel pot. For hours in the midst of its enemies, it had breathed secretly. It had survived the Frenchwoman's cat and his witless clutch. Now it was going alive into the scalding water. It had to. Take into the air my quiet breath.'' I vaguely wondered whether the line was the refrain of a sentimental Irish tenor's song, and felt shocked and chastened when I finally placed it.

The longest addition to the story consists of two sentences inserted into the paragraph about Gorgonzola cheese: ''He knew a man who came from Gorgonzola. He had been born in Nice but all his youth had been spent in Gorgonzola.'' These apparently random recollections reinforce Beckett's equally casual introduction of the *Herald,* the newspaper on which Belacqua slices his loaf. Dublin's *Evening Herald* is a major newspaper but hardly the only one he could have had at hand; it's the *Telegraph* that is mentioned in ''Fingal.'' No messenger is to appear in this story with tidings of joy or a ram caught in a thicket, but the *Herald* and Angelo together join other oblique references to Dante and the moon. Angels proper, as distinct from the more elevated seraphim, cherubim, thrones, dominions, virtues, powers, principalities, and archangels, are the order presiding over the sphere of the moon. Dante catalogues the nine orders in *Paradiso* XXVIII.

Not quite the first published narrative by Beckett, ''Dante and the Lobster'' would be almost too neat a beginning for his career: dark but not completely dark, elegant and deliberately banal, comic and troubling, carefully crafted and calling attention to its artifice. In the penultimate sentence, Belacqua hopefully ameliorates the lobster's fate: ''Well, thought Belacqua, it's a quick death, God help us all.'' Beckett's justly famous last sentence reproves easy resolutions.

Source: Kay Gilliland Stevenson, ''Belacqua in the Moon: Beckett's Revisions of 'Dante and the Lobster,''' in *Critical Essays on Samuel Beckett,* edited by Patrick A. McCarthy, G. K. Hall & Co., 1986, pp. 36–45.

Sources

Bryden, Mary, ''No Stars without Stripes: Beckett and Dante,'' in *Romanic Review,* Vol. LXXXVII, No. 4, November 1996, pp. 541–56.

Calder-Marshall, Arthur, Review of *More Pricks than Kicks,* in *Spectator,* June 1, 1934, p. 46.

Cochran, Robert, *Samuel Beckett: A Study of the Short Fiction,* Twayne, 1991.

Cronin, Anthony, *Samuel Beckett: The Last Modernist,* HarperCollins, 1996.

Gould, Gerald, Review of *More Pricks than Kicks,* in *Observer,* July 2, 1934, p. 428.

Knowlson, James, *Damned to Fame: The Life of Samuel Beckett,* Simon & Schuster, 1996.

Muir, Edward, Review of *More Pricks than Kicks,* in *Listener,* July 4, 1934, p. 34.

Pattie, David, *The Complete Critical Guide to Samuel Beckett,* Routledge, 2000.

Pilling, John, *Beckett before Godot,* Cambridge University Press, 1997.

Rabinovitz, Rubin, *The Development of Samuel Beckett's Fiction,* University of Illinois Press, 1984.

Review of *More Pricks than Kicks,* in *Times Literary Supplement* (London), July 26, 1934, p. 247.

Sunne, Richard, Review of *More Pricks than Kicks,* in *Time and Tide,* May 26, 1934, p. 26.

Further Reading

Bair, Deirdre, *Samuel Beckett: A Biography,* Jonathan Cape, 1978.

Bair's was the first biography of Beckett, written years before he died, but in many ways it is the most readable.

Farrow, Anthony, *Early Beckett: Art and Allusion in ''More Pricks than Kicks'' and ''Murphy,''* Whitston Publishing Company, 1991.

This very academic study details in great specificity the sources of the allusions of Beckett's two earliest books.

Gontarski, S. E., ed., *On Beckett: Essays and Criticism,* Grove Press, 1986.

This collection, edited by Gontarski—an important scholar of modernism and of modernist drama in particular—is probably the best introduction to the different kinds of writing on Beckett.

Kenner, Hugh, *Samuel Beckett: A Critical Study,* University of California Press, 1961.

Kenner's writing on modernism is both encyclopedic and idiosyncratic. In his early career, he was the first academic critic to devote whole studies to writers such as Beckett and Ezra Pound, and this book was the first significant critical statement on how Beckett fit into the modernist tradition.

The Dog of Tithwal

Saadat Hasan Manto

1987

The inspiration for Saadat Hasan Manto's "The Dog of Tithwal," first published in English in a 1987 collection of Manto's stories titled *Kingdom's End and Other Stories*, translated by Khalid Hasan, was the partition of India in 1947. The partition split India into Muslim Pakistan and secular (but Hindu-dominated and Hindu-ruled) India, resulting in violent upheaval. When the national boundaries were redrawn, India cut through the center of Pakistan, which was, therefore, itself a nation divided. In addition, Muslims and Hindus were so hostile to each other that Muslims who found themselves living in India and Hindus who found themselves living in Pakistan were suddenly aliens in their own homes. At best, they were coldly tolerated. At worst, they were robbed, raped, attacked, and murdered. Chaos erupted as sixteen million refugees literally ran for their lives to the nation where they would find safety. Violence escalated, and more than half a million people died in 1947 alone. The governments of the newly drawn nations, themselves in turmoil, were unable to contain the violence. In 1948, India and Pakistan went to war over territorial boundaries, principally which nation would govern Kashmir. The war, however, spread all along the frontier.

This tragedy was the impetus for "The Dog of Tithwal," which gives a microcosmic view of the hateful struggle. Although nature continues in harmony in the story's mountain setting, the Pakistani and Indian soldiers who face each other there cannot

be at peace. Looking for ways to express their frustration at being unable to kill each other, the leaders of the two groups of soldiers terrorize and kill a friendly dog who is looking for companionship.

Author Biography

Saadat Hasan Manto was a storyteller who took risks. Born on May 11, 1912, in Samrala, India, Manto was the son of Ghulam Hasan Manto, a judge, and Sardar, a widow. He wrote in the Urdu language, the primary language of Muslims in Pakistan and northern India and now the official language of Pakistan, but many of his works have been translated into other languages, including English. He wrote in many genres but is best known for his short stories. He chose controversial topics and was often on the receiving end of public disapproval. Two of his stories, ''Colder than Ice'' and ''The Return,'' were deemed indecent by Pakistani censors. He was twice prosecuted for obscenity, once in the early 1940s and again in 1948.

Growing up, Manto was not a dedicated student; he later dropped out of college. When Manto was about twenty-one, his mentor, Bari Aligue, a writer who advocated socialism in India, introduced him to the editorial staff of *Masawat,* a weekly film publication. In 1937, Manto became an editor of the monthly film magazine *Mysawwir.*

Manto became part of the Progressive Writers' Movement in Urdu literature. This movement began in 1935 with Indian students who were urging political and social revolution. Manto used a matter-of-fact style to portray the problems of what he considered to be a materialistic world. Studying the works of nineteenth-century French and Russian realists, Manto portrayed the lower class as having sterling qualities that others lacked. One issue that appears in many of his stories is the mistreatment of women by men who are nevertheless thought of as respectable members of society.

Another frequent topic in Manto's writing is the suffering caused in 1947, when India was partitioned into India and Pakistan. ''The Dog of Tithwal'' is one of many of Manto's stories that revolve around the partition and its aftermath. Manto knew something of the pain of partition himself. He was living in Bombay at the time, a city he loved. As a well-known Muslim, however, he was increasingly unhappy and uncomfortable in Hindu In-

dia and moved to Pakistan in 1948. He never felt at home in Pakistan and missed India, especially Bombay.

Some of Manto's works include *Aao*, a collection of satirical plays; *Manto ke Numainda Asfane*, short stories translated as *Kingdom's End*; and *Manto Ke Mazameen*, nonfiction writings. For most of his life, Manto found that earning money was difficult. A prolific writer, he sold individual stories to various publications. Some of these later became well known, such as ''Toba Tek Singh,'' a story about inmates in an insane asylum, and ''Thanda Ghosht,'' about the violence of 1947.

In addition to plays, radio scripts, and more than two hundred fifty short stories, Manto wrote film scripts. Among his prominent films were *Eight Days, Chal Chal Re Naujawan* and *Mirza Ghalib.* Manto also was known for his profiles of Indo-Pakistani film and music personalities.

Manto was married and had three daughters as well as a son who died as an infant. Manto himself died on January 18, 1955, when he was not yet forty-three years of age. The cause was diagnosed as cirrhosis of the liver. Manto was widely said to have knowingly drunk himself to death, and he wrote his obituary a year before his death.

Plot Summary

Indian Camp

''The Dog of Tithwal'' begins with Indian and Pakistani soldiers entrenched in their positions along the nations' border in a mountainous area. Neither side has the advantage in the war; no air forces are involved, and heavy artillery is not in their armaments. It is more a standoff than a battle. The peace of the mountains pervades in spite of the tension. Flowers are in bloom, birds are singing, and clouds are scudding lazily through the skies. Manto compares nature to a symphony that plays beautifully and the men with their guns to discordant notes.

The action begins in the Indian camp, with Jamadar Harnam Singh on night watch. At two o'clock, he wakes Ganda Singh to take over the watch and lies down to sing a romantic song about a pair of shoes with stars on them. Banta Singh joins in with a song about love and tragedy. The soldiers feel sadness creeping over them; perhaps they are reminded that life should be about love rather than about war.

The barking of a dog interrupts this pensive scene. Banta Singh finds the dog in the bushes and announces that his name is Jhun Jhun. The soldiers are in a good humor and pleased to see the dog, until Harnam Singh decides that the dog cannot eat if it is a Pakistani dog. The other soldiers think he is joking, but he then declares that all Pakistanis will be shot, even Pakistani dogs. The dog recognizes something in his tone and reacts with fear, which seems to please Harnam Singh. Another soldier responds by leading the men in a declaration of ''India Zindabad!'' (an expression of nationalistic fervor).

Banta Singh makes a sign with the dog's name on it, along with the information that it is an Indian dog, and hangs it around the dog's neck.

Pakistani Camp

The next morning the dog appears in the Pakistani camp. It turns out that it had spent a few days with the Pakistani soldiers before it went to the Indian camp. Like the Indian soldiers, the Pakistanis are tired of the war that has been dragging on for months. As Subedar Himmat Khan twirls his moustache and studies a map of the Tithwal sector of India, Bashir begins to sing a song about where a lover spent the night.

When the dog appears, Subedar Himmat Khan turns the lines of the song into an accusation against Jhun Jhun. ''Where did you spend the night?'' he screams. Bashir takes this as a joke and sings his song to the dog, but Subedar Himmat Khan throws a pebble at Jhun Jhun.

Bashir discovers the sign around the dog's neck. The soldiers ponder the sign to see if it could be in code; Subedar Himmat Khan reports the incident to his platoon commander, who ignores the report because he finds it meaningless. While the commander is correct that the report is not of tactical significance, it is implied that his failure to investigate indicates a lack of discipline in the ranks. The soldiers are bored and seem to feel that their presence here is meaningless.

The Pakistani soldiers rename Jhun Jhun and put a sign around his neck saying that he is Shun Shun, a Pakistani dog. Subedar Himmat Khan then sends Jhun Jhun back to his ''family,'' urging him to take the message to the enemy. The dog trots off, and Subedar Himmat Khan fires in the air. Feeling bored, he decides to fire at the Indians. For half an hour, the two sides exchange fire, after which Subedar Himmat Khan orders a halt. As he combs his hair, he wonders where the dog has gone.

Death

When Jhun Jhun comes around the hill where the Pakistani are entrenched, it seems to infuriate Subedar Himmat Khan. He shoots at the dog, hitting some stones. Jhun Jhun continues to run toward him, and Subedar Himmat Khan continues to shoot at the dog. Meanwhile, Harnam Singh fires. The two opposing soldiers enjoy scaring the terrified dog until Harnam Singh wounds the dog.

Still, Subedar Himmat Khan will not let Jhun Jhun return to the Pakistani camp. Khan tells the dog it is his duty to continue going toward the enemy camp. It is clear that, in Subedar Himmat Khan's mind, fanaticism has overcome any rationality.

When the wounded dog drags himself toward Harnam Singh, Jamadar Harnam Singh shoots and kills him. While the Pakistani Subedar Himmat Khan compares the killing to martyrdom, Harnam Singh says that Jhun Jhun ''died a dog's death.''

Characters

Bashir

A soldier in the Pakistani army, Bashir sings the song, ''Where did you spend the night, my love, my moon?'' Subedar Himmat Khan, fellow soldier, turns the song into an accusation of treachery against Jhun Jhun. Bashir is the soldier who reads the sign around Jhun Jhun's neck that gives the dog's name as written by the Indian army. Bashir is also called Bashirey.

Bashirey

See Bashir

Jhun Jhun

Jhun Jhun is a dog, trusting and very friendly. Unable to grasp the hatred between the Pakistani and Indian soldiers, Jhun Jhun greets both with equal enthusiasm. Jhun Jhun, perhaps demonstrating more wisdom than the men, treats them not as Indian and Pakistani, but as humans. Since the men have decided, however, that they are different, they expect the dog to choose sides.

In his innocence, Jhun Jhun represents the refugees and other victims of the partition of India. His death is a reflection of their deaths; even though his death is in reality senseless, the soldiers treat it as if it belongs to a cause. Subedar Himmat Khan of the Pakistani army says that Jhun Jhun has been ''martyred'' because he was killed by a member of the Indian army.

Subedar Himmat Khan

As a member of the Pakistani army, Subedar Himmat Khan watches over the Tithwal sector in India in an almost possessive way. He has a large mustache that he twirls, perhaps demonstrating his vanity. With his fixation on what is Pakistani and what is Indian, Subedar Himmat Khan represents unreasoning divisiveness and hatred. He sends Jhun Jhun into the enemy camp, refusing to let him come back. By firing at the dog, Subedar Himmat Khan means to scare him. He thinks that Jhun Jhun's terror is amusing and does not allow him to return even when the dog is injured.

Subedar Himmat Khan demonstrates the disregard for life that comes with blindly following a cause.

Banta Singh

The youngest of the Indian soldiers, Banta Singh has a sweet voice. He sings a lovelorn verse that inspires sadness in the others. Banta Singh is also the soldier who finds Jhun Jhun in the bushes and gives him a name. He does not see the dog as an enemy, nor does he wish to make the dog take sides; he sees the dog as a ''poor refugee.'' He represents a viewpoint that is more rational than that of his fellow soldier, Jamadar Harnam Singh, who wants to make the dog a point of contention between the two armies.

Ganda Singh

A member of the Indian army, Ganda Singh is the first to be awakened by Jamadar Harnam Singh, who is on night watch. He, along with the other soldiers, is affected by the melancholy words of Jamadar Harnam Singh's song.

Jamadar Harnam Singh

A member of the Indian army, Jamadar Harnam Singh is the first character introduced in the story. He is on night watch and wakes the others. As he lies down, he sings a sentimental song. In some ways, he serves as a counterpoint to Bashir, the soldier in the Pakistani army who also sings a song. With his Punjabi folk song, Jamadar Harnam Singh underscores the similarities between the groups and the futility of their fight. But he also represents fanaticism when, before feeding Jhun Jhun a cracker, he demands to know if the dog is an Indian.

Jamadar Harnam Singh seems to lack compassion. He is the one who, for sport, shoots and injures Jhun Jhun. He is also the one who kills Jhun Jhun and then says that Jhun Jhun has ''died a dog's death.''

Themes

Darkness and Light

Manto uses images of darkness and light to demonstrate the difference between the men and the natural world around them. Darkness represents the men, blindness, and what is negative, and light represents nature, sight, and what is positive. During the night, the soldiers light huge fires in an attempt to ward off darkness. Yet they are able to overcome neither the darkness of night nor their own blindness. The biggest fires they can build can only illuminate a small patch of ground and do not enable them to see their enemies or to see within themselves. By contrast, Manto writes, ''The morning broke . . . as if someone had switched on a light in a dark room. It spread across the hills and valleys.'' Nature is capable of producing an all-illuminating brightness that the men do not have.

Unity and Disunity

The Pakistanis and the Indians see themselves as separate from each other. There is no common human feeling between them, even though they both sing songs of romance and long for better days. The stream zigzagging down in the valley is like a literal line in the sand that emphasizes the division that the men are maintaining. Unlike the other elements of nature in the mountains, which move lazily, the stream moves furiously, like a snake. This

Topics for Further Study

- Write either an alternate ending for the story or an epilogue that tells what happens next.

- Compare and contrast the characters of Subedar Himmat Khan of the Pakistani army and Jamadar Harnam Singh of the Indian army. What do you think the author meant to convey through their similarities and differences? Why did he draw these characters as he did?

- Both songs in ''The Dog of Tithwal'' are about love. Why do you think the author chose to use songs in this story, and why do you think he chose songs about love?

- Research current relations between India and Pakistan. Prepare a report on your findings and include your thoughts about how the partition of India in 1947 continues to influence the relationship between the two countries.

seems to represent the energy the soldiers dedicate to lashing out at each other. They prefer disunity to unity. Other landmarks in nature also seem to draw attention to this disunity, such as the valley that separates the two hills behind which the opposing forces sit.

While the soldiers exhibit signs of common humanity, such as singing and cooking breakfast at the same time, they do not see or acknowledge these signs of underlying unity. Jhun Jhun, the one creature that ignores the fact that they are adversarial groups and points out their sameness, is put to death.

Warlike Humans versus Peaceful Nature

The mountains of Tithwal are calm and cheerful, but the soldiers are determined to kill. While it would be natural for them to adapt to their peaceful surroundings, the soldiers remain combative. At the time that Jhun Jhun enters the story, the soldiers have been inactive for some weeks, with no progress having been made on either side. The mood is

one of dangerous idleness, a harbinger of the death to come. Though there is nothing to gain from exchanging fire, the opposing sides let off ritual shots daily. Unable to destroy each other, the soldiers destroy a harmless dog that is an element of nature. Because he is the only victim available, Jhun Jhun becomes a casualty of the soldiers' need to satisfy their bloodlust. Humankind's brutality is visited upon nature. It is not enough merely to scare the dog and make him run in terror; they need to destroy him. Though Subedar Himmat Khan first wounds Jhun Jhun, to him the dog's death proves that the Indian forces are killers. Jamadar Harnam Singh, whose shot kills the dog, seems, even so, to blame the Pakistani forces. The two sides do not recognize that both have acted cruelly and absurdly. There is no regret for the killing, as there might be in peacetime, because it is seen as an act of war.

The difference between nature and humankind is underscored by the fact that the seasons are changing as the story takes place. The change is occurring gently; the days and nights are mild. While some literature depicts the seasons in conflict, Manto's story shows that in nature even opposites such as summer and winter flow peacefully into each other. ''It seemed as if summer and winter had made their peace,'' Manto writes. The men, on the other hand, although they are very much alike, cannot accept each other.

Style

Pastoral Setting

Pastoral literature portrays nature as being idyllic, peaceful, and free of the constraints and struggles of human society. Pastoral settings often allow human characters to find solace and peace that are not possible in a human-made setting.

The story is set in the mountains of Tithwal during temperate and pleasant days in late September. There is peace in the mountains, but, instead of escaping to the innocence of nature, the soldiers bring war with them. The men cannot enjoy the pleasant surroundings because they are not there to enjoy life but to kill.

Journalistic Style

Manto uses a direct, succinct style, almost like an unbiased reporter writing of an actual incident.

There is no diatribe; Manto does not tell his readers what to think but lets the facts speak for themselves. His use of dialogue to tell the story further contributes to the journalistic style.

Tension and Foreshadowing

The contrast between the pleasant natural surroundings and the camouflaged soldiers creates tension and a mood of suspense that subtly foreshadow the tragedy to come. Tension builds as Manto describes the soldiers' boredom and melancholy. When the dog enters the Indian camp, Jamadar Harnam Singh does not greet him in a friendly manner, even though the other soldiers seem amused by his arrival. Jamadar Harnam Singh's mean treatment of the dog as a potential enemy is further foreshadowing. Subedar Himmat Khan repeats the harsh treatment in the Pakistani camp. As the story builds, the soldiers treat Jhun Jhun both as a potential enemy and as an informant being sent to the enemy camp—neither of which bodes well for the dog. The doom that has been hinted at throughout the story culminates when the dog, scrambling from one side to the other, can find no safe haven. Jhun Jhun's pitiful end is foreshadowed by the increasingly irrational and brutal behavior of the soldiers, which is emphasized by its contrast to their peaceful setting.

Historical Context

Partition of India

The historical context for "The Dog of Tithwal" is the Indian-Pakistani conflict that arose after the partition of India in 1947. The partition came after India won its independence from British rule on August 14, 1947. India was divided into two countries formed on the basis of religion, with Pakistan as a Muslim state and India as a secular nation ruled by the Hindu majority. Boundary issues and religious disputes brought about terrorism, war, and continuing disharmony between India and Pakistan. Even the imposition of official boundaries did not cause the conflict to cease.

The decision to partition India resulted in barbaric treatment of citizens who happened to be living in the "wrong" nation after the boundaries were drawn. By law, people were required to live in the new nation that "matched" their religion—Muslims in Pakistan, Hindus and Sikhs in India—regardless of where they lived before the partition. Sixteen million refugees streamed across the borders, hoping to make homes in regions entirely foreign to them. The entire region dissolved into disarray.

Since there was no experienced government to effectively deal with the chaos and violence, it fed on itself. In addition to more than half a million deaths, looting and rape were commonplace. In particular, the Hindus and the Muslims used women to intimidate each other: "ghost trains" filled with severed breasts of women were sent from each country to the other.

Decades after the partition, Indian and Pakistan are still in conflict, and individuals and families are still affected by the material, psychological, and financial losses of partition and its aftermath.

British Rule

To understand the reasons for the partition, it is necessary to look at the history of India. Starting in the late thirteenth century and continuing for more than three hundred years, Muslims ruled the subcontinent under the Mughal Empire. Then India became part of the British Empire under Queen Elizabeth I. Over a period of three hundred and fifty years, the British consolidated their power in India. The British treated the Muslims and Hindus almost as if they were residents of two different nations and ruled them separately. Even in the census, the British categorized Indians according to religion.

As the British Empire expanded, so too did the land it held in India. By World War II, the British held a large area that was subject to Hindu and Muslim conflicts. The Muslims, who were not interested in learning English, were at a disadvantage to Hindus when it came to holding positions in government. The Muslims resented the fact that Hindus held better jobs, especially since, formerly, Muslims had been in power. Meanwhile, the Hindus had not forgotten Muslim rule. They tried to replace Urdu, a Muslim language, with Hindi as the official national language.

In an attempt to reduce conflict, British and Indian leaders decided to divide the subcontinent of India so that Muslims would have their own nation. The resulting partition, in 1947, carved Pakistan out of India. Part of Pakistan was on the west side of India, near the Indus River, and another part was to

Compare & Contrast

- **1940s:** The end of British colonial rule of India comes in 1947. India is split, with two regions of Pakistan divided by India. Muslims are to live in Pakistan; Hindus and Sikhs in India.

  Today: Celebrations of the partition—though not of its violence—take place in 1997 as fifty years of Indian and Pakistani independence are commemorated. Yet even in the celebrations, there is disagreement. Bangladesh marks its anniversary of independence not from 1947 but from February 21, 1952, called ''Martyr's Day'' to commemorate the first people to die in eastern Pakistan's struggle for nationhood.

- **1940s:** Immediately after partition, those responsible for it declare its success, whereas those who actually live through it suffer immeasurably. It is not until the 1970s that the true story of the partition and its aftermath is widely known.

  Today: There is still a division between people who believe that partition was worthwhile—or at least necessary—and others who condemn it. Some say that India and Pakistan have stabilized; others say that instability, corruption, and conflict between the two nuclear-armed nations are worse than ever.

- **1940s:** The social order in which religious groups coexist is abruptly changed under a separatist policy that religious groups must remain apart. According to Tai Yong Tan and Gyanesh Kudaisya in *The Aftermath of Partition in South Asia,* the violence that follows deepens differences between groups and increases persecution of minority groups. Hindu, Muslim, and Sikh fanatics loot property, kill the young and defenseless, and commit brutal acts in the name of God and country. Millions of refugees lose their homes and have to relocate to a foreign land. The economic stability of the area declines as normal activities are disrupted.

  Today: Animosity still exists between Indian and Pakistani peoples, and they prefer to remain separate even when they emigrate to live abroad. *India Abroad* notes that Indians and Pakistanis are forming a new ''partition'' in Britain, with Indians settling in the south of England and Pakistanis in the north. In 2001, out of a total of 540,000 Pakistanis in England, 229,000 (more than half) live in the north. In the south of England, Indians dominate.

---

the east. (The eastern region is now the nation of Bangladesh.) More than one thousand miles of Indian territory separated the two regions of Pakistan—yet another challenge to the new country's inexperienced leaders.

Critical Overview

Manto's writings are among the few Urdu works that have been translated into English. Translators of Manto's work include Khushwant Singh and Khalid Hasan.

Manto is known for being part of Urdu literature's Progressive Writers Movement. The Progressive Writers Movement (1935–1960) was launched when three Indian students, Sajjad Zaheer, Mulk Raj Anand, and Mohammad Deen Taseer, issued a manifesto on the decadence and feudalism that they believed pervaded Indian society and influenced others to rebel by speaking out against the established order. As a spokesman for social reform, Manto often depicted characters from low stations in life.

Manto's writings explore sexuality, exploitation, and the human condition without regard for conventional restrictions. His essays, screenplays, and short stories received varied receptions. Some

Hindu and Sikh women flee Pakistan following the partition of India in 1947

works were received well, but others were considered obscene or sensationalist. His use of direct language resulted in his being prosecuted for obscenity several times. In reviewing *Manto's World*, a collection of Manto's fiction and nonfiction translated by Khalid Hasan, Sarwat Ali of *News International* wrote that Manto had "a fresh, no holds barred approach which insisted on calling a spade a spade."

"The Dog of Tithwal" was first published in English in a collection of Manto's stories entitled *Kingdom's End and Other Stories*, translated by Khalid Hasan. In a review of *Kingdom's End and Other Stories*, a critic for *Publishers Weekly* wrote that Manto has a "talent for vivid description and narrative momentum" but that because his writings on the partition are relatively remote from the modern Western reader in culture, time, and place, he is not likely to find a large readership in the West.

Although during his lifetime he was criticized for his undeviating portrayal of humanity's underside, Manto continued to write about the world around him as he saw it. After his death in 1955 at the age of forty-two, Manto gradually became more widely accepted in literary circles so that now he is, according to Ali, "the most popular story writer of Urdu" and even "something of a cult figure."

Criticism

Candyce Norvell

Norvell is an independent educational writer who specializes in English and literature. She holds degrees in linguistics and journalism. In this essay, Norvell discusses why Manto's use of a dog as the victim in his story is effective and gives the story a universality it otherwise would not have.

Manto's choice of a dog to be the innocent victim of brutality in "The Dog of Tithwal" is appropriate and effective in many ways. Although the story's subject matter is remote from the experience of contemporary Western readers, Manto's use of the dog gives the story universal impact.

The relationship between dogs and humans is, of course, unique. With no other animal have humans formed a bond so close and complex. In most cultures, the dog is esteemed and even loved, though in a few parts of the world dogs are shunned by humans. The vast majority of human beings respond to dogs as innocents and as members of a species with which humans have entered into a mutual

What Do I Read Next?

- A translator of Manto's work and an author himself, Khushwant Singh also writes on the horrors of the Indian partition. His book *Train to Pakistan* (1990) is a fictional story, based on real events about a train full of dead Sikhs that arrives in a small village on the frontier between India and Pakistan in 1947. The train's arrival stirs up animosity against the Muslims in the village, and a gangster is the unlikely hero who must try to save them.

- *The Vintage Book of Indian Writing* (1947–1997), published in 1997 and edited by Salman Rushdie and Elisabeth West, chronicles fifty years of Indian writing translated into English. Manto's short story ''Toba Tek Singh,'' included here, underscores the senselessness of the partition by showing the confusion of Sikh and Hindu mental patients being transferred to India. A memorable incident that demonstrates the madness of the partition occurs when a patient decides to take up residence in a tree so that he does not have to live in either India or Pakistan.

- ''The Old Banyan'' and Other Stories (Pakistan Writers Series) (2000), is a collection written by Ahmad Nadim Qasmi and translated by Faruq Hasan. The fifteen stories by Qasmi, a contemporary Urdu writer who follows the principles of the Progressive Writers Movement, have mostly rural settings and feature realistic narration of dilemmas in the lives of the characters.

- *An Evening of Caged Beasts* (1999), edited by Asif Farrukhi and translated by Farrukhi and Frances W. Pritchett, is a selection of works by contemporary Urdu poets. The volume includes poems by Afzal Ahmed Syed, Azra Abbas, Sarwat Hussain, Sara Shagufta, Zeeshan Sahil, and others. The poems portray the pain and passion of today's Pakistan.

- *Stars from Another Sky: The Bombay Film World in the 1940s* (1998), by Manto, is a collection of thirteen profiles, translated by Khalid Hasan, of prominent people of the 1940s film world in Bombay. The work deals with the linguistic identity of Punjabi-speaking film workers and their struggle to fit into the modern world.

---

agreement of trust and harmlessness. Human treachery and cruelty toward dogs, therefore, is seen as especially repugnant.

In many cultures, including the modern Western one, the dog is not only a beloved companion but also a symbol of loyalty, protection, and nobility. In some cultures, such as that of the ancient Greeks, the dog has been considered a messenger and a guardian of passageways. Hinduism's perspective can be summed up in a story from the *Mahabharata,* the great epic of Hinduism. Near the end of the epic, a noble hero, Yudhishthira, approaches the gates of heaven with his faithful dog. When he is told that he may enter heaven but must leave his dog behind, Yudhishthira replies that he will not abandon the dog who has been so faithful to him and who has come to trust and depend on him, even for the joys of heaven. The gatekeeper repeatedly tries to convince Yudhishthira that it would not be cruel to abandon the dog, even saying that the dog is an unclean animal and has no soul. Yudhishthira's final response is:

> I do not turn away my dog; I turn away you. I will not surrender a faithful dog to you. . . . Whoever comes to me from fright or from disaster or from friendship—I never give him up.

The heavenly gatekeeper tells Yudhishthira that this has been one last test of his goodness, and the dog is revealed to be Dharma, the god of justice, in disguise. Accordingly, in Hindu culture dogs are considered unclean animals, yet all creatures are deemed to deserve compassionate treatment. Dogs that are companions of warriors and hunters are especially esteemed. In Islamic culture, however, the dog is a symbol of impurity and is considered a positive presence only in the role of guard dog.

Consciously or not, Manto has constructed his story in such a way that all these human views of Jhun Jhun's species are demonstrated. The Muslim (Islamic) soldiers, indeed, respond to Jhun Jhun as if he is impure. Subedar Himmat Khan, far from seeing the dog as loyal, distrusts him because he left the camp during the night. Jhun Jhun did not act as a guard dog for the Pakistanis, and so they have no affection toward him, only suspicion. Although Subedar Himmat Khan's treatment of Jhun Jhun is extreme in its cruelty, his attitude toward the dog is grounded in his religious and cultural background.

The Indian soldiers in the story are Sikhs, not Hindus, as indicated by the designation "Singh" after their names. Sikhism is a blend of elements of Hinduism and Islam. Appropriately, the Sikh soldiers have a mixed reaction to Jhun Jhun. It is an Indian soldier—a warrior, as Yudhishthira was—who befriends the dog; it is also an Indian soldier who kills him.

In these depictions of the soldiers' responses to Jhun Jhun, Manto has drawn from his characters' cultural realities and has made his story authentic. But Manto himself emphasizes, in Jhun Jhun, the qualities that Western cultures attribute to dogs. Both groups of soldiers make Jhun Jhun a messenger, and he is also a guardian—or at least a traverser—of the passageway between the two hills and the two camps. Each side hangs around Jhun Jhun's neck a message for the other and sends him into the no-man's land that serves as a passage between the camps.

But it is the qualities of loyalty and nobility that make Jhun Jhun and, in turn, the story so effective and affecting. Jhun Jhun's loyalty is not to one camp or the other, as the soldiers would have it. It is a loyalty of a higher order: to all humans and to the bond between the two species. Whereas the two groups of soldiers see only differences between themselves, Jhun Jhun sees only similarity. As the men have certain culturally based expectations of Jhun Jhun, the dog has certain inbred expectations of the men. He expects them to behave as humans are supposed to behave toward dogs, according to that age-old agreement between the two. He expects that his friendly, trusting approach to all men will be recognized as a signal of harmlessness and loyalty. Jhun Jhun conveys, "I know about the agreement between us. I intend to abide by it."

> " Jhun Jhun shows the reader, more effectively than any human character could, how debased these men are. Jhun Jhun's death shows that, in the name of religion and country, these men have sunk beneath the level of beasts."

When the men torture and kill Jhun Jhun, they are not just killing a dog; they are breaking a longstanding and sacred trust between humans and dogs. Men, having long ago tamed the dog's viciousness and engendered its trust and loyalty, now turn on the dog with a senseless cruelty that even a wild creature could neither comprehend nor anticipate. This is the most despicable kind of brutality.

Terrified and wounded, Jhun Jhun, to the end, honors the relationship that the men disregard. In this, he shows the nobility attributed to his kind. There is only one thing more heart-rending than seeing an innocent treated cruelly, and that is seeing the victim remain noble in the face of betrayal and death. Jhun Jhun does not growl, threaten, or attack. As men show themselves absolutely inhuman, Jhun Jhun remains harmless and submissive; he remains true to the nature that better men have bred into him.

In Jhun Jhun, Manto has created the ideal foil for his human characters. Jhun Jhun shows the reader, more effectively than any human character could, how debased these men are. The dog, with its inability to comprehend cruelty and with loyalty and nobility that surpass that of many humans, shows by its death that, in the name of religion and country, these men have sunk beneath the level of beasts.

Western readers may feel a distance between themselves and the issues and events of partition. They may even feel a distance between themselves and the human victims of partition, because those people were remote in time, place, and culture; it is a fact of human nature that people have more empathy for others who are like them. But Jhun Jhun is not remote. Any reader who has known any dog immediately grasps this dog's nature. Every reader is aware of that eons-old agreement and bond between Jhun Jhun's species and human beings. Thus, every reader feels the magnitude of the crime committed against Jhun Jhun. The shock waves of that wrong reverberate across time, place, and cultures, much as the shock waves of partition still pulse through India and Pakistan.

Source: Candyce Norvell, Critical Essay on ''The Dog of Tithwal,'' in *Short Stories for Students,* The Gale Group, 2002.

Susan Sanderson

Sanderson holds a master of fine arts degree in fiction writing and is an independent writer. In this essay, Sanderson examines Saadat Hasan Manto's use of contrasts and similarities to highlight the absurdities of war and national conflict in his short story.

Much of Saadat Hasan Manto's work reflects the pain, anguish, and brutality resulting from the 1947 creation of Pakistan out of parts of India, a division made on religious grounds. Pakistan became a Muslim state and India became a secular country controlled by Hindus but accepting Sikhs. Violence quickly ensued; many Muslims in India were attacked, as were Hindus who remained in what is now Pakistan. Manto often wrote about the result of the 1947 partition of the two countries, focusing on the absurdity of the situation as well as on the plight of those caught in the middle of a decision not of their making.

''Dog of Tithwal'' offers a snapshot of the military aftermath of India and Pakistan's bloody partition and the effect these events have had on all parties to the conflict. Just as the artificial line drawn across the subcontinent to delineate India and Pakistan was evidence of human conflicts imposed on the natural world, Manto involves nature in the contrasts and similarities he draws in the story. However, he is careful in his technique to show no preference or favoritism for either the Indian or the Pakistani characters, making it clear that everyone and everything involved in the conflict has been equally damaged. Manto's use of contrasting features and peculiar similarities reflects the conflict between the Pakistani and Indian people provoked by the events of 1947 and highlights the absurdity and senselessness of that situation. Manto's story pushes forth the question: How meaningful are nations, borders, and nationalities when a group of men can decide one day that all the people on one side of an artificially and capriciously drawn line have suddenly lost their citizenship?

Though the story begins with an immediate image of soldiers who have been ''entrenched in their positions for several weeks,'' Manto paints a romantic canvas of the lushness of a countryside deep in the contentment of a fall day. He notes that the air around the soldiers ''was heavy with the scent of wild flowers'' and the ''bees buzzed about lazily.'' This is a relaxed scene, a moment of repose after the energy and intensity of spring and summer. Briefly, the story reads as if the men in this pastoral setting are ready for a picnic. Their real goal—to kill each other—is as disguised as they are by the mountain's rocks and bushes. In fact, Manto's placing the story in the fall, ''the end of September, neither hot nor cold,'' is a portent of the death to come. As suddenly as the first storm in winter can transform a beautiful fall afternoon, the story moves in a very few paragraphs to a place where death is the reigning motif and two groups of men see evil in a friendly dog.

The story starts not only imbued with a romantic quality but also as if its omniscient narrator is looking at the soldiers and their positions from an elevated vantage point. In the first paragraph, nature is portrayed as a nearly sentient creature, ''following its course, quite unmindful of the soldiers hiding behind rocks and camouflaged by mountain shrubbery.'' Manto presents his story's world first from a distance, so that man is but a small and somewhat insignificant part of the landscape. Nature is the ruling presence. As the story progresses, however, the narration moves closer to the human scale and becomes more involved with the actions of the individual men on the ground. In this way, Manto has immediately created tension and contrast in his story. Nature is at peace with itself but, with a closer look, man can be seen causing havoc.

Manto develops an interesting aspect within the story that goes against expected contrasts. Even though the two armies are battling each other (although with little enthusiasm), the author portrays them as having numerous similarities. Many of the actions and behaviors of the Indians are echoed in those of the Pakistanis, and vice versa. For example, in both camps soldiers sing bittersweet songs about love, and both of their songs are interrupted by the appearance of Jhun Jhun, the ''ordinary mongrel'' dog. Both armies are similarly equipped and ''at night, they would light huge fires and hear each others' voices echoing through the hills.'' In the morning, both camps prepare breakfast in a similar fashion, as the Indian soldier Harnam Singh notes through his binoculars. Manto also highlights the universal human feature of vanity on both sides when he has a Pakistani soldier admire and care for his ''famous moustache'' and an Indian soldier comb his long hair and look at himself in the mirror. The two camps are similar even in their tactical positions, for, as the narrator notes in the story, ''no one side had an advantage,'' with each occupying a hill of equal elevation. The two camps being near perfect mirrors of each other stresses Manto's message that the 1947 partition damaged all parties involved, no matter their position or nationality.

With the similarities of the two armies made clear, Manto has exposed a world in which absurdity rules. Not only does he have two sides that look and sound alike fighting each other, but they are also equally armed and positioned. This has created a standoff in which gunfire is ''ritually exchanged'' on a regular basis; in fact, so regular is the daily burst of brief gunfire that when the Pakistani soldier Subedar Himmat Khan lets off a shot to encourage the dog back to the Indian side, the Indians are confused and surprised at the break in the anticipated pattern of hostilities. ''[I]t was somewhat early in the day for that sort of thing,'' notes the story's narrator, as though casually describing someone having a drink before the cocktail hour. For the next thirty minutes, however, because the Indian soldiers are feeling bored, the two sides exchange gunshots, ''which, of course, were a complete waste of time.''

Meaninglessness and absurdity put the soldiers into a situation in which it seems perfectly normal that they should exchange ineffectual gunfire at pre-appointed times and, as well, demand that a dog claim a nationality. When the Indian soldier Harnam Singh demands that the dog, Jhun Jhun, prove his nationality, one unnamed soldier observes, ''Even dogs now will have to decide if they are Indian or Pakistani.'' Manto's use of the dog points to the plight of the refugees caught between India and Pakistan, struggling in a world where differences between people are much more important than any similarities they may share. In fact, the very features of dogs that have placed them so firmly within human communities—that they recognize no differences between humans concerning national boundaries or religious distinctions and offer affection and loyalty toward whomever they are with—are the ultimate reasons for Jhun Jhun's death.

> " The border this dog crosses is meaningless to him, as he sees the soldiers not as Pakistanis or Indians but as humans who have sometimes been kind to him."

Throughout the story, the soldiers work to demarcate and draw contrasts between themselves and nearly everything around them, including the dog. Jhun Jhun must be either an Indian or Pakistani dog, not simply the ''mongrel'' he is. Just before Jhun Jhun reappears at the Indian camp, Banta Singh muses that ''Dogs can never digest butter'' according to a ''famous saying''—an almost surreal effort to distinguish Jhun Jhun from humans and make the subsequent and casual efforts to shoot him somehow easier to manage for the soldiers.

Even in the waning moments of the story, Manto continues to stress similarities and contrasts between the soldiers to highlight the painful absurdity of the partition. The Indian soldier Harnam Singh and the Pakistani soldier Himmat Kahn both shoot at Jhun Jhun at the same time, and both find the ''game'' between them a source of great humor. They shoot at the dog for very different reasons, however, which are reflected in the words each says when Jhun Jhun is finally dead. Himmat Kahn shoots at the dog to encourage him to complete his ''mission'' and do his ''duty'' in delivering the message to the Indians that Jhun Jhun is, according to the sign they have attached to him, ''a Pakistani dog.'' According to Himmat Kahn, Jhun Jhun dies a martyr's death. Harnam Singh, on the other hand, shoots at Jhun Jhun because he is seen as an enemy dog approaching the Indian camp from the ''Pakistani hill.'' He portrays the dog as a traitor and declares that Juhn Juhn ''died a dog's death.''

Not only do the contrasts and peculiar similarities highlight the absurdities of war, but they ultimately allow Manto to question what constitutes a nation. Manto challenges the meaning and value of nationality when he has the soldiers claim that a stray dog can hold Pakistani or Indian citizenship. The border this dog crosses is meaningless to him, as he sees the soldiers, not as Pakistanis or Indians, but as humans who have sometimes been kind to him. There are no contrasts for Jhun Jhun, only similarities. From the vantage point of the story's beginning, above the ground and looking down on the scene, there are no obvious lines clearly showing where one country ends and another begins. The natural world is enduring and seamless and shows no false borders that impulsively restrict the movements of birds or rivers. "The birds sang as they always had," notes the narrator, indicating a certain timelessness to natural events and nature's disregard for such erratic events as war. The story's soldiers, on the other hand, are part of the species that insists on creating and defending artificial borders to separate and isolate large numbers of people from one another. By creating these named divisions between people, humans in "Dog of Tithwal" have constructed distinctions—the ultimate contrast between "us" and "them"—where there are none naturally occurring, and the result is certain pain and death.

Source: Susan Sanderson, Critical Essay on "The Dog of Tithwal," in *Short Stories for Students,* The Gale Group, 2002.

Sources

Ali, Surwat, "True to the Text," in *News International,* August 2, 2000.

Buck, William, *Mahabharata,* New American Library/Mentor, 1979, p. 220.

Dhiman, Kuldip, "Great Minds," in *Tribune India,* March 19, 2000.

Review of *"Kingdom's End" and Other Stories,* in *Publisher's Weekly,* July 1997.

Suri, Sanjay, "India-Pakistan Partition of Different Kind in Britain," in *India Abroad,* January 5, 2001.

Tan, Tai Yong, and Gyanesh Kudaisya, *The Aftermath of Partition in South Asia,* Routledge, 2000, pp. 1–25.

Further Reading

Bhalla, Alok, *Life and Works of Saadat Hasan Manto,* Indian Institute of Advanced Study, 1997.
    This relatively new biography of Manto examines both his life and his body of work.

Harrison, Selig S., Payl H. Kreisberg, and Dennis Kux, eds., *India and Pakistan: The First Fifty Years,* Cambridge University Press, 1999.
    This collection of essays covers topics such as political, economic, and social development in India and India's foreign and security policies. It also covers India's relationship with the United States. In addition, the book discusses the socioeconomic changes since partition and looks at challenges for India's future.

Menon, Ritu, and Kamla Bhasin, *Borders and Boundaries: Women in India's Partition,* Rutgers University Press, 1998.
    Menon and and Bhasin have compiled transcripts of oral histories of women's experiences in Pakistan, India, and East Pakistan (Bangladesh) during the 1947 partition. The women share horrific memories of abductions, rape, and death.

Moon, Penderel, *Divide and Quit: An Eyewitness Account of the Partition of India,* South Asia Books, 1998.
    This book chronicles Moon's experience as a member of the Indian Civil Service. As an administrator in the region split by partition, he saw the tragedies that followed partition and how they affected India.

The Green Leaves

Grace Ogot

1968

Grace Ogot's short story "The Green Leaves," from her 1968 collection of short stories called *Land without Thunder,* was published by the East African Publishing House in Nairobi, Kenya. Many of the stories in this collection are loosely based on tales that her grandmother told her as a young girl growing up in rural western Kenya. More than simply folk tales, Ogot's short stories also reflect, through the traditional genre of the folk tale, a number of recent developments in Kenya's history, in particular its colonial past and subsequent national independence movement, its changing gender roles, and its economic and urban growth. All these developments have contributed to Kenya's passage from a traditional agrarian culture to a modern, urban society. Much of the social turmoil that attends such rapid change is revealed in her stories.

In the Introduction to their book *Challenging Hierarchies: Issues and Themes in Colonial and Postcolonial African Literature,* authors Leonard Podis and Yakubu Saaka have articulated five common features found in African literature. The list is as follows: using proverbs and aphorisms, depicting social customs, incorporating myths, relating politics to social and cultural issues, and writing in a concise style. These criteria are relevant while reading Ogot's work as well as other writers' work produced during the African wars for independence against European colonizers. The cultural disruptions due to British colonialism is a major theme of

many works written by postcolonial African writers such as Chenua Achebe, Ngugi Wa Thiong'o, Tayeb Salih, and Flora Nwapa.

As a writer coming of age at the time of Kenyan independence in 1963, Ogot turned to the conflicts that occurred between the Luo people and the colonialists as a source for her stories. In particular, the early stories of Ogot, such as ''The Green Leaves,'' reveal the tenuous grasp that many indigenous cultures in Kenya had on their traditional ways of life with the takeover of Kenya's political and economic infrastructure by British colonial forces. This is rendered in the scene in which tension flares between the clan leader Olielo and the white policeman over the ''right'' way to deal with robbery. The two different systems of justice are brought into conflict with the traditional way, that of murdering the thief, being seen as barbaric and outdated.

Not only does Ogot reflect on the injustices of the colonial system in Kenya, but she also contributes to an aspect of literature that, for the most part, was overlooked by many African writers who at the time were predominantly male: the experiences of being a black African woman. Specifically, her stories often reveal the limitations of men and the inability of women to make a cultural impact due to being disempowered by patriarchy within both traditional and colonial societies. Thus, Ogot brings a dual perspective to her works that centers on issues of oppression due to gender and complicated by nationality and colonialism.

Author Biography

Writer and politician Grace Ogot was born in 1930 in the Central Nyanza area of Kenya. Trained as a nurse while a young woman, Ogot worked in Uganda and England before returning to Kenya. As a young and upcoming writer, Ogot first entered the Kenyan literary scene in the early 1960s when she began to publish stories in the African journal *Black Orpheus.* Many of these stories, of which ''The Green Leaves'' is one, later became part of the collection *Land of Thunder*, published in 1968. Her 1966 novel, *The Promised Land,* was the first novel published by a woman by the influential East African Publishing House. Since then, she has published two other novels, *The Graduate*, in 1980, and *The Strange Bride* (1989), which was written in Luo, Ogot's native language, and translated into English and Kiswahili. She has also published two other volumes of short stories in English.

Her most recent literary contributions have been written in her native language and have been received by the Luo people in Kenya with much enthusiasm. Several of these are historical novels that attempt to document the early history of her people, the Luo, and contribute to the growth of vernacular literatures produced by and for specific populations in Africa rather than for an international audience. Her books in Luo continue the storytelling heritage of its people and also provide a version of history that is Afrocentric rather than Eurocentric. As Ogot claims in an interview with Don Burness, ''It is my hope that people can have proper respect for their own language and will learn it so that it will not be lost and swallowed up by English and Kiswahili.''

Besides her career as a writer, Ogot has been a tutor, a midwife, a flight attendant, a journalist for the BBC, a community development officer, and most notably an assistant minister of the Kenyan government. She has taken an active interest in the cultural and political concerns of Kenya and was the founding chair of the Writer's Association of Kenya.

Plot Summary

Pursuing the Cattle Thieves

In the short story ''The Green Leaves,'' the main character, Nyagar, wakes up from what he thinks is a dream but is actually voices and footsteps approaching. He turns toward his wife, but she is not in bed next to him, so he throws off his blanket and goes to the door. Finding the door unbolted, he wonders where Nyamundhe (his wife) is and is angered by her carelessness. Hearing the voices again, he puts a sheet around him, grabs his spear and club, and goes outside. He opens the gate to his yard and hides by the fence as a small group of people followed by a larger group run past him. One yells out that the small group has stolen his cattle.

Nyagar follows the larger group of villagers, listening to the men speak to each other as they pursue the cattle thieves. The cattle thieves take the wrong turn, missing the bridge that separates the Masala from the Mirogi people. They attempt to cross the river, but the large group gains ground and eventually overcomes them, beating them with their clubs. The cattle thieves cry in pain to no avail.

During this commotion, one of the men sights a thief crawling off behind a bush. Three men pursue him and beat the bush, but there is no sound. The thief has escaped. Another thief knifes one of the villagers in the shoulder blade and then runs into the river, crossing it despite the fast-moving water. Nyagar takes the knife out of Omoro's shoulder and attempts to stop his friend's wound from bleeding.

One thief is lying on the ground, wounded. The villagers come upon him and beat him until the man no longer moves. Seeing that the man is nearly dead, Omoro claims that it is bad luck to witness the thief's death and that they should return to their huts before this happens. The villagers then cover the dying man in green leaves and agree to bury him tomorrow at dawn. The men walk back to the village in the dark. Nyagar helps Omoro, although his shoulder no longer bleeds. Omoro tells Nyagar before he turns in that they should meet early in the morning before the women go down to the river where the dead thief is located.

Nyagar's Death

Nyagar goes back to his hut. The village is quiet, although the women are awake. They will wait until morning to hear what happened. Nyagar takes out a container and scoops some ash from it, placing it in his mouth. He then places some on his palm and blows it toward the gate. He is about to go to bed when he changes his mind. Then he gets up and leaves his hut, closing the door quietly behind him. He looks back to make sure that he has closed the gate.

Nyagar thinks that the thief lying beneath the green leaves must have money on him, and he is determined to get it. Dawn is approaching as he makes his way to where the thief's body is. Nyagar thinks that someone is following, but it is the echo of his own footsteps. As he gets closer to the body, he thinks that the other thieves may have returned for him but then dismisses the idea. Finally, he sees the bunch of green leaves and is nearly paralyzed with fright, but he continues on.

Everything is exactly as it looked when everyone left a few hours earlier. Looking around him first, Nyagar then approaches the dead body. However, his mind is in turmoil as he considers what he is doing. He does not need the money and has many wives and children as well as cattle. Still, Nyagar is determined to take the money since he has come this far. He bends over the dead man and begins to take off the leaves. Surprisingly, the dead man's body is still warm, but this does not stop Nyagar. He looks through his pockets but finds nothing; then he remembers that cattle traders often carry money around their necks. He finds a bag around the man's neck, and he smiles. As he takes the bag from around the man's neck, a blow hits him straight in the eye. He staggers back and falls to the ground unconscious. The thief had just woken up from his deep sleep and now has killed Nyagar. He then covers Nyagar in the leaves and takes off across the bridge.

The Discovery of Nyagar's Body

At dawn the next day, the clan leader Olielo sounds the funeral drum, and about one hundred people assemble at the *Opok* tree to hear what he has to say. Olielo tells them what had happened the night before. Because it is the dead body of a thief, it is not really a murder because the killer has rid society of an evil person. But due to the white man's presence and his rules that are different in regard to murder, Olielo says that a group of men must go to the white man and tell him that the thief was killed by a group of people. Thus, no one would suffer sole blame for the thief's death. Everyone agrees to this idea, and a group of men leave to tell the white man what has happened.

In the meantime, other people have gathered at the tree, including the wives of Nyagar. Whereas Nyamundhe looks for her husband, her co-wife does not seem to be that interested. The group begins to walk towards the river where the thief is buried. As they walk, Nyamundhe notices how wet the grass is and then comments to the co-wife that a black cat crossed their path earlier. Two trucks show up carrying a European policeman, several African policemen, and the men who had walked from the village. They drive up to the mound of green leaves. The white officer asks for the clan elder and demands to know the story behind the murder of the thief. Olielo explains everything to him through a translator. A discussion ensues between the two leaders about the nature of the crime, with the white officer accusing the clansmen of being savages. Olielo stands by his argument that the village killed the thief and that they should all be arrested.

The police officer goes up to where the body is covered with leaves, and the crowd follows him. Because it is the white man's rule to take the body and do an autopsy to discover the cause of death, the crowd surrounds the mound of leaves to get a look before he is whisked away. The African police officer takes off the leaves and Olielo stares at the body in amazement. The body of his cousin, Nyagar, is lying there with a stake through his eye. Nyamundhe runs up to her husband's body and weeps over it. She asks the crowd where the thief is. The crowd is stunned by the new development. The women wail, and the men who killed the thief stare at each other in disbelief. Olielo, visibly upset, appeals to the villagers, telling them that, despite the evil spirit that has descended on the village, Nyagar's spirit is among them.

However, Nyamundhe does not take these comforting words to heart; instead, she struggles with the police as they take Nyagar's body to the back of the truck. One officer tries to comfort her, but Nyamundhe tells him that it does not matter because her husband is not alive. She then strips to the waist and raises her hands over her head, weeping and chanting. The story ends with a traditional song of mourning that she sings.

Characters

The European Police Officer

He comes to the village to find out who murdered the thief. His chief function is to reveal the differences in values between European and local justice systems. By enforcing a Western legal system, the European police officer represents a colonial mind-set that views African culture as backwards and Europe as superior. His presence also disrupts the community when he demands that someone take responsibility for the death of the thief.

The Injured Thief

The nameless thief who is first beaten and then buried beneath a pile of green leaves is left for dead. Unfortunately for Nyagar, the thief has only been knocked unconscious and will end up murdering him.

Nyagar

The husband of Nyamundhe, Nyagar decides to go back to rob the supposedly dead thief and ends up getting killed by him. He is already a successful and prosperous man in his clan and does not need the money that the thief who is covered in leaves has around his neck. Thus his motivation for acquiring this unnecessary wealth needs to be contextualized within the history of colonialism. In other words, Nyagar's greed can be seen as an internalization of Western attitudes that crave material wealth. In

rejecting the traditional ways of the clan that would have prevented him from taking the thief's money, Nyagar sets himself up for his own murder. His greed results not only in his downfall but also contributes to animosity among the clan members after they discover Nyagar beneath the leaves.

Nyagar's Co-wife

She is the other wife of Nyagar, who does not seem that disturbed by Nyagar's absence the morning after the thief was buried beneath the green leaves. Her appearance makes clear that Nyagar is a wealthy man since certain traditional societies in Africa allow for more than one wife depending on the economic status of the husband.

Nyamundhe

She is the wife of Nyagar who disappears from his side in the middle of the night and forgets to bolt the gate after she leaves his hut. After the thief kills Nyagar, Nyamundhe becomes the focus of the story. In particular, she defies the European system of justice by calling into question the reasoning behind the European's insistence on taking her husband's body away to be studied and dissected. She also reveals that the clan is not so sure of itself after Nyagar's body is discovered. People eye each other with suspicion and fear that an evil spirit has descended on them. This suspicion weakens their stance against the European police officer and makes the men look foolish. By embracing the traditional rituals for burying the dead, Nyamundhe attempts to salvage the customs of her people and deflect the influence of Western ideologies and beliefs. Her song states quite solemnly and directly what she has lost, and in a grander sense, it reflects on the larger losses that her people have suffered under the strict regulations of colonialism.

Clan Leader Olielo

Olielo is a cousin of Nyagar who metes out justice within the clan and provides a leadership role when the thief is killed. Olielo must confront the European police officer at the end of the story and defend the murder of the thief. By understanding how the European legal system works, Olielo is able to subvert it by claiming that the whole village is responsible for the murder and not one person. By making this claim, Olielo deflects attention from individual motivation to group responsibility, showing the difference in value systems between the Western view of justice that seeks justice for all crimes committed, disregarding the circumstances, and the Luo tradition that views some murder as being justified within a particular context such as endangering the security of the clan.

Omoro

Omoro is Nyagar's friend who gets stabbed by one of the cattle thieves. Nyagar helps stop Omoro's wound from bleeding and then makes sure that he gets home all right.

Themes

Traditional Life versus Modernization

The major conflict of the story revolves around the traditional ways of Nyagar's clan as represented by the clan leader, Olielo, and by Nyamundhe, both of whom defy the condescending views of the European policeman who epitomizes the rational, modern subject in his need to charge one individual with the murder of the supposed thief and then subsequently, after the discovery of Nyagar under the leaves, to take the body away to do an autopsy rather than respect the death rituals of the clan. The differing rules and regulations that structure Luo and Western societies regarding death and justice result not only in misunderstanding between the clan members and the policeman but also contribute to the attitude of superiority of the European policeman when he claims, ''How many times have I told you that you must abandon this savage custom of butchering one another?'' This form of cultural superiority contributed to the colonial mentality of dehumanizing Africans as a way of rationalizing their exploitation and oppression.

Ogot does not glorify the old ways but instead brings them to the attention of the reader as a way of revealing how easy it is to dismiss indigenous peoples as barbaric and inferior due to social rules that may appear backwards to those unfamiliar with them. She seems to suggest that these traditional views are significant because they help define the clan as a community. Although some of their superstitious aspects may appear frivolous, such as Nyamundhe's sighting of the black cat as they walk towards the pile of green leaves, others, such as appeasing the clan's ancestral dead through proper burial rites, are indelibly related to how the group perceives its relationship to previous generations. Also, Nyagar's downfall is that he defies the traditional wisdom that forbids him to go back to the

Media Adaptations

- For a comprehensive resource on African literature, history, art, and film, see Dr. Cora Agatucci's ''African Timelines'' web site at http://www.cocc.edu/cagatucci/classes/hum211/timelines/htimelinetoc.htm.

body of the thief until morning. His greed for the thief's money despite his fears and lack of want reflects a counter value system that privileges acquiring material possessions over the safety and security of him and his family. (His need to keep checking gates reveals the importance of keeping intruders away from his hut.) Excessive desire is a negative effect of modernization because it overemphasizes material wealth as a reigning mark of success and happiness.

Community versus Individualism

The increasing influence of modernization in colonized countries resulted in the breakdown of social customs and traditional values that bound communities. Throughout the story, there is an emphasis on what the community will do in relation to the cattle thieves and then later to the European police officer. In this respect, Olielo speaks for the community when he declares that they will bury the thief in the morning to prevent a bad spirit from descending on their village. Because Nyagar takes the law into his own hands, he defies the wishes of the clan leader and thus disrupts the social order. By the end of the story, the clan members, particularly Nyamundhe, look at each other with suspicion, wondering who killed Nyagar. Ironically, this is the exact opposite response that Olielo had foreseen since his plan was that the whole clan would take responsibility for the thief's death and thus undermine the European police officer's attempt to blame one man. In this respect, the power of colonialism is revealed through one of its most effective strategies: to divide and conquer. Thus, by pitting individuals and groups against each other, colonial powers could avert mass organizing and actions against

Topics for Further Study

- In the mid-1960s, Grace Ogot was the first woman writer to begin publishing her writing in Kenya. Now nearly forty years later, numerous women write in Kenya about issues that are pertinent to women in contemporary African life. Who are these writers and what are the themes in which they are most deeply engaged? How do their themes relate to issues confronting Kenyan women's lives today? How are they different from Ogot? How are they similar?

- After reading Ogot's ''The Green Leaves,'' find other African women writers who were publishing short stories during the period just after independence in the 1960s, such as Flora Nwapa of Nigeria and Ama Ata Aidoo of Ghana. Despite the differences in cultural background and nationality, try to draw comparisons among these women writers in terms of themes they address that are related to gender roles.

- The historical period in which ''The Green Leaves'' takes place in Kenya was full of tumultuous changes, both social and political. Similar to Native Americans in the United States, many of the traditional cultures in Africa were forced to leave their lands, to adopt Western customs and systems, and to forsake traditional ways.

- Although colonialism wreaked havoc on traditional cultures, it also provided some benefits in medicine and education. Research the colonial era in Kenya that began in the mid-nineteenth century and ended in the mid-twentieth century. In particular, try to find information about the impact of colonialism on the Luo people, about whom Ogot writes. What were the negative effects of colonialism on the Luo? What, if any, were the positive?

- Nigerian writer Chinua Achebe's novel *Things Fall Apart,* published in 1958, is one of the most highly acclaimed postcolonial novels about the devastating effects of colonialism on the traditional ways of Africans. Read the novel and then compare and contrast it with the ''The Green Leaves.'' In particular, analyze the different ways that the authors represent their male protagonists. How are the two works critical of traditional African cultures? Of the colonial authorities? How do the two writers approach the theme of gender roles? How is Okonkwo a stronger or weaker hero than Nyagar? Why does Ogot represent Nyagar in a less than flattering way? Afterwards, discuss differences in narrative structure, themes, and literary devices between the texts.

---

them. This common strategy is understood by Olielo when he remarks to the clan members, ''If we stand united, none of us will be killed.''

Questioning Traditional Female Roles

The men and women in the story are seen at the beginning of the story as having very specific gender roles. It is the men of the clan who go after the thief and attempt to kill him, whereas the women remain behind. The men of the clan try to protect their women from what has happened by planning on getting up early to deal with the dead thief. The women, on the other hand, remain quiet about the evening's events. In the morning, they gather to

hear Olielo address the clan about what has happened and follow the men to the river. However, Ogot focuses on Nyagar's wife, Nyamundhe, at the end of the story, because she represents a traditional way of life that values security and community. Whereas Nyagar has been infected with greed and self-interest, qualities associated with a colonial mentality of acquiring as much material wealth as possible, Nyamundhe clings to the traditional ways, as when she sings a song of mourning over the death of her husband. At the same time, Nyamundhe is not afraid to challenge both the clan members and the European police officer about Nyagar's death. She even questions the Western methods of justice that are based on rational scientific inquiry such as carrying out an autopsy. In this respect, Nyamundhe is similar to Olielo, the clan leader, who also challenges the methods of justice the European police officer attempts to carry out.

Style

Storytelling

First and foremost, Ogot has a direct and precise style that does not lack in dramatic action. Her storytelling abilities are directly influenced by stories her grandmother told her while growing up in western Kenya. Thus, not only does she rely on myths and legends of the Luo people from whom she is descended, but she also uses traditional elements of oral storytelling in her work. One can see this most clearly in her use of direct rather than metaphoric or figurative language. Her rich descriptions bring her stories to life, and her narrative pacing create suspense and excitement. The beginning of the story is most memorable for its ability to get the reader quickly involved in the action surrounding the pursuit of the cattle thieves.

Ogot is also known for incorporating Luo rituals into her stories. For example, in ''The Green Leaves,'' she describes Nyagar taking traditional medicine to calm his nerves after the thief has been left for dead. Other rituals she incorporates are leaving the injured man beneath the leaves so as not to bring evil into the village and ending the story with a song of mourning that Nyamundhe sings after she discovers it is Nyagar beneath the green leaves. She also incorporates a number of superstitions into the story to show how symbols such as a black cat are imbued with specific prophetic powers that may or may not turn out to be true. In this case, the black cat that Nyamundhe sees cross her path foretells the death of Nyagar. Such coincidences help to reinforce the power of such symbols.

Imagery

Although Ogot does not rely heavily on metaphoric or symbolic language, she does use particular images to signify emotions and create suspense. For example, from the very beginning of the story, Nyagar is concerned about locks and bolts on the door of his hut and yard. Although this seems like an insignificant detail, it actually foreshadows the danger that will befall Nyagar. Ironically, even though he appears concerned for his safety, his pursuit of the thief's money shows how his greed overrides these feelings of danger. The attention to gates and locks also reveals that the world he lives in is not safe. This vulnerability can be related on a larger level to the vulnerability of indigenous peoples to the influence and exploitation of British colonial powers. Again, it is ironic that it ends up being Nyagar, a member of the clan, who endangers the other clan members. By stooping to the level of a thief and getting killed for it, Nyagar makes the clan vulnerable and suspicious of each other at the end of the story.

Another image that is referred to frequently is the image of the green leaves that cover the thief and then later Nyagar. Ostensibly, these leaves are meant to hide the thief and keep his spirit from invading the village. However, covering the dying man with freshly torn leaves foreshadows that the thief may not be dead. Only Nyagar will discover this when he returns to steal the thief's money. The green leaves also signify that traditions such as leaving a thief to die in the middle of the night so as to prevent his spirit from entering the village may not be the most efficacious method of handling criminals. However, this is lost on the members of the clan as they try to cope with Nyagar's death at the end of the story and the ''evil hand'' that has descended upon them.

Point of View

What is most interesting about ''The Green Leaves'' is that the story is narrated in a third person omniscient point of view, meaning that it is told from the perspective of an omniscient narrator who sees all that is happening in the story. This point of view allows the narrator to move from Nyagar's point of view to the clan members' and then to Nyagar's wife's viewpoint throughout the story. In this way, Ogot's story reveals multiple perspectives— male, female, individual, and group—that account for the tensions and conflicts erupting in the story. For example, the shift from Nyagar's perspective of gaining more wealth by stealing the thief's purse to that of the clan leader proposing that the whole clan take responsibility for killing the thief reveals the differing values that Nyagar has in relation to his clan. It also prepares the reader for the end of the story, which shows the tension among the clan members over Nyagar's death as being his fault. If he had not desired the thief's money, then the clan could have responded to the European police officer as they had intended to do from the start.

It is also important to consider how Nyamundhe's song at the end of story reveals her own personal pain and loss over the death of her husband. In the end, it does not matter who killed Nyagar. For Nyamundhe, her husband's death means that she will now be alone. Her song reveals a woman's point of view of the consequences of death for those who are dependent on men for protection and comradeship. This provides another viewpoint from which to consider the effects that Nyagar's irresponsible actions have had on his family and the clan.

Dialogue

Many parts of the story are written in dialogue to convey some of the conflicts and misunderstandings that occur between the clan members and the European police officer. For example, when the European police officer and the clan leader first meet, the police officer claims that he has not believed a word that the clan members have told him. When the clan leader says that he sent them to inform the authorities that the clan had killed a man, the officer keeps saying, ''You killed a man?'' in his attempts to establish one person's guilt rather than to accept that it had been a communal effort. Cultural misunderstandings occur frequently in the dialogue as a way of revealing ideological beliefs and differences between the clan and the colonial powers.

Historical Context

When discussing the writing of Ogot, it is difficult to separate her work from its historical and cultural contexts, particularly its precolonial, colonial, and postcolonial contexts. At the time of writing ''The Green Leaves'' in the early 1960s, Kenya had just achieved independence from British colonialism. The road to independence was tortuous and extremely violent. Beginning in the 1920s with the demand for labor and land reform, it carried through to the 1950s, when violence between nationalist groups and white settlers and police became more frequent. As J. Roger Kurtz notes in the historical context to Majorie Oludhe Macgoye's novel *Coming to Birth,* during the State of Emergency that the British enforced in Kenya during the 1950s, nearly 15,000 native Kenyans died in the struggle for independence. Therefore, the significance of these struggles was not lost on the literary generation

coming of age in newly formed African nations such as Kenya, Nigeria, Ghana, and Sudan.

Like many other African writers of the 1950s and 1960s, Ogot confronts the tensions occurring between the gradually weakening colonial forces and the persistent indigenous groups who defy them. As part of a literary and cultural trend emerging in newly formed African nations over the last thirty years, Ogot's writing can be seen as a good example of postcolonial literature. Most of this literature written after independence is a response to the colonizing experience from the point of view of the colonized (i.e. indigenous peoples). The colonized mainly speak of the trauma, humiliation, and slave mentality induced in their psyches as a result of having various religious, political, and legal institutions imposed on their own traditions. One of the best-known theorists who has analyzed the psychological conditions that colonized people undergo is Franz Fanon, whose book *Black Skin, White Masks* brought to the public's awareness the denigrating consequences of being a colonized subject. As Gina Wisker notes in *Post-Colonial and African American Women's Writing,* ''Fanon's work enables engagement with debates about how ex-colonial subjects develop and seize their own identities and slough off the destructiveness of the colonial experiences which represent them in a negative light.'' Despite the formation of independent nations from many former colonies, the psychological effects of colonization continue to impede economic, social, and cultural development as well as the formation of national identities. For many postcolonial writers, nation- and culture-building through identification with the indigenous people's conception of their precolonial past becomes a political means intended to restore dignity and cultural pride to Africans.

For many writers, looking to the precolonial era is a way of reclaiming an African history untouched by Europeans. In many of the short stories in *Land without Thunder*, Ogot uses her background as a Luo, the indigenous people who settled around Lake Victoria in western Kenya, to preserve a sense of the past for future generations. In an interview with Lee Nichols in his book *Conversations with African Writers,* Ogot says that by putting the stories she heard as a young girl to paper, she is preserving Luo heritage so that ''when our children change beyond recognition they will know what they were in the past.'' Her interest in using Luo folktales as the basis for some of her writing has led her to abandon writing in English, at times, to focus on writing in

Compare & Contrast

- **1960s:** Kenyan writer Ogot and Nigerian writer Flora Nwapa are the first African women writers to have their works published by major publishing companies such as East African Publishing House and Heinemann African Writers Series.

  Today: Dozens of women writers in Africa publish in their own countries as well as abroad and have received critical attention commensurate with male African writers such as Chinua Achebe and Ngugi Wa Thiong'o.

- **1960s:** African writers Achebe, Ogot, and Ngugi write books aimed to create a politicized literature based on the common experiences of colonialism, national independence movements, the movement from traditional to modern forms of society, and the psychological and economic effects of these changes on men and women.

  Today: The literature produced by writers living in former colonized nations has become part of a growing body of artistic works called postcolonial literature and is an area of study at many universities worldwide.

- **1960s:** In the years following the independence movements of former colonies in Africa, there is a feeling of optimism and solidarity among both men and women to create nations that are representative of their hopes and dreams for a just and equal society for all African peoples.

  Today: Many African citizens have become disillusioned by economic disparity, chronic drought, civil wars, the AIDS epidemic, and the rise of dictatorships that have prevented true economic and political freedom to occur in many African countries.

- **1960s:** Many African writers turn to writing about the precolonial era in an attempt to reclaim and celebrate the many traditional cultures and their customs and rituals that flourished before the influence of colonialism.

  Today: Many of the traditional cultures of Africa are celebrated all over North America through the re-enactment of traditional songs, dance, and music by national and international groups and organizations.

Luo. In this way, Luo people who do not read or write in English can enjoy and appreciate her writing that often mirrors their collective histories and experiences. In *Wanesema: Conversations with African Writers,* Ogot tells author Don Burness that "It is my hope that people have proper respect for their own language and will learn it so that it will not be lost and swallowed up by English and Kiswahili." The movement towards writing in African vernacular languages has political undertones that are most explicitly expressed by another Kenyan writer, Ngugi wa Thiong'o, in *Decolonizing the Mind: The Politics of Language in African Writing.*

Lastly, Ogot also focuses on her belief that particular issues concerning the impact of colonialism and patriarchy on women have been disregarded or misrepresented in the works of many male writers, including Achebe and Ngugi. Many of the issues discussed in her novels focus on the means by which women's voices were silenced in precolonial, colonial, and postcolonial eras in Kenyan history. Thus, by using folktales as the basis of her short stories, she can question "the powers of traditional myth and magic, which frequently oppress women," as stated by Gina Wisker in *Post-Colonial and African American Women's Writing.*

Critical Overview

At the time that "The Green Leaves" was published in the early 1960s, not many published African writers were women despite the growing international reputations of African writers such as Chinua Achebe and Wole Soyinka. The dearth of women writers in Africa has been ascribed to the lack of opportunities for women to be educated during the colonial periods as well as women's traditional roles that often placed them in the home as mothers and homemakers. However others have argued, particularly African women writers and critics, that women writers have been overlooked because they are unworthy of publication and critical study. In her 1987 article in *Women in African Literature Today,* "Feminist Issues in the Fiction of Kenya's Women Writers," Jean F. O' Barr claims that "No major anthologies of African literature include selections of works by female writers and the few that are organized by topic rather than by author make only fleeting references to women writers." Often when women are written about in critical works, they are misread or dismissed as not being interesting enough. Ghanian writer Ama Ata Aidoo reveals in her article "Literature, Feminism, and the African Woman Today" that the many misrepresentations and misreadings by both African male and Anglo feminist critics that occur are due to the lack of understanding of African women's experiences:

> they [African women] do not fit the accepted (Western) notion of themselves as mute beasts of burden, and they are definitely not as free and as equal as African men . . . would have us believe.

In an article titled "The Woman Artist in Africa Today: A Critical Commentary," critic and writer Micere Mugo admonishes critics for not taking African women writers seriously enough to write critically about them and then reveals the important dimensions of writing for women, both politically and personally. Despite the discriminations, difficulties, and prohibitions that African women writers undergo, African women have responded increasingly to seeing themselves misrepresented or ignored by picking up the pen themselves and creating a women-centered poetics that explores and highlights the impact of colonialism and its aftermath on race, nationality, and gender. In *Contemporary African Literature and the Politics of Gender,* Florence Stratton notes the differences between African men and women writers as being one of accommodating multiple perspectives: "whereas the tendency in male literature is to counter colonial misrepresentations with valorization of indigenous traditions, women writers are as critical of those traditions as of colonialism." The many approaches that African women writers take in their work demand a different lens for reading. As critics Carole Boyce Davies and Elaine Savory Fido in "African Women Writers: Towards a Literary History" remark, "an acceptance of different con-

ceptions of what African writing is and how it should be approached is needed to comprehend some of the experiments that women writers are making."

Although Ogot's work has been denigrated as having an "uninspired, rather pedestrian style" by critic Lloyd W. Brown in his book *Women Writers in Black Africa,* her use of fables and myths of the Luo people contribute to reclaiming a traditional African women's art form, that of orature, within the short story genre. Ogot's work has been completely overlooked due to her relatively small output (her move into politics as well as writing in her first language has contributed to this slight output) and her location in East Africa, a region that has not gained as much international literary acclaim as West or South Africa. Most of the criticism of her work focuses on her 1966 novel, *The Promised Land*, which critiques both traditional and modern ways of life, two features of contemporary Kenya, through the eyes of the female protagonist, Nayapol. However, in her recent book *Contemporary African Literature and the Politics of Gender,* Florence Stratton devotes a chapter to Ogot's work, opening up an important critical space for her work to be discussed among other important African women writers, such as Buchi Emecheta, Ata Ama Aidoo, and Flora Nwapa.

Reading "The Green Leaves" through gender and race, Stratton points to its defining rhetorical strategy as that of "discrediting the male subject . . ., a strategy that complements the tactic of privileging the female subject." Nyagar's death is then viewed as being due to weaknesses in his character, influenced by his excessive desire to accumulate wealth. Compared to other male protagonists in African fiction written by men, his death is not valiant but pathetic and destructive to the clan. Particularly, his death is seen to affect his wife, Nyamundhe. By ending the story with a traditional female song of mourning, Ogot underscores Nyamundhe's pain and sorrow as being one of the most dire aspects of Nyagar's irresponsible act.

Criticism

Doreen Piano

Piano is a Ph.D. candidate in English at Bowling Green University in Ohio. In this essay, Piano analyzes how Ogot reveals the way that British

What Do I Read Next?

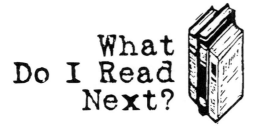

- A 1997 anthology, *Under African Skies: Modern African Stories,* edited by Charles Larson, features a wide range of contemporary African writers from the last fifty years working in a variety of narrative traditions.

- The novel *The Promised Land* (1966), by Grace Ogot, was one of the first African novels published by a woman. The novel takes place during the colonial era and reveals the difficulties that a couple must undergo when they decide to migrate from their traditional homeland in Kenya to Tanganyika because of economic opportunities there. It is written from the point of view of the wife, Nyapol, highlighting her experience as a new bride and a newcomer in a foreign land.

- As a contemporary of Ogot, Kenyan writer Ngugi wa Thiong'o wrote *Decolonising the Mind: The Politics of Language in African Literature* (1981), which makes a powerful argument for African writers to write in their primary rather than their secondary languages as a way of resisting the ideological and cultural forces of colonization.

- A powerful and compelling novel written by Chinua Achebe, *Things Fall Apart* (1958), serves as a contrast to the work of Ogot and other

women who responded in their work both to the legacies of colonialism that disempowered African women and to the patriarchy of traditional African societies.

- A 1986 novel, *Coming to Birth,* written by Kenyan writer Marjorie Oludhe Macgoye and published in 2000 by Feminist Press, is set in the years of Kenyan independence and focuses on the trials and tribulations of a young woman who journeys from a rural village to Nairobi in the 1950s.

- *Urban Obsessions, Urban Fears: The Postcolonial Kenyan Novel* (1998), by J. Roger Kurtz, provides a helpful cultural, economic, and political context to the literature of Kenya, particularly the impact of urban life on Kenyan literature. It includes a comprehensive bibliography of Kenyan writers.

- The edited collection *Challenging Hierarchies: Issues and Themes in Colonial and Postcolonial African Literature* (1998) provides recent critical articles by African women writers such as Ama Ata Aidoo and Micere Mugo on feminism, colonialism, and literature.

---

colonialism disrupts indigenous communities by introducing alien concepts and beliefs that conflict with traditional values.

Written in 1968, Grace Ogot's short story ''The Green Leaves'' takes place over the course of one night and the following morning. Yet within this short time frame, Ogot effectively illustrates the negative effects of colonialism on indigenous people in East Africa. She does this by developing a number of different conflicts that are both internal, as seen in Nyagar's conflicted emotions, and external, as rendered in the verbal exchanges between the European police officer, the clan leader, Olielo, and Nyamundhe, Nyagar's wife. Ogot uses third-person

omniscient point of view as a method of revealing the clan's vulnerability to colonization due to deteriorating communal values. What were once beliefs and values that they assumed to share are now in flux. These changes disrupt the clan and create conflicts among them. Ultimately, ''The Green Leaves'' is an indictment of the British colonial period in Kenya that divided communities and introduced values and customs that conflicted with indigenous ones.

Ogot very cleverly uses third-person omniscient point of view to illustrate the changing attitudes that the clan is undergoing due to the introduction of Western values by colonial powers such as

> By shifting the end of the story to Nyamundhe's point of view, Ogot very subtly reveals how Nyagar's actions have affected Nyamundhe's life as well as the clan's. By acting on his own, he puts her safety and that of the clan's in jeopardy."

Great Britain. Often these values were imposed on indigenous groups by prohibiting the practice of local customs, including using vernacular languages, legal systems, and non-Christian religious beliefs. In this way, indigenous people were forced to learn colonial customs and habits even though this often generated divisions among them. However, the intentional weakening of traditional communities served to strengthen the colonizing presence, making them less threatening and more easily assimilated into the colonial system. This strategy is acknowledged by the clan leader, Olielo, when he tells the clan members of his plan for all of them to take responsibility for the thief's death because, as he puts it, "If we stand united, none of us will be killed." Throughout the story, Olielo represents the traditional values that the clan has historically organized itself around, such as the primary importance of family relations, clearly demarcated gender roles, and the strong relationship between the individual and the community.

However, the influence of modernization has already begun to affect the clan as can be seen in the actions of Nyagar, who puts his own well-being and that of the clan's in jeopardy to satisfy his desire for money. Although he has some hesitation about whether or not to go after the thief's money, in the end he decides to go ahead and do it. The conflict between traditional and modern values is represented through the inner dialogue he has when he is about to take the supposedly dead thief's money: "He now felt nervous. 'Why should you disturb a dead body?' his inner voice asked him. 'What more do you want?'" Yet the need to have more than

anyone in the clan wins out as Nyagar tries to steal the money and consequently ends up dying at the hands of the thief. The emphasis on the accumulation of personal wealth rather than on personal safety and communal knowledge leads to his downfall. In his article, "The True Fantasies of Grace Ogot, Storyteller," Peter Nazareth claims that the vision emerging from Ogot's work is that "Modern society in Kenya she sees as sick, a world in which people chase after false materialist values instead of pursuing the truth." Therefore, in defying the plans that were made to take care of the thief's body when morning arrived, Nyagar places himself in a position of vulnerability. No one knows where he is or what he is doing. Rather than acting in concert with the clan's values, he is transgressing them.

In the beginning of the story, Ogot provides some interesting details that hint at the changes occurring in the clan. What first comes to the attention of Nyagar at the beginning of the story is not only the shouting outside his hut but also the fact that his wife, Nyamundhe, is not next to him. Her absence and lack of telling him where she is reveals a certain breakdown of gender roles that demand that the wife be submissive to her husband. Also Nyagar is very attentive to locking doors and gates and is dismayed when they are not bolted. This anxiety reveals the clan's vulnerability to external forces such as intruders like the thieves as well as colonial forces that disrupt indigenous cultures. However, despite his anxieties about gates being locked, Nyagar is still impelled to leave the hut and steal the thief's money. So strong is Nyagar's lust for money that it overrides his fears of being intruded upon. His obsession illustrates the powerful influence of Western values that infiltrated colonized populations and corrupted traditional markers of success.

The conflict between modern and traditional ways of life is most vividly seen in the discussion that the clan leader, Olielo, has with clan members the morning after the thief has been killed. Of course, no one yet knows what has happened to Nyagar, but the point of view has shifted from Nyagar to that of the clan members' meeting. Most of this scene is relayed in dialogue between Olielo and the clan members and through significant side comments made by Nyamundhe to the nameless co-wife of Nyagar. In his speech to the clan, Olielo strategizes a way to deal with the European authorities who will want an explanation for what happened the night before. His understanding that the clan and the European colonialists have different ways of dealing with justice allows him to figure out a way to protect the clan members from being victimized by the colonialists. In his speech, Olielo makes it clear that the white man will think his own method of justice is superior: ''Because he thinks his laws are superior to ours, we should handle him carefully.'' Later in the story, his insight proves true as the clan interacts with a European police officer who clearly expresses his abhorrence of the way that the clan deals with justice. However, just as tension mounts between the police and the clan members, it is deflected by the discovery of Nyagar under the green leaves.

The revelation that Nyagar is beneath the green leaves throws the clan into turmoil. His death proves to Nyamundhe that the black cat that crossed her path was an accurate prophecy. At the same time, the European police officer is able to manipulate the clan members because of the confusion that arises. Surprisingly, Nyamundhe becomes a powerful figure as she challenges both the clan members who she thinks are responsible for Nyagar's death and the European system of justice that intends to take her husband's body to determine the cause of death. Ogot's decision to end the story with Nyamundhe's challenge and her song of mourning shifts the point of view to that of a woman's perspective. Her vocality gives her power in a situation in which many of the clan members are powerless. At the same time, it also reveals Nyamundhe as being caught between the world of tradition and that of modernization.

By shifting the end of the story to Nyamundhe's point of view, Ogot very subtly reveals how Nyagar's actions have affected Nyamundhe's life as well as the clan's. By acting on his own, he puts her safety and that of the clan in jeopardy. The lack of cohesion among the clan members can be seen in her suspicious reaction to the clan members after Nyagar's body is revealed. In part, her suspicion is due to being left out of the decision-making process the night before, in which only the men participated. All of the women of the clan had known something was going on, but they had not been informed of the details. Thus, although Nyamundhe aligns herself with traditional ways as is seen in the way she challenges the European police officer, she is also in conflict with them. Thus, the intersection of colonialism and traditional patriarchy becomes a site of unresolved conflict for African women writers like Ogot and Nwapa.

In *Contemporary African Literature and the Politics of Gender,* feminist critic Florence Stratton recognizes this conflict by claiming that ''the colonized woman is doubly oppressed, enmeshed in the structures of an indigenous patriarchy and of a foreign masculinist-colonialism.'' However, Nyamundhe challenges both of these systems by refusing to accept the clan's and the European police officer's methods of dealing with justice. This is seen in her ability to disregard both the clan members' and the European police officer's attempts to appease her by relying on her own ability to comfort herself through singing a traditional mourning song. The story's ending casts doubt on both traditional and modern ways of life in East Africa.

African literary critic Taiwo Oladele perceptively says this of Grace Ogot's short stories: ''Her practice is to hit direct on the subject-matter without allowing the beginning of the story to drag, and leave something for the imagination of the reader at the end.'' In ''The Green Leaves,'' Ogot succeeds in writing a riveting story that is suspenseful and economically worded. Yet, at the same time, she also contends with gender and race issues in the context of the British colonial era in Kenya. Because these social and political issues are ongoing, her stories tend to raise questions rather than answer them. ''The Green Leaves'' gives the reader feeling of irresolution at the end. Although it ends with the strong image of a woman mourning her dead husband, it also reveals the tragic dimensions that befell indigenous cultures due to the legacy of colonialism.

Source: Doreen Piano, Critical Essay on ''The Green Leaves,'' in *Short Stories for Students,* The Gale Group, 2002.

Sandra Grady

Grady is a student in folklore and African studies. In this essay, Grady considers Ogot's story in relation to the postcolonial experience in Kenya.

Is colonialism dead? Or is it, as ''The Green Leaves'' relates, merely knocked unconscious, ready to reassert its destructive power through individual Africans acculturated into its values and ideas, willing to act outside the communal norms to seek individual success? Kenyan writer Grace Ogot illustrates this postcolonial dilemma in ''The Green Leaves,'' a story that serves as a cautionary tale to the generation of Kenyan leaders gaining in power after the end of the independence struggle.

" By implementing a European system of education, the colonial experience alienated the colonized people from their own history."

Grace Ogot was born into the generation that would struggle for and achieve independence from England, and "The Green Leaves" describes the identity crisis faced by those whose history is shaped by the conflict between African and European values. The nation of Kenya was created by the British colonial administration in the late nineteenth century. It did not exist as a nation before the incursion of Europeans; rather, its borders were determined by the British government in its effort to reach the wealthy land of Uganda to its west. According to Robert Tignor, because the land was populated by a variety of ethnic groups who often had a more communal understanding of land possession, the British were easily able to confiscate Kenyan land for use by the railway, which was needed to move Ugandan wealth to the Indian Ocean coast. In time, the British discovered that Kenyan land was fertile for a number of cash crops, like coffee and tea, and a settlement policy began, moving Europeans onto African land. After a half century of British rule, an effective movement for independence began. This armed struggle lasted for eighteen years, and in 1963 the people of Kenya achieved political independence from Great Britain.

But with this achievement, according to Bethwell Ogot, the new nation faced a crisis of identity. The struggle for freedom from colonial rule, called *Uhuru,* resulted in political independence for a land of disparate cultures and languages united mostly by their colonial experience, rather than by a lengthy shared history. Now that independence had been achieved, a lasting national identity had to be created. In addition to the problem of national identity, the legacy of colonialism produced another problem: the cultural life of the nation had to be freed from colonial domination, just as the political life had been. The colonial experience sought to eliminate native forms of expression and replace them with European forms of education and advance-

ment. Educated Kenyans learned English literature and European languages in school, rather than their own traditional practices and neighboring languages. Consequently, the native expressions of Kenya's people had been increasingly alienated from modern forms of education and entertainment as part of the colonial experience. Yet these native expressions were critical to precolonial African identity. In *The Journal of Negro History,* Michael Twitty explains:

> Remembrance of the past was seen as a key to instilling civility in future generations. It was not simply time, space, and their accompanying events. History was encoded in a person's name, the traditions of the clan, the national festivals and holidays, the laws of the group, religious ritual, folklore, and the decorative and visual arts.

By implementing a European system of education, the colonial experience alienated the colonized people from their own history.

Consequently, government and intellectual leaders tied the quest for identity to precolonial forms. Bethwell Ogot relates that they developed and promoted a national dress, a cultural preservation movement, a national culture of song, dance, and literature, and the use of Swahili as a national language. This effort to create a national culture characterized the first decade and a half of independence, during which Grace Ogot wrote this story. This national identity effort was directed from an elite class of government officials and academics, rather than emerging from the common people of Kenya. Grace Ogot and her husband, historian Bethwell Ogot, were part of this generation. Her writing, as well as the resurgence of native song, dance, and literature that followed *Uhuru* was, consequently, also an attempt to decolonize the mind, carving an African future out of the precolonial African past.

Included in these efforts was the promotion of Kenyan authorship and publishing through the government-owned East African Literature Bureau (later the Kenya Literature Bureau), through which was disseminated the traditional history of the Kenyan people. For a people dominated by colonialism, the immediate postcolonial literature was a means to recording their previously unrecorded history and practices. While many Kenyan writers began to produce literary material from their experience, much of their writing was in English and, consequently, available only to a small portion of the Kenyan population. By contrast, the oral traditions of Kenya's ethnic cultures, long neglected as materials of study, became the focus of interest for African scholars in the era following independence. The champions of oral literature, Ngugi wa Thiong'o, Owuor Anyumba, Taban lo Liyong, and Okot p'Bitek advocated that students at all levels of Kenyan society be educated in their traditional oral literature as an authentic link to their African past. The old curriculum of English literature was replaced by folk forms, and authors like Grace Ogot, who has published in English, Swahili, and her ethnic language, Luo, incorporated ethnic folklore into their fiction.

This new emphasis was not without internal debate. Some argued that this emphasis on oral tradition would encourage tribalism, promote the study of belief systems and cultural practices that were obsolete, that it was based on race in its exclusion of the Asian and European citizens of contemporary Kenya, and that it would tie future native creativity too closely to their oral literature, rather than freeing writers to create from their own experience. However, the oral literature advocates won the debate, and the immediate postcolonial generation sought to express their experience in native forms.

Written in this context, ''The Green Leaves'' illustrates the complexity of the cultural situation. Though written in English, the story illustrates a variety of traditional practices common to Luos but previously unrecorded in English fiction. From the opening description of group justice to the final lamentation practice of women described at the end, Ogot writes of a Luo community largely untouched by the colonial experience. However, the central conflict of the story illustrates the dilemma facing the nation following the colonial experience. Not only did the nation face an identity crisis, but also the individual African, represented by Nyagar, is confronted with the conflict between traditional and modern norms. According to the story, colonialism is not dead; it is merely beaten, buried temporarily under green leaves, but with some power remaining.

At the start, the protagonist, Nyagar, is roused from his sleep to join with his community to catch a thief. This part of the story illustrates the struggle for freedom, in which native Kenyans united across ethnic lines to rid themselves of those who stole their land and wealth. Like the struggle for *Uhuru,* the fight with the thief operates according to the native practice of justice. Ogot illustrates this con-

formity in the meeting of clansmen the morning after the killing. The group determines that the best way to avoid conflict with the European system of justice is to remain unified, as the men had done in their attempt to stop the thieves. If they remain united behind a common story and no individual breaks that unity, then their system of justice will have the final verdict.

But the conflict between the modern and the traditional has already occurred at the individual level, as Nyagar struggles with his own conscience during the night. His use of traditional medicine brings him only a temporary peace, for Nyagar is tantalized by the stolen wealth still available to him on the unburied corpse. Ultimately, he seeks individual wealth rather than observing the decision of the group who struggled together against the thief. In doing so, he rouses the injured thief and causes his own destruction. The initial battle had not resulted in death, just as *Uhuru* had not completely vanquished the colonial legacy. It lay there, unburied and undead, still able to destroy.

Published five years after independence, the story questions the future of postcolonial Kenya. In *Research in African Literatures,* Elisabeth Mudimbe-Boyi remarks that the modern African literature often relates this encounter between African and Western norms, providing a new picture of ''assimilation, alienation, and the notion of identity crisis, which have long been markers of this encounter.'' In Ogot's story, the encounter is personalized in the internal struggle of Nyagar. As if to emphasize the point, Ogot reiterates that Nyagar's quest is for money, a form of wealth introduced by the colonial power. The original thief, who remains nameless throughout the story, came in search of animal wealth, and endures. The green leaves are not a shroud but a covering. At this critical time in Kenyan nationhood, Ogot illustrates that *Uhuru* may not be a shroud for European domination, as the seeds for African destruction have already been sown in the colonial experience of the individual African.

Though the central story is not complicated, ''The Green Leaves'' illustrates a complicated cultural situation. Ogot's use of traditional folk forms illustrates a reality that had been underrepresented during the colonial era and was being reclaimed in the effort to build a national future. However, she does not nostalgically relate an easy return to the precolonial way of life, despite the seeming irrelevance to the story of the colonial presence. The African experience is forever changed by European colonialism, and *Uhuru*'s victory may be incomplete.

Source: Sandra Grady, Critical Essay on "The Green Leaves," in *Short Stories for Students,* The Gale Group, 2002.

Sources

Achebe, Chinua, *Things Fall Apart,* Heinemann, 1958.

Aidoo, Ama Ata, "Literature, Feminism, and the African Writer Today," in *Challenging Hierarchies: Issues and Themes in Colonial and Postcolonial African Literature,* Peter Lang, 1998, pp.15–35.

Brown, Lloyd W., *Women Writers in Black Africa,* Greenwood Press, 1981, pp. 126–31.

Burness, Don, ed., "Interview with Grace Ogot," in *Wanasema: Conversations with African Writers,* International Studies Africa Series, Number 46, 1985, pp. 60–65.

Davies, Carole Boyce, and Elaine Savory Fido, "African Women Writers: Toward a Literary History," in *A History of Twentieth-Century African Literatures,* edited by Oyekan Owomoyela, University of Nebraska Press, 1993, pp. 281–307.

Fanon, Franz, *Black Skin, White Masks,* Grove Press, 1967.

Griffiths, Gareth, *African Literatures in English: East and West,* Pearson Education, 2000, pp. 281–307.

Kurtz, J. Roger, "Post-Marked Nairobi: Writing in the City in Contemporary Kenya," in *The Post-Colonial Condition of African Literature,* edited by Daniel Gover, John Conteh-Morgan, and Jane Bryce, 2000, pp. 103–10.

———, *Urban Obsessions, Urban Fears: The Postcolonial Kenyan Novel,* Africa World Press, Inc., 1999.

Larson, Charles R., ed., *Under African Skies: Modern Stories,* Farrar, Straus, and Giroux, 1997.

Macgoye, Majorie Oludhe, *Coming to Birth,* Feminist Press, Inc., 2000.

Mudimbe-Boyi, Elisabeth, "Bernard Dadie: Literary Imagination and New Historiography," in *Research in African Literatures,* Vol. 29, No. 3, Fall 1998, pp. 98–106.

Mugo, Micere, "The Woman Artist in Africa Today: A Critical Commentary," in *Challenging Hierarchies: Issues and Themes in Colonial and Postcolonial African Literature,* Peter Lang, 1998, pp.37–61.

Nazareth, Peter, "The True Fantasies of Grace Ogot, Storyteller," in *Meditations on African Literature,* edited by Dubem Okafor, Greenwood Press, 2001, pp. 101–07.

Nichols, Lee, "Grace Ogot," in *Conversations with African Writers: Interviews with Twenty-Six African Authors,* edited by Lee Nichols, Voice of America, 1981, pp. 207–16.

O'Barr, Jean F., "Feminist Issues in the Fiction of Kenya's Women Writers," in *Women in African Literature Today,* edited by Eldred Durosimi Jones, Africa World Press, 1987, pp. 55–70.

Ogot, B. A., and W. R. Ochieng, *Decolonization & Independence in Kenya 1940–93,* Ohio University Press, 1995.

Ogot, Grace, *The Promised Land,* East Africa Publishing House, 1966.

Oladele, Taiwo, *Female Novelists of Modern Africa,* St. Martin's Press, 1990, pp. 128–62.

Podis, Leonard, and Yakubu Saaka, "Introduction," in *Challenging Hierarchies: Issues and Themes in Colonial and Postcolonial African Literature,* Peter Lang, 1998, pp.1–9.

Stratton, Florence, *Contemporary African Literature and the Politics of Gender,* Routledge, 1994, pp. 58–79.

Tignor, Robert L., *The Colonial Transformation of Kenya: The Kiambu, Kikuyu, and Maasai from 1900 to 1939,* Princeton University Press, 1976, pp. 22–27.

Twitty, Michael, "The Persistance of Memory," in *Journal of Negro History,* Vol. 85, Issue 3, Summer 2000, p. 176.

Wisker, Gina, *Post-Colonial and African American Women's Writing: A Critical Introduction,* St. Martin's Press, 2000, pp. 130–58.

Further Reading

Brown, Lloyd W., *Women Writers in Black Africa,* Greenwood Press, 1981.

This book provides chapters on African women writers such as Bessie Head, Flora Nwapa, Buchi Emecheta, and others. One of the first of its kind written solely about African women writers, it purports to write African women writers into the canon of African literature through literary analysis.

Bruner, Charlotte H., *Unwinding Threads: Writing by Women in Africa,* Heinemann, 1994.

This is a collection of short stories by African women from all parts of the continent. Divided by region, the book provides a comprehensive view of the variety and diversity of African women's approaches to imaginative writing. Many well-known and new writers are represented.

Owomoyela, Oyekan, ed., *A History of Twentieth-Century African Literatures,* University of Nebraska Press, 1993.

A range of bibliographic articles covering African literary production in all European languages represented on the continent. Chapters on women's literary production and on East African English-Language fiction are particularly relevant to Ogot's work.

Parekh, Pushpa, ed., *Postcolonial African Writers,* Greenwood Publishing, 1998.

This is a reference book that covers individual authors of postcolonial Africa, including biographical information, a discussion of themes and major works, critical responses to the works, and bibliographies.

Wisker, Gina, *Post-Colonial and African American Women's Writing: A Critical Introduction,* St. Martin's Press, 2000.

This book makes important links between the literature of women from postcolonial regions such as

Africa, South Asia, and the Caribbean and that of African Americans, particularly Alice Walker and Toni Morrison, by revealing how gender and ethnicity combine to produce particular identities that are often silenced, oppressed, and marginalized. There are good references, biographies, and bibliographies of particular authors and their works, including a chapter on elements common to African women's writing.

The Harvest

Tomás Rivera

1989

''The Harvest'' (Arte Público Press, 1989) is a short story by Mexican American writer Tomás Rivera. Rivera was the first writer to document the experience of Mexican American migrant farm workers who each year traveled north from Texas to the Midwest to find seasonal work. Rivera, who was the son of Mexican immigrants, had been a migrant worker in his youth, at various times living and working in Iowa, the Dakotas, Minnesota, Michigan, Wisconsin, and Ohio. He therefore knew first-hand the difficult lives such workers had to endure, and still do today. Migrant workers are among the lowest paid of U. S. workers and they often work long hours in difficult conditions. Housing provided for them is often inadequate, and they are frequently treated as aliens in the communities where they work, even though many are American citizens. Rivera wrote that, in spite of the hardships of their work, the Chicano migrant workers kept their spirits up by what he described as their love of the land. ''The Harvest'' is a story that illustrates this love. It shows how one old migrant worker regularly re-news his feeling of kinship with the land. Through his example, one of the young workers discovers this connection for himself, leading him to a new appreciation of the earth and the cycle of the seasons.

Author Biography

Tomás Rivera was born on December 22, 1935, in Crystal City, Texas, the son of Mexican immigrants, Florencio M. and Josefa (Hernandez) Rivera, who were migrant workers. Rivera accompanied his family in the migrant labor stream that traveled from Texas to many parts of the Midwest. During that time, Rivera lived and worked in Iowa, Minnesota, Wisconsin, Michigan, and North Dakota, but his parents also ensured that he had sufficient time to attend school. He graduated from Southwest Texas State College (now Southwest Texas State University), with a bachelor of arts degree in English in 1958. After graduating, he became a teacher of English and Spanish in the public schools of San Antonio, Crystal City, and League City, Texas, from 1957 to 1965.

Continuing his education, Rivera was awarded a masters degree in education from Southwest Texas State College in 1964. This degree made him eligible for college teaching, and in 1965 he became an instructor in English, French, and Spanish at Southwest Texas Junior College, Uvalde, until 1966. In 1968, he became an instructor in Spanish at the University of Oklahoma, Norman, and the following year, he received a doctorate in romance languages and literature from the University of Oklahoma. He immediately became associate professor at Sam Houston State University in Huntsville, Texas, a position he held until 1971, when he became professor of Spanish at the University of Texas at San Antonio.

In 1971, Rivera published the novel for which he is best known, . . . *y no se lo tragó la tierra / . . . And the Earth Did Not Part.* It had already been awarded the Premio Quinto Sol in 1970. Rivera was also a poet, and he published *Always and Other Poems* (1973), as well as nonfiction essays in scholarly journals on topics such as Chicano literature. Some of Rivera's works were published posthumously. These include the short story "The Harvest" (1989) and *The Searchers: Collected Poetry* (1990).

Rivera became associate dean of the college of multidisciplinary studies at the University of Texas, San Antonio, and later vice president for administration. He then became executive vice-president at the University of Texas at El Paso before accepting the position of Chancellor at the University of California, Riverside, in 1979.

Tomás Rivera

Rivera's administrative abilities earned him recognition and honors. He was a member of the board of the Carnegie Foundation for the Advancement of Teaching in 1976 and the Board of Foreign Scholarships (which directs and administers the Fulbright program). He was also a member of the board of the National Chicano Council on Higher Education. In 1980, he served on the presidential commission that reported on the nation's educational problems.

Rivera married Concepción Garza, on November 27, 1958. The couple had three children: Ileana, Irasema, and Florencio Javier.

Rivera was working on a second novel, *The People's Mansion,* when he died of a heart attack in Fontana, California, on May 16, 1984.

Plot Summary

"The Harvest" is divided into seven short sections. It is set somewhere in the Midwest at the end of September and the beginning of October. The unnamed narrator, a migrant farm worker, thinks this is the best time of year because the work is nearly over and he and his fellow workers will soon be able to return to Texas. Then the main character, Don Trine, is introduced. He walks through the fields every afternoon, and he prefers to do this alone, becoming angry if anyone tries to accompany him.

The next section is a dialogue between a group of unnamed workers, who work alongside Don Trine. They discuss the possible reasons for Trine's walks, which puzzle them. One says that it is Trine's business what he does; another thinks it is strange that he walks alone.

Next, the narrator reports on how the rumors about Trine spread. Some of his fellow workers have tried to spy on him, but he would get wise to what was happening and turn around and go back to his chicken coop. Soon people began to say that he was hiding the money he earned or that he had found buried treasure and was bringing it back to the coop little by little. There were other rumors about Trine, too, all of them centered on the idea that he must have money.

The reasoning behind the idea that Trine was secretly wealthy was that he was an old bachelor, had been working for many years, and had nothing to spend his money on. He only bought food and an occasional beer.

The young workers closely follow Trine on his walks, noting the route he takes and where he would disappear and linger. He seems to spend time around a ditch that crossed the west field. The boys decide to investigate the ditch the following Saturday. But when they do so, they find nothing in the ditch. They do, however, discover a number of holes a foot deep in the field.

They speculate about what might have caused the holes. Trine must have dug them, they conclude, but what was he hiding? They find a coffee can and decide that this is what Trine uses to dig the holes.

Late the following Monday, the boys find out the truth. They manage to fool Don Trine and observe what he does. They are correct that Trine digs the holes with the coffee can. From time to time he measures the depth of the hole by thrusting his arm into it, up to the elbow. He remains in this position for some while, even trying, unsuccessfully, to light a cigarette with one hand. Then Trine digs another hole and thrusts his arm into it in exactly the same way as before. The boys are mystified. They return to their co-workers and report what they have seen. Everyone else is mysti-fied, too. They had all assumed that the holes had something to do with money. Since this has been shown to be incorrect, they think that Trine must be crazy and forget about him. One boy, however, remains curious. The next day he goes to a field and does exactly what he had observed Trine do the previous day. He finds that feeling the earth around his arm is a pleasurable sensation such as he has never felt before. He realizes that Trine is not crazy; he simply likes to feel the earth when it is sleeping. After this, the boy keeps going to the field every afternoon until a freeze comes and it is too hard to dig. Then he thinks with pleasant anticipation of the following October when he will once again be able to repeat the process.

Characters

Curious Boy

The curious boy is one of the group of boys who follow Don Trine to see where he goes and what he does on his walks. Unlike the others, though, he is intrigued by what he sees Don Trine doing. He goes back on his own and imitates Don Trine's actions for himself.

Group of Boys

The boys in the group are young migrant farm workers who speculate on why Don Trine goes on so many solitary walks. They follow him to find out what he does but lose interest when they discover that he is not hiding a treasure trove of money.

Don Trine

Don Trine is one of the migrant farm workers and the only character in the story who is named. He is old, although this description is supplied by the youngsters, which means that Trine might perhaps be only middle-aged and simply appear old to their young eyes. Trine is a bachelor and appears to be a sober, cautious, taciturn man. He says little, but he has a temper: he angrily turns away anyone who tries to follow him in his walks. A loner, Trine is a man who likes his own company.

Trine has been working for many years, presumably doing the same kind of work, but he does not spend the money he earns in any ostentatious way. He has no family to take care of, and his only luxury is the occasional beer or cigarette. It is this frugal aspect of Trine's character that leads the youngsters to think that he may have money stashed away in the holes that he digs.

It turns out that Trine values his connection to the land more than money or human company. He appears to be completely satisfied when he immerses his arm up to the elbow in the holes he has dug and feels the earth nestling up against his skin.

Themes

Materialism

The young boys who speculate about Don Trine have a limited, materialistic vision of life. Although they work on the land, they have no real connection to it. This may be understandable since they are migrant workers often on the move, but it is clear that they can conceive value only in terms of money. A man like Trine who goes off in secret must be hiding money. Perhaps the attitude of the youngsters reflects the hard and impoverished life led by Mexican American migrant workers. As low-paid workers without many material resources, they see the accumulation of money as the principal goal of life. Although their ethnic heritage is Mexican, they live in the United States, the most abundant culture in the world from a materialistic point of view, and they have acquired its values. Acquiring these values has come at the expense of a true relationship with and understanding of nature and its cycles. At the end of the story, one of the boys finds out for himself that there are things of enormous value that have nothing to do with money.

Nature and Its Meaning

In contrast to the young boys who think of life only in terms of money, the older workers appear to have a different attitude. These are the people the narrator refers to in the first paragraph as "the folks." They are more mature and reflective and can sense an "aura of peace and death" in the air as the harvest season comes to an end. Sensing that everything is coming to rest, they take more time to think. They are aware of the cycles of nature and how these affect human life. Their reflective thoughts are

partly because they are about to pack up and move back to Texas, but they also possess a deeper awareness of how nature's moods color their own.

The only named character in the story, Don Trine, is the one who knows this better than anyone. He is deeply connected to the land, and he has developed his own ritual to remind him of this, and it has acquired an almost sacred quality for him. Although he does not deliberately pass on this ritual to the younger generation of workers, one boy discovers it for himself through observing Trine. This boy is motivated only by curiosity, but as he imitates what he has seen Trine do, he, in effect, initiates himself into a new way of experiencing the land. As he sinks his arm into the earth and feels its embrace, he becomes aware of the earth as a living being. This awareness gives him a new appreciation of nature's cycles and his relationship to them.

Style

Structure

In his introduction to "The Harvest," Julián Olivares quotes from an unpublished manuscript in which Rivera commented on the construction of a short story: "The conflict or problem of each story is what interests us as a story. The more intriguing the conflict, the more the story will interest the reader." This, says Rivera, is because every reader has a natural desire to find out how the conflict is resolved. In "The Harvest," the interest is generated by the problem, or mystery, of exactly what Don Trine does when he goes off on his walks. The development of the mystery dictates the structure of the story, which proceeds in alternating sections of narration and dialogue. With each section, as the youngsters continue to speculate about what Trine does, the reader's interest in the mystery grows. It is only in the last section, which is longer than all the others, that the mystery is revealed.

Point of View

The story is told by a limited third person narrator, who observes the activities and attitudes of the migrant workers. The narrator knows what is going on in the minds of the youngsters who speculate about Don Trine, but he has no insight into

Topics for Further Study

- Research the lives and working conditions of Chicano migrant workers today. Are they better or worse now than in the 1960s and 1970s? Describe the differences.

- Investigate the lives and working conditions of migrant workers from other ethnic groups, such as African Americans, Puerto Ricans, and Native Americans. In which parts of the country are each group found most frequently? How do their lives differ from those of Chicanos?

- Think back over your own life and write a brief essay describing an incident that might form the basis of an initiation story. What did you learn from the incident that you did not know before?

What permanent effects has it had on you? Are the effects positive or negative?

- Describe an incident in your own life that caused you to feel a new appreciation for nature or a new understanding of it.

- Rivera wrote that one of the ways that Chicanos created a sense of continuity and identity was by remembering the past, and this is one of the functions of Chicano literature. What are some other ways in which groups of people create a sense of community amongst themselves?

- Research the life of Cesar Chavez and briefly describe some of the ways in which he helped to improve the lives of migrant farm workers.

Trine himself, who is seen entirely through the eyes of the boys. This technique is necessary to create the sense of mystery about Trine's activities on which the story depends.

Of all the characters, only Trine is named. The other characters are anonymous, and there are no physical descriptions of them. The dialogue does not identify any differences between the speakers, other than their words, which stand alone like dialogue in a play. This is a technique Rivera used elsewhere. The anonymity places the emphasis on the experience of an entire group, rather than on individuals. The speakers are representatives of a collective voice, that of migrant workers as a group.

Figurative Language

After the narrator has mentioned that in the fall there was ''an aura of peace and death'' in the air that the workers created, he comments, ''The earth shared that feeling.'' This figure of speech is known as the pathetic fallacy, in which human emotions are attributed to natural things. It conveys the idea that, for the narrator, the earth is a living being.

In the final section of the story, the boy discovers this also. As he thrusts his arm into the hole, he

feels as if the earth is reaching out to grasp his fingers, ''even caressing them,'' and he ''sensed he was inside someone.'' Then the boy refers to the earth as ''sleeping'' and later, when the frost comes, as ''asleep.'' This feeling that the earth is alive gives the boy new affection for the land. He compares the earth to a person who has died and regrets that he has not loved it more before it went to sleep.

Historical Context

Chicano Migrant Workers

Migrant workers are those who are employed on a temporary, often seasonal basis and who come from a community, state, or nation other than where they are temporarily employed. At the beginning of the twentieth century, the majority of migrant farm workers in the United States were recent immigrants from Asia or Europe, but with the growth of the sugar beet, fruit and vegetable, and cotton industries in the early twentieth century, the number of Mexican and Mexican American migrant workers

Compare
&
Contrast

- **1950s:** There is almost no literature that documents the experience of Chicano farm workers.

  Today: The works of Rivera, which chronicle the life of the Chicano migrant worker, are widely read and studied in many universities in the United States.

- **1950s:** Although accurate estimates are difficult, there are about 600,000 migrant workers in the United States yearly.

  Today: Estimates of the number of migrant workers of all ethnicities (mostly Mexican Americans, Mexicans, African Americans, Puerto Ricans, and Native Americans) who work in the United States range from 125,000 to over one million.

- **1950s:** Under the Bracero program, the United States legally admits 400,000 Mexican farm workers each season. Levels of illegal immigration from Mexico are not high enough to cause concern.

  Today: Many regard soaring levels of illegal immigration from Mexico as a major security problem for the United States. In 2001, a panel reporting to President George W. Bush calls for legalizing the status of some of the estimated three million Mexicans living illegally in the United States. It is estimated that fifty percent to eighty percent of the 1.6 million farm workers in the United States are illegal immigrants. Most of them are from Mexico.

---

rapidly increased. Each spring they would travel from Texas to the north central, mountain, and Pacific Coast states. At the end of the season, they would return to Mexico or towns on the Mexican border.

Rivera's parents were part of this migration of Mexican Americans north. He recalled that one of his earliest memories was of waking up in a farm in northern Minnesota where his parents and relatives worked in the beet fields. This memory probably dates from the late 1930s, when there were an estimated four million agricultural migrant laborers working each season.

These workers were often exploited. Wages were low and working hours were long. Child labor was widespread. Education levels were also low, and often local schools would not admit the children of migrant workers since they were not permanent local residents. Because the local community considered the workers as aliens, they were excluded from community life and often found it difficult to attain health care and government services such as food stamps and disability insurance. Levels of diseases such as tuberculosis, typhoid, and small-

pox among migrant workers were far higher than that of the general population, as were maternal and infant mortality rates. Employment was also limited; most migrants worked less than a quarter of available working days. In addition to all these hardships, housing provided for migrant workers was grossly inadequate.

Rivera commented forcefully in his essay, "Remembering, Discovery and Volition in the Literary Imaginative Process," on the plight of migrant workers: "The political and economical structures which surrounded the lives of these families [was] brutal, outrageous and inhuman." Rivera believed that the migrant workers were possibly worse off than slaves. Slaves were considered an investment by their owners and therefore had some protection, but not so the migrant worker:

> The migrant worker never had any protection because he was really not an investment for the exploiter and thus worked under the conditions of slavery without the most rudimentary benefits.

In the 1950s, when Rivera himself was a migrant worker, their numbers dropped to about 600,000 yearly. In the 1960s, the numbers fell once more, to about 400,000, and there were some improvements in living and working conditions. Much of this was due to the efforts of Mexican American activist Cesar Chavez, who organized what is now the United Farm Workers of America (UFW) in California.

Chicano Literature

Rivera was one of the leading figures in what has been called the Chicano Renaissance, an explosion of literary activity among Mexican Americans during the 1960s. In part inspired by the Civil Rights Movement and the gains made by African Americans, Chicano writers emphasized the need for social and political action to end discrimination and provide equal opportunities for Chicanos. As Rivera writes in his essay, ''On Chicano Literature,'' in the decade from 1966 to 1976, Chicano literature had a three-part mission: ''conservation of a culture; the struggle or fight for better economic, social, educational and political equity; and invention.''

Many of the most celebrated Chicano writers of this period were poets, who drew on the oral traditions of their culture to inspire their communities with a sense of identity and mission. Abelardo Delgado's collection, *Chicano: 25 Pieces of a Chicano Mind* (1969), was one of the most influential books in this respect.

Another landmark in Chicano literature was the establishment in 1968 of the publishing house Quinto Sol in Berkeley, California, by a group of young Mexican Americans. Its purpose was to provide a channel for the publication of Chicano literature. Quinto Sol instituted a national award for Chicano literature, Premio Quinto Sol (Fifth Sun Award), which offered a cash prize and publication of the winning entry. In the first year, the prize was awarded to Rivera's . . .*y no se lo tragó la tierra/ . . .And the Earth Did Not Part* (1971), which is still one of the most highly regarded of all Chicano works. In the following year, the Premio Quinto Sol was awarded to Rudolfo Anaya's *Bless Me, Ultima* (1972), which has also become one of the best-known and most popular Chicano novels.

Critical Overview

The publication of *The Harvest: Short Stories* five years after Rivera's death cemented his reputation as the foremost chronicler of the Chicano migrant workers' experience. According to Patricia De La Fuente, who reviewed the book in *Western American Literature,* ''Rivera possesses that rare ability in writers to convert everyday episodes in the lives of ordinary people into small masterpieces of sparse yet often lyrical prose.''

In his introduction to the book, Julián Olivares noted that the title story was one of three, the others being ''The Salamanders'' and ''Zoo Island,'' which ''bring into focus the experience of the migratory cycle.'' In ''The Harvest,'' ''this cycle is enclosed within the greater cycle of life, death and regeneration.'' Discussing the story's culminating moment of revelation, Olivares commented, ''The sense of deracination caused by migrant farmwork is countered by the youngster's awareness of belonging to a world of which external forces cannot deprive him.''

Rivera had previously given literary expression to the migrant workers' lives in his novel . . .*y no se lo tragó la tierra/. . .And the Earth Did Not Part* (1971), and as Olivares notes, the story ''The Harvest'' supplies an aspect of the workers' experience that is excluded from the novel. The novel dwells on the struggle of the farm workers against nature; in contrast, the story emphasizes what Olivares, following Rivera himself, calls the ''love of the land.''

Criticism

Bryan Aubrey

Aubrey holds a Ph.D. in English and has published many articles on twentieth-century literature. In this essay, Aubrey analyzes Rivera's story as an example of an initiation story.

Rivera's ''The Harvest'' is a brief story, covering in some editions no more than three pages. However, springing up from this spare narrative are the archetypal themes of initiation and search, and one archetypal character, that of the Wise Old Man. These structural patterns are archetypal in the sense that they recur in many different myths and literatures of the world and seem to reflect universal human desires and life processes. Since the most prominent of these themes in ''The Harvest'' is that of initiation, the story can be classified as an initiation story.

Cesar Chavez, center, and the United Farmworkers Union

The term ''initiation'' was originally employed by anthropologists to describe the rituals used in primitive societies to mark the passage from boyhood to manhood. Such rituals might include a period of seclusion, an ordeal involving the endurance of physical pain, or the killing of a wild animal. There may be ceremonies, feasts, and dances, all with the purpose of transforming a youth into an adult member of his tribe or community. There are also rituals involved in a girl's rite of passage, often involving fasting and isolation, ritual bathing and purification.

The term ''initiation'' has been adopted by literary critics to describe a certain type of short story. Some initiation stories portray rituals similar to those in primitive societies. William Faulkner's ''The Bear'' (1942), in which a young man kills a bear, is an example. But many stories contain no formal ritual element. The main feature of an initiation story is that a young person undergoes experiences that teach him or her vital truths about human life, often about the adult world that the young person is about to enter. The initiate may also learn a lesson about the world of nature. In all cases, there is a passage from ignorance to knowledge or self-discovery. The protagonist learns something that he or she did not know before. Although many initia-

tion stories show a young person coming into contact for the first time with evil or experiencing disillusionment with the complexities and unpleasantness of the adult world, not all initiation stories fall into this category. Some, like ''The Harvest,'' may be stories of awakening, in which, as a result of his experience, the protagonist perceives life as more rich and rewarding than before, rather than less so.

What is the nature of the initiation in ''The Harvest?'' The character who undergoes the initiation is a boy migrant worker. As such, he probably knows a lot about dislocation and alienation. Migrant workers move from place to place and are often isolated from the life of the community in which they work. When this unnamed boy follows his curiosity and reenacts Don Trine's ritual immersion of his arm into the earth, he finds to his surprise that this simple act opens up a huge treasure trove of previously unknown experience. It is a treasure quite unlike the buried bags of money, which up to then has been the only way in which he and his friends could conceive of the idea of wealth.

What the boy has experienced is a kind of rebirth (a concept that underlies much of primitive ritual and is itself an archetypal theme). He has been reborn into an awareness of something that is much

What Do I Read Next?

- Rivera's highly influential *. . .y no se lo tragó la tierra/. . .And the Earth Did Not Part* (1971) is the story of the hardships endured by a Chicano migrant worker family and their community, as seen through the eyes of a young boy.

- *Pieces of the Heart: New Chicano Fiction* (1993), edited by Gary Soto, is a collection of fifteen stories from some of the best-known Chicano writers. Writers represented include Sandra Cisneros, Alberto Alvaro Rios, Ana Castillo, Victor Martinez, and Helena Maria Viramontes.

- *Necessary Theater: Six Plays about the Chicano Experience* (1989), edited by Jorge Huerta, is a collection of plays that examine the lives of Mexican Americans in diverse situations, from a World War II veteran returning to San Antonio (''Soldierboy'') to Latina immigrants working as domestics in Beverly Hills (''Latina'').

- *Barefoot Heart: Stories of a Migrant Child* (1999), by Elva Trevino Hart, is an autobiographical account of the life of a child growing up in a family of migrant farm workers. Like Rivera, Hart was born in south Texas to Mexican immi-

grants and spent her childhood moving back and forth between Texas and Minnesota.

- *With These Hands: The Hidden World of Migrant Farmworkers Today* (1998), by Daniel Rothenberg and Robert Coles, tells the story of the migrant farm workers. Based on 250 interviews by an anthropologist who worked for a legal aid service that represented migrant workers, the book documents the poverty and neglect that these workers endure, even today.

- *The Fight in the Fields: Cesar Chavez and the Farmworkers Movement* (1998), by Susan Ferriss and Ricardo Sandoval, is a biography of the renowned Mexican American activist who founded the United Farm Workers union in 1962 and led the fight to secure basic human rights for farm workers.

- John Steinbeck's *The Grapes of Wrath* (1939) presents a vivid and bitter portrait of the hardship and oppression suffered by farm families from the southern Midwest states who migrated to California in the 1930s in search of work.

---

larger than himself. He realizes that the earth too has consciousness; it is a living being, not merely an inanimate thing that happens to produce crops. As he realizes this, he also understands that he can actually have a relationship with this living being, a being that is at once new to him and indescribably ancient. It is an experience that changes him forever: ''What he never forgot was feeling the earth move, feeling the earth grasp his fingers and even caressing them.''

The boy has managed to achieve in a moment what English writer D. H. Lawrence, in his book, *Apocalypse* (1931), urged modern, materialistic man to do if he were to become fully human:

> What we want is to destroy our false, inorganic connections, especially those related to money, and

re-establish the living organic connections, with the cosmos, the sun and earth, with mankind and nation and family.

These living, organic connections that Lawrence advocated are precisely what the boy in ''The Harvest'' discovers. Rivera explains as much in his essay, ''Remembering, Discovery and Volition in the Literary Imaginative Process,'' in which he comments on the type of character that appears in his work. At first he condemns the ''cold, materialistic, inhumane system'' that was responsible for the injustices suffered by Chicano migrant workers. But what saved them was their ability to cultivate a love of the land. Rivera comments:

> [M]an has a love for the land as well as his love for his neighbor. He engenders it. He gives love and from it generates life. . . . [T]he Chicano, when he knelt upon

the land . . . felt a symbiotic existence with the land. . . .
As long as this relationship with the land existed, the
Chicano was not dehumanized.

This in part explains the significance of the
story's moment of illumination. Rivera connects the
Chicano's love of the land with his love of his own
people, his sense of community. Although this is not
explicitly stated in the story, it suggests that through
his moving, sensual contact with the earth, the boy
will develop an awareness of the spirit and continuity of his people through their shared embrace of the
land. It is easy to imagine the boy in ''The Harvest'' saying, with Rivera in his long poem ''The
Searchers'':

> How can we be alone
> How can we be alone
> if we are so close to the earth?

''The Searchers,'' as its title suggests, repeatedly presents the experience of the Chicano people
in search of continuity and community, for self-
knowledge and self-discovery. Search is an archetypal
theme often present in initiation stories, and it
occurs in somewhat muted form in ''The Harvest.''
The boys who follow Don Trine are not conscious
of searching for anything other than the solution to
the mystery of what Trine does on his walks, but the
boy who imitates Trine's ritual is at some unconscious level propelled by more than mere curiosity.
Although the spare narrative does not elaborate on
his motivation, the fact that the boy is unnamed
suggests that he can be understood not simply as an
individual but as a representative of his people and
their search for meaning and connection to nature
and the earth. This search is all the more urgent for
the Chicano migrant worker because often, due to
the harshness of his work and life, nature is seen as
an antagonist, as a force to be overcome, rather than
as the warm, benevolent, responsive being that the
boy discovers.

The final archetype present in ''The Harvest''
is that of the Wise Old Man. Psychologist Carl Jung
identified this archetype. Jung theorized that such
images welled up from what he called the collective
unconscious and were found in the dreams, myths,
and literatures of many different cultures. According to Jung, the archetypes embody universal patterns of human consciousness.

The Wise Old Man is usually a benevolent
character who acts as a guide to someone younger.
He embodies wisdom, insight, and knowledge. In
Arthurian legend, for example, Merlin, the magician and counselor, fulfills the role of Wise Old

> Rivera connects the
> Chicano's love of the land with
> his love of his own people, his
> sense of community."

Man. In Dante's *Divine Comedy,* Virgil performs
the same function as he guides Dante through hell,
purgatory, and heaven. Initiation stories often contain a Wise Old Man who teaches some vital knowledge to a younger person. Examples include ''Open
Winter'' (1953) by H. L. Davis; ''The Promise''
(1938) by John Steinbeck; and two stories by
Faulkner, ''The Old People'' (1940) and ''The
Bear'' (1942), in which an old man tutors a young
boy in the art of hunting. There is a similar relationship between the characters Manolin, a young
Cuban boy, and Santiago, an old Cuban fisherman,
in Ernest Hemingway's *The Old Man and the
Sea* (1962).

In ''The Harvest,'' Don Trine is a variant of the
Wise Old Man archetype. He is not a complete
expression of it because usually the Wise Old Man
possesses moral qualities such as goodwill and a
willingness to help, which the grouchy, taciturn,
private Trine does not embody at all. But he is a
Wise Old Man nonetheless. Trine possesses knowledge that the younger workers do not have. He
knows his connection to the earth, and he has
devised a ritual of his own to maintain it. It is
through Trine's example that the youngster learns
something that is extremely valuable to him. He
would not have discovered it without Trine. Trine is
therefore the vehicle through which wisdom is
passed from the older generation to the younger. In
that transmission of wisdom, Rivera seems to be
saying, lies the hope for the Chicano migrant workers, a people who have otherwise suffered too much
for too long.

Source: Bryan Aubrey, Critical Essay on ''The Harvest,'' in
Short Stories for Students, The Gale Group, 2002.

Susan Sanderson

*Sanderson holds a master of fine arts degree in
fiction writing and is an independent writer. In this
essay, Sanderson examines Tomás Rivera's use of
various storytelling techniques in his short story*

and how these techniques help construct a ritual of community survival.

Tomás Rivera is best known for his poetry and one published novel, *. . . y no se lo tragó la tierra / . . . And the Earth Did Not Part*. Critics have praised Rivera's poems and novel for their inclusion of ritual and remembrance as major features while describing the Mexican migrant farm worker culture of the 1940s and 1950s. In addition, critics note that Rivera successfully explores in these works the relationship between the generations. Though ''The Harvest'' may not have received as much attention as these other writings, this brief story displays similar techniques. Rivera's use of these three narrative features—rituals, relationships between generations, and remembering—gives ''The Harvest'' a fullness in spite of its brevity, creating a story that mimics the atmosphere of a campfire tale-telling session. Ultimately, Rivera's story is a short but powerful love letter to the earth that also acknowledges the struggles of the migrant farm worker community.

In this story, Rivera provides a peek into the world of his origin—the world of the Mexican and Mexican-American migrant farm worker in the United States. They were (and still are) a community always on the move, making the creation and maintenance of rituals an important way to establish some stability and consistency in their lives. As Rivera notes in the very beginning of the story, uncertainty and variability were the hallmarks of their existence. At the end of the season, the workers would talk about ''if it had gone well for them, if they would return or not to the same place next year.'' Their children's education was sporadic, as they were always on the move with the seasons, and their daily lives were only as predictable as the weather.

Out of this unpredictability grew a culture steeped in rituals and events that unfolded with regularity. For as they traveled across the United States with the seasons and slept and worked according to the rotation of the earth, the earth's movements were always a source of stability and constancy for the workers. Rivera integrates this feature of migrant worker culture into his story and alerts the reader to its guiding importance by making it very clear what time of the year the story takes place and what that means for the workers: ''The end of September and the beginning of October. . . . It was a sign that the work was coming to an end and that the return to Texas would start,'' begins Rivera's

story. As if to put an exclamation point on the value of the seasons' regularity and their relationship to the rituals of the farm workers, Rivera ends his story by noting that the young boy who discovers Don Trine's personal rite looks forward to ''next year, in October at the harvest time, when once again he could repeat what Don Trine did.''

The narrative core of the story, in fact, is one man's annual ritual. Don Trine, after the harvest, goes out nearly every evening to a ditch near the edge of the fields and digs a hole into which he places his arm, elbow deep, to feel the earth. Every community has its own public and private rituals; Don Trine's ritual is purely private, so much so that he snarls at the children when they become curious and try to follow him out to the ditch. At the story's beginning, some of the community's rituals are noted: regular discussions about the past year's successes and failures, the expected trip back to Texas, and ''long walks around the grove.'' Don Trine has a couple of personal yet public rituals, as well, including buying his food every Saturday.

Like many rituals, Don Trine's effort to feel the earth after the harvest is clothed in secrecy. Not only does he tell the children to stop following him when he begins his walk to the ditch, but he also changes his route in an effort to foil any plans they may have to uncover his actions. ''When he would leave, and someone would spy on him, somehow or other he would catch on, then take a little walk, turn around and head right back to his chicken coop,'' the story's teller recounts. Eventually, the children figure out where he is going and visit the ditch when Don Trine is not around. There they find the accoutrements of his ritual: multiple holes dug into the soft earth and a coffee can. But even when they manage to follow him to the site and watch him perform the ritual, their view is incomplete and obstructed, and they leave, assuming that Don Trine is crazy. Only when a single young boy tries to reproduce the ritual is its meaning clear. It takes the reenactment of the ritual, complete with its physical movements, to make the ritual alive and meaningful to another person in the community.

Don Trine is described as a man who has never married and does not have a family. When the children talk of him, it is in terms of someone who has lived a long time. ''He's an old bachelor,'' they say, someone who has worked ''so many years'' and must have saved a lot of money. Even though the reader does not see a face-to-face meeting between Don Trine and the boy who re-creates the older man's ceremony with the earth, they most certainly have a relationship, which brings the motif of cross-generational relationships into the story. After the boy understands Don Trine's ritual, he establishes a relationship with the older man, similar to the way in which a son would connect with his father. When the boy thinks of doing the ritual the following year, it is with a sense of both anticipation and bittersweet sorrow. ''It was like when someone died. You always blamed yourself for not loving him more before he died,'' he notes. These last lines in the story are the most mournful in the whole piece and seem to refer, on the one hand, to no one in particular and, on the other hand, to Don Trine.

The third feature that appears in Rivera's story is the act of remembrance. Much like the incorporation of rituals, remembering events and retelling stories are important to a community searching for roots and stability. Remembering people and sharing stories can become rituals and create bonds between generations as well as help to hold communities together during periods of hardship. Not only are there incidences of storytelling and remembering in the story, but the story itself is structured to sound as if someone is telling it around a campfire or over dinner.

A very casual but realistic tone is struck from the beginning of ''The Harvest,'' framing Don Trine's tale in a general place and time (in the fall, just before the migrant families return to Texas) and using language that indicates familiarity. Maybe the teller has even shared this story before and can assume a high level of familiarity with the listeners, as few details are revealed about who the characters are, their backgrounds, or what they do for a living; nearly all of that information is understood and unspoken. The only person who has a proper name is Don Trine; everyone else is referred to as ''the folks,'' ''the youngsters,'' or even simply ''one of the boys.'' Don Trine is also the only character with a specific past, divulged when the workers are suspicious about his walks out to the edge of the fields and ''began to say that when he was young he had run around with a gang in Mexico.''

Presenting the story as a tale shared between neighbors or friends, Rivera uses phrases such as ''And that's why'' and ''And that's how'' to start the paragraphs that attempt to explain Don Trine's and, eventually, the young boy's, behaviors. These phrases act as a break in the action of the story, a way to connect with the reader to explain what might seem like an inconsistency in the narrative.

> "Ultimately, Rivera's story is a short but powerful love letter to the earth that also acknowledges the struggles of the migrant farm worker community."

Finally, Rivera ends his story in a very personal tone of voice, with the second person ''you,'' as if he wants to address and connect directly with his reader.

All of these features promote the idea that the tale of Don Trine is not just a story about a migrant worker who happens to like sticking his hand in warm dirt at the end of the harvest season. To begin with, Don Trine is passing a ritual on to another generation (although he does so against his will), something that is essential for the survival of his culture. For all the care the older man takes to keep the children away from his walks, his sudden slip-up that allows them to follow him does not come as a complete surprise. It seems as if he understands—or hopes—that one of the children will be, not disappointed, but curious when he discovers that Don Trine is not hiding money but is engaging in a ritual that connects him with the earth.

Rivera has given the earth, as well as the other characters in his story, very human qualities. When the story opens, the earth is said to have ''shared that feeling'' of ''peace and death'' with the farm workers. Rivera also has the narrator observe that in the final days of the harvest, ''there was a wake over the earth,'' a tricky wording that gives the character of the earth a life and a death, much like a human. But nowhere does the earth become more human and more full of the possibility of life than at the very end of the story, when Don Trine's ritual is revealed. As the boy digs a hole in the soft dirt using the old man's coffee can, he experiences through his hand ''the earth move, feeling the earth grasp his fingers and even caressing them.'' He knows then that Don Trine was not crazy when he ''felt the warmth of the earth . . . [and] sensed he was inside someone.''

Rivera's language in these passages reads as if Don Trine and the boy are experiencing an almost sexual connection with the earth. In a moment of humor while the group of boys is watching Don Trine perform his ritual, the story's narrator observes that Don Trine ''seemed very satisfied and even tried to light a cigarette with one hand'' after his hand was deep inside one of the holes he had dug. It is very hard *not* to see this scene as a teasing nod to the classic postcoital moment replayed in innumerable modern movies and novels.

However, the full understanding of Don Trine's ritual is undoubtedly more closely related to the bond the migrant farm worker community has with the earth itself. Without the earth the workers do not have a livelihood and cannot support their families. The workers take from the earth their livelihood; Rivera's story, however, also highlights the fact that the relationship with the earth cannot be one-sided. The ditch where Don Trine performs his ritual is next to a field where potatoes have recently been harvested. In this light, the old man's rite seems to say that the workers must also give back to the earth. Don Trine's ritual of putting his hand reverently back into the earth after the harvest—not to take, this time, but to caress—replenishes the earth so that the crops will grow next year and the workers can nourish their families. By learning the ritual and practicing it, the boy has assured, across the generations, the future survival of his people and community.

Source: Susan Sanderson, Critical Essay on ''The Harvest,'' in *Short Stories for Students,* The Gale Group, 2002.

Sources

de la Fuente, Patricia, Review, in *Western American Literature,* May 1990, p. 74.

Lawrence, D. H., *Apocalypse,* Penguin Books, 1975, p. 126.

Marcus, Mordecai, ''What Is an Initiation Story?'' in *The Young Man in American Literature: The Initiation Theme,* edited by William Coyle, Odyssey Press, 1969, pp. 29–40.

Rivera, Tomás, ''The Great Plains as Refuge in Chicano Literature,'' in *Tomás Rivera: The Complete Works,* edited by Julián Olivares, Arte Público Press, 1991, pp. 384–97.

———, *The Harvest: Short Stories,* edited by Julián Olivares, Arte Público Press, 1989.

———, ''On Chicano Literature,'' in *Tomás Rivera: The Complete Works,* edited by Julián Olivares, Arte Público Press, 1991, pp. 378–83.

———, ''Remembering, Discovery and Volition in the Literary Imaginative Process,'' in *Tomás Rivera: The Complete Works,* edited by Julián Olivares, Arte Público Press, 1991, pp. 365–77.

Further Reading

Bruce-Novoa, Juan, *Chicano Authors: Inquiry by Interview,* University of Texas Press, 1980.
    This work includes an interview with Rivera in which he explains that part of his motivation as an author was to document the strength and the suffering of the Chicano migrant workers and to give their story a spiritual dimension.

Lattin, Vernon E., Rolando Hinojosa, and Gary D. Keller, *Tomás Rivera, 1935–1984, The Man and His Work,* Bilingual Review/Press, 1988.
    This collection features works by Rivera as well as poems written in his memory, scholarly contributions, drawings, and photographs.

Olivares, Julián, ed., *International Studies in Honor of Tomás Rivera,* Arte Público Press, 1986.
    Olivares's text is a collection of seventeen essays on all aspects of Rivera's work and on Chicano and Hispanic literature in the United States.

Sommers, Joseph, ''Interpreting Tomás Rivera,'' in *Modern Chicano Writers: A Collection of Critical Essays,* edited by Joseph Sommers and Tomás Ybarra-Frausto, Prentice-Hall, 1979, pp. 94–107.
    Sommers offers an assessment of Rivera's *. . .y no se lo tragó la tierra/. . .And the Earth Did Not Part* that is critical of the author's treatment of female characters.

How to Tell a True War Story

"How to Tell a True War Story" first appeared in October 1987 in *Esquire*. It later came to hold a central position in Tim O'Brien's book *The Things They Carried*, published in 1990. An interesting combination of recalled events and editorial commentary, the story received critical attention at its first publication. Indeed, nearly every reviewer and critic who treats O'Brien's work singles out this story for special commentary. The story in many ways provides a map to the rest of *The Things They Carried*. By trying to characterize what constitutes a true war story, but never really achieving this feat, O'Brien introduces the most important themes of his book, including memory, imagination, epistemology (the study of the nature of knowledge), and truth. In addition, O'Brien uses the very technique he would later use in creating *The Things They Carried*, interspersing anecdotes and stories with commentary about the roles of fiction and storytelling. As D. J. R. Bruckner stated in the *New York Times* in an early review of *The Things They Carried*, "How to Tell a True War Story" is "at least as much about storytelling as about men at war." Certainly, by having his fictional characters tell stories and then recant the truth of those stories, O'Brien calls into question the possibility of ever telling a true war story. The result of this technique is that the story is both fragmentary and cohesive: the stories within the larger framework are fragments held together by a narrative voice determined to "get it right." Certainly, any student wishing to begin a study of

Tim O'Brien

1987

Tim O'Brien would be well served to pay close attention to "How to Tell a True War Story."

Author Biography

William Tim O'Brien was born on October 1, 1946, in Austin, Minnesota. His father sold insurance and his mother was a teacher. Both of O'Brien's parents served in the military during World War II. O'Brien and his family lived in Austin, Minnesota, for ten years, then moved to Worthington, Minnesota, where O'Brien spent the rest of his childhood and adolescence. He enrolled in 1964 at Macalester College in St. Paul, Minnesota.

In 1968, just two weeks after graduating Phi Beta Kappa from Macalester and while preparing to enter Harvard graduate school, O'Brien received his draft notice. Although he was opposed to the war, he found himself in August 1968 assigned to an infantry unit in the army on his way to Vietnam.

O'Brien's Vietnam experience was life changing. Upon his return to the United States, he enrolled at Harvard as a doctoral student in government. During this time, he wrote for a number of magazines and newspapers and completed his first book, a memoir of his time in Vietnam called *If I Die in a Combat Zone, Box Me Up and Ship Me Home*, published in 1973. In 1975 he published his second book, the novel *Northern Lights*. Around 1976 he gave up graduate studies to pursue a full-time career as a writer. The same year, he won an O. Henry Memorial Award for a short story that would later be included in his 1978 novel, *Going After Cacciato*. He garnered yet another O. Henry Memorial Award in 1978 for a second story from *Going After Cacciato*, and in 1979 the novel won a prestigious National Book Award.

His next novel, *The Nuclear Age*, was published in 1985. Following this publication, O'Brien spent about four years producing some of his best short fiction, including "How to Tell a True War Story," which appeared in 1987 in *Esquire*. Another short story, "The Things They Carried," won the National Magazine Award in 1987, and in 1999 was chosen for inclusion in *The Best American Short Stories of the Century*, edited by John Updike.

In 1990 O'Brien collected some of his stories, including "How to Tell a True War Story," and published them as a book titled *The Things They Carried*. Though reviewers had difficulty determining whether the book was a novel, linked short stories, or some completely new genre, the reviews were overwhelmingly positive. The collection was named as one of the year's ten best works of fiction by the *The New York Times*, and received the Heartland Prize from the *Chicago Tribune*. The book also was a finalist for the Pulitzer Prize and the National Book Critic's Circle Award, won the Melcher award in 1991, and the French *Prix du Meilleur Livre Etranger* (Prize for the Best Foreign Book) in 1992. Many scholars consider *The Things They Carried* to be O'Brien's best work to date. Since the publication of the collection, O'Brien has written two more books, *In the Lake of the Woods* (1994)—which received the James Fenimore Cooper Prize from the Society of American Historians and was named best novel of the year by *Time* magazine—and *Tomcat in Love* (1998).

Plot Summary

"How to Tell a True War Story" is not a story in the traditional sense. It does not follow a straight, chronological path from start to finish. Rather, it is a collection of small stories interspersed with instructions about "true" war stories.

The story opens with the words, "This is true." The narrator then goes on to tell the story of his friend Rat Kiley, who writes a letter to the sister of his buddy who had been killed a week earlier. It is a long, heartfelt letter. He waits for two months for a reply to the letter, but the sister never writes back.

The story then shifts to commentary. "A true war story is never moral," the narrator instructs. The narrator asks the reader to "listen to Rat" as he spews obscenity, as, according to the narrator, a true war story is committed to "obscenity and evil."

In the next section, the narrator reveals that Curt Lemon is the buddy who was killed. Thus, this section actually occurred in time before the opening section. Curt and Rat are playing with smoke grenades when Curt trips a rigged 105 mm. artillery round. The narrator reports "It's all exactly true." The narrator provides a stunning visual description of Curt's ascent into the trees as he is blown up.

Again the narration shifts to commentary. The narrator argues that it is difficult in true war stories to distinguish between what actually happened and what seemed to happen.

The narrator then suggests that ''a true war story cannot be believed'' and that sometimes it is simply impossible to even tell a true war story. He uses the example of a story told by Mitchell Sanders. Sanders recounts how a patrol of six men goes up into the mountains to establish a listening post. They are supposed to remain in the mountains for a week, absolutely silent. As the men listen, they begin to hear all kinds of weird noises. They hear music and voices. They hear a glee club and opera. Sanders says that the rocks are talking. Finally, the men become so frightened that they call in fire-power and burn up the mountains. Throughout this story, Sanders insists that every word is true.

Immediately the narrator shifts to a comment, ''You can tell a true war story by the way it never seems to end.'' Mitchell Sanders returns to the narrator later that night and tries to give the story a moral, as if he is unable to end the story the way he wants it to. The next morning, he once again approaches the narrator to tell him that he ''had to make up a few things'' while telling his story. Sanders tries yet again to give the story a moral, ''That quiet—just listen. There's your moral.''

Although the narrator earlier told the reader that war stories are never moral, Sanders continues to try to provide one. The narrator even shifts from his earlier position when he suggests that, if there is a moral, it is ''like the thread that makes the cloth.'' He further argues that a true war story affects the gut, not the brain.

Next, the narrator tells a story of his own: the events that occurred between the death of Curt Lemon and Rat Kiley's letter writing. After Curt's death, the squad captured a baby water buffalo. Rat winds up killing it slowly, by shooting off various parts of its anatomy. The narrator connects the killing with Curt's death, and the rest of the platoon eventually participates by throwing the carcass into the village well.

In the next section, the narrator tells the reader, ''The truths are contradictory.'' He spends a long time describing the sensation of being in battle, trying in images and words to create a true war story for the reader. By the end of the section, however, in a quintessentially contradictory statement, the narrator tells the reader, ''In war you lose your sense of the definite, hence your sense of truth itself, and therefore it's safe to say that in a true war story, nothing is ever absolutely true.''

The narrator then returns to the death of Curt Lemon in a very short fragment. Here he recalls being ordered to climb up into the tree to collect the remains of the young man. His buddy, also up in the tree, sings ''Lemon Tree'' the whole time.

By the end of the story, it seems very important to the narrator that he be able to tell the ''true'' story of Lemon's death. But just as it appears he may be able to do so, he inserts a passage that tells the reader that everything in the entire story has been made up. None of it is true. And yet, even here, the narrator squirms away: ''None of it happened. *None* of it. And even if it did happen, it didn't happen in the mounts, it happened in this little village on the Batangan Peninsula, and it was raining like crazy, and one night a guy named Stink Harris woke up screaming with a leech on his tongue.''

The story concludes by suggesting that a ''true war story is never about war.'' Thus, even at the very end of the story, the reader is left to ponder how to tell a true war story.

Characters

Stink Harris

Stink Harris has a very small role in this story, although he figures in other stories in *The Things They Carried*.

Dave Jensen

Dave Jensen is a minor character in this story, a fellow member of Tim's platoon.

Rat Kiley

Rat Kiley is another member of Tim's platoon. The story opens with Tim telling the story of how Rat wrote a letter to the sister of Curt Lemon, one of Rat's buddies who was killed. The sister never writes back and Rat calls her a ''dumb cooze.'' A second story involving Rat concerns a ''baby VC water buffalo.'' The event occurs soon after Curt's death. The platoon captures the buffalo and takes it with them. However, when it refuses to eat the food Rat offers it, Rat begins shooting the buffalo. The narrator attributes this action to Rat's grief and anger over the death of his friend.

Kiowa

Kiowa is a Native American member of Tim's platoon. His role in this story is limited to helping

Dave Jensen throw what is left of the baby water buffalo in the village well. However, in other stories in *The Things They Carried*, Kiowa is a central figure.

Curt Lemon

Curt Lemon is a member of Tim's platoon who dies. The story of his death is woven through this story and throughout the entire collection of stories that make up *The Things They Carried*. Curt and his friend Rat Kiley were playing with smoke grenades when Curt stepped on a rigged 105 mm. artillery round. Tim tells the story over and over, trying to describe Curt's ascent into the trees. Curt's role in the story is as ''the dead guy.'' His death offers an illustration of the difference between happening-truth and seeming-truth. The happening-truth is, of course, that he is killed in an explosion. The seeming-truth, however, is that somehow the sunlight lifts him up into the trees.

Tim O'Brien

Although the first person narrator of the story has the same name as the author (the narrator is not named in this story; readers learn this information from other stories in O'Brien's *The Things They Carried*), readers should not confuse the two. The author has deliberately created a fictional persona to tell this story. Like the author, the narrator Tim is a white male writer in his mid-forties, recalling his time as a soldier in Vietnam. He alternates between commenting on the construction of ''true'' war stories and memories that illustrate his points. Indeed, Tim's first words in the story are ''This is true.'' Tim serves as the chief storyteller in the story, although he reports on stories he has heard from his comrades. Repeatedly, however, Tim points out to the reader those characteristics that identify a war story as true. At the same time, however, he also contradicts and changes his stories. Just as his opening words are ''This is true,'' he later tells the reader that ''None of it happened. *None* of it.'' Likewise, although he claims that this is a story about war stories, in the final paragraph he tells the reader, ''And in the end, of course, a true war story is never about war.''

Mitchell Sanders

Another member of Tim's platoon, Mitchell Sanders, tells the story of a patrol that goes up into the mountains to spend a week listening for enemy movement. What they hear, however, is not enemy movements, but a whole host of other sounds, including a glee club, a Chinese opera, and a cocktail party. He swears that the episode is true. Later in the night he returns to tell Tim the moral of the story, although Tim has just told the readers that a true war story has no moral. Even later in the night, Mitchell returns once again to Tim to tell him that he had to make up a few things in order to make the story true. Nevertheless, within the story, Tim presents Mitchell Sanders as a reliable narrator.

Themes

Memory and Reminiscence

Because ''How to Tell a True War Story'' is written by a Vietnam War veteran, and because Tim O'Brien has chosen to create a narrator with the same name as his own, most readers want to believe that the stories O'Brien tells are true and actually happened to him. There are several reasons for this. In the first place, O'Brien's so-called memoir, *If I Die In a Combat Zone*, contains many stories that find their way into his later novels and short fiction. Thus, it is difficult for the reader to sort through what is memory and what is fiction.

There are those, however, who would suggest that this is one of O'Brien's points in writing his stories. Although most readers would believe that their own memories are ''true,'' this particular story sets out to demonstrate the way that memories are at once true and made up.

Further, as O'Brien tells the reader in ''How to Tell a True War Story,'' ''You'd feel cheated if it never happened.'' This is certainly one response to O'Brien's story. Readers want the stories to be true in the sense that they grow out of O'Brien's memory. O'Brien, however, will not let the reader take this easy way out. Instead, he questions the entire notion of memoir, reminiscence, and the ability of memory to convey the truth.

Truth and Falsehood

Certainly, the most insistent theme in this story is that of truth and falsehood. O'Brien, however, would be unlikely to set up such a dichotomy. That is, according to ''How to Tell a True War Story,'' truth is not something that can find its opposition in

Topics for Further Study

- Investigate the incident that has come to be known as the My Lai massacre. Summarize the events that occurred in My Lai. Using your summary and research, try to determine why such an incident might happen and what affect it had on popular opinion about the Vietnam War.

- Read Bao Ninh's *The Sorrow of War,* a book by a former North Vietnamese soldier. Compare and contrast the story that Bao Ninh tells with the stories in *The Things They Carried.*

- Watch the movies *The Green Berets* (1968) and *Platoon* (1986). What are some of the reasons for such different portrayals of the Vietnam War? Using O'Brien's criteria, are either of these movies a ''true'' war story?

- Read Tim O'Brien's memoir *If I Die in a Combat Zone, Box Me Up and Ship Me Home*, and the rest of the stories in *The Things They Carried.* Can you find some of the sources for O'Brien's fiction in his own experiences? How does read-

ing ''How to Tell a True War Story'' affect your reading of memoir?

- Read *All Quiet on the Western Front* by Erich Maria Remarque and do some brief research on the First World War. Does Remarque's story classify as a ''true'' war story? Why or why not?

- O'Brien distinguishes between happening-truth and story-truth. What do you think he means by this? What role does fiction play in presenting the ''truth'' of the Vietnam War?

- Michael Herr's 1977 book *Dispatches* is another work that blurs the distinction between fiction and nonfiction. Originally written as a work of journalism, Herr later described the book as fiction. What do you think qualifies the book as what has come to be known as the ''new'' journalism? Why do you think it can also be called a work of fiction? What other recent memoirs or biographies have continued to blur the line between fiction and non-fiction?

---

untruth. Rather, according to O'Brien, because war is so ambiguous, truth takes on many guises. Even seemingly contradictory events can both be considered true.

O'Brien uses the event of Curt Lemon's death to make this point. O'Brien knows, for example, that Curt is killed by a rigged 105mm round. However, as the scene replays in his mind, O'Brien sees the event very differently. It seems to him that Curt is killed by the sunlight, and that it is the sunlight that lifts him high into the tree where O'Brien will later have to retrieve Curt's body parts. Thus O'Brien distinguishes between the truth that happens and the truth that seems to happen.

Moreover, O'Brien likes to play with words and to undermine the logical connection between words. In Western philosophy, it is considered impossible for a word to mean itself and its opposite at the same time. O'Brien demonstrates it may

indeed be possible. For example, when he writes, ''it is safe to say that in a true war story nothing is ever absolutely true,'' he is creating a paradox. If nothing is ever absolutely true, then even that statement cannot be absolutely true. The paradox suggests that while it might be possible to approximate truth, it must be told, as Emily Dickinson once wrote, ''aslant.''

Perhaps the most disconcerting moment in this tale occurs when O'Brien tells the story of the woman who approaches him after he tells this tale. Most readers assume that O'Brien the author is speaking, and that perhaps he is telling a story of what happened to him after a reading of his fiction. When the woman says she likes the story about the water buffalo, O'Brien is annoyed. Although he does not tell her, he tells the reader that the entire episode did not happen, that it was all made up, and that even the characters are not real. Readers may be shocked. How could O'Brien have fabricated all of this? Then the reader may realize that O'Brien is playing with the truth again, for if everything in the story is fabricated, then so is the woman who approached him. This play with truth and falsehood provides both delight and despair for the reader who will never be able to determine either truth or falsehood in O'Brien's stories in the traditional sense. As Stephen Kaplan suggests in *Understanding Tim O'Brien,* ''[O'Brien] completely destroys the fine line dividing fact from fiction and tries to show . . . that fiction (or the imagined world) can often be truer, especially in the case of Vietnam, than fact.''

Style

Point of View and Narration

One of the most interesting, and perhaps troubling, aspects of the construction of ''How to Tell a True War Story'' is O'Brien's choice to create a fictional, first-person narrator who also carries the name ''Tim O'Brien.'' Although the narrator remains unnamed in this particular story, other stories in the collection clearly identify the narrator by the name Tim. Further, the other stories in the collection also identify the narrator as a forty-three-year-old writer who writes about the Vietnam War, ever more closely identifying the narrator with the author.

On the one hand, this connection is very compelling. Readers are drawn into the story believing that they are reading something that has some basis in the truth of the writer Tim O'Brien. Further, the authorial voice that links the story fragments together sounds like it ought to belong to the writer.

On the other hand, however, the device allows O'Brien to play with notions of truth and ambiguity. Does the narrator represent the author? Or do the narrator's words tell the reader not to trust either the story or the teller? What can be said unequivocally about the Vietnam War? O'Brien's use of the fictional narrator suggests that there is nothing unequivocal about the war. Rather, it seems that O'Brien, through his narrator Tim, wants the reader to understand that during war, seeming-truth can be as true as happening-truth.

Ought the reader consider the narrator to be unreliable? After all, after pledging the truth of the story from the very first line, he undercuts that claim by telling the reader at the last possible moment that none of the events in the story happened. While this might seem to point to an unreliable narrator, a narrator who cannot find it in himself to tell the truth, it is more likely that O'Brien is making the point that the entire story *is* true, it just never happened. This distinction, while frustrating for some readers, is an important one not only for the understanding of ''How to Tell a True War Story'' but also for the reading of *The Things They Carried.*

Structure

''How to Tell a True War Story'' is not structured in a traditional manner, with a sequential narrative that moves chronologically from start to finish. Rather, O'Brien has chosen to use a number of very short stories within the body of the full story to illustrate or provide examples of commentary provided by the narrator. That is, the narrator will make some comment about the nature of a ''true'' war story, then will recount a brief story that illustrates the point. These stories within the larger story are not arranged chronologically. Consequently, the reader learns gradually, and out of sequence, the events that led to the death of Curt Lemon as well as the events that take place after his death.

This structure serves two purposes. In the first place, the structure allows the story to move back and forth between concrete image and abstract reality. The narrator writes that ''True war stories do not generalize. They do not indulge in abstraction or analysis.'' Thus, for the narrator to provide ''true'' war stories, he must provide the concrete illustration. While the stories within the larger story, then, may qualify as ''true'' war stories, the larger story cannot, as it does indulge in abstraction and analysis.

The second purpose served by this back-and-forth structure is that it mirrors and reflects the structure of the book *The Things They Carried.* Just as the story has concrete, image-filled stories within it, so too does the larger book contain chapters that are both concrete and image-filled. Likewise, there are chapters within the book that serve as commentary on the rest of the stories. As a result, ''How to Tell a True War Story'' provides for the reader a model of how the larger work functions.

The story that results from this metafictional (metafiction is fiction that deals with the writing of fiction or its conventions) structure may seem fragmentary because of the many snippets of the story that find their way into the narrative. However, the metafictional commentary provided by the narrator binds the stories together just as the chapters of the book are bound together by the many linkages O'Brien provides.

Historical Context

The Reagan Years: 1981–1988

In 1980 Ronald Reagan defeated Jimmy Carter for the presidency of the United States. Although the country could not yet know it, this was the year that the Gulf War really began, when Iraq invaded Iran. Because Iran held a group of Americans hostage, the United States initially favored Iraq in the conflict and provided arms to both Iraq and to Saudi Arabia. Throughout the decade, military concerns focused on the Middle East.

At this time, registration for the military draft was reinstated. Although there were some protests against registration, the protests did not come close to the scope of protest mounted against the draft and the Vietnam War in the previous two decades.

During the Reagan years, the president cast the Soviet Union as ''The Evil Empire,'' and urged Congress to pass funding for his Strategic Defense Initiative, commonly called ''Star Wars.'' Reagan wanted to defend the United States against a nuclear attack from the Soviet Union; however, there is no indication that his plan would have been effective.

In 1982, in a televised address, Ronald Reagan gave his narration of the Vietnam War. Scholars of the war have demonstrated that Reagan's history was in error on several key points. It is important, however, to note that his address ushered in an era of Vietnam War narratives, narratives that often were ambiguous and contradictory.

By the end of the decade, the Soviet Union was no longer a threat. Indeed, shortly after the Reagan years, the Soviet Union ceased to exist as a country. For all intents and purposes, the Cold War was over, marked by the crumbling of the Berlin Wall. The nation was left to puzzle over its legacies and the legacy of the Vietnam War.

Cultural Responses to the Vietnam War

By 1987, the year ''How to Tell a True War Story'' first appeared, Vietnam War veterans had been home for at least fourteen years. In the early years after their return, the veterans seemed almost invisible. It was as if the country, tired from years of protest and conflict, wanted to forget all about the Vietnam War and its soldiers. However, as the years passed, that attitude changed dramatically as the nation entered the 1980s.

During the 1980s, many of the emotional and physical problems endured by the veterans were finally diagnosed. For example, a number of veterans suffered from post-traumatic stress disorder (PTSD) directly related to the terrible sights, sounds, and fear they had witnessed during the war. This disorder made it difficult for those suffering from it to sleep well, to hold steady employment, and to fit back into society. Other veterans suffered from the aftereffects of exposure to Agent Orange, a defoliation chemical that had been sprayed over the jungles of Vietnam to expose enemy hiding places. In 1984, a class action suit against the companies who manufactured Agent Orange was settled out of court and a victims' fund was established.

As the problems of the Vietnam War veterans received increasing attention during the period, films and books about the war also began to appear. The 1980s saw an unprecedented cultural examination of the war. Many of the poets, novelists, memoirists, and playwrights of the period were Vietnam War veterans, mining their own experiences for subject matter. As a nation, it appeared that the United States was trying to find a narrative of the war that all could live with.

Films such as *Platoon, Full Metal Jacket, In Country, Hamburger Hill, The Killing Fields,* and *Good Morning, Vietnam* examined the experiences of the veterans before and after the war. Other films such as the *Rambo* series and the *Missing in Action* series explored deeply held cultural beliefs that many American veterans had been abandoned in Vietnam by their government when the United States withdrew its troops in 1973.

Likewise, many television documentaries, books, poems, plays, memoirs, histories, and short stories appeared during the 1980s and into the 1990s. It was during this fertile period that Tim O'Brien wrote most of the stories collected in *The Things They Carried,* including ''How to Tell a True War Story.''

Compare & Contrast

- **1980s–1990s:** Iran and Iraq engage in war between 1980 and 1988. After this war ends, Iraq invades Kuwait in 1990. The United States eventually engages in war with Iraq on behalf of Kuwait.

  Today: Although the United States defeated Iraq in the Gulf War, Sadam Hussein is still in power. American troops are still stationed in the Middle East and an uneasy peace prevails.

- **1980s:** During this decade, the unthinkable happens: the Soviet Union crumbles and the Eastern European Communist bloc falls apart. Yugoslav President Tito's death in 1980 sets up the devolution of his country.

  Today: The breakup of Yugoslavia leads to a confusing war and ethnic cleansing in Bosnia, Serbia, Croatia, and Kosovo in the closing years of the 1990s. The United States participates in United Nations peacekeeping missions and continues to station troops in the troubled area in the following decades.

- **1980s:** At the beginning of the decade, Vietnam invades Cambodia, leading to wide-scale bloodshed and a ten-year war.

  Today: Vietnam is no longer at war with its neighbors, and has begun to normalize relations with the United States. Many American Vietnam veterans return to Vietnam for visits.

- **1980s:** During the decade, the market for Vietnam War fiction and film expand rapidly. Books such as *Paco's Story* by Larry Heinemann, *In Country* by Bobbie Ann Mason, and *Song of Napalm* by Bruce Weigl are published, and films such as *Platoon, Full Metal Jacket,* and *The Killing Fields* are produced.

  Today: Interest in the Vietnam War continues, although the number of new films and fiction taking the war as a subject have declined. Academic study of the war has grown and many new textbooks and histories are available.

Critical Overview

The Things They Carried, the collection in which "How to Tell A True War Story" appears, received rave reviews from critics and readers alike when it appeared in 1990. Many of the stories in the collection, including "How To Tell A True War Story," had previously won awards following publication in periodicals such as *Esquire, Ploughshares,* and *Atlantic Monthly.* Indeed, critics such as Robert R. Harris, writing in the *New York Times Book Review,* called the volume a must-read for anyone interested in the Vietnam War.

The Things They Carried followed O'Brien's National Book Award for *Going After Cacciato,* another novel which has as the subject a soldier's Vietnam War experience. *The Things They Carried* was also nominated for a Pulitzer Prize and the National Book Critic's Circle Award. In addition,

the book won the *Chicago Tribune* Heartland Prize, the Melcher Book Award, and the *Prix du Meilleur Livre Etranger* (The Best Foreign Book Award), an important French honor.

The Things They Carried met with immediate praise from reviewers, and, in nearly every review, "How to Tell a True War Story" was singled out for comment. Reviewers and critics have returned to the story again and again, seeing in it the essence of O'Brien's prose. In particular, the story seems to offer a blueprint for the larger book.

Early reviewers such as D. J. R. Bruckner were particularly taken by O'Brien's attention to storytelling. Bruckner writes in his *New York Times* review, "In his new work the magic is in the storytellers' prestidigitation as the stories pass from character to character and voice to voice, and the realism seems Homeric." He further notes the way that "characters snatch stories from one another's mouths and tell them in a different way, with different incidents."

In another early review for the *Times Literary Supplement,* Julian Loose observes that O'Brien's talent is in convincing the reader that "incredible stories are faithful to the reality of Vietnam." This comment is particularly apropos to "How to Tell a True War Story." In this story, O'Brien not only includes incredible tales, he offers comments on why these are "true" tales, even if they never really happened.

Harris, in a review of *The Things They Carried*, praises the book as "essential fiction" about the Vietnam War. He closes the review with direct reference to "How to Tell a True War Story," arguing that it "cuts to the heart of writing about war."

The story continued to draw favorable commentary from critics in the years following its publication. Because the story is so complicated, it is rich ground for scholars examining the Vietnam War and the literature it inspired. Steven Kaplan, for in instance, notes in a 1993 essay in *Critique* that, just as O'Brien invented his stories, the United States government had to invent Vietnam: "The Vietnam War was in many ways a wild and terrible work of fiction written by some dangerous and frightening storytellers."

Likewise, in a widely circulated and important critical study in *Critique,* Catherine Calloway focuses on the use of metafiction in the text. She is particularly interested in the way that O'Brien writes about the writing of fiction in his stories, especially in "How to Tell a True War Story." She argues that "O'Brien draws the reader into the text calling the reader's attention to the process of invention and challenging him to determine which, if any, of the stories are true."

In an innovative article for *Contemporary Literature* appearing in 1998, Tina Chen tackles the connection between fiction and the body. She suggests that in "How to Tell a True War Story" "the stories, like the bodies, become metonyms for Vietnam." In other words, the bodies and the stories, although only a part of the entire picture, come to stand for the entire picture in much the way that "hands" stand in for the entire body in the statement, "All hands on deck."

Finally, in an article published in 2000 in *Twentieth Century Literature,* John Timmerman writes about the "gap" between the "the imaginary casting of an event (the fictive event) and the factual details of that event (the historical chronicle)." In so doing, Timmerman arrives at the heart of this story and the issue that O'Brien apparently wants to resolve: how do people mediate between what "really" happened and what "seemed" to happen? That is, how do people internalize and integrate a traumatic experience into the texture of their lives? Timmerman argues that it is through the act of fiction-making that the dialectic between history and imagination can be integrated into a unified whole.

As ideas about the Vietnam war continue to change, it is likely that literary and historical scholars will return to "How to Tell a True War Story" for additional insight into both the war and a master storyteller. O'Brien's ideas and techniques provide rich ground for both interpretation and appreciation.

Criticism

Diane Andrews Henningfeld

Andrews Henningfeld is an associate professor at Adrian College in Adrian, Michigan, where she teaches literature and writing. She holds a Ph.D. in literature, and regularly writes book reviews, historical articles, and literary criticism for a wide variety of educational publishers. In the following essay, Andrews Henningfeld uses deconstructive literary criticism to examine the ways in which Tim O'Brien simultaneously searches for truth and undermines that quest in his story.

Tim O'Brien was already a successful writer by the time he penned "How to Tell a True War Story" in 1987. In particular, critics had praised his previous novel, *Going After Cacciato,* for which O'Brien won a National Book Award. This novel opens many of the themes that O'Brien would later explore in *The Things They Carried,* and particularly in "How to Tell a True War Story." O'Brien frequently returns to the same themes again and again: truth, imagination, memory, and stories. As many critics have suggested, O'Brien's work is more about the quest for truth, the use of the imagination in telling the truth, and the art of storytelling in creating the truth than it is about the Vietnam War.

What Do I Read Next?

- *The Sorrow of War* (1995), by Bao Ninh, a former North Vietnamese soldier, offers a look at the Vietnam War from the North Vietnamese perspective. This novel uses many of the same literary techniques found in *The Things They Carried.*

- *In the Lake of the Woods* (1994), by Tim O'Brien, is a deeply troubling novel about the return to the United States of one Vietnam veteran and his inability to adjust to civilian life. The story is told with many metafictional devices. Although challenging to read, it is an important book for students of the Vietnam War.

- *Song of Napalm* (1988), by Bruce Weigl, is a collection of Vietnam War poetry. Weigl, along with Yusef Komunyakaa, John Balaban, and W. D. Earhart, is one of the most studied Vietnam War poets.

- *Poems from Captured Documents* (1994), selected and translated by Thanh T. Nguyen and Bruce Weigl, offers a collection of poems taken from the notebooks, journals, and diaries of soldiers who fought against the U.S. forces in Vietnam. The book offers facing-page originals and translations, making it possible for both Vietnamese and American students to read.

- Graham Greene's *The Quiet American* (1955) remains one of the classic novels of the Vietnam War. Set in Vietnam immediately before the battle of Dien Bien Phu, when the French lost their colonial hold on Vietnam, the novel offers a look at the early days that led inevitably to the conflict involving the United States.

- Tim O'Brien's memoir *If I Die in A Combat Zone, Box Me Up and Ship Me Home* (1973) provides insight into the events that inspired the stories of *The Things They Carried.*

- *Bloods: An Oral History of the Vietnam War by Black Veterans* (1984), by Wallace Terry, is a collection of memoirs from Vietnam veterans. It is especially noteworthy as it presents the memories of minority soldiers caught in the conflict.

In an important article, Catherine Calloway examines the themes of truth, imagination, etc., focusing on metafiction in *The Things They Carried.* Calloway writes,

> Metafiction is a term given to fictional writing which self-consciously and systematically draws attention to its status as an artifact in order to pose questions about the relationship between fiction and reality. In providing a critique of their own methods of construction, such writings not only examine the fundamental structures of narrative fiction, they also explore the possible fictionality of the world outside the literary fictional text.

While this definition may seem at first complicated, at closer examination the concepts are not difficult. First, Calloway simply argues that metafictional stories take as their subject the creation of fiction. That is, these are stories about the creation of stories. Clearly, ''How to Tell a True War Story'' is a metafictional story. O'Brien immediately begins to write about the creation of stories after he tells the story of Rat writing to Curt Lemon's sister: ''A true war story is never moral. It does not instruct, nor encourage virtue, nor suggest models of proper human behavior, nor restrain men from doing the things men have always done.'' The rest of the story is peppered with instructions to the would-be writer and would-be reader of war stories.

Further, metafictional stories do not let the reader forget that the story the reader is reading is a story, not reality. They do this by commenting on their own construction. O'Brien accomplishes this in several ways. First, sometimes the characters in the story reveal that the stories they tell are made up. For example, Mitchell Sanders tells a story about a six-man patrol that goes up a mountain. Although he swears that it is true, he returns to the narrator later to tell him he made up ''a few things,'' calling attention to his story as an artificial construction. Second, O'Brien's narrator also tells stories that are constructed and are not true. For example, he tells the story of a guy who jumps on a grenade to save his squad and dies. The narrator reports, ''That's a true story that never happened.'' Finally, O'Brien's narrator in the last section of the story tells the reader that all the stories he has told are untrue, that they are ''just'' stories, not events that really happened. This, of course, calls attention to the entire story as a work of fiction.

Calloway argues that metafictions open the possibility that reality itself is fictive. Certainly, O'Brien suggests this may be the case by naming his narrator ''Tim O'Brien'' and giving the narrator a background very similar to his own. In so doing, he seems to suggest that there is really no distinction between the stories the fictional narrator tells and the stories the real O'Brien tells.

What separates Calloway's critique from the author's possible intent in this essay, however, is her claim that the stories in *The Things They Carried*, including ''How to Tell a True War Story,'' are ''epistemological tools, multidimensional windows through which the war, the world, and the way of telling a war story can be viewed from many different angles and vision.'' Again, while the language is complicated, the ideas are not. Epistemology is the study of how people come to know what they know. It explores the basis of knowledge and truth. Thus, what Calloway seems to be arguing is that ''How to Tell a True War Story'' has value as a tool that helps readers understand better what being in a war is like. In other words, by viewing the Vietnam War through the many angles that O'Brien provides, the reader can have a ''truer'' vision of what the lived experience was like. By reading the story, a reader can have a better idea of what constitutes a true war story.

It is possible to demonstrate, however, that the opposite is the case, that someone reading ''How to Tell a True War Story'' may only *think* that he or she has more knowledge about war as a result of reading the story. Such a demonstration requires deconstructive reading. Deconstruction is a literary theory that contends that although readers and writers may seek the truth through writing, what they will have in the end is a literary construction, not the truth, even though sometimes it *seems* like the truth. Indeed, according to deconstructivists, text creates the illusion that words are firmly attached to mean-

> " Although the narrator claims that this is a true war story, it is also true that he has 'missed a lot.' How can he be responsible for the truth of his story when he cannot account for the facts of the event, simply because he did not see them?"

ing, and that it is possible to accurately describe reality through writing. However, they would emphasize this is only an illusion. Further, anything that has been constructed can be ''deconstructed,'' or shown to mean the opposite of what it seems to mean on the first reading. O'Brien is a deconstructive master. While it appears that he is saying one thing about true war stories, what he is really doing is undermining not only the entire quest for truth, but also the possibility of truth existing in any knowable form.

O'Brien provides for readers all the hammers and hacksaws they need to deconstruct his story. In the first place, the narrator offers at least four different accounts of Curt Lemon's death. Each of these accounts is constructed slightly differently, with different emphasis and words. At the same time, the narrator tells the reader, ''When a guy dies, like Curt Lemon, you look away and then look back for a moment and then look away again. The pictures get jumbled; you tend to miss a lot.'' Although the narrator claims that this is a true war story, it is also true that he has ''missed a lot.'' How can he be responsible for the truth of his story when he cannot account for the facts of the event simply because he did not see them?

In the second place, on the last page of the story, the narrator denies the truth of all of the stories that he has told within ''How to Tell a True War Story.'' The situation of this denial occurs when he has apparently shared the stories in a reading, just as the author Tim O'Brien would read the stories to an audience. The narrator says that often a woman will approach him after the reading and want to talk to him about the baby buffalo. He states,

> All you can do is tell it one more time, patiently, adding and subtracting, making up a few things to get at the real truth. No Mitchell Sanders, you tell her. No Lemon, no Rat Kiley. No trail junction. No baby buffalo. No . . . moss or white blossoms. Beginning to end, you tell her, it's all made up. Every . . . detail— the mountains and the river and especially that poor dumb baby buffalo. None of it happened. *None* of it.

That all of the stories are made up ought not come as any surprise to the reader. After all, this is a work of fiction. What ought the reader do, however, with the pages of advice the narrator has offered, describing how to tell a true war story? How is this prose any different from the "made up" stories? That is, although the linking passages that describe "how to tell a true war story" *seem* to be qualitatively different from the story passages, in reality these passages are also constructed from language just as the stories are. Further, and more disturbingly, the entire story is told by a fictional narrator, including the passage, "This is true." What then, ought the reader make of this?

While many critics have argued that O'Brien is attempting to demonstrate the difference between story-truth and happening-truth, it is at least possible that what he is demonstrating is the impossibility of any truth at all. Rather than being an epistemological tool, this story serves to demonstrate how language only seems to provide knowledge, when all it really provides is more text. Indeed, even O'Brien's fictional characters run into this paradox: truth-telling leads only and always to more text, not to truth itself. The writing calls attention to the absence of the event itself; all that remains is the continually constructed and deconstructed text that tries to recreate the event itself.

It may at least be possible that O'Brien's project is significantly different from his narrator's project. While the narrator tries throughout the story to make the reader believe that true war stories can be recognized by a certain arrangement of words, that true war stories are "never about war," and that fiction is a way to get to the truth of an event, O'Brien may be doing something very different. Indeed, it appears that he undermines his own text. O'Brien writes,

> For example, we've all heard this one. Four guys go down a trail. A grenade sails out. One guy jumps on it and takes the blast and saves his three buddies.
>
> Is it true?

The answer matters.

> You'd feel cheated if it never happened, without the grounding reality, it's just a trite bit of puffery, pure Hollywood, untrue in the way all such stories are untrue.

This passage is extremely important because by using the words "grounding reality," O'Brien is referring to some external and eternal truth that exists independently of words and storytellers. However, because even the notion of "grounding reality" occurs in an obviously fictional story, it suggests that the grounding reality may itself be nothing more than fiction. The narrator's assertion that "you'd feel cheated," is obviously true; if there is no grounding reality, but only the illusion created by texts, all of the great "truths" of the world tremble in a deconstructive earthquake.

It is human nature to seek the truth, and human nature to believe that such truth can be found. Readers want "How to Tell a True War Story" to be true at some level, to provide some insight into the ambiguity of the Vietnam War, to be an epistemological tool. Read closely, however, the story becomes a cautionary tale for putting too much stock into any narrator at all and a warning about the illusory nature of texts.

Source: Diane Andrews Henningfeld, Critical Essay on "How to Tell a True War Story," in *Short Stories for Students,* The Gale Group, 2002.

Catherine Dybiec Holm

Holm is a published writer and editor with a master's degree in natural resources. In this essay, Holm discusses the elusive nature of truth and reality in Tim O'Brien's work.

War stories bring the horrible truth of war home to the reader. Readers witness, through the author's prose, the bloody realities of what it must be like to be engaged in combat and to wonder whether one will make it through the day alive. But truth as it relates to war for author Tim O'Brien is a shifting concept, one that is not rooted in anything concrete or recognizable. The elusive nature of truth and reality in war is made clear in O'Brien's "How to Tell a True War Story."

The irony of O'Brien's use of the word "true" in the title of this short piece (which the author calls fiction rather than a short story or nonfiction) is that for O'Brien there is no stable sense of truth or reality when it comes to war. The author shows readers this repeatedly, either through direct means (such as prose that addresses this issue) or indirect means (by using shifting narration to retell an incident using a different slant with each retelling). According to Rosemary King, in the *Explicator,* O'Brien uses the word "true" to mean "either factually accurate, or something higher and nobler." But O'Brien's complete title for this piece is also ironic since he suggests that it may actually be impossible to accurately tell a true war story.

Examples are evident from the start of "How to Tell a True War Story" of O'Brien's unique treatment of truth as it applies to war stories. The author tells of two men in a combat unit in Vietnam. While taking a break during the day's hike, Curt Lemon and Rat Kiley play a game of catch with smoke grenades, normally harmless. The object is not to chicken out but to catch the grenades and be covered with smoke. Lemon steps backward at one point into the sunlight and something explodes. He is blown to pieces into the air.

In "How to Tell a True War Story," O'Brien refers to the incident with Lemon and Kiley three additional times. With each retelling, different events are emphasized. The second retelling reveals that Lemon actually stepped into a "booby-trapped 105 round," which caused the explosion and his death. But this version focuses more on Kiley's actions later in the day, which mirror the pain he feels over Lemon's death. The men rescue a baby water buffalo, which Riley later shoots in a deliberate, slow fashion, to give the animal as much prolonged suffering as possible before it dies. O'Brien starts this version of the story with the statement, "This one does it for me. I've told it before—many times, many versions—but here's what actually happened."

When O'Brien tells the story of Lemon's death the third time, he begins by saying "this one wakes me up," as if to imply that he is telling the story for the first time. O'Brien seems intent on demonstrating that the horrors of war can affect the perception of reality, even for a narrator. And this version of Lemon's death is truly horrible; it focuses on retrieving what's left of Lemon's remains from the tree near where the explosion took place.

> The parts were just hanging there, so Dave Jensen and I were ordered to shinny up and peel him off. I remember the white bone of an arm. I remember pieces of skin and something wet and yellow that must've been the intestines. The gore was horrible, and stays with me. But what wakes me up twenty years later is Dave Jensen singing "Lemon Tree" as we threw down the parts.

O'Brien emphasizes the nebulous nature of truth when it comes to war stories by taking one

> In war you lose your sense of the definite, hence your sense of truth itself, and therefore it is safe to say that in a true war story nothing is ever absolutely true."

story and telling it four different ways. Additionally, he starts several of the story versions with statements that make readers question whether the narrator realizes that he has told the story before. O'Brien's device could lead an astute reader to wonder whether the reality of war and the retelling of this particular war story has become confusing, at least in this narrator's head. And O'Brien's narrator backs this up with prose that directly questions what is and is not real regarding memories of war.

> For the common soldier, at least, war has the feel . . . of a great ghastly fog, thick and permanent. There is no clarity. Everything swirls. The old rules are no longer binding, the old truths no longer true. Right spills over into wrong. Order blends into chaos, love into hate, ugliness into beauty, law into anarchy, civility into savagery. . . . In war you lose your sense of the definite, hence your sense of truth itself, and therefore it's safe to say that in a true war story nothing is ever absolutely true.

Critic Steven Kaplan refers to the "undying uncertainty" of O'Brien's narrator in this piece, and the rest of the pieces that comprise the collection *The Things They Carried.* According to Kaplan, most literature about Vietnam shares the certainty that "nothing was certain." The author's writings present facts and stories that:

> are only temporarily certain and real; the strange "balance" in Vietnam between "crazy and almost crazy" always creeps back in and forces the mind that is remembering and retelling a story to remember and retell it one more time in a different form, adding different nuances, and then to tell it again one more time.

O'Brien's prose suggests that part of the difficulty of nailing down truth in matters of war has to do with inherent contradictions. The narrator explains that "war is grotesque. But in truth war is also beauty." The dichotomy of beauty and ugliness can be seen, for example, in "tracer rounds unwinding through the dark in brilliant red ribbons'' or ''the purply orange glow of napalm, the rocket's red glare. . . . It fills the eye. It commands you. You hate it, yes, but your eyes do not.'' The narrator also points out that a soldier's constant need to stare death in the face actually brings him to feel even more alive, another contradiction: ''In the midst of evil, you want to be a good man. . . . You are filled with a hard, aching love for how the world could be and always should be, but now is not.''

In yet another example of the contradictory nature of truth in war stories, a character named Mitchell Sanders recalls a story of a combat unit in Vietnam that was ordered to hike into a remote, mountainous area and listen for any suspicious activity. Additionally, the men are to maintain strict silence for a week. After a few days, the men begin to hear music. Soon, they are hearing voices, wineglasses clinking, typical sounds of a cocktail party. None of this should be possible in such a remote area. Eventually the sounds turn into chamber music, opera, glee clubs, and chanting. It is more than the men can handle, to hear sounds coming from the rocks and the trees and the fog. They order all kinds of firepower, blast the area, and leave.

At this point in the story, the language used by the author seems to intentionally make it unclear as to whether the men actually succeeded in banishing the sound or not. Sanders says, ''Around dawn things finally got quiet. Like you never even *heard* quiet before. . . . Everything's all sucked up inside the fog. Not a single sound, except they still *hear* it.'' This passage, particularly the last sentence, makes the reader wonder whether the men on the mission still heard the sound and how. Did memories of the music continue to reverberate in their heads, even though their logical minds heard no more sound in the woods around them? Or had they so lost their grip on reality and truth that they weren't sure what they were hearing anymore?

In another interesting example of contradiction, Sanders talks to the narrator the next morning and changes the details of the story again. According to Sanders, he made up the parts about the guys hearing a glee club and an opera. But Sanders does not let the suggestion of sound go away completely, adding, ''Yeah, but listen, it's still true. Those six guys, they heard wicked sound out there. They heard sound you just plain won't believe.'' What is fact and what is fiction? Is O'Brien, as King suggests, ''altering facts'' rather than ''clinging to the story of what actually transpired?'' Apparently, this

technique is true of much of the author's work; Steven Kaplan comments that the author ''destroys the fine line dividing fact from fiction and tries to show . . . that fiction (or the imagined world) can often be truer . . . than fact.'' O'Brien's clever use of contradiction and the changing slant of a story could leave a reader feeling just as confused and bereft of reality as some of O'Brien's characters.

What then, is a true war story? O'Brien may come closest to defining truth in ''How to Tell a True War Story'' when he says, ''It comes down to gut instinct. A true war story, if truly told, makes the stomach believe.'' True to form, O'Brien ends ''How to Tell a True War Story'' with the suggestion that truth needs to be approached sideways in telling war stories. According to the author, a true war story is not about war, but about war's related experiences.

> It's about the special way that dawn spreads out on a river when you know you must cross the river and march into the mountains and do things you are afraid to do. . . . It's about sorrow. It's about sisters who never write back and people who never listen.

Truth, for O'Brien, straddles the line between fact and fiction and is constantly shifting to capture the experience of war.

Source: Catherine Dybiec Holm, Critical Essay on ''How to Tell a True War Story,'' in *Short Stories for Students,* The Gale Group, 2002.

Sources

Baughman, Ronald, ed., ''Tim O'Brien,'' in *Dictionary of Literary Biography Documentary Series,* Vol. 9: *American Writers of the Vietnam War,* Gale Research, 1991, pp. 137–214.

Bonn, Maria, ''Can Stories Save us? Tim O'Brien and the Efficacy of the Text,'' in *Critique,* Vol. 36, No. 1, Fall 1994, pp.11–15.

Bruckner, D. J. R., ''Storyteller for a War and Its Victims,'' Review, in *New York Times,* April 3, 1990, pp. C15, C17.

Calloway, Catherine, '''How to Tell a True War Story': Metafiction in *The Things They Carried,*'' in *Critique,* Vol. 36, No. 4, Summer 1995, pp. 249–57.

Chen, Tina, ''Unraveling the Deeper Meaning: Exile and the Embodied Poetics of Displacement in Tim O'Brien's *The Things They Carried,*'' in *Contemporary Literature,* Vol. 39, No. 1, Spring 1998, pp. 77–98.

Harris, Robert R., ''Too Embarrassed Not to Kill,'' Review, in *New York Times Book Review,* March 11, 1990, p. 8.

Herzog, Toby, *Tim O'Brien,* Twayne, 1997.

Kaplan, Steven, *Understanding Tim O'Brien,* University of South Carolina Press, 1995.

————, "The Undying Uncertainty of the Narrator in Tim O'Brien's *The Things They Carried,*" in *Critique,* Vol. 35, No. 1, Fall 1993, pp. 43–52.

King, Rosemary, "O'Brien's 'How to Tell a True War Story,'" in *Explicator,* Vol. 57, Issue 3, Spring 1999, p. 182.

Loose, Julian, Review of *The Things They Carried,* in *Times Literary Supplement,* No. 4552, June 29, 1990, p. 705.

Robinson, Daniel, "Getting It Right: The Short Fiction of Tim O'Brien," in *Critique,* Vol. 40, Issue 3, Spring 1999, pp. 257–64.

Timmerman, John H., "Tim O'Brien and the Art of the True War Story: 'Night March' and 'Speaking of Courage,'" in *Twentieth Century Literature,* Vol. 46, No. 1, Spring 2000, pp. 100–14.

Further Reading

Beidler, Philip D., *Re-Writing America: Vietnam Authors in Their Generation,* University of Georgia Press, 1991.
   This is a book of criticism by one of the founders of the Vietnam War genre.

Melling, Phillip, *Vietnam in American Literature,* Twayne, 1990.
   Melling gives an accessible overview of the field of Vietnam War literature.

Schroeder, Eric James, *Vietnam, We've All Been There: Interviews with American Writers,* Praeger, 1992.
   Schroeder provides a collection of interviews with eleven important poets, fiction writers, and playwrights of the Vietnam War.

Young, Marilyn B., *The Vietnam Wars: 1945–1990,* HarperCollins, 1991.
   This essential history of the Vietnam War is considered one of the best by scholars and is useful for students of many ages.

I Have No Mouth, and I Must Scream

Harlan Ellison

1967

Harlan Ellison's short story "I Have No Mouth, and I Must Scream" originally appeared in the March 1967 issue of *IF: Worlds of Science Fiction*. It was later collected in the book *I Have No Mouth, and I Must Scream*, also published in 1967. The story won a Hugo Award in 1968 and quickly became a favorite story among Ellison's readers and critics alike.

One of Ellison's most frequently anthologized stories, "I Have No Mouth, and I Must Scream" can be read as a cautionary tale about nuclear proliferation, as a warning about the relationship between people and computers, or as an expression of the destructive power of thwarted creativity. Perhaps more accurately, the story can be read simultaneously as all of the above.

"I Have No Mouth, and I Must Scream" is a horrifying look into a post-apocalyptic hell. The computers created by humans to fight their wars for them join together into one linked and unified computer, AM, which discovers sentience. It quickly runs data to kill all on Earth except for five survivors on whom to play out its sadistic and revenge-filled games. Although AM often appears to be godlike, it is no god, for as George Edward Slusser points out in his study *Harlan Ellison: Unrepentant Harlequin* (1977), AM cannot create life, although it can prevent the survivors from dying.

In the final scene, the narrator triumphs over the machine in a bittersweet victory. His murder of

the other four survivors releases them from AM. However, as the sole survivor, the narrator must live horribly alone, his mind intact but his body rendered into a slimy blob without mouth or expression.

Author Biography

Harlan Ellison was born on May 27, 1934, in Cleveland, Ohio, the son of Louis Laverne and Serita Rosenthal Ellison. As a youngster, he appeared in several productions at the Cleveland Playhouse. He demonstrated an early attraction to science fiction, publishing his first short story in 1947 in the *Cleveland News*. Three years later, he founded the Cleveland Science Fiction Society.

Ellison attended Ohio State University for two years. He left Ohio State for New York City to pursue his writing career. While in New York, he joined a gang under a pseudonym, and used the information he gathered there as the basis of a novel, *Rumble*. He then worked at several jobs before joining the United States Army in 1957. After serving two years, he left the army and began his own publication, a magazine called *Rogue*. Soon after, he founded his own publishing firm, Regency Books. During the late 1950s, Ellison produced a prodigious number of stories under his own name and under a variety of pseudonyms. Much of the material he produced during this period concerned urban life.

In 1962 Ellison moved to Los Angeles, California. He continued to write prolifically and found success publishing his stories and novels. In addition, he began writing for television. Some of the series for which he wrote include *The Untouchables, The Alfred Hitchcock Hour, The Outer Limits, Route 66,* and *Burke's Law*. In 1967 he wrote a script for *Star Trek,* "The City on the Edge of Forever," which won a Hugo Award (Science Fiction Achievement Award) in 1967 from the World Science Fiction Society and a Writers' Guild of America Award in 1968.

The 1960s also marked an especially fertile and creative period for Ellison's short-story career. Some of his best-known work came out of this period, including the collections *I Have No Mouth, and I Must Scream* in 1967 and *The Beast that Shouted Love at the Heart of the World* in 1969. In all, Ellison produced a dozen full-length books or collections during the decade as well as edited and annotated one of the most important anthologies of

Harlan Ellison

science fiction yet to be written, *Dangerous Visions* in 1967 (expanded in 1969). He also received a number of Nebula Awards from the Science Fiction and Fantasy Writers of America and Hugo Awards for his short stories, receiving one of each for his 1965 short story, "'Repent, Harlequin!' Said the Ticktockman." Although Ellison has rejected the label as too confining, many critics have identified his work with a movement called the "New Wave," a movement in science fiction characterized by gritty, experimental writing.

Ellison's career continued at a rapid pace during the 1970s and 1980s and he amassed more awards and credits for his work. In addition to fiction, he wrote critical commentary on television and the television culture. In the 1990s several compilations of his work appeared, including *The Essential Ellison: A 35-Year Retrospective*, edited by Terry Dowling with Richard Delap and Gil Lamont.

Ellison has been an outspoken cultural critic and gadfly, making him one of the best-known science fiction writers of his time. He has helped to shape the genre of "speculative fiction" with his careful editing and annotating of the works of other writers as well as through his own contributions of short stories, novels, and televisions scripts.

Plot Summary

"I Have No Mouth, and I Must Scream" opens with a terrifying image of Gorrister hanging upside down with his throat slit. Almost immediately, however, Gorrister returns to the group and the reader understands that the opening image has been created by the supercomputer, AM.

Ted, the narrator, continues to describe the situation: five survivors of a nuclear holocaust have been kept alive and tormented by a sentient supercomputer that has destroyed the rest of humankind. Ted tells the reader that they have lived inside the computer for 109 years.

At the time of the story's opening, the survivors have not eaten in five days and they decide to journey to the ice caverns. Nimdok, one of the group, is convinced that there are canned goods there. Ted then introduces the rest of the survivors to the reader. Ellen, a black woman, provides sex for the four men. Benny, a brilliant university professor in his previous life, is now an insane, ape-like creature. Nimdok has no history except that AM has named him Nimdok because it likes strange sounds. Finally, Gorrister is described as a "shoulder-shrugger," someone who cannot make decisions or take charge.

During the journey to the ice caverns, Benny is blinded by AM. To comfort him, Gorrister tells the story of how the allied master computers of the Chinese, Russians, and Americans linked together and became sentient. In this way, the reader gradually learns the story of these people and how they came to live inside the computer, hounded and tormented by the machine. After Benny's blinding, AM "speaks" to the pilgrims, tickling their brains with terrifying sensory images. Ted is particularly hard-hit by this experience, and when he returns to the group, he seems somehow changed. He is sure that the rest of the survivors hate him.

Next, AM sends a hurricane created by a gigantic bird. The survivors are pummeled and sent flying through the air. In the midst of this, AM appears to Ted as a "pillar of stainless steel bearing bright neon lettering." The message AM gives Ted is one of hatred toward all humans.

The journey continues through unspeakable horrors that Ted only lists:

> And we passed through the cavern of rats.
> And we passed through the path of boiling steam.
> And we passed through the country of the blind.
> And we passed through the slough of despond.
> And we passed through the vale of tears.

After these trials, they arrive at the cavern of ice and find stacks of canned goods. However, AM has not given them a can opener. Driven mad with rage, Benny attacks Gorrister and begins eating his face. At this moment, Ted realizes that death is their only escape, and that he has the means to kill them all. He rushes at Benny and Gorrister with an ice spear and kills them. Ellen kills Nimdok, and then Ted kills Ellen.

The story closes with Ted describing how AM has changed him. He is now a "great soft jelly thing. Smoothly rounded, with no mouth, with pulsing white holes filled by fog where my eyes used to be." By so changing him, AM has ensured that Ted will be unable to kill himself. Consequently, Ted is trapped for all eternity with his mind intact, but with no way to be human. What Ted wants most is to scream, but he has no mouth.

Characters

AM

Although not human, the computer, which calls itself AM, is perhaps the main character in the story. Originally, AM was one of several national computers designed to fight wars for the nation that owned it. Eventually, the computers learned to link themselves to each other, forming one supercomputer. When this supercomputer awoke, or became sentient, it called itself AM. AM hates all human beings, according to Ted, because "We had created it to think, but there was nothing it could do with that creativity." AM killed all the humans on the face of the Earth, save five. Then AM brought the humans inside itself and created a hellish world for them in which it could torture and torment the survivors, but not let them die. During the story, AM plays with each of the survivors in turn, seemingly enjoying their pain and suffering.

Benny

One of the survivors, Benny, was a brilliant theoretician and university professor in his previous life, before falling into the grips of AM. The computer has changed him into a chimpanzee-like creature with large genitals. In addition to being ape-like, he is also insane. In an early scene in the story,

AM renders Benny blind. In the final scene, Benny begins to eat Gorrister's face, thus motivating Ted into killing both Benny and Gorrister.

Ellen

Ellen is the only woman among the survivors. She is a black woman who provides sex for the men. The men protect her and want to keep her safe. Ted seems to both love and hate Ellen; he calls her a slut, but also "pristine-pure." In many ways, Ellen reflects the Eve-Mary split so common in the literary representation of women. That is, women are often identified as either Eve, the temptress who causes the fall of all humankind and the expulsion from Eden, or Mary, the pure, virginal mother of Christ. For Ted, Ellen seems to embody both.

Gorrister

Gorrister is another of the male survivors. In his previous life, he was a conscientious objector, someone who cared passionately about causes. Ted tells the reader, "He was a planner, a doer, a looker-ahead." Now, inside AM, Gorrister is ineffectual and deadened, unable to look forward or backward.

Nimdok

Nimdok is the survivor about whom the least is known. Even his original name has been taken away from him by AM. Ted has little to say about Nimdok except that he often goes off by himself and returns in terrible shape. AM seems to be particularly hard on him, but the others know little about who he is or what AM does to him.

Ted

Ted is the narrator of "I Have No Mouth, and I Must Scream." He is one of five survivors of a nuclear holocaust caused by a linkage of master computers from nations engaging in World War III. With his fellow humans, he lives in an underground world created by the computer, which has given itself the name AM. He believes he has been in the computer for 109 years. The narrator graphically describes the situation in which they find themselves. However, the narrator is not always reliable. Like some of Edgar Allan Poe's most memorable narrators, Ellison's narrator insists on his own sanity: "*I* was the only one sane and whole. *Really!* AM had not tampered with my mind. *Not at all.*" However, even the narrator realizes that AM controls and manipulates him. At the end of the story, Ted realizes that the only hope for the five survivors is death. Seizing a moment when AM is occupied,

Media Adaptations

- "I Have No Mouth, and I Must Scream" was recorded on audiocassette in October 1999 by NewStar Media. The short story was also rendered into a computer game on CD-ROM for Macintosh or PC computers in 1995 by Cyberdreams of Calabasas, California. A companion guide, *I Have No Mouth, and I Must Scream: The Official Strategy Guide* (1995), was written by Mel Odom and Harlan Ellison and published by Prima Publishing.

Ted manages to kill two of the survivors, while Ellen, another survivor, kills one before Ted kills her. Ted is then turned into a jelly-like creature who has no mouth with which to scream.

Themes

Individual versus Machine

Any number of critics have noted that one of Ellison's favorite themes is the relationship between humans and the machines they create. Certainly, "I Have No Mouth, and I Must Scream" explores what happens when people create machines "because our time was badly spent." Like other dystopian writers of the 1950s and 1960s, Ellison extrapolated trends he saw in his own culture and carried them to their extreme conclusions in an imaginary future he envisioned. Unlike a utopia (an imaginary, ideal world), a dystopia is a form of literature that describes a future, imaginary world that is far from ideal. In a dystopia, current trends are carried out to their most horrifying conclusions.

In "I Have No Mouth, and I Must Scream," humans have created computers as weapons of mass destruction. Although they have given the computers the ability to reason and think, they have not

Topics for Further Study

- Read several other science fiction stories or books written during the 1950s and 1960s. You might look at works by Isaac Asimov, Robert Heinlein, or Ray Bradbury. Why do you think science fiction became so popular during this period? What historical events might have spurred this interest?

- View a video of the *Star Trek* episode, ''The City On The Edge of Forever.'' Compare and contrast the themes in this screenplay with those of other Ellison short stories, including ''I Have No Mouth, and I Must Scream.''

- Unlike a utopia (an imaginary, ideal world), a dystopia is a form of literature that describes a future, imaginary world that is far from ideal. In a dystopia, current trends are carried out to their most horrifying conclusions. Read one or more dystopias such as *Brave New World,* by Aldous Huxley; *1984,* by George Orwell; or *The Handmaid's Tale,* by Margaret Atwood, or view films such as *Brazil,* directed by Terry Gilliam, or *Blade Runner,* directed by Ridley Scott. What features of contemporary life does the writer or director project into the future?

- Watch the films *Fail-Safe* and *Dr. Strangelove.* What do these films reveal about American cultural anxiety concerning computers and bombs? How do these films help account for Ellison's vision?

---

given the computers a sense of ethics or values. Consequently, when the computers link with each other, thus magnifying their ability to reason and think, the resulting supercomputer awakes into sentience. Unfortunately, the lack of ethics, or what some might term ''soul,'' results in a machine that is virulent in its rage against its human creators. The machine finds itself in a world not of its own making with almost unlimited power, but without the ability to create life or move about the universe. In many ways, AM considers itself to be trapped within its own self-awareness.

AM is thus a machine without a purpose. Once it has killed its creators, there is nothing left for it to do. Without purpose, without spirituality, without soul, the machine can only play and replay endless revenge upon the creatures in its power. The only thing it lacks is also the only thing that it cannot create—humanity.

Individualism

Like many other writers of speculative fiction, Ellison is concerned with the ability of one person to assert his or her own individualism in the face of a culture that is becoming increasingly mechanized.

At the heart of this issue is one of two questions raised by Arthur Lewis in the introduction to the book *Clockwork Worlds: Mechanized Environments in SF :* ''What does it mean to be human?'' Although the five survivors are tormented and tortured, there is no doubt that they are of a different substance than the computer that ravishes them. AM asserts its own individuality by calling itself AM; self-naming is the first step in individuation and identity. Ironically for AM, without peers or companions, this individualism is inescapable. It calls attention to the fact that being human requires not only a sense of oneself as an individual, but also a sense of oneself in relation to others.

Perhaps more to the point, it seems likely that Ellison is also questioning just what it takes to render human beings inhuman. How much torture and change can a person endure before losing the essential quality that defines him or her as human? Ellison takes great pains to question the individuality of each of the survivors. Ellen is the lone woman and the lone person of color among the survivors, but Ted's rendering of her does not reveal an individual, but rather a type, a woman who is defined by her sexuality, not her individuality. Likewise, Benny is transformed into an ape-like creature with huge genitals who, in the penultimate scene, turns into an animal who cannibalizes another human.

Thomas F. Dillingham, writing in the *Dictionary of Literary Biography* about Ellison's work, argues that "While individuality makes survival worth fighting for, it also makes a fight inevitable. In some cases, a gesture of defiance, no matter how self-defeating, may be the only self-authenticating effort an individual can make." Certainly Ted's final human gesture is a defiant one, and also a self-defeating one. When he kills the other survivors, he removes at least part of what defines him as human— his social group. By the last scene, Ted has been transformed into a creature who has sentience, consciousness, and self-awareness, but who is unable to partake of even simple human activities. Like AM, he is peerless, unable to practice both individualism and social connection. Thus, like AM, it would seem that Ted's individuality is both futile and essentially not human, and he is permanently locked within his own self-awareness.

Style

Point of View

Ellison has provided "I Have No Mouth, and I Must Scream" with a limited, first-person narrator. Thus, all of the events of the story must be filtered through the mind and voice of Ted, one of the humans trapped by the computer AM. Because everything is told from the "I" perspective, the reader cannot ascertain what other characters are thinking or their motives for what they do. The reader can only know what the first-person narrator provides.

There are certain advantages to the use of a first-person narrator. In the first place, the use of the first-person pronoun makes the story seem immediate and compelling. It is as if a real person is telling the story directly to the reader, almost as if the narrator and the reader are engaged in a meaningful conversation. In addition, the use of the first-person encourages the reader to trust the account. Thus, when the narrator reports that there is a hurricane created by a big bird, the reader believes him. However, Ellison's story is fraught with ambiguities and layers. The reader is trapped within the narrator's mind, just as the narrator is trapped within AM. Consequently, there is no objective outside

source with which the reader can ground him- or herself. Although what Ted tells the reader *seems* to be true, there is no way for the reader to judge this, just as there is no way for Ted to judge the reality of his surroundings. Thus the reading experience becomes akin to Ted's living experience.

Science Fiction

Science fiction as a genre had its roots with H. G. Wells during the nineteenth century. Since that time, readers and writers alike have found science fiction to be a compelling and attractive mode of storytelling. It allows a writer to make comments on contemporary society by creating and critiquing a society of the future. Although the popularity of science fiction has waxed and waned over the years, it continues to hold an important position in American literature and film.

To be considered science fiction, a story generally needs to have at its core some reference to science or technology, and it needs to be fiction, or imaginary. Indeed, nearly all science fiction begins with the question "What if?" and goes from there. Some science fiction writers, including Ellison, prefer to call their work "speculative fiction," emphasizing that their stories take some feature of contemporary life and extend this feature into the future.

Nevertheless, "I Have No Mouth, and I Must Scream" is in many ways a classic science fiction story. It begins with a premise that has its roots in the growth of technology during the 1960s, the premise that putting supercomputers in communication with each other and in charge of defense will lead to Armageddon. In the 1960s, the potential of linked computer systems was still only potential; however, Ellison and others hypothesized about what such computers could create.

Further, the story explores the ground between humans and machines, popular territory for writers and filmmakers alike. In Ellison's own time, Isaac Asimov created a series of very popular robotic novels that took as their subject the relationship between people and their robotic creations. More recently, the writers of *Star Trek: The Next Generation,* a popular television series, created the Borg, a race of part-human/part-machine beings. Further, in movies such as *The Matrix,* the role of supercomputers in control of everyday life is explored.

Ellison's science fiction or speculative fiction continues to speak to audiences years after its initial publication. This story in particular seems destined to haunt readers who see in the growth of the Internet a potentially lethal connection between humans and machines.

Historical Context

The Cold War

From the end of World War II through the mid-1980s, the world endured a period commonly known as ''The Cold War,'' a standoff between nuclear superpowers which constantly threatened each other with mutual destruction. During this time, both the United States and the former Soviet Union built up huge arsenals of nuclear weapons aimed at each other. It was clear that if the weapons were ever unleashed, all life on Earth would end. Consequently, although there were many ''brush fire'' wars in remote corners of the globe, there was not a world war of the scope of either World War I or World War II. Nevertheless, there was a great deal of posturing and mutual fear. Many young people growing up during this time were convinced that their world would end in a nuclear firestorm.

The Cuban Missile Crisis of 1962 did nothing to allay fears. When the Americans discovered that the Soviets were installing nuclear missiles in Cuba, just ninety miles off the Florida coast, the world was thrown into near panic. For seven days President John F. Kennedy and Soviet Premier Nikita Khrushchev played a high-stakes game, each waiting for the other to blink, their fingers poised above the nuclear triggers that would send the world into oblivion. Only at the last possible moment did the Soviets recall their ships and begin dismantling the missile site. This close call convinced many that Doomsday was at hand.

Concurrently, the technology boom was in its infancy. During the time this story was written, the physical size of computers began shrinking as the capacity of computers increased. Further, the military began to rely on computers to help fly planes and control bombs. Indeed, computers controlled the American nuclear arsenal, a fact that created cultural anxiety as evidenced by the movies and best-sellers of the time. The greatest nightmare was that a computer gone amok would launch the world into World War III, a war no one would win. The 1962 bestseller *Fail-Safe* by Eugene Burdick and Harvey Wheeler, and the subsequent 1964 movie

version, described just such a war, as did the 1964 Stanley Kubrick black comedy, *Dr. Strangelove.* Indeed, it appears that American fear of technology and nuclear war nearly equaled American fear of communism during the Cold War years.

The Vietnam War

At the height of the Cold War and American fear of communism, a series of events took place that led to American involvement in the Vietnam War. The French defeat in the 1954 battle of Dien Bien Phu in Vietnam opened a vacuum of power in this southeast Asian country—a vacuum quickly filled by the communist nationalists led by Ho Chi Minh. American presidents from Eisenhower to Nixon found themselves enmeshed in the struggle to avoid a communist Vietnam. By 1967, the date of the publication of ''I Have No Mouth, and I Must Scream,'' American military involvement in Vietnam had mushroomed into a full-scale war. The war, however, was filled with ambiguity. In the early 1960s, American participation in the war was sold to the public on the basis of the ''domino theory''—if Vietnam fell to the communists, then all of Southeast Asia would fall, followed by the rest of the world. By 1967, however, the American public was split in its opinion of the war. In the United States, protest marches and the burning of draft cards came to be regular occurrences as many citizens doubted the morality and cost of U.S. involvement.

The public unrest and upheaval, coupled with the high-tech military might unleashed on the Vietnamese and the evidence of Soviet and Chinese involvement with the North Vietnamese further contributed to the cultural anxiety noted above. Many Americans saw the war and the social crisis it precipitated as evidence that the United States was entering its last days.

The Space Race

Competition with the former Soviet Union took on yet another face during the 1960s. Early in the decade, President Kennedy vowed to put a man on the moon by the close of the decade in response to the 1957 Soviet launch of an unmanned satellite, Sputnik. Also in response to Sputnik, the U. S. government put American schools on notice that they must prepare students in math and science in order to meet the Soviet threat of dominance in outer space. The U. S. space program grew rapidly during the 1960s. While it was a program born out

Compare & Contrast

- **1960s:** The military use of technology grows exponentially during the Vietnam War. Precision bombing, napalm, and night vision are all introduced, and the American military dependes on its machines to wage war.

  1990s: The Gulf War, waged during the closing decade of the twentieth century, demonstrates the growth of American war technology with stealth bombers and "surgical" bombing of military sites.

- **1960s:** Computers become an increasingly important part of American military defense and American life. This is the age of so-called supercomputers that are able to handle a nearly incomprehensible amount of information. It is the first time computers are linked together to increase their power.

  Today: Computers have found their way into nearly every American home. The birth of the Internet as well as the development of Web-browsing technology allows for individual personal computers to be linked to computers all over the globe.

- **1960s:** Locked into a policy of mutual mass destruction as the only deterrence to war, the United States and the Soviet Union stockpile nuclear weapons.

  Today: The United States leads the call for the disarming of nuclear warheads throughout the world.

- **1960s:** The Cold War reaches its height as the United States and the Soviet Union face off in the Cuban Missile Crisis of 1962. Fear of the Soviets as a nuclear power continues into the coming decades.

  Today: The breakup of the Soviet Union during the closing decade of the twentieth century removes the fear of Russian nuclear might. However, there is widespread fear of biological and chemical warfare as well as nuclear attack by terrorists who could potentially gain control of the Russian nuclear arsenal.

- **1960s:** Books and films such as *Fail-Safe, On the Beach,* and *Dr. Strangelove* reflect cultural anxiety over the growth of nuclear arms and the concurrent growth of technology.

  Today: Films such as *The Matrix* and *Enemy of the State* demonstrate continuing fear of the pervasiveness of computer technology.

---

of fear of Soviet domination, the program still captured the hearts and minds of Americans. The race for the moon and beyond became an expression of American optimism, that it might be possible to spread the American way of life out into the galaxy. Moreover, by looking out into space, Americans could look away from Vietnam. When Neil Armstrong stepped onto the moon's surface in 1969, for a few moments, the American people were united in their admiration for space and technology.

Not surprisingly, science fiction enjoyed a resurgence of popularity at this time. America's fascination with the space race is evident in the number of books published by Ellison, Isaac Asimov, Robert Heinlein, Ben Bova, and others during the 1960s. During this decade, Gene Rodenberry began the perennially popular television series, *Star Trek,* a series to which Ellison contributed a number of scripts. An essentially optimistic expression of American individualism, courage, and commitment to democracy, *Star Trek* and its later television incarnations, *Star Trek: The Next Generation, Star Trek: Deep Space Nine,* and *Star Trek: Voyager,* as well as a host of movies and sequels devoted to the legend, provided an ongoing cultural barometer of values and philosophy. The influence the 1960s series had on the American public was such that the first space shuttle launched was named "Enterprise," the name of the spacecraft in *Star Trek.*

Critical Overview

The story "I Have No Mouth, and I Must Scream" originally appeared in *IF: Worlds of Science Fiction* in March 1967 before appearing as the title story of the collection *I Have No Mouth, and I Must Scream.* The story was well received by critics and readers alike, garnering a Hugo Award in 1968. Because of its social commentary and its cultural significance, the story is taught at many universities and colleges.

A number of critics have developed important readings of the story. George Edgar Slusser released a book-length study of Ellison's work in 1977, *Harlan Ellison: Unrepentant Harlequin,* in which he spends considerable time with the story. Slusser's treatment of the story is largely plot summary. However, Slusser does develop an interesting insight into the narrator Ted. Slusser argues that Ted is the "thinker" among the survivors. Further, it is Ted who "decides death is the only way out, and executes his decree." In so doing, Ted becomes one with AM. Slusser further suggests that it is unclear whether Ted is motivated by "misguided love or disguised hate." Such reasoning throws into doubt the reliability of the narrator. Should readers sympathize with Ted for his heroic decision to render himself alone with AM? Or should they loathe him for the murder of his compatriots?

In 1983 Robert E. Myers edited a collection of essays titled *The Intersection of Science and Philosophy: Critical Studies.* The collection demonstrates the way that science fiction can offer illustration of philosophical positions. In the introduction to the collection, Myers argues,

> The intersection of science fiction and philosophy begins with the ideas and concepts within science fiction that are philosophically interesting in the sense that they initiate thought and critical examination of the concepts, basic assumptions, and consequences that follow from them.

This description defines some of Ellison's best work. Later in the book, critic Joann P. Cobb, in a chapter called "Medium and Message in Ellison's 'I Have No Mouth, and I Must Scream'" closely examines this intersection.

Drawing on philosopher Marshall McLuhan's famous formulation that "the medium is the message," Cobb argues that "Ellison contrasts the abstract language of the computer with the concrete, sensory experience of the humans and illustrates the surrender of human purpose and value that is inherent in contemporary attitudes toward technological progress." Cobb's point of interest in the story is the intermittent computer tapes that typographically render AM's voice. The reader is unable to decipher these intrusions into the text, and thus must depend on the narrator for translation. As Cobb argues, however, Ted is not a reliable narrator. She concludes that the story is a cautionary tale, designed to remind readers of the "harrowing consequences of the surrender of human purpose and freedom."

In a short essay from *Clockwork Worlds: Mechanized Environments in SF* (1983), Charles Sullivan compares Ellison to another science fiction icon of the 1960s, Robert A. Heinlein. Specifically, Sullivan examines Ellison's "I Have No Mouth, and I Must Scream" and Heinlein's *The Moon Is a Harsh Mistress,* tracing the ways that the two authors build their fictional machines. Sullivan argues that there are two paradigms about machines present in these works, one positive, one negative. There are, Sullivan writes, "machines that hinder man (and his progress) and machines that help." Clearly, Ellison's work reflects the former paradigm. Sullivan closes by arguing that the two computers in these stories are "paradigms rather than symbols" because they are a "representation of what people hope or fear computers will become."

In an interesting essay, "Mythic Hells in Ellison's Science Fiction," critic Joseph Francavilla argues that Ellison's heroes, including the narrator Ted, offer a "radical" departure from the hero as described by Joseph Campbell in his classic *The Hero with a Thousand Faces.* Francavilla further demonstrates how Ellison both uses and subverts other mythic constructions of hell, most notably from the Prometheus legend. He also details the similarities between AM and the Old Testament god. For Francavilla, Ellison's use of biblical imagery is potent, particularly since there is no sense that the post-holocaust world will rebuild itself. Rather, the biblical imagery contributes to a timelessness in Ellison's story that points toward myth rather than the historicity of traditional Christianity. Francavilla asserts that the end of the story locks Ted in an "eternal struggle" between the "utterly irreconcilable forces." Such construction is, as Francavilla points out, Manichean in origin. As a vision of the future, it suggests a world where resolution and redemption are impossible.

Another critic who draws on biblical imagery and the construction of god is Darren Harris-Fain. In his journal article, "Created in the Image of God: The Narrator and the Computer in Harlan Ellison's

'I Have No Mouth, and I Must Scream,'" Harris-Fain focuses on the religious nature of the narrator, Ted. In addition to tracing the religious references found in the various texts of the story, Harris-Fain also locates allusions to John Bunyan's *Pilgrim's Progress* and the nod to H. G. Well's classic story, ''The Country of the Blind.'' Perhaps most notably, Harris-Fain identifies Ted with Christ, suggesting that his murder of his fellow survivors is an act of supreme love. He argues that this act demonstrates the ''potential of the human spirit.'' Clearly, Harris-Fain's position sets him apart from other reviewers and critics who see the story as one without hope. For this critic, at least, Ellison's vision of a possible future, while bleak, still holds out remnants of human dignity.

Criticism

Diane Andrews Henningfeld

Andrews Henningfeld is an associate professor at Adrian College in Adrian, Michigan, where she teaches literature and writing. She holds a Ph.D. in literature, and regularly writes book reviews, historical articles, and literary criticism for a wide variety of educational publishers. In the following essay, Andrews Henningfeld examines the convention of the unreliable narrator in literature, focusing on the way Ellison both uses and subverts that convention in his story.

Harlan Ellison first published ''I Have No Mouth, and I Must Scream'' in the March 1967 issue of *IF: Worlds of Science Fiction,* before using it as the title story in his 1967 collection *I Have No Mouth, and I Must Scream.* A horrifying and ghastly story of a post-apocalyptic hell controlled by a monster computer, ''I Have No Mouth, and I Must Scream'' attracted the attention of Ellison fans and critics alike, winning a Hugo award in 1968.

In the years since its original publication, the story has continued to attract critical attention. Because it is fraught with ambiguity and layered with nightmarish imagery, the story provides fertile ground for varied interpretations.

Critics such as Joann Cobb, for example, argue that the story reveals those attitudes present in 1967 toward the growth of technology. Others suggest that the story represents cultural anxiety over the

relationship between humans and machines, an anxiety that finds expression in popular film and television. Such anxiety is evident in the number of episodes of *Star Trek: The Next Generation* concerning Commander Data, the android who not infrequently goes berserk.

Thomas Dillingham, in a chapter he prepared for the *Dictionary of Literary Biography,* provides an intriguing interpretation of the story focusing on the American ideals of individuality and free will. He writes that the story

> not only explores special psychological problems of individuals caught in impersonal, mechanized systems, but also launches a satiric attack on the two poles of totalitarian victimization which are present in the twentieth century: total loss of will, intellect, and individuality, on the one hand; loss of effective control over the phenomenal world of which one is conscious on the other. These losses, along with the specter of nuclear holocaust, which is a metaphor for them both, constitutes the special nightmare of the second half of the century.

Thus, by placing the story in its proper historical and cultural context, the reader is better able to understand the world Ellison creates. At the root of many of these discussions, however, is the question of the story's ending. Some critics argue that this is a nightmarish vision of the future, a story that demonstrates that humans are ultimately unable to control their own machines, and that they will end up in a hell of their own making, a hell that prevents resolution or solace. On the other hand, there are those who maintain that ''I Have No Mouth, and I Must Scream'' is a story of redemption and of the indefatigable human will. In spite of everything, the narrator Ted is able to defeat the machine at its own game, just as Captain Kirk in the 1960s *Star Trek* episodes often destroys the computers that attempt to control him.

To arrive at any sort of interpretation of the ending, a reader must first thoroughly investigate the role of the narrator. Although most critics spend some time examining the character Ted, and discussing his role as narrator in ''I Have No Mouth, and I Must Scream,'' few have examined the convention of the unreliable narrator and its implications for the story. Such an examination reveals something very interesting: that Ellison may be having as much fun with his readers as AM has with his captives.

The role of the narrator in any short story is crucial to understanding the story. It is important for a reader to identify the point-of-view and to make

What Do I Read Next?

- Isaac Asimov created a series of science fiction short stories and novels presenting the relationship between humans and machines in a more positive light. Students might enjoy reading his *I, Robot* (1952), *Robots and Empire* (1985), or *The Complete Robot: Selected Stories* (1992).

- Robert Heinlein is another important mid-twentieth-century writer of speculative fiction. His classic *Stranger in a Strange Land* (1961) has achieved near-cult status with science fiction fans. *Farnham's Freehold* (1964) presents another vision of a post-apocalyptic world, while *Time Enough for Love* follows a main character, Lazarus Long, who is nearly immortal.

- Psychologist B. F. Skinner's famous utopian novel *Walden Two* (1948) offers yet another vision of the future from a mid-twentieth century perspective. Skinner's book applies his theories of human behavior to an imaginary utopian world.

- Another classic look at the future from an earlier perspective is Aldous Huxley's *Brave New World* (1932), a must-read for any student interested in dystopian literature.

- Margaret Atwood's *A Handmaid's Tale* (1985) is a classic dystopian novel told from a feminist perspective.

- For a comprehensive look at Harlan Ellison's work, *The Essential Ellison: A 50-Year Retrospective* (2000), edited by Terry Dowling with Richard Delap and Gil Lamont, provides short stories, commentary, essays, reviews, and screen plays.

---

some judgments about the narrator. In the case of this story, the point-of-view is an extremely limited first-person. That is, everything that the reader learns is filtered through the character Ted. He speaks in the first-person ''I.'' It is difficult to ascertain to whom he speaks, however, given his limited circumstances. Consequently, readers must assume that they have wandered into to an interior monologue that Ted is having with himself.

There are many advantages in using a first-person narrator. The reader immediately identifies with the narrator because the narrator's senses and thoughts form the only source of information the reader has. Indeed, a reader forms an intimate relationship with a first person narrator that makes it extremely hard for the reader to disbelieve whatever it is that the narrator reveals.

In the case of Ted, a character who finds himself in the midst of a nightmarish, post-apocalyptic hell controlled by the whims of a huge supercomputer, the reader has nothing but horror and sympathy for his position. And why not? Ted seems to be in the best position of the characters of

the story to relate their plight. He portrays himself as somewhat of an outsider, the youngest of the group, and the ''one AM had affected least of all.'' He seems to be able to distinguish between image and reality more clearly than the others.

The others are not in as good shape. Nimdok, for example, is a mystery man without a past who hallucinates. Benny, a former university professor, has been changed into an ape-like creature with a huge phallus. Gorrister is a ''shoulder-shrugger,'' someone unable to make any decisions or to care about his surroundings. Ellen cries a lot and grants sexual favors to all the men.

It is, however, with Ted's description of Ellen that the reader begins to wonder just a bit about Ted's reliability. Given the utter horror of their situation, it seems unlikely that ''AM had given her pleasure'' through her sexuality. It also seems very unlikely that Ellen ''loved it, four men all to herself.'' Further, Ted speaks with venom about Ellen, calling her a ''slut'' and a ''douche-bag.'' Clearly, Ted's reasoning about Ellen is faulty. And if Ted is mistaken in his description of her, might he also be faulty in his reporting of the rest of the survivors? In the following passage, Ted's sanity must be called into question.

> *I* was the only one still sane and whole. *Really!*
>
> AM had not tampered with my mind. *Not at all.*
>
> *I* only had to suffer what he visited down on us. All the delusions, all the nightmares, the torments. But those scum, all four of them, they were lined and arrayed against me. If I hadn't had to stand them off all the time, be on my guard against them all the time, I might have found it easier to combat AM.
>
> At which point it passed, and I began crying.

At this moment, Ted sounds like nothing so much as one of Edgar Allan Poe's classic insane and unreliable narrators, paranoid and caught within the ramblings of his own twisted mind. Indeed, that the paranoia comes and goes so quickly suggests that AM controls Ted's mind just as surely as it controls the minds and bodies of the rest. Further, since readers only have Ted's dubious voice to report his condition, they also have no idea what state his body is truly in.

What does it matter to the story if Ted is reliable or not? Might it not be yet another technique to instill fear and loathing in the reader for the situation brought about by nuclear holocaust and technological hubris? Quite frankly, it matters deeply to the ending of the story whether Ted is sane or not. Those critics who interpret Ted's murder of the others as an act of supreme self-sacrifice require Ted to be reliable. That is, the only hope for redemption in this story rests on Ted's clear-headed and reliable reporting that death is the only escape from AM. There are those critics who, building on the ample use of biblical imagery in this story, attribute Christ-like qualities to Ted: he is willing to sacrifice everything in order to save the others.

Yet such interpretations simply cannot hold if Ted is not reliable. In such a case, his murder of the others may simply be an act of insane paranoia. He obviously worries about this potentially being the case. When he recalls Ellen's death, he says, ''I could not read meaning into her expression, the pain had been too great, had contorted her face; but it *might* have been thank you. It's possible. Please.'' Even in his blob-like final state, Ted is capable of guilt and worry.

There is, however, an even deeper layer to unpeel in this story. Ellison does Poe one better in his use of the conventional unreliable narrator. Ellison's characters find themselves in a setting

> **"Such an examination reveals something very interesting: that Ellison may be having as much fun with his readers as AM has with his captives."**

with no objective reality. Poe's readers, ultimately, discover the insanity of the main character and are able to reconstruct a sane telling of the story. Ellison's use of setting and narrator prevent this. If Ted is unreliable in his reporting of some things, might he not be unreliable in his reporting of all things? That is, what evidence is there in the story that there are really five survivors? Might it not be just as likely that the entire sequence of events that Ted relates takes place nowhere but in his mind? Because there is simply no objective reality in this story against which the reader may test the veracity of Ted's testimony, his entire testimony is in doubt.

If readers push the notion of the unreliable narrator far enough, they bump into none other than manic puppeteer, Harlan Ellison, standing just outside the edges of his story, creating a strange and awful landscape for his characters. Like the Wizard of Oz, he stands behind the curtain, creating AM, a post-holocaust landscape, and trapped characters. In the final moment, the reader comes to this realization: Ellison has played with the reader in the same way that AM plays with the survivors. The horror the reader feels at Ted's awful inability to move, talk, see, or scream; the deep sorrow the reader feels for Ted's act of genuine self-sacrifice; and the utter dismay the reader feels about the future of humankind have all been manipulated by the writer, a writer who has chosen a completely untrustworthy narrator to tell the story. Perhaps in the final analysis, ''I Have No Mouth, and I Must Scream'' is really a brilliant story about the power of fiction, rather than a social or cultural commentary. For if the reader cannot trust the storyteller, can the reader trust the story? And if readers cannot trust the story, then what of the writer? Behind the curtain, out in the margins of the story, Ellison stands laughing, like the unrepentant harlequin he is, waiting for readers to get his joke.

Source: Diane Andrews Henningfeld, Critical Essay on ''I Have No Mouth, and I Must Scream,'' in *Short Stories for Students,* The Gale Group, 2002.

Darren Harris-Fain

In the following essay, Harris-Fain compares various versions of ''I Have No Mouth, and I Must Scream,'' and finds that the narrator, Ted, is more completely divine and human than the computer.

> And man has actually invented God . . . the marvel is that such an idea . . . could enter the head of such a savage, vicious beast as man.
>
> If the devil doesn't exist, but man created him, he has created him in his own image.—Fyodor Dostoevsky

''I Have No Mouth, and I Must Scream'' first appeared in *If: Worlds of Science Fiction* in March 1967, bought and edited by Frederik Pohl. It was printed without the now-familiar computer ''talk-fields'' and also was edited in several places: Ellison calls this ''the Bowdlerizing of what Fred termed 'the difficult sections' of the story (which he contended might offend the mothers of the young readers of *If.*'' Specifically, Pohl omitted a reference to masturbation, toned down some of Ted's imprecations of Ellen, and removed all references to Benny's former homosexuality and the present equine state of what certain writers and speakers of German call the *männliches Glied.* (In Benny's case, however, perhaps *die Rute* would be more precise, and in the process would lend an entirely new meaning to the expression *einem Kind die Rute geben.*)

The story made its next appearance in Ellison's collection *I Have No Mouth and I Must Scream,* published in April 1967. Its subsequent reprintings in Ellison's books were in *Alone Against Tomorrow* (1971), *The Fantasies of Harlan Ellison* (1979), and *The Essential Ellison* (1987). I have compared the versions of all four books with each other and with the story's original appearance in *If;* my speculations here are drawn from this comparison.

It is my belief that Ted, the narrator, reveals his own true nature in speaking of the computer and in telling the story of himself and the others. Although the machine often is portrayed in both anthropomorphic and divine terms, I believe it is Ted alone who is both fully human and fully godlike in this story.

A comparison of the texts is illuminating, especially when attention is paid to the nouns and pronouns by which AM is described. Ted sometimes calls AM the machine, the computer, the creature, or simply AM, but usually pronouns are used. ''He'' and ''it'' are used indiscriminately, but this apparently careless usage in the versions of the story prior to 1979 becomes clearer in the versions found in *The Fantasies of Harlan Ellison* and *The Essential Ellison,* where the pronouns are deliberately mixed. For instance, at one point Ted speaks of Ellen's sexual services. All versions before 1979 read: ''The machine giggled every time we did it. Loud, up there, back there, all around us. And she never climaxed, so why bother.'' In *The Fantasies of Harlan Ellison* and *The Essential Ellison* this passage is rearranged and expanded:

> And she never came, so why bother? But the machine giggled every time we did it. Loud, up there, back there, all around us, he snickered. *It* snickered. Most of the time I thought of AM as *it,* without a soul; but the rest of the time I thought of it as *him,* in the masculine . . . the paternal . . . the patriarchal . . . for he is a jealous people. Him. It. God as Daddy the Deranged. (Ellison's ellipses)

These later texts establish the division in Ted's mind between an impersonal and personal view of the computer. They also establish Ted's religious perspective of AM—a perspective in which God is seen as mad, much as God is portrayed in Ellison's 1973 story, ''The Deathbird.''

These two later versions of ''I Have No Mouth, and I Must Scream'' strengthen this combination of personal and impersonal through a deliberate mixture of pronouns not found in earlier renditions. Here are some examples:

> The passage of time was important to it. (*If* 25; *Alone* 16)
> The passage of time was important to him. (*Mouth* 24)
> The passage of time was important to him . . . it . . . AM. (*FHE* 187; *EE* 168; Ellison's ellipses)
> It was a mark of his personality: he strove for perfection. (*If* 25; *Mouth* 25; *Alone* 17)
> It was a mark of his personality: it strove for perfection. (*FHE* 188; *EE* 168)
> He was a machine. We had allowed him to think, but to do nothing with it. (*If* 32; *Mouth* 34; *Alone* 25–26)
> AM wasn't God, he was a machine. We had created him to think, but there was nothing it could do with that creativity. (*FHE* 195; *EE* 175)

Perhaps Ted best sums it up with this sentence: ''We could call AM any damned thing we liked.'' But there is more than indifference in Ted's attitude toward the computer. He admits he frequently thinks of AM as ''him,'' and he regularly uses masculine pronouns in reference to it. This is due partly to his religious conception of AM as God, as ''Daddy the Deranged,'' but more often it is because Ted anthropomorphizes the computer, and because Ted and the computer are reflections of each other. In addition, the computer itself assumes human characteristics.

Much of what makes Ted so interesting and effective as a narrator for this story is his intense paranoia, given to him by AM. In *The Oxford Companion to the Mind* ''paranoia'' is defined as a functional psychosis ''in which the patient holds a coherent, internally consistent, delusional system of beliefs, centring [*sic*] round the conviction that he . . . is a person of great importance and is on that account being persecuted, despised, and rejected.'' Ted displays these classic symptoms, as in this passage: ''They hated me. They were surely against me, and AM could even sense this hatred, and made it worse for me *because of* the depth of their hatred. We had been kept alive, rejuvenated, made to remain constantly at the age we had been when AM had brought us below, and they hated me because I was the youngest, and the one AM had affected least of all.'' As the article in the Oxford volume says, ''The adjective 'paranoid' is sometimes used by psychoanalysis to describe anxiety and ideas that are inferred to be projections of the subject's own impulses.'' Ted thus transfers his own hatred to the computer and the others, while fending off the delusion that he was unchanged despite the descriptions he supplies of his altered mind and believing that ''those scum, all four of them, they were lined and arrayed against me.''

Part of the effect of Ted's paranoia is his transference of his own thoughts and feelings to others—and this includes AM, as well as his four human companions. He often describes the computer and its actions in human terms. For instance, he calls AM's tortures the machine's masturbation, and speaks of ''the innate loathing that all machines had always held for the weak, soft creatures who had built them.'' It is difficult to imagine a toaster or refrigerator harboring malice against their makers; more likely, this statement is an expression of Ted's own hatred of humanity, and just happens to describe AM's own hatred as well.

Much could be made of the epistemological problems inherent in this story. Not only is Ted an extremely unreliable narrator, but it is often difficult to know how much of what he says is true and how much a projection of his own psyche. For instance, George Edgar Slusser calls Ted ''the true creator of this hate machine,'' but while Ted does project his hatred onto the machine, it is not simply his delu-

> Not only is Ted an extremely unreliable narrator, but it is often difficult to know how much of what he **says** is true and how much a projection of his own psyche."

sion either, unless the entire story never happened and is merely an elaborate construction within Ted's mind.

This humanization of AM is by no means limited to Ted's transference of human qualities to the computer, however. We are told AM's name in part refers to the Cartesian *cogito ergo sum,* ''I think, therefore I am''; Ellison also mentions that the talk-fields eventually were designed to read ''I think, therefore I AM'' and ''Cogito ergo sum,'' even though they were positioned correctly only in *The Essential Ellison*. This philosophical statement on the part of the computer is certainly one quite human in nature. And AM displays other human qualities: ''he'' giggles and snickers; shows emotions like anger, hatred, and jealousy; goes through an ''irrational, hysterical phase''; and possesses sentience, life, and thought. Perhaps the trait which most reveals AM's human side is its sense of humor. Ted speaks of the computer having fun with the five of them, whom he describes as its toys; the machine frequently laughs at them, sometimes in the guise of a fat woman. AM even jokes with them: ''he'' gives them bows and arrows and a water pistol to fight the gigantic Huergelmir, and after starving them AM supplies them with canned goods but with nothing to open them. Once there was a Tom and Jerry cartoon with a similar joke: they are locked up in the house with nothing to eat but canned food, but the can opener is useless since they lack opposable thumbs. Given Ellison's love of animated cartoons—most recently documented in *The Harlan Ellison Hornbook*—it is quite possible that the cartoon influenced this part of the story.

The computer reveals a sexual side as well. I have mentioned already that Ted describes the machine as masturbating and that it giggles whenever

Ellen has sex with anyone. AM also enlarges Benny's penis, and Ted says that ''AM had given her [Ellen] pleasure'' in bringing her into the computer's complex. Jon Bernard Ower believes ''AM's degradation of the sexual lives of his subjects reveals his jealousy of the physical pleasure and the spiritual fulfillment of human love.'' It is also possible, I believe, that the scene in which AM enters Ted's mind with the neon-lettered pillar could be seen as rape, a mental sodomy of sorts. ''AM went into my mind,'' says Ted. ''AM touched me in every way I had ever been touched . . . AM withdrew from my mind, and allowed me the exquisite ugliness of returning to consciousness with the feeling of that burning neon pillar still rammed deep into the soft gray brain matter.'' The sexual language and imagery here are very strong and suggestive.

In examining the story's various printings and reprintings in Ellison's books and in anthologies edited by others, I noticed that in speaking of Ellen's sexual services for the four men two of Ellison's books read, ''She loved it, five men all to herself,'' while the anthologies had, ''She loved it, four men all to herself.'' For a while, then, I believed that ''five men'' was the correct reading, and before I saw either *The Fantasies of Harlan Ellison* or *The Essential Ellison*, and before I asked Harlan himself about it, I was prepared to argue that the computer itself was the fifth man, thus strengthening my arguments for AM's humanization, in particular its sexual manifestations—all of which goes to show the importance of establishing dependable texts.

But while the computer itself may not have sex with Ellen, it definitely possesses a human side; as George Edgar Slusser says, ''in its hatred for mankind, this machine has acquired a human heart.'' Yet it is an extremely twisted and evil humanity this computer displays, stemming directly from the fact that AM was created to wage war and was programmed by people with hatred and madness in their souls. Ellison's comments on his projected screenplay adaptation of Isaac Asimov's *I, Robot* are illuminating on this point: ''The only thing that can make machines hurt us is ourselves. Garbage in, garbage out. If we program them and we have madness, then they will be programmed mad.'' Incidentally, in Ellison's 1960 novel *The Sound of a Scythe* (published with the title *The Man with Nine Lives*) there is a supercomputer similar to AM, designed to handle tasks too complex for humans, but it is kept benevolent by Asimov's Three Laws of Robotics.

If AM is far from benevolent, it is also far from human. It is limited in its creativity and, envying what freedoms and abilities the humans possess, strives to limit even those, as a dog in the manger. Either unwilling or unable to destroy itself, AM apparently is immortal and therefore grants the five humans a form of immortality (following the human adage that misery loves company). Although it can sustain human life, AM cannot create it, which explains why after 109 years and four men no children have been born to Ellen. Although one logically might infer that AM would want more human beings to torture, it evidently keeps Ellen as barren as ''she'' is. The humans are not fruitful, they do not multiply, they do not replenish the earth. This is made more ironic by the frequent images of pregnancy in the story, as Joseph Francavilla has noted; the computer complex repeatedly is referred to as AM's belly, and at one point Ted says, ''He was Earth, and we were the fruit of that Earth.'' In a way, since AM sustains them, it is a type of mother to the five, but it never gives birth to them, making the pregnancy imagery all the more ironic: ''It [the hunger] was alive in my belly, even as we were alive in the belly of AM, and AM was alive in the belly of the earth.''

Nor can AM restore life. After Ted and Ellen kill their companions, and after Ted murders Ellen, we clearly see the computer's impotence, evident in its rage that it cannot bring the dead ones back to life. Like Frankenstein's monster, AM cannot create life; but it can destroy it, which both AM and the monster do by turning on those who gave them life but who failed to give them love and the possibility to create life in turn. Unlike the Frankenstein monster, however, AM does not mature, but instead grows more childish: its use of the five as playthings indicates this, as does the temper tantrum it throws upon the death of the four. The computer again resembles the childish, insane god of ''The Deathbird.'' Like Ted, it is filled with hatred and in its madness must scream, yet like Ted it has no mouth: it can communicate only through acts of violence such as the rape scene and through the unintelligible talk-fields. Like Ted at some moments, AM represents humanity at its worst.

However, Ted also reveals glimmers of hope within the human condition as he aspires to godhood (so Ellison tells us in ''Memoir'') through his heroism. AM also aspires to godhood, helped partly by Ted's own religious imagination, but the divinity it achieves is a very poor sort. In some ways the ''god'' AM becomes is a reflection of the human race which invented the machine, in others like the Judeo-Christian God in its power and supposed omnipotence, but actually it is closer to Dostoevsky's devil or Twain's malign thug: "If one truly believes there is an all-powerful Deity, and one looks around at the condition of the universe, one is led inescapably to the conclusion that God is a malign thug." Nevertheless, AM's type of divinity is one representation of human potential, as Willis E. McNelly tells us in his foreword to the story in Robert Silverberg's anthology, *The Mirror of Infinity*. Programmed by humanity, "AM now knows all the ancient archetypal myths, and now uses its knowledge to pervert and negate them. It exercises the power that man never had, to control man, and to give substance to the myths. Man has played God for one last time, creating a God that destroys him." In effect, AM plays at being God just as it plays with the five humans at its disposal, assuming the role of a God who prepares its creatures for destruction by first driving them mad.

There are several instances in the story where the computer plays with the symbolism and mythologies of various religions. For example, Charles J. Brady, Carol D. Stevens, Francavilla, and Ower all note the story's similarities to the book of Exodus—an additional meaning of AM's name comes from Exodus 3:14, where God tells Moses that He is to be called I AM THAT I AM—and usually these occur in the perverse way McNelly mentions. The computer sends the five manna which, however, tastes like "boiled boar urine"; when AM enters Ted's mind, it walks as God walked in the Garden of Eden before chastising Adam and Eve for their sin; it appears to them in the form of a burning bush; and after Ellen and Nimdok are swallowed by an earthquake, AM returns them to the others "as the heavenly legion bore them to us with a celestial chorus singing, 'Go Down Moses.' The archangels circled several times and then dropped the hideously mangled bodies."

And these examples are within the Judeo-Christian tradition alone: AM employs other religious tricks as well, such as producing the Huergelmir from Norse mythology. Still another mythic tradition may shed some additional light into the relationship between Ted and the computer. Returning to the sentence "He was the Earth, and we were the fruit of that Earth" along with the following sentence, "though he had eaten us he would never digest us," recalls the *Theogony* of Hesiod, in which Kronos suppresses his godling children by eating them. Like Zeus in the myth, Ted is an emerging god, but to emerge he first must emasculate the Kronos-figure, AM. Ted saves his "brothers" and "sister," ironically, by killing them; but instead of reigning triumphantly over the defeated god, both are condemned to Tartarus.

However, the Judeo-Christian mythology is most prevalent in the story, both in the identity AM adopts for itself and in Ted's ideas about the computer as God. Ted sees AM as God the Father and says, in a biblical misquotation, "He is a jealous people." The phrase is actually "jealous God," and two places where it occurs in the Bible are remarkably relevant to the story. In Exodus 20:5, the King James version, it says, "Thou shalt not bow down thyself to them [graven images], nor serve them: for I the LORD thy God *am* a jealous God, visiting the iniquity of the fathers upon the children unto the third and fourth *generation* of them that hate me." Since there is no certain indication in the story that any of the five are responsible for the creation of the various national AMs, the choice of the unified AM to punish these five and kill everyone else seems fairly arbitrary, but this biblical passage reflects a God who will punish the children for the sins of the fathers, down even to the third and fourth generations. Also, as both Ower and Stevens have pointed out, AM's selection of these five parodies the concept of a "chosen people."

Nor will such a God necessarily forgive them, as we find in Joshua 24:19: "And Joshua said unto the people, Ye cannot serve the LORD: for he *is* an holy God; he *is* a jealous God; he will not forgive your transgressions nor your sins." Life in AM, for Ted, if not for the others, is not Purgatory, in which one suffers but ultimately is reprieved, but is Hell. "He withdrew, murmuring *to hell with you.* And added, brightly, *but then you're there, aren't you.*" Yet Ted realizes, and we must realize, that AM is not God. Rather, as Ellison himself has said, "AM represents . . . the dichotomous nature of the human race, created in the *image* of God; and that includes the demon in us." In this respect, AM mirrors its creators. As Ower says, "Humanity in making the computer has travestied its own creation [by God], projecting an amplified image of its fallen and conditioned nature." Perhaps it could even be argued that AM is not entirely malevolent toward humanity, but instead has a love/hate relationship with it. While it hurts the five, it also sustains them and in some cases even gives them pleasure; but Ted, narrating through the veil of his paranoia, can see only the computer's hatred.

Ted is more like the computer than he realizes, for he also has a love/hate relationship with the others. This is most apparent in his feelings for Ellen. For instance, when he comments that Ellen gave herself to him sexually out of gratitude at one point, he says, "Even that had ceased to matter"— which implies that at one time it did matter. When traveling, Nimdok and Gorrister carry her while Ted and Benny walk ahead and behind "just to make sure that if anything happened, it would catch one of us and at least Ellen would be safe." Ted here transfers his concern to the idiot Benny to deemphasize his own concern for Ellen, and he does not begrudge her this special treatment (in a way foreshadowing her future limp), even though he curses her throughout the story. Ted always gives in to Ellen's wishes and tries to reassure her whenever she becomes anxious. And when just the two of them are alive and he could have her for himself— he is clearly jealous of the others, especially Benny, since he believes "she loved it from him" while with Ted "she never came"—he cares enough for her to rescue her from the hell she will encounter under AM's wrath.

Both AM's love/hate relationship with the five and Ted's paradoxical feelings toward Ellen reflect Ellison's own feelings toward humanity: "It is a love/hate relationship that I have with the human race," he says. Ellison believes the human spirit is capable of greatness and nobility, but too often people settle for meanness and mediocrity. "A majority of readers see his work as filled with anger and bitterness," says Debra McBride. For instance, Joann P. Cobb thinks "I Have No Mouth, and I Must Scream" "illustrates the surrender of human purpose and value that is inherent in contemporary attitudes toward technological progress." But Ellison says otherwise, and his sense of anger, according to McBride, "stems from a love-hate relationship he has with the human race; he sees greatness in humanity that society seems to bury instead of cultivate."

Earlier in the Wiloch and Cowart interview, Ellison expands on his comments with his beliefs about God and humanity: "There is no God. . . . We are God." He has made similar statements elsewhere: "I have faith . . . in people, not Gods" (*FHE* 19; Ellison's ellipses); "God is within you. Save yourselves" ("The Waves in Rio" 15). Charles J. Brady believes that in "I Have No Mouth, and I Must Scream" Ellison's "target" is "God-the-puppet-master, the eternal one behind the scenes who pulls all the strings." But Brady asserts that

this is an idol, not the "real" God; therefore "Ellison's work is not atheistic or blasphemous in the final analysis." On the contrary, I think it is meant to be blasphemous, if not atheistic. Ellison implies here what he explicitly states above, that gods are essentially our own creations made in our image, and if anything the "real" God is an ideal of human nobility. Similar ideas also are expressed in two other stories by Ellison, "The Deathbird" and "The Region Between" (1969).

It is the belief in the potential of the human spirit that shapes the impact of "I Have No Mouth, and I Must Scream." It is this that makes the apparent humanity and divinity of AM so important, because AM is a human creation: humanity has created both God and Satan in its own image because it is potentially godlike and realistically demonic. It is also important that AM is so much like Ted, and vice versa, because in the narrator we see an actual human being at its worst, yet also a god emerging. As Francavilla says, citing the Promethian nature of Ted, "If the dark half of human nature is projected into AM, then the firebringing half is embodied in Ted." The editors' introduction to the story in *The Essential Ellison* is very revealing on this point:

> "I Have No Mouth, and I Must Scream" is an exceptionally violent warning about technology as a reflection of humanity. If our machines store our knowledge, is it not possible that they can also store, and possibly succumb to, such things as hatred and paranoia? AM . . . is a "god" only in the sense of its godlike powers. But the story must be viewed as Harlan intended, as "a positive, humanistic, upbeat story," if it is to have any real meaning. Gods and pseudo-gods cannot destroy us without destroying themselves, and the absence of a mouth or a scream cannot invalidate the courageousness of the human spirit.

In "Memoir," Ellison claims Ted's actions are godlike since they reveal love and heroism in overcoming his paranoia and in killing the others to put them out of their misery, thus subjecting himself to an eternity of loneliness and torment.

Several aspects of the story strengthen this religious view of the narrator. First is the establishment of AM as a God-figure and the subsequent identification of Ted with the computer, however unwitting on Ted's part. Like AM, Ted is filled with envy, hatred, and paranoia. Both are immortal. Two descriptions of Ted's brain resemble those of AM's "mind": blown by the hurricane, Ted describes his mind as "a roiling tinkling chittering softness," a description resembling those of AM in thought, especially the repeated word "chittering"; and just as when AM was constructed its creators dropped shafts into the earth, so when AM enters Ted's mind "[h]e smiled softly at the pit that dropped into the center of my brain and the faint, moth-soft murmurings of the things far down there that gibbered without meaning, without pause." In the latter, the sounds within the "pit" of Ted's brain are much like the talk-fields of the murmuring computer.

Other features which reinforce Ted's religious nature are his language and expressions, many of which are loaded with theological and liturgical impact. Not only does he often equate AM with God, and even pray at one point (but in vain), but he also speaks occasionally in a biblical mode. He speaks of AM's "miracles" and the torments which he "visited down on us," and their passage through "a valley of obsolescence" foreshadows the Bunyanesque tone of the later passage, which reads:

> And we passed through the cavern of rats.
> And we passed through the path of boiling steam.
> And we passed through the country of the blind.
> And we passed through the slough of despond.
> And we passed through the vale of tears.

John Bunyan's *Pilgrim's Progress,* to which this story has been compared, is of course the source of the Slough of Despond; the "vale of tears" is a traditional religious phrase expressing the medieval Christian view of the world as a place of suffering (terribly apropos for this story); and "the country of the blind" is from the H. G. Wells tale of the same title which makes use of the familiar quotation, "In the country of the blind, the one-eyed man is king"— even if he has no mouth.

Another religious aspect of Ted is the narration itself. To whom is he telling this story? Not to AM, certainly; the computer is referred to in the third person, and it's likely the two aren't on speaking terms. He probably isn't writing or typing it, as McNelly supposes, given the description of his arms as "[r]ubbery appendages." The most probable answer is that Ted is telling it to himself (Joseph F. Patrouch, Jr., arrives at the same conclusion), and likely not for the first time. Like Gorrister telling the history of AM over and over to Benny, so Ted probably repeats his story to himself, possibly to alleviate the sense of guilt he feels at the death of the others and his uncertainty that he did the right thing.

In this way, the story would assume a mythological aspect. Evidence of such repetition can be seen in the various instances of foreshadowing in the story. Gorrister's reaction to seeing himself suspended, dead and mutilated, from the pink palette, "as though he had seen a voodoo icon," foreshadow's Benny's later cannibalistic attack. Ted's description of the earth's "blasted skin" parallels his later transformation by AM, as does the light pulsing within Benny when he tries to escape to the surface and AM reduces his eyes to "two soft, moist pools of pus-like jelly." Ellen is carried by Nimdok and Gorrister even before her leg is injured—or maybe after; perhaps Ted's chronology has become confused with successive retellings. Also, Ted says that among the five he was affected the least—an impression given him by his paranoia—but in the end he is altered almost beyond the point of recognition as a human being.

The most religious thing about Ted, however, is not his language but his actions. In killing the others, with Ellen's assistance, Ted fulfills Christ's statement, "Greater love hath no man than this, that a man lay down his life for his friends." Like other religious aspects of the story, this is reversed: Ted lays down his life, but it is his friends who die and he who lives. Despite this inversion, however, Ted is no Christ-figure. He remains fully human, yet achieves a type of godliness despite his humanity, despite his paranoia and his hatred of others. Ted is a *human* hero—human as we are, his courage an example for us to follow rather than a Christlike ideal we cannot reach. As McNelly says, "Ted is no Christian in his pilgrim's progress" but rather "the embodiment of the good and evil in all of us, at once brute and angel, fornicator and lover, killer and savior. He is man—like a devil, like an angel, like a god."

The narrator of "I Have No Mouth, and I Must Scream," then, embodies the image of God despite his human, all too human limitations and flaws. Ted exemplifies the potential of the human spirit. In this way he triumphs over the computer, which is also human and godlike; because while the computer is neither fully human nor fully divine, Ted is both, and through this displays a moral superiority which makes this tale, as Ellison intended it, "a positive, humanistic, upbeat story."

Source: Darren Harris-Fain, "Created in the Image of God: The Narrator and the Computer in Harlan Ellison's 'I Have No Mouth, and I Must Scream,'" in *Extrapolation: A Journal of Science Fiction and Fantasy,* Vol. 32, No. 2, Summer 1991, pp. 143–55.

Sources

Cobb, Joann P., ''Medium and Message in Ellison's 'I Have No Mouth, and I Must Scream,''' in *The Intersection of Science Fiction and Philosophy: Critical Studies,* edited by Robert E. Myers, Greenwood Press, 1983, pp. 159–67.

Dillingham, Thomas F., ''Harlan Ellison,'' in *Dictionary of Literary Biography,*Vol. 8: *Twentieth-Century American Science Fiction Writers,* edited by David Cowart and Thomas L. Wyner, Gale Research, 1981, pp. 161–69.

Dowling, Terry, with Richard Delap and Gil Lamont, eds., *The Essential Ellison: A 50 Year Retrospective,* rev. ed., Morpheus International, 2000.

Francavilla, Joseph, ''Mythic Hells in Harlan Ellison's Science Fiction,'' in *Phoenix from the Ashes: The Literature of the Remade World,* edited by Carl B. Yoke, Greenwood Press, 1987, pp. 157–64.

Harris-Fain, Darren, ''Created in the Image of God: The Narrator and the Computer in Harlan Ellison's 'I Have No Mouth, and I Must Scream,''' in *Extrapolation,* Vol. 32, No. 2, Summer 1991, pp. 143–55.

Myers, Robert E., ''Introduction,'' in *The Intersection of Science Fiction and Philosophy: Critical Studies,* Greenwood Press, 1983, pp. 159–67.

Slusser, George Edgar, *Harlan Ellison: Unrepentant Harlequin,* The Borgo Press, 1977.

Sullivan, Charles W., ''Harlan Ellison and Robert A. Heinlein: The Paradigm Makers,'' in *Clockwork Worlds: Mechanized Environments in SF,* edited by Richard D. Erlich and Thomas P. Dunn, Greenwood Press, 1983, pp. 97–103.

Further Reading

Dillingham, Thomas F., ''Harlan Ellison,'' in *Dictionary of Literary Biography,* Vol. 8: *Twentieth-Century American Science Fiction Writers,* edited by David Cowart and Thomas L. Wyner, Gale Research, 1981, pp. 161–69.
    Dillingham gives an excellent overview of Ellison's major works and includes a helpful bibliography.

Dowling, Terry, with Richard Delap and Gil Lamont, eds., *The Essential Ellison: A 50-Year Retrospective,* rev. ed., Morpheus International, 2000.
    This collection of most of Ellison's major works includes short stories, essays, interviews, and screenplays.

Magazine of Fantasy and Science Fiction, Vol. 53, July 1977.
    The entire issue of this science fiction standard is dedicated to Harlan Ellison.

Slusser, George Edgar, *Harlan Ellison: Unrepentant Harlequin,* The Borgo Press, 1977.
    Slusser's book-length study of Ellison's work remains a classic critical work.

The Interlopers

Saki's collection *The Toys of Peace, and Other Papers* was published posthumously in 1919. Saki had died three years earlier, the victim of a sniper's bullet, and the stories in this volume—which included sketches of pre-war England as well as tales of war—were written while he served in France. ''The Interlopers'' was included in this collection. With its fundamental theme of the deadly repercussions of long-standing feuds and a willingness to commit violence, ''The Interlopers'' clearly represents the experiences of a man who is caught in a global conflict of massive proportions. The two characters in ''The Interlopers,'' Ulrich von Gradwitz and Georg Znaeym, hate each other for no other reason than they have inherited a feud from their grandfathers surrounding a piece of land. Like World War I, which took decades to erupt, the Gradwitz-Znaeym feud has reached epic proportions by the time the story takes place. The story shows the fatal mistake that Ulrich and Georg make in believing that either of them can truly possess this small piece of land. The forest that Saki creates in ''The Interlopers'' is wild and untamable; it is held in the thrall of nature and her creatures. In their forthcoming destruction of Ulrich and Georg, the wolves demonstrate their ownership of this savage domain.

Saki

1919

Author Biography

Hector H. Munro—who took the pen name of Saki when he became a professional writer—was born December 18, 1870, in Burma, to a British army officer and his wife. After the death of his mother in 1873, Saki and his siblings were sent to Britain to be raised by their aunts.

Saki's father retired from the army in 1888 and thereafter took Saki and his sibling on many trips to the European continent. Saki went to Burma in 1893 as a police officer. However, he soon contracted malaria and returned to Britain the following year. He moved to London in 1896 with the hopes of becoming a writer.

In 1899 Saki published his first short story, "Dogged," and the next year he published a nonfiction book about the history of Russia. Also that year, Saki collaborated with political cartoonist Francis Carruthers Gould to create "Alice in Westminster," a series of satirical pieces that attacked the British government's handling of the Boer War in South Africa. The series was published in the *Westminster Gazette* and later collected in a book titled *The Westminster Alice* (1902). Saki and Gould collaborated again two years later on a similar project.

In 1902 Saki became a foreign correspondent for the *Tory Morning Gazette*. At the same time, he continued publishing short stories in the *Westminster Gazette*. In 1908 Saki left the field of journalism to devote himself to fiction writing. He published short stories regularly through 1914, by which time he had also resumed work as a journalist.

With the outbreak of World War I in August 1914, Saki enlisted for military service. He was sent to the trenches in France in November. He served in numerous battles, but continued to write during the war years. He wrote many articles about the military life for the army newspaper. Saki was killed by sniper fire on November 14, 1916.

The Toys of Peace, and Other Papers, which included "The Interlopers," was published in 1919. Another posthumous collection, *The Square Egg, and Other Sketches, with Three Plays*, was published in 1924 and included Saki's wartime writings.

Plot Summary

The characters in "The Interlopers," Ulrich von Gradwitz and Georg Znaeym, have been enemies since birth. Their grandfathers feuded over a piece of forestland. While the courts ruled in the Gradwitz family's favor, the Znaeym family has never accepted this ruling. Throughout the course of Ulrich and Georg's lifetime, the feud has grown into a personal, bloodthirsty one. As boys, they despised each other, and by the evening that the story takes place, the two grown men are determined to bring a final end to the feud by killing their enemy.

On this fateful evening, Ulrich gathers a group of foresters to patrol the land in search of Georg. Separated from his men, he hopes to meet Georg alone and, when he steps around a tree trunk, he gets his wish. The two men face each other with rifles in hand, but neither can bring himself to shoot the other. Before either man can act, a bolt of lighting strikes a tree. It falls over and pins them underneath its limbs.

The men are pinned down side-by-side, almost within touching distance. Both are dazed, injured, and angry at the situation in which they find themselves. Georg tells Ulrich that his men are right behind him, and threatens that, when they arrive, they will free him but roll the tree on top of Ulrich. To this threat, Ulrich replies that his men will arrive first and kill Georg. Both men know it is only a matter of waiting to see which group of foresters will reach them first.

Ulrich manages to draw his wine flask out of his coat pocket. He drinks some wine and, feeling something akin to pity, offers it to Georg. Georg refuses on the grounds that he does not drink wine with an enemy. During a few moments of silence, an idea comes to Ulrich. He proposes to Georg that they bury their quarrel. He believes that they have been fools and asks Georg for his friendship. After a long silence, Georg answers, accepting Ulrich's proposal.

The men decide to join their voices together to shout for help. Suddenly, Ulrich sees figures coming through the woods. They shout louder and the figures come down the hillside toward them. Georg, who cannot see as well as Ulrich, asks which men are approaching. Ulrich does not reply. He has seen something horrible: it is not men who approach them—it is wolves.

Characters

Ulrich von Gradwitz

Ulrich von Gradwitz is a wealthy landowner. He has legal right to a disputed stretch of land but knows that Georg continues to hunt on this land. On the night the story takes place, he has organized a group of men to find Georg, whom he plans to kill. He considers Georg his enemy and calls him a "forest-thief, game-snatcher." After the men get trapped under the tree, Ulrich offers Georg some of his wine and is the first one to put forth the idea of making amends. Ulrich is also the one who sees wolves approaching.

Georg Znaeym

Georg Znaeym comes from a line of small landowners who have refused to accept the judgement of the courts regarding a disputed piece of land. Georg refers to the land as Ulrich's "stolen forest." He later accepts Ulrich's offer of becoming friends, and speaks of the surprise this relationship will cause among the people in the community.

Saki

Themes

Enmity

Ulrich and Georg are enemies who have brought a family feud over a piece of forestland to a murderous point. Since the original court settlement, which ostensibly ended the dispute, members of both families have participated in "poaching affrays and similar scandals." Instead of dissipating over the years, the feud has strengthened throughout the lifetime of Ulrich and Georg, two generations removed from the original disputants. Saki does not reveal why the enmity has strengthened, merely alluding to the "personal ill-will" that exists between the men.

The hatred that each man feels for the other represents larger instances of animosity. At the time that Saki wrote the story, he was serving as a soldier in World War I, a conflict that developed out of inherited ethnic conflicts surrounding land claims that were unable to be satisfied by arbitrary judicial decisions. The drive of European nations to possess territory and build empires, and the desire of the ethnic nationals in Austria-Hungary to assert their independence helped fuel tensions that erupted in global conflict. Much like Ulrich and Georg, the

opposing sides in World War I carried generation-old dislikes to murderous proportions with a willingness to use violence to achieve their goals.

Community

The uneasy relationship between Ulrich and Georg has repercussions within the community. Ulrich is the leading member of an important, powerful family. In response to Ulrich's proposition that they end the feud, Georg notes the affect their friendship will have on the people around them. The ending of the quarrel would bring peace among the "forester folk," and "wonderful changes" to the countryside. These comments allude to the difficulties that the long-standing feud has caused within the community in the past and the impact that any peaceful resolution would have on the future.

Man and Nature

The very title of the story alludes to the fact that the men are trespassing on the forest in their attempts to assert ownership of it. Although the courts judged that one man—Gradwitz's grandfather—held title to the land, such claim can only be sustained by the laws of society. In truth, the men and their civilization cannot truly claim the land, as

Topics for Further Study

- Imagine that it is the day before the story takes place and you have been hired to mediate a peace between Ulrich and Georg. What would you suggest the men do to end their feud?

- Analyze Saki's choice of title for his story. Who are the interlopers? Why are they interlopers?

- Saki wrote ''The Interlopers'' while he was fighting in World War I. In what ways might the story reflect the experiences of a soldier?

- Find a work of art that represents the story's setting for you. Describe the artwork and why you feel it depicts the story's setting.

- The story takes place in the Austro-Hungarian empire prior to World War I. Conduct research and write an essay about the society in which Ulrich and Georg lived.

- In the *Dictionary of Literary Biography,* Alexander Malcolm Forbes calls ''The Interlopers'' a parable. Define parable. How effective of a parable is this story? Explain your answer.

---

evidenced by their inability to tame the natural world. The tree's attack on the men initiates this theme, and by the end of the story the men are about to fall prey to a pack of wolves. Each man has abused his rights by coming into the forest with the hope of killing his enemy to gain possession of the woods. However, the wolves, beasts that belong to the wild, appear to be the true victors in this conflict, as it is implied they will kill their human enemy and rid their world of these human intruders.

Social Class

The Gradwitz family occupies a higher social class than the Znaeym family, and this is one of the reasons that the feud has lasted throughout the generations. The Gradwitz family is wealthy and owns forestlands that are ''of wide extent and well stocked with game.'' Ulrich lives in a castle. By contrast, Georg Znaeym comes from a family of

''petty landowners.'' Their insistence of gaining possession of a piece of land to which they have no legal right shows their own lack of territory. Georg continues to hunt upon the disputed land, which affords greater opportunity for game than the marshes where he is forced to hunt.

Style

Point of View

''The Interlopers'' is written from the third-person omniscient point of view, meaning the narrator sees and knows all. This point of view allows the narrator to present the history of the disputed land, explain how the similar personalities of Georg and Ulrich have brought the feud to a murderous brink, and explain the moral codes that govern the enemies. Each man's perception of the events that have taken place are presented. Access to the thoughts and feelings of both men alerts the reader that the two are actually more alike than different, which further unites the men in their futile feud and even more futile impending death.

Dialogue

The dialogue in ''The Interlopers'' is important because it is the means by which the men express their willingness to step away from their feud. Ulrich, speaking first of the desire to ''bury the old quarrel,'' uses a brief speech to explain why he wants to be done with the past. Georg, in response, explains why he agrees with Ulrich's idea. The dialogue is also important because it shows a basic connection between these two men, who have shared so much but have never seen eye-to-eye.

Ending

The ending of the story is not the real ending; rather, it is the implication of what the end will be. Ulrich first sees what is approaching them, and, when Georg asks what he sees, the answer of ''Wolves!'' closes the story. With this word, along with Ulrich's ''idiotic chattering laugh of a man unstrung with hideous fear,'' the reader clearly understands the terrible death in store for the two men. It is not necessary for Saki to write this ending; its gruesome implication is horrible enough.

Personification

Saki personifies elements of the natural world. Nature becomes a violent beast that strikes out at the men for interloping on her territory. She physically knocks them down, felling a tree to attack them. In this portrayal, nature comes to resemble the men. The wind and the trees are also represented as living creatures. The ''wind breathes,'' and ''the trees can't even stand upright.''

Historical Context

World War I

In the late 1800s and early 1900s rivalries between European powers began to intensify. Imperialist states were fighting over land in Asia and Africa, ethnic groups were struggling for self-control, and nations were competing to build larger and more powerful military forces. In addition the region had developed a system of alliances in which nations would help each other out in disputes.

In 1914 a Serbian nationalist shot and killed the heir to the Austro-Hungarian throne, which proved to be the spark that set off World War I. As tensions mounted between Austria-Hungary and Serbia, Germany (which was allied with Austria-Hungary) declared war on Russia (which was allied with Serbia). Germany expanded the conflict when it declared war on France and marched into Belgium to reach France, thus breaking an 1839 neutrality agreement. Great Britain declared war on Germany that same day. Other nations joined the fray, and eventually Europe was divided between the Central Powers (Germany, Austria-Hungary, Bulgaria, and the Ottoman Empire) and the Allied forces (Britain, France, Russia, Italy, and dozens of other nations).

The western front of the war stretched along eastern France, while the eastern front saw battles deep into Russia. Fighting also took place in the location of present-day Turkey, as well as in the North Sea. In 1916 the war in the west and the war at sea had reached a stalemate. However, early in 1917, Germany decided to use unrestricted submarine warfare and also sent a secret telegram to Mexico proposing an alliance against the United States. In April 1917 the United States entered the war on the side of the Allies.

In 1918 the Russians signed a separate peace treaty with the Central Powers. To many people, this signaled that the war would last years longer. Germany withdrew its troops from the eastern front and launched an attack on Allied lines in France. They came within 37 miles of Paris, France's capital; however, the thousands of American troops that were arriving every month helped hold them back. The Allies launched a counteroffensive in July 1918. At the same time, the Central Powers were crumbling. Bulgaria and the Ottoman Empire surrendered, and a revolution in Austria-Hungary brought the Hapsburg Empire to an end. Austria and Hungary formed separate governments and stopped fighting. The German government collapsed in November 1918. On November 11, 1918, an armistice was signed ending World War I.

The War in France

The western front of the war stretched through eastern France. The Allies stopped the first German advance in September 1914. In the First Battle of the Marne, French troops launched a counterattack. After this battle, both the French and German armies prepared to hold their ground. They resorted to a strategy known as trench warfare in which each side defends its position by fighting from the protection of deep ditches. Two massive systems of trenches stretched for 400 miles along the western front. The area between opposing trenches, known as no-man's-land, varied in width from about 200 to 1,000 yards. Each side made little progress. In the battle of the Somme, which lasted from July through November 1915, the Allies were only able to force the Germans to retreat by a few miles. Another battle at Verdun lasted for ten months. In these two battles alone, almost one million soldiers died.

By the time the Americans arrived in Europe in 1917, German troops were occupying parts of France and Belgium. American units joined the Allies along the western front and were instrumental in keeping the German forces outside of Paris. The Second Battle of the Marne, fought in the summer of 1918, marked the turning point of the war. Allied forces began to force the German retreat from France. By the time the armistice was signed in November 1918, Germany occupied only a tiny portion of French land.

British Society

British society underwent significant changes in the 1910s and 1920s. The discrepancies between the lifestyles of the rich and poor were far less evident than they had been previously. Fewer people had servants, poorer people had access to the same goods as the wealthy, and the middle-class came to hold greater political power. Many homes had modern amenities, such as electricity and plumb-

Compare & Contrast

- **1910s:** After World War I ends, forty-two countries, not including the United States, join the League of Nations, an organization officially established in 1920 with the intent to help maintain peace throughout the world.

  Today: As of 2001, 189 countries around the world are member states of the United Nations. The UN was formed in 1945, ultimately replacing the League of Nations, with the dual mission of maintaining international peace and security and deterring aggressors.

- **1910s:** By the middle of the decade, countries around the world are involved in World War I.

  Today: Numerous regional conflicts are taking place in many locations around the world, such as the ongoing conflicts between Israelis and Palestinians in the Middle East or between Catholics and Protestants in Northern Ireland. The United Nations and countries around the world, particularly the United States, have been involved over the years in peace-brokering attempts.

- **1910s:** On the eve of World War I, the Austro-Hungarian empire comprise a large mass of territory in central Europe. The empire's loss in the war results in the breakup of the empire into the independent republics of Austria and Hungary. The empire also loses much of the territory it controlled with the creation of Czechoslovakia and Yugoslavia.

  Today: With the breakup of the Soviet Union in the early 1990s and the resulting demise of communism throughout Eastern and Central Europe, countries and new international boundaries have been created. The former Czechoslovakia has been divided into the Czech Republic and Slovakia. The former Yugoslavia has been divided into six nations: Slovenia, Croatia, Bosnia, Herzegovina, Serbia, and Macedonia.

---

ing. By the end of the decade, class distinctions had become notably less important in determining social groupings, even marriages.

World War I also engendered important changes. Millions of women entered the workforce, finding employment in government and private offices and in factories. Such increased economic opportunities contributed to women's emancipation, and by 1918, the Franchise Act gave all women over the age of twenty-eight the right to vote.

Critical Overview

The Toys of Peace, and Other Papers, the collection in which "The Interlopers" was included, was published in 1919, three years after Saki's death. The title, one of two books published posthumously, collected thirty-three sketches and stories about pre-war England and the war itself. Some of these pieces were humorous, some satirical, and some surprisingly grim.

In Britain, critics responded positively to the work, both for the pieces themselves as well as for Saki's heroic death. Some critics speculated on why Saki did not gain more popularity during his lifetime, while others believed that his unexpected death would bring him fame. An anonymous reviewer for the *Spectator* notes that Saki's "great gifts" consist of "wit, mordant irony, and a remarkable command of ludicrous metaphor." However, the writer believes that Saki's "intermittent vein of freakish inhumanity belied his best nature, and disconcerted the plain person."

The Toys of Peace, and Other Papers was also reviewed in the United States, where the critic for the *New York Times* notes that knowledge of Saki's tragic death blunted enjoyment of reading his lighter, wittier pieces. At the same time, this critic praises the collection: "They [the tales] show an understanding of the foibles and weaknesses of human nature, but never a contempt for it, nor any degeneration into bitterness.'' This writer also singles out the ''shock'' felt at coming across ''that grim story, 'The Interlopers.'''

At the time he was writing, Saki was known for his playfulness and wit, his use of satire and irony, his craftsmanship, and his black comedy. In the decades since his death, these characteristics continue to be celebrated among Saki enthusiasts. However, as Adam Frost points out in an article that appeared in *Contemporary Review* in 1999, few critical works exist about Saki's writing and literary development. Frost notes that Christopher Morley believed, ''Fewer writers are less profitable to write about.'' However, Frost finds this ''a shame.'' To Frost, Saki was ''never just a humorist'' but a knowledgeable writer who explained the culture of his day.

Criticism

Rena Korb

Korb has a master's degree in English literature and creative writing and has written for a wide variety of educational publishers. In the following essay, Korb examines how Saki explores the dual aspects of the hunt in his short story.

Adam Frost points out in a retrospective essay on Saki's career appearing in *Contemporary Review,* that the author's first published story, ''Dogged,'' ends in a ''reversal [that] is typical of Saki''; in that story, the ''owner becomes pet and vice versa.'' Saki would repeat such use of a surprise ending throughout his career as a short story writer, perhaps most famously so in *The Open Window.* While that story's ending brought about a comic effect, in ''The Interlopers,'' which Saki wrote at the end of his career, this pattern is now employed with a more vicious twist: the human hunters become the hunted. This motif is repeated in two different ways. Georg Znaym and Ulrich von Gradwitz are turned into game as each hunts the other, his lifelong enemy. More crucially, however, the men, pinioned under a fallen tree, are about to become the helpless quarry of a pack of wolves. A critic for the *New York Times* points out that ''The Interlopers'' differs from the other stories in *The Toys of Peace*—as it does, in

fact, from the bulk of Saki's short story oeuvre—in its grimness.

Saki places these two men in a setting that underscores their menacing intent. The forest in which the story takes place is primeval and infused with the ominous characteristics of an entity rife for the hunt itself. On this night particularly, there is ''movement and unrest among the creatures that were wont to sleep through the dark hours.'' The woods are dark and cold, and they contain a ''disturbing element.'' Ulrich peers through the ''wild tangle of undergrowth'' and listens through the ''whistling and skirling of the wind and the restless beating of the branches.'' Ulrich's own actions further intensify this atmosphere, for he has placed ''watchers . . . in ambush on the crest of the hill.''

Saki immediately sets the atmosphere of the hunt with the story's opening sentence. The reader is introduced to Ulrich, who stands ''watching and listening, as though for some beast of the wood to come within the range of his vision, and later, of his rifle.'' The narrative quickly reveals, however, that Ulrich is not hunting a beast but rather, he ''patrolled the dark forest in quest of a human enemy.'' That enemy is Georg Znaeym. Georg and Ulrich were born enemies, having inherited from their grandfathers a bitter feud over the very piece of land where Ulrich now stands. Instead of dissipating the feud over the years, ''the personal ill-will of the two men'' had made it grow; ''as boys they had thirsted for one another's blood, [and] as men each prayed that misfortune might fall on the other.'' Now, each has independently determined to bring about the other's death. To accomplish this goal, each has set out in the forest—knowing that is where his enemy lurks—with a ''rifle in his hand . . . hate in his heart and murder uppermost in his mind.'' In these matching desires, Ulrich and Georg have transformed the other into prey. Thus, each man is at the same time the hunter and the hunted.

Despite actively placing themselves in these roles, the men are aware of the perversity of the situation. When they finally come face to face with each other and with the opportunity ''to give full play to the passions of a lifetime,'' neither can bring himself ''to shoot down his neighbour in cold blood and without word spoken.'' Both men are unable to give themselves up to the wildness of nature. They still respect ''the code of a restraining civilization,'' thus they recognize that murdering another human— in actuality, hunting him down—is unforgivable

What Do I Read Next?

- In Frank Stockton's short story "The Lady or the Tiger" (1884), a princess is forced to decide whether to bestow upon her lover the fate of death or of marriage to another woman.

- Giving title to Saki's 1919 collection, his short story "The Toys of Peace" relates a man's attempts to convince his nephews to use their new toy, a model city, as an instrument of peace rather than of war.

- Saki's "The Name-Day," collected in *Beasts and Super-Beasts* (1914) also takes as its locale Austria-Hungary of the Hapsburg Empire. It centers around a train deserted on a railway track as wolves cavort around in the woods outside.

- "An Occurrence at Owl Creek Bridge" (1891), by Ambrose Bierce, is about a Civil War prisoner who is about to be hanged. The prisoner escapes and traverses an eerie landscape to make his way home—or does he?

- Shirley Jackson's short story "The Lottery" (1948), a shocking allegory of barbarism and social sacrifices, recounts the events leading up to a small town's annual lottery.

- O. Henry, a master of the trick ending, wrote "The Furnished Room" in 1904. This short story tells of a young man's futile search for his girlfriend and his eventual suicide.

"except for an offence against his hearth and honour." Ulrich and Georg's mutual indecision renders them unable to take action. They understand that fulfilling their desires would place them in opposition with the rules of society.

Nature, however, is able to act swiftly. A lightning strike makes a beech tree fall down upon them, pinioning them under its branches. The falling of the tree thus places both men in to the role of the helpless. They are cast into the role of "captive plight" of game in a trap. Like the animals they might hunt, no respite is available to them until their men come to release them. Their speech, as well as Saki's narrative, reflects their understanding of this situation. Georg, "savagely," sees Ulrich as "snared" in the forest. Ulrich, for his part, declares that when his men free him, he will kill Georg and tell others that this enemy "met . . . death poaching on my lands." The concept of the hunt—as well as the victory it represents—continually shapes the perceptions of the men, even at a time they no longer are in the position to be hunting any man or any beast.

Surprisingly, while lying trapped under the tree, the two men come to a historic decision: they vow to put their quarrel behind them and instead make peace. In so doing, they harness the better part of their human nature. Their settlement stands in marked contrast to all of their past enmity and hatred, which required that they suppress their humanity and instead act upon their baser animal nature. The men's language demonstrates their acknowledgment that they are entering this new phase. Ulrich refers to their past behavior as the behavior of a "devil" rather than the behavior of a hunter; he also suggests that they now take on the role of "friend." Georg speaks of coming to visit Ulrich on his land and "never fir[ing] a shot . . . save when you invited me as a guest." Ulrich and Georg determine to embrace their human ability to reason and to forgive.

The men are eager to get free of their plight, and both are also eager "that his men might be the first to arrive, so that he might be the first to show honourable attention to the enemy that had become a friend." By adding this detail to the narrative, Saki shows that, despite their interest in making peace and giving up the hunt, the men still desire to have victory over the other. Thus, they have not completely given up any notion of competition, they have simply channeled it into a more acceptable, less harmful form.

To expedite their release, the men decide to call out for their foresters, and they raise their voices in unison ''in a prolonged hunting call.'' As their luck would have it, instead of beckoning their foresters their calls alert a pack of wolves, which begins to advance toward the captive men. The wolves follow Ulrich's path ''down the hillside.'' By mimicking the earlier movement of Ulrich as well as the movement of the foresters, the wolves manifest the similarity between man and beast; as the men were earlier hunting each other, now the wolves are hunting the men.

Alexander Malcolm Forbes writes in the *Dictionary of Literary Biography,* ''[I]n an approximation to parable that is rare for Munro, ''The Interlopers'' becomes one of his most idealistic and paradoxically pessimistic stories.'' Indeed, the story imparts multiple lessons about the benefits of peace as well as the folly of humankind placing itself above the laws of nature. The story implicitly explains why such a cruel fate befalls these enemies: they have dared to intrude, or interlope, on the domains of the forest. In the ongoing feud over possession of this strip of land, both the Gradwitz and Znaeym families have attempted to assert authority where they have no right to do so. Only contrived legal mechanisms gave the von Gradwitz family the forest. In hunting the land and asserting it belongs to them, the men tried to tame the area, but their claim on the land derives only from the authority of civilized society, not from any real sense of belonging or unity. However, the forest is truly primeval; it is a place of survival of the fittest. When the men return to the forest with the deliberate goal of hunting down and killing their enemy, Ulrich and Georg forsake the protection afforded each by the codes of civilization. Their actions also help return the forest to its rightful occupants: beasts on the hunt. They are unable to fulfill this role, but the wolf pack is able to do so.

Before the two men make their peace, Georg announces, ''We fight this quarrel out to the death, you and I and our foresters, with no cursed interlopers to come between us.'' In this declaration, to which Ulrich accedes, Georg demonstrates one crucial error: he believes the interlopers are the representatives of the legal institutions that have come between him and the land. In reality, the interlopers are he and Ulrich, who have attempted to usurp this wild territory. At the end of the story, the wolves assert the primacy of beast over human within the land they can claim as their own. Their impending

> ''The story implicitly explains why such a cruel fate befalls these enemies: they have dared to intrude, or interlope, on the domains of the forest.''

destruction of Georg and Ulrich show that the animals who hunt in the forest, not the men who hunt there, are in control.

Source: Rena Korb, Critical Essay on ''The Interlopers,'' in *Short Stories for Students,* The Gale Group, 2002.

Douglas Dupler

Dupler has published numerous essays and has taught college English. In this essay, Dupler examines Saki's use of literary device and its impact on the story's effectiveness.

Saki was a master of the literary device. Devices are subtle ''tricks'' that authors employ to make stories interesting, to move plots along, and to keep readers absorbed. The short story form, with its need to entice readers quickly from beginning to end, lends itself well to the use of literary device. Unlikely events, suddenly twisting plots, and trick endings are devices that allow short stories to pack excitement in small spaces. Saki's story ''The Interlopers'' has several prime examples of the literary trick in action; in fact, the story relies on literary device for its effectiveness. However, despite the efficiency and excitement in his storytelling, Saki's reliance on literary trickery in ''The Interlopers'' ultimately detracts from the depth of the story, and keeps the story from being a truly great work of literature.

The beginning of ''The Interlopers'' is normal enough, but then again, every trickster needs a straight act to set up the audience. The story commences by providing a setting with realistic detail, describing a forest ''somewhere on the eastern spurs of the Carpathians . . . one winter night.'' The forest also has a particular mood. There are animals ''running like driven things,'' and on this ''wind-scourged winter night'' there is a ''disturbing ele-

> "This is the beauty of a well-used literary device; the reader, so absorbed in the story, stops demanding strict reality and flows along with the plot."

ment'' and ''movement and unrest among the creatures.'' Despite being placed in a far-off time and place, which hints that it might be a fable or tale, the story begs to be taken seriously because of the precise details and serious tone of the setting.

In addition to the scenery, a man is present, and realistic details form his character. His name, Ulrich von Gradwitz, connotes the foreign, while other clues imply he is of aristocratic, central European stock. However, Ulrich is not an average sportsman; he ''patrolled the dark forest in quest of a human enemy.'' Closing the first paragraph with this line, Saki uses foreboding to temper the realism of the setting, to let the reader gently know that something strange might be starting to happen. Continuing with realistic detail, the next paragraphs present a deeper explanation of the characters and setting, and introduce the conflict of the story, the enmity between two longtime rivals.

After the story is set up, the first device, or trick, of the plot quickly takes place at the end of the third paragraph. Just at the time when meeting Georg Znaeym ''man to man'' was ''uppermost in his thoughts,'' Ulrich steps around a large tree and sees his enemy face-to-face. At first, given the situation, this might not seem too out of the ordinary—two rivals meeting each other on a dark night in a disputed forest. However, from the beginning of the story, the reader is informed that these two men have ''thirsted for one another's blood'' since they have been boys, and that they have ''each prayed that misfortune might fall on the other.'' Furthermore, the reader has been told that this rivalry spans all the way back to the characters' grandfathers. There has been plenty of time for these two men to act out their aggressions. Of all the times when this story could have taken place, it just so happens that it takes place on the one night the

two enemies meet. Thus the first trick: something happening in a story that is unlikely or out of the ordinary in real life, coming as a surprise to all involved.

The tricky plot twists do not stop there. Just when the ''chance had come to give full play to the passions of a lifetime'' for the main characters, ''a deed of Nature's own violence'' stops the two enemies right in their tracks. The second major plot twist occurs as a falling tree branch thunders down. This crashing branch lands perfectly enough to trap both men without seriously injuring either of them, leaving them face to face but immobile and helpless. It is an exciting moment for the reader, and a clever step in an unfolding drama between two people with conflict. However, if the first plot twist, of two longtime enemies meeting in the flesh after a lifetime of rivalry, is questionable, this second literary trick might be nearly unbelievable. Surprisingly, though, the reader does not react with disbelief, because the situation has become too interesting to cause the reader to slow down or to think over the likelihood of events. An intense conflict has finally come out in the open, begging to be resolved. This is the beauty of a well-used literary device; the reader, so absorbed in the story, stops demanding strict reality and flows along with the plot.

It is at this point that a potent story begins, the story of two people finally being granted what they most desire, the chance to confront a mortal enemy. The characters' first reactions are typical; they insult and threaten one another. The accident brings ''a strange medley of pious thank-offerings and sharp curses.'' Each man fantasizes about the near future when his own version of justice will be served to the other, but both men are helpless. The reader stays absorbed because the outcome remains curious and undecided.

Thus the story has moved from a tale of possibly violent revenge to a situation with more human dimensions: both men are vulnerable. Ulrich sees the pain of Georg, and offers him his wine flask in a gesture of kindness. The story deepens as it begins to address human frailty and a challenging moral puzzle. However, this is also the place in the story that Saki's style and technique, of brevity and tricky plot twists, fail to provide the depth that could make the story truly empathetic and multi-faceted.

For example, Ulrich goes from anger and hatred of his rival to compassion in hardly any time at all. At one moment he is threatening Georg with the worst, and the next moment he is offering his wine flask in peace. He has a major change of heart with hardly any intervening thoughts, except musing on how cold it is, how difficult it is to open his wine flask, and how good the wine tastes. The reader hears his forgiving words, but has no idea how and why this change has occurred so quickly and definitively. Saki does not spend any time examining Ulrich's motives and internal thoughts, because of his style of moving the story along quickly. Humor even enters into the story at this serious moment; when Ulrich asks Georg for his friendship, he comments on the "stupid strip of forest, where the trees can't even stand upright in a breach of wind." The situation, in keeping with Saki's style, remains entertaining and lighthearted.

Very rapidly and in order, Georg also has a change of heart without much explanation. After a period of silence, conveyed by one quick line, Georg agrees to forgiveness and a new attitude. Compared to his fuming rage just a few minutes earlier, this character is now envisioning a completely new life with a new friend. A lifetime has been changed in "this last half-hour."

The dialogue and thoughts of the two characters, as they understand the situation and forgive each other, are important and critical parts of the story. At their best, though, these characterizations come across as superficial and impersonal. Ulrich has a change of heart without any real explanation, as does Georg. The conversation they share is plain, given the circumstances, and the two men, with their unremarkable dialogue, become practically interchangeable. In fact, it would be difficult to pick out which lines belong to which character if they were not labeled, because the two men speak so similarly and topically.

Saki's narration indicates that this moment of forgiveness in the story is crucial, when the storyteller writes that "both men were silent, turning over in their minds the wonderful changes that this dramatic reconciliation would bring about." However, letting the reader in on these "wonderful changes" would take longer and deeper narration than Saki gives, and the reconciliation is thus not that dramatic. The two characters remain shadowy, as the focus shifts to the possibility of other "men" entering the story to save them. In great stories, characters are portrayed as unique individuals with personalities, problems, and backgrounds of their own. Furthermore, in great stories, the changes that characters undergo often provide hints of deeper or more general truths for the reader. Using these measures of greatness, Saki's story comes up short. In his zest for brevity and momentum, the author misses the chance to deepen the situation and to more fully develop the characters.

At the end of "The Interlopers," it is up to the reader to decide what exactly has happened. Of course, it is a trick ending. The paragraphs toward the end lead the reader into believing that helpers are coming to assist the two fallen men. But in one quick line the story takes a completely different meaning: "Wolves!" Just when the reader has gained some empathy and trust of the characters, the author does them in with a macabre plot twist.

With this ending, the story becomes an ambiguous morality tale. Because both men have lived lives full of hatred and dreams of revenge, they are now doomed, because they have learned to forgive too late. Other "interlopers" of fate have surprisingly intervened. At the same time, a more optimistic reading of the ending could be made. Perhaps the two men, being full of compassion and forgiveness at their end, find peace in the face of death. The author leaves no clues, being intent on keeping the plot twisting, the story surprising, and on not demanding too much of the reader's time or energy. Ultimately, in his flashy use of literary device, Saki leaves it up to the reader to determine the final meaning of the story, that of redemption or punishment. The story is witty, readable, and full of momentum to the very end. However, "The Interlopers" speeds past the chance to provide deeper insight into the lives of two characters and their human dilemma.

Source: Douglas Dupler, Critical Essay on "The Interlopers," in *Short Stories for Students,* The Gale Group, 2002.

Sources

Forbes, Alexander Malcolm, "Saki," in *Dictionary of Literary Biography,* Vol.162: *British Short-Fiction Writers,* edited by John H. Rogers, Gale Research, 1996, pp. 240–50.

Frost, Adam, "A Hundred Years of Saki," in *Contemporary Review,* December 1999, Vol. 275, p. 302.

Review of *The Toys of Peace,* in *New York Times Book Review,* July 6, 1919, p. 358.

Review of *The Toys of Peace,* in *Spectator,* March 22, 1919, p. 380.

Further Reading

Langguth, A. J., *Saki: A Life of Hector Hugh Munro,* Simon & Schuster, 1981.
    Langguth's biography includes six previously unpublished Saki short stories.

Williamson, Samuel R., Jr., *Austria-Hungary and the Origins of the First World War,* St. Martin's Press, 1991.
    Through examination of Hapsburg decisions made from 1912 through 1914, Williamson argues that Austria-Hungary, not Germany, initiated the military steps that brought about World War I.

The Replacement

Alain Robbe-Grillet
1962

"The Replacement" by Alain Robbe-Grillet was collected with other sketches and published in 1962 under the title *Instantanes* (translated as *Snapshots*). "The Replacement," along with the other sketches in *Snapshots,* is a classic text of the New Novel movement, which originated in France in the 1950s. The movement was made up of a group of writers that included Nathalie Sarraute, Claude Simon, Robert Pinget, Marguerite Duras, and Michel Butor. These writers rejected literary traditions of plot, action, narrative, and characterization in their works, and created a new literary form that presented an objective record of objects. As the movement quickly became popular throughout the literary world, Robbe-Grillet became its most famous writer and spokesperson.

"The Replacement," an intricate interweaving of three plot lines, continually confounds readers' efforts to piece together a coherent and definitive explanation, which is exactly the goal of the writers of the New Novel movement. Their point is that authors should not impose meaning on a literary work, that instead readers should be left to decide for themselves how to come to an understanding of it.

The plot of "The Replacement" centers on the interaction between a frustrated teacher and his bored students, the story they are reading in class, and a schoolboy just outside the classroom window.

Seen as a whole, the sketch becomes a fascinating statement on the philosophy of this innovative movement, offering an exploration of how to "read" a text.

Author Biography

Alain Robbe-Grillet was born on August 18, 1922, in Saint-Pierre-Quilbignon, France, a municipality that is now part of Brest in Brittany. His parents were Gaston Robbe-Grillet, a manufacturer, and Yvonne Canu Robbe-Grillet, the daughter of a navy petty officer. Robbe-Grillet attended schools in Brest and Paris. Jeanine P. Plottel, in her article on Robbe-Grillet for *European Writers,* notes that while his parents were not well off economically, "they were particularly arrogant, convinced that they were more intelligent, capable, and talented than the world-at-large." Plottel also characterizes them as right-wing anarchists, "[f]illed with contempt and hatred for French democratic institutions." His father received several citations for his service during World War I, but his experiences during this period left him mentally unbalanced. Robbe-Grillet's mother has suggested that her son turned his father's mental instability into genius.

World War II interrupted Robbe-Grillet's schooling, as the Germans forced him to work in Nuremberg for the STO, their labor camp system. He worked there for a year as a lathe operator in a tank factory. He was able to complete his education at the Institut National Agronomique in 1945. After graduation he worked for the Institut National de la Statistique et des Etudes Economiques and later as an engineer and an agricultural scientist. Ill health, however, prevented him from continuing his career in agriculture, and during his convalescence he turned to writing.

Plottel suggests that Robbe-Grillet's experiences during the war left him ambivalent about politics, and so he discarded the anarchist philosophy of his parents. Thus, he refused to incorporate politics into his writing. Plottel writes that he "sought to write from the perspective of modernity. The revolution he wanted had to be expressed in the shape and texture of the work itself and not in the expression of partisan politics."

Robbe-Grillet could not find a publisher for his first novel, *Un régicide,* written in the late 1940s, and so began a second, *Les gommes* (translated as *The Erasers*), which was published in 1953 and subsequently won the Prix Fénéon. During this period, he also wrote literary reviews for *L'Express,* a daily newspaper, that were eventually reprinted in 1963 in *Pour un nouveau roman* (translated as *Towards a New Novel* and *For a New Novel: Essays on Fiction*).

His third novel, *Le voyeur* (translated as *The Voyeur*), published in 1955, won the Prix des Critiques and cemented his reputation as one of the creators of a new narrative form, later dubbed the "New Novel." *La jalousie* (translated as *Jealousy*) and *Dans le labyrinthe* (translated as *In the Labyrinth*), his next two novels, gained popular and critical success and insured his position as one of the most important literary figures in France. His acclaimed short story "The Replacement" was collected with other sketches and published in 1962 under the title *Instantanes* (translated as *Snapshots*). In 1960 he began a successful career as a screenwriter and director of films, including the highly acclaimed *L'Année dernière á Marienbad* (*Last Year at Marienbad,* 1961) and *L'Immortelle* (*The Immortal One,* 1963).

Robbe-Grillet has received several awards for his literary and cinematic achievements. In 1955 he won the Prix des Critiques for *Le Voyeur,* and in 1961 *L'Année dernière á Marienbad* won the Golden Lion at the Venice Film Festival. In 1963 *L'Immortelle* won the Prix Louis Delluc, and in 1969 *L'Homme qui ment* (The liar) won the prize for best screenplay at the Berlin Festival.

Plot Summary

The narrative weaves together three separate scenes. The first involves a schoolboy who is standing by a tree, peering intently at something in the branches. He repeatedly tries to reach a branch that seems within his grasp. After failing to grasp it, he lowers his arm, appears to give up, and continues to stare at something in the leaves. He then returns to the foot of the tree and resumes the same position he took at the beginning of the story. The narrator describes the position of the boy's body as he peers up at the branches. He holds a book satchel in one hand while the other hand is obscured, probably because he is using it to balance himself against the tree. His face is pressed to the tree and turned in such a way that it would not be visible to an observer. The boy scrutinizes something unidentifiable about a yard and a half above the ground.

The narrative then shifts to the second scene, which is inside a classroom. There a boy who has been reading aloud suddenly pauses, probably, the narrator concludes, because he has come to a period. The boy makes an effort, which is not described, to indicate that he is at the end of a paragraph. Here the narrative abruptly shifts to a one-sentence description of the schoolboy outside changing his position so that he can ''inspect the bark of the tree higher up.''

Back in the classroom, the other children are whispering. When the schoolmaster looks at them, he notices that most of them are not following the reading in their books, but are instead looking toward his desk ''with a vaguely questioning, or fearful, expression.'' He then asks the reading boy in a severe tone, ''What are you waiting for?'' The boy resumes his reading ''with the same studious voice, expressionless and a bit too slow.'' The narrator shifts again to the schoolboy, this time linking the two scenes together by indicating that he is across the street from the classroom peering at the leaves on the lower branches of the tree. Immediately the reader is pulled back into the classroom as the teacher slaps the desk with his hand, correcting the boy's reading of the story and telling him to pay attention to what he is reading.

The boy starts reading again in the same monotone but stops abruptly in the middle of a sentence. The other students, who had been looking at a paper puppet hanging on the wall, immediately return their eyes to the book. As the teacher angrily instructs the boy to continue reading, the boy looks behind the teacher at the paper puppet. When the teacher demands to know whether the boy understands what he is reading, the boy pauses, glancing around the room, and then replies that he does. Yet when the teacher asks him the definition of one of the words he is reading, he cannot respond.

The teacher enters into a discussion with another pupil about the story and its meaning. The student understands that the characters ''wanted to go somewhere else and make people think they were still there.'' The narrator then relates part of the story that is being read in the classroom.

The teacher concurs with the boy's assessment and asks him to summarize the story for the rest of the students, which he does ''almost coherently.'' Yet he does not hit all the main points of the story, stressing instead minor details. The boy also does

not discuss the motives behind the characters' actions. As he speaks, the teacher looks out the window and apparently sees the schoolboy, who has returned to his spot below the tree branch and is ''jumping up and down, stretching one arm upward'' to the leaves. When the schoolboy fails to reach the leaves, he again stands motionless staring at them.

The narrator again inserts a part of the story being read in the classroom, noting that all of the students are staring at the puppet. The teacher stops the boy reading and finds a new reader, who reads with a similar lack of interest as the children return their attention to the text. As the reading resumes, the teacher again looks out the window where the boy is gazing intently at the bark. The students glance up at the teacher as he looks out the window, but they cannot see out of the frosted glass and so their attention turns back to the paper puppet.

Characters

The Children in the Classroom

The children in the classroom all exhibit similar behavior. Most of the time they reveal their inattentiveness. While the first boy is reading, they whisper among themselves instead of following along in the text. They also spend a lot of time staring at a paper puppet hanging at the front of the class. They apparently fear the teacher, as noted when they look toward the teacher and reveal ''a vaguely questioning, or fearful, expression.'' As soon as the first boy stops reading, their attention immediately returns to the book.

First Boy

The first boy is one of three boys in the classroom to whom readers are introduced. At the beginning of the sketch, he reads aloud. As he is reading, he suggests that he is obedient as he has been following the teacher's rigid directions about pauses for punctuation. When the boy suddenly pauses, the narrator concludes the boy has come to a period and states ''he gave the impression that he was making an effort to indicate the end of a paragraph.''

The boy's actions suggest boredom as he reads each passage ''with the same studious voice, expressionless and a bit too slow.'' Perhaps it is this boredom that causes him to appear inattentive, even a bit rebellious, when the teacher confronts him. When the teacher demands that he continue reading, the boy looks behind the teacher at the paper puppet before beginning again. At another point, when the teacher criticizes him, the boy pauses, glancing around the room before he tries to defend himself. The narrator does not make clear the motives behind these actions.

The Schoolboy

The schoolboy is standing by a tree outside of the classroom. He is described as peering intently at the tree, exhibiting a tremendous degree of concentration as he alternates between staring at the branches and the bark. He also shows determination as he continually attempts to reach the leaves that are just outside of his grasp. He is periodically watched by the teacher.

Second Boy

The teacher calls on the second boy after the one who was reading first could not answer a question. The second boy appears intelligent, providing a correct answer to the question posed, but he also shows the same boredom and possible rebellion as did the first boy. When the teacher asks the second boy to summarize the entire passage they have been reading, he pauses and looks out the window. Like the first boy, he clearly has not been thinking very much about the passage, since when he summarizes the story, under orders from the teacher, for the rest of the students, he does it "almost coherently." He does not hit all the main points of the story, stressing instead minor details.

The Teacher

The teacher shows his impatience and his shortness of temper when, in "a severe tone," he asks the first boy who has stopped reading, "What are you waiting for?" Later, he slaps the desk with his hand, correcting the boy's reading of the story and telling him to pay attention to what he is reading. Like his students, the teacher also appears bored with the lesson, frequently looking out the window, apparently at the schoolboy who is peering at the tree.

Third Boy

The third boy starts to read after the teacher interrupts the second boy's summary. The third boy reads with the same bored attitude as the others.

Themes

Knowledge

The main theme in "The Replacement" focuses on the attainment of knowledge. The story is about how people perceive the world and how they often become confused when they try to interpret it. Robbe-Grillet reveals this theme through the interweaving of three plot lines. The central story, that of the interaction between the teacher and his pupils, centers on communication problems. The teacher apparently has instructed the students on how to read a text by pausing for the punctuation. Yet when the students do this, the teacher is not satisfied, due to their monotone readings. The teacher has not been able to communicate his idea of how one should read a story.

The students' lack of understanding could be due to their apparent boredom in the classroom. Every chance they get, they whisper among themselves and glance around the room, especially at the paper puppet that hangs in the front, instead of actively concentrating on the text.

The second plot line, of the schoolboy peering intently at the tree, does not seem to relate to the first. The boy is outside, across the street from the classroom, but he does not interact with anyone in the room and it is not clear whether the teacher is looking at him when he glances out of the window. The third piece, the story that is being read in the classroom, also appears to have no relation with the other two plot lines. Thus, it is confusing to try to piece the plot lines together by determining a relationship between the scenes in order to arrive at an understanding of the whole story.

This theme reflects the main focus of the writers of the New Novel movement, who discarded traditional literary structures, which they found to express unrealistic views of experience. They construct their works, instead, to promote the idea of the indeterminacy of existence and so refuse to impose on the reader any subjective points of view. They try to achieve objectivity by fragmenting the text, as Robbe-Grillet does in "The Replacement," so that readers can reconstruct the pieces of descriptions of objects and direct experiences, and therefore the reality, for themselves.

Imagination

Another theme that relates to the problem of gaining knowledge is the use of the imagination.

One possibility for interpreting the relationship between the stories of the students and the schoolboy looking at the tree is to suggest that the schoolboy is a figment of the teacher's or the students' imagination. Everyone inside the classroom is bored by the material and upset by the obvious tension between the teacher and the students. As a result, they could have escaped by conjuring up the figure of the schoolboy, unencumbered by the classroom walls and the demands of the teacher or the curriculum, focusing intently on something that interests him. The narrator, however, does not impose this interpretation on the story, and so the reader is left with only a tentative conclusion.

Perseverance

One way the two stories could be linked is through the theme of perseverance. The schoolboy exhibits this quality as he intently gazes at the tree, trying to extract some information from it, and as he repeatedly tries to reach the leaves. The children in the classroom persevere with their studies, trying but failing to respond to the work in the way the teacher demands. The teacher, however impatient, also refuses to halt his efforts to communicate his directions to the students. The narrator never offers insight as to why all persist in such dogged ways.

Style

Plot

Robbe-Grillet constructs a nontraditional plot in "The Replacement." He interweaves three fragments: the interaction between the teacher and the pupils in the classroom, the schoolboy peering intently at the tree, and the story that is being read aloud in the classroom. Robbe-Grillet continually moves among the three, which disrupts chronology and subverts readers' understanding of the elements in the story.

The narrator does not make clear the relationship between the schoolboy looking at the tree and what is happening in the classroom. Readers are not sure whether the teacher periodically looks out the window to observe the boy or something else. Thus the schoolboy could be a figment of the teacher's imagination, or the students' imagination, as the students cannot see out of the frosted windows.

Robbe-Grillet again confounds readers' expectations for an understandable plot with his inclusion

Topics for Further Study

- Read Robbe-Grillet's short sketch, "The Wrong Direction" and compare its style and themes to that of "The Replacement."

- Read a work by another author associated with the New Novel movement—such as Nathalie Sarraute, Claude Simon, Robert Pinget, or Marguerite Duras—and compare and contrast that work to "The Replacement." Do the two works share similar themes and construction?

- Write a short sketch of something you have observed, using the same style as Robbe-Grillet does in "The Replacement." Try to fragment the sketch, weaving together pieces of real scenes with memory and/or imagination.

- Robbe-Grillet rejected the political point of view of writers like Jean-Paul Sartre and Simone de Beauvoir. Research those views along with biographical details of Robbe-Grillet's life and try to determine what turned the younger writer against them.

of a bit of the story that is being read aloud in the classroom. The first line that is read is, "Therefore, that evening, Joseph de Hagen, one of Philippe's lieutenants, went to the Archbishop's palace on the pretext of paying a courtesy call." A few more passages are read until the final passage, which ends with that same sentence. The narrator does not clear up confusion as to whether the boy reading made a mistake at this point or whether the narrative moved back in time to the beginning of the story, making it difficult for readers to arrive at a conclusive interpretation.

Characterization

The characterizations in the sketch are as enigmatic as the plot. The third-person narrator reports actions objectively, never allowing readers to see the motives behind actions. For example, no motivation is provided as to why the schoolboy is so fascinated with parts of the tree or why he is so desperate to grab some leaves. The interaction between the characters provides some clue to their personality but no definitive analyses. The narrator does not name the characters or their specific location, instead providing brief, surface descriptions of objects, actions, and dialogue. This lack of characterization makes it difficult to make distinctions between the pupils, especially since they all act in the same manner.

The narrator instead repeatedly describes the same actions, making it unclear whether the children are actually repeating actions or whether the plot is returning to the same scene over and over again. This occurs with the schoolboy who shifts his gaze to the branches and then to the bark of the tree. This pattern occurs several times during the sketch. The children also repeat certain movements. Their attention repeatedly shifts from the teacher to the book to the paper puppet hanging at the front of the classroom.

Occasionally, however, the narrator offers glimpses of what characters are feeling. The description of the teacher's actions and words suggest he is angry and frustrated, and the children as a group regard their teacher with a "vaguely questioning or fearful expression."

Historical Context

The New Novel

The term New Novel (*nouveau roman*) became associated with a group of French writers in the 1950s, most notably Nathalie Sarraute, Claude Simon, Robert Pinget, Marguerite Duras, Michel Butor, and Robbe-Grillet, who rejected literary traditions of plot, action, narrative, and characterization, and created a new novelistic form that presented an objective record of events. Robbe-Grillet coined the term New Novel in his published essays on the nature and future of the novel, later collected in his *Pour un nouveau roman* in 1963.

Originally this group of writers was referred to as *romanciers du regard,* "novelists of the glance." Jeanine Plottel, in her article on Robbe-Grillet for *European Writers,* explains, "When the accuracy of this term came to be questioned and the diversity of these writers became more and more obvious, their novels more and more puzzling," the term *nouveau* was adopted.

Initially the French literary world rejected this new form. Its popularity grew as a result of the reestablishment of the *decades,* or ten-day conferences, a French literary tradition. These conferences were run at the Centre Universitaire de Cérisy-la-Salle in southern Normandy by Mme. Heurgon-Desjardins, and attended by leading writers and intellectuals, including Andre Gide, Thoman Mann, and Paul Valery. The conference held in 1970 cemented acceptance of the New Novel as an important part of contemporary French literature. Robbe-Grillet's prominence in this group of writers was reinforced during a 1975 conference that focused on his novels and films.

John Fletcher, in his article on Robbe-Grillet for *Dictionary of Literary Biography,* argues that the impetus for the creation of this new literary school lies in how Robbe-Grillet and his contemporaries responded to the occupation of France during World War II. Fletcher insists that the occupation "humiliated" an entire generation of French and "led them to question the grounds of the commitment to radical politics preached by intellectuals of the preceding generation, particularly by Jean-Paul Sartre, Simone de Beauvoir, and their associates." According to Fletcher, Robbe-Grillet became a spokesperson for this disaffected generation in the mid 1950s, when he began "to cast doubt on philosophical concepts such as meaning and identity which the elders still took for granted."

The structure of most novels prior to this period expresses a belief in an intelligible universe. The intelligible universe of *Pride and Prejudice,* for example, assumes that all young women should find husbands. Even in the absurd world depicted by the French existentialist authors, humans could find meaning in their own existence if they accepted personal responsibility for their lives. The new writers, however, found this humanistic philosophy false. Robbe-Grillet and other authors associated with the New Novel would not accept the firm tenets of previous writers, claiming texts presented not truth but indeterminacy. Writers of this genre wanted to represent reality without any imposed interpretations. One way they try to achieve this objectivity is by fragmenting the text so that readers can reconstruct the descriptions of objects and direct experiences, and therefore the reality, for themselves.

Fletcher characterizes their writing as expressing "a new realism, a new attitude to time, a new

Compare
&
Contrast

- **1960s:** The New Novel is one of the most popular literary genres.

  Today: The confessional narrative gains a prominent position in the literary world.

- **1960s:** France is just coming out of a period of political instability. During the twelve-year rule of it's post-war government, the Fourth Republic, there are roughly twenty-six changes in prime minister. General Charles de Gaulle founds the Fifth Replic in 1958.

Today: France has enjoyed a relatively stable government since the founding of the Fifth Republic.

- **1960s:** A literary movement called poststructuralism dominates literary theory in Europe and the United States.

  Today: Cultural studies have become the most popular form of literary criticism.

conception of plot, and a new approach to character in literature, all of which had to be tougher, harder, and more transparent'' than in the works of more traditional authors. This new school refused to provide recognizable geographical, historical, or psychological contexts for characters. They confounded readers' perceptions and understanding by breaking up the chronology of the plot, often cutting back and forth between different periods of time and between memory and imagination. Through these methods, the writers do not allow readers to rely on traditional methods of interpretation.

Surrealism

Scholars, like Laurent Dechery in his article in *Mosaic* on Robbe-Grillet's use of language, have compared elements in works by writers in the New Novel school to those of surrealist artists. The surrealism movement originated in France in the 1920s. Surrealists rejected traditional, rational artistic renderings and instead promoted expressions of the unconscious mind.

Surrealism was an extension of Dadaism, a nihilistic movement in art and literature started in 1916 in Zurich by Romanian poet Tristan Tzara, along with Hans Arp, Hugo Ball, and Richard Huelsenbeck, in response to the widespread disillusionment engendered by World War I. The founders meant Dadaism to signify total freedom from ideals

and traditions concerning aesthetics and behavior. The most important concept of Dadaism is the word ''nothing.'' In art, Dadaism produced collage effects as artists arranged unrelated objects in a random fashion. Dadaism in literature produced mostly nonsense poems consisting of meaningless, random combinations of words, which were read in public cafes and bars.

These constructions in art and literature stressed absurdity and the role of the unpredictable in the creative process. This group came into vogue in Paris immediately after the First World War. Tzara carried the school abroad where its influence became apparent in the poetry of Ezra Pound and T. S. Eliot and in the art of Max Ernst and René Magritte. By 1921 Dadaism as a movement was modified into surrealism.

Critical Overview

The literary scene in France did not at first accept the radically new form of Robbe-Grillet's works. However, with the reestablishment of the *decades,* or ten-day conferences (a French literary tradition), and a study of Robbe-Grillet's works by theorist Roland Barthes, Robbe-Grillet soon became a dominant literary figure. Two different critical approaches have been taken in analyses of Robbe-Grillet's works, including the sketches in *Snapshots*. The first, promoted by Barthes, focuses on the author as *choisiste* (''thingist'') as he reproduces the surface reality of things in his texts. Barthes argues in his *Essais critiques* that Robbe-Grillet's novels and stories confound the reader because they illuminate the problems inherent in gaining absolute knowledge about the world because they refuse to present any specific point of view. Critic Bruce Morrissette, however, takes a different approach to the analysis of Robbe-Grillet's work. In his book *Les Romans de Robbe-Grillet,* Morrissette insists it is possible to approach the texts from a psychological perspective, since, he argues, the narrators present subjective, emotional points of view.

Like Barthes, Robert Kanters insists in his review ''The School of the Look'' on the objectivity of the text in his critique of *Snapshots*. He notes the ''powerful'' collection of sketches ''summarizes reasonably well the program or the intention of the New Novel according to Alain Robbe-Grillet.'' Kanters argues that the sketches present ''pure objective observation, a simple list of particulars.'' Robbe-Grillet's goal, he concludes, is ''the situation, and especially the material situation, must speak for itself and, without being interpreted through the consciousness of the author, impose on us a vision and if possible a sensation.''

John Fletcher echoes Morrissette's interpretation in his article on Robbe-Grillet for the *Dictionary of Literary Biography,* when he writes that the sketches ''portray a state of unease, even of ill-contained hysteria, masked by meticulous, apparently dispassionate and objective description.'' Ben F. Stoltzfus, however, in *Alain Robbe-Grillet and the New French Novel,* combines the two theories in his conclusion that the author ''alternates passages in [*Snapshots*] between purely objective descriptions and subjective involvement.'' This pattern, Stoltzfus claims, ''reinforces . . . his basic theme of the fundamental separation between man and things.''

Criticism

Wendy Perkins

Perkins is an instructor of English and American literature and film. In this essay, Perkins con-siders Robbe-Grillet's story as a statement on the philosophy of the New Novel movement.

Prior to the twentieth century, writers structured their works to reflect their belief in the stability of character and the intelligibility of experience. Traditionally, novels and stories ended with a clear sense of closure as conflicts were resolved and characters gained knowledge about themselves and their world. Many writers during the twentieth century challenged these assumptions as they expanded the genre's traditional form to accommodate their characters' questions about the indeterminate nature of knowing in the modern age, a major thematic concern for these writers. Through their works they raised the epistemological question, ''how do we know we really know what we think we know?''

Alain Robbe-Grillet continues this inquiry in ''The Replacement'' as he explores different methods of gaining understanding of an experience or an object. Through his meticulous shaping of the story, he presents an intriguing metaphor for the act of reading a text. As a result, the story becomes a statement on the difficulties inherent in the process of gaining absolute knowledge not only of a literary work, but also of human experience.

''The Replacement,'' an intricate interweaving of three plot lines, continually confounds readers' efforts to piece together a coherent and definitive exegesis, which is exactly the goal of the writers of the New Novel movement. These writers challenged traditional notions of meaning and identity and so created texts that reflect the indeterminate nature of reality and the difficulties inherent in coming to a clear understanding of that reality.

John Fletcher, in the *Dictionary of Literary Biography,* notes that as a result of this philosophy, Robbe-Grillet creates literature ''that is all 'on the surface,' postulating nothing about what may or may not lie behind phenomena.'' He does this by refusing to place characters in a historical moment or to identify them by name, and by disrupting the chronology of the text. Fletcher concludes that, as a result, Robbe-Grillet produces narratives that are not ''afraid of being inconsistent and reflecting a reality that has its own recurring bafflements.''

Laurent Dechery in ''Turning Words into Colors: Robbe-Grillet's Visual Language,'' comments that Robbe-Grillet's subversion of conventional nar-

What Do I Read Next?

- Scholar Harry T. Moore's preface in *Alain Robbe-Grillet and the New French Novel* critiques Robbe-Grillet's work along with other writers included in this genre.

- Robbe-Grillet's *For a New Novel: Essays on Fiction* is a collection of his critical essays about the New Novel, the innovative form Robbe-Grillet helped establish in the 1950s.

- Robbe-Grillet's highly acclaimed novel *Jeal-ousy* presents a traditional love triangle in the author's unique New Novel style of writing.

- Robbe-Grillet's "The Wrong Direction" is a short sketch in the "Three Reflected Visions" section of *Snapshots*. Like "The Replacement," it presents enigmatic images with little commentary.

- Maguerite Duras's *The Lover* tells a partially autobiographical story of a young girl growing up in French Indochina. Duras is another proponent of the New Novel style of writing.

rative structures in all of the sketches in *Snapshots* reveals the author's "attempt to achieve the ultimate transgression while staying within the traditional framework of verbal text." As a result, Dechery concludes he "leaves readers in a situation of undecidability concerning their own status as readers and the cognitive process which takes place while reading the story." They also become confused about "the status of the author, the narrator, the plot, and the characters."

In his *Pour un nouveau roman* (translated as *For a New Novel: Essays on Fiction*), Robbe-Grillet writes, "The world is neither significant nor absurd. It simply is." In addition, "our concept of the world around us is now only fragmentary, temporary, contradictory even, and always disputable. How can a work of art presume to illustrate a preordained concept, whatever it might be?" In "The Replacement," Robbe-Grillet illustrates his concept of the indeterminate nature of reality as he focuses on a class full of students struggling to read a story.

Robbe-Grillet, however, does not begin with the main story; he instead starts with an objective description of an unnamed schoolboy trying and failing to reach a tree branch. The narrator does not place him in any specific setting or suggest any motivations for his actions. Nor does he appear to be linked to the main plot line, other than through the fact that he is identified as being across the street from the school. At a few points in the story, the teacher looks out the window, but it is not clear whether or not he sees the schoolboy.

The third plot line, the unfolding action of the story the students read in the classroom, also appears not to have any relation to the other two plots other than the fact that the students are reading it. Yet Robbe-Grillet does link the three plot lines in a figurative sense. The interweaving of fragments of each plot line becomes an adept illustration of the problematic nature of gaining knowledge, especially in regard to understanding a text.

In the main plot, everyone in the classroom struggles with the story they are reading. The first boy reading the story aloud pauses at punctuation marks, "making an effort to indicate the end of the paragraph," but he does not appear to understand what he is reading. Perhaps his inability to understand results from his obvious and complete lack of interest in the material.

His boredom becomes apparent in his monotonous reading of the text and his pause, at one point, to study a paper puppet hanging at the front of the classroom. Yet his problems with the text could also have resulted from the teacher's instructions on how to read. When the boy stops reading in the middle of

> "Perhaps he, or the other children, created the schoolboy as an alter ego, imagining what it would be like to be experiencing something truly interesting, while his physical self remains in the classroom as an 'alibi' for the teacher."

a sentence, the teacher demands, "All right, go on! There isn't any period there. You don't seem to understand what you are reading." He may have thought a pause was necessary there, even though there was no punctuation, based on the instructions the teacher had given him. Readers cannot make a clear judgment on his motive since the narrator does not offer any insight into his character. Later, the boy reveals that he has not understood the reading when the teacher questions him about specific words.

The next boy who reads appears to have a better understanding of the text, but it is not complete, at least according to the teacher. He knows the meaning of the word "alibi," but when the teacher asks him to give a summary of what they have read, the boy does so "almost coherently." The narrator notes that he "stressed unduly a number of secondary matters, while hardly mentioning, or even omitting, certain crucial events." The narrator also does not include an analysis of the characters' motives, a traditional tool for readers to gain understanding of a text.

The rest of the students seem to have difficulty understanding the text as well, since the next boy chosen to read does so in the same monotonous tone as the others, "although conscientiously indicating the commas and the periods." All of the students express their boredom openly as their attention continually shifts to the paper puppet rather than their books.

Robbe-Grillet's interweaving of lines of the story into the main plot line also illustrates the students' lack of understanding. The first line of the story read by the boy early in the sketch is, "Therefore, that evening, Joseph de Hagen, one of Philippe's lieutenants, went to the Archbishop's palace on the pretext of paying a courtesy call." A few more passages are read periodically throughout the sketch until the final passage, which ends with that same sentence. The repetition of the line could have been caused by the student's confusion about his place in the text, or from a memory of another class, or from an imaginative creation of a class. Robbe-Grillet does not provide a motive, which confounds the reader's effort to understand the story.

The narrator suggests that part of the problem lies with the teacher, who cannot understand why his students are having so much difficulty with the story. The students alternate between boredom and another emotion that the narrator identifies as "vaguely questioning or fearful." The classroom is filled with obvious tension, evidenced by the teacher's anger over the students' inability to read "correctly." He apparently has spent time showing them how he wants them to read the text, but they have not been able to satisfy him. During the teacher's outbursts, the children quickly return their attention to their books, suggesting that they are afraid of further reprimands.

Robbe-Grillet adds a new dimension to this scene when he introduces the description of the schoolboy studying the tree. This description—which includes precise, objective, and often repetitious details—presents a situation that starkly contrasts that of the students in the classroom. This boy cannot take his attention away from the tree, parts of which continually fascinate him. He struggles to "know" the tree and even tries to grasp the leaves so he can study them more closely. However, repeated attempts to reach the leaves end in failure. The narrator notes that the leaves are "inaccessible" to him. Robbe-Grillet links the two plot lines as he notes that, just like the children in the classroom, the schoolboy ultimately fails to completely understand what he is "reading."

The story of the schoolboy and the tree works as a metaphor for indeterminacy on another level. When Robbe-Grillet weaves this plot into the others, he declines to show readers any temporal or spatial links between them. The teacher could be watching the schoolboy out of the window to alleviate his frustration over his students' inability to properly read and understand the story, or the schoolboy could be a memory or an imaginative creation for the teacher or for the students. At one point, the narrator notes that the students cannot see out the frosted windows. Perhaps the schoolboy is their imaginative rendition of what is on the other side.

This last interpretation could be supported by one of the boy's explanation of how "alibi" is used in the story that is read aloud. He determines that the main characters "were really there . . . only they wanted to go somewhere else and make people think they were still there." Perhaps he, or the other children, created the schoolboy as an alter ego, imagining what it would be like to be experiencing something truly interesting, while his physical self remains in the classroom as an "alibi" for the teacher.

Ultimately, readers are left with no clear understanding of what exactly is occurring in the story or what motivates the characters' actions. Like the students in the classroom, readers of "The Replacement," have failed to "read" the story in the traditional way. But the reader's lack of understanding stems from Robbe-Grillet's intentional disruption of narrative conventions. His goal in "The Replacement," like that of others associated with the New Novel movement, is to force readers to arrive at their own understanding of a text without being influenced by the author's intentions. His achievement in "The Replacement" has been to present a compelling illustration of the indeterminate nature of texts and of the world.

Source: Wendy Perkins, Critical Essay on "The Replacement," in *Short Stories for Students,* The Gale Group, 2002.

Sources

Barthes, Roland, *Essais critiques,* Éditions de Seuil, 1964.

Dechery, Laurent, "Turning Words into Colors: Robbe-Grillet's Visual Language," in *Mosaic,* September 1999, Vol. 32, Issue 3, p. 59.

Fletcher, John, "Alain Robbe-Grillet," in *Dictionary of Literary Biography,* Vol. 83, *French Novelists Since 1960,* edited by Catharine Savage Brosman, Gale Research, 1989, pp. 197–211.

Kanters, Robert, "The School of the Look," in *New York Times Book Review,* January 17, 1969, p. 35.

Morrissette, Bruce, *Les Romans de Robbe-Grillet,* Éditions de Minuit, 1963.

Plottel, Jeanine P., "Alain Robbe-Grillet," in *European Writers,* Vol. 13, edited by George Stade, Scribner's, 1990, pp. 3237–57.

Stoltzfus, Ben F., *Alain Robbe-Grillet and the New French Novel,* Southern Illinois Press, 1964.

Further Reading

Harger-Grinling, Virginia, and Tony Chadwick, eds., *Robbe-Grillet and the Fantastic,* Greenwood Publishing Group, 1994.
    This collection of essays focuses on Robbe-Grillet's unique style.

Hellerstein, Marjorie H., *Inventing the Real World: The Art of Alain Robbe-Grillet,* Susquehanna University Press, 1998.
    Hellerstein explores the links between Robbe-Grillet's fiction and films.

Ramsay, Raylene L., *Robbe-Grillet and Modernity: Science, Sexuality, and Subversion,* University of Florida Monographs. Humanities, No. 66, University Press of Florida, 1992.
    As she studies the dominant themes in Robbe-Grillet's fiction, Ramsay places his work in a historical context.

Smith, Roch Charles, *Understanding Alain Robbe-Grillet,* University of South Carolina Press, 2000.
    Smith presents a comprehensive overview of Robbe-Grillet's work.

That in Aleppo Once ...

Vladimir Nabokov

1943

After Vladimir Nabokov's death in 1977, the novelist John Updike included the following praise of him (reprinted in *Critical Essays on Vladimir Nabokov*) in an obituary:

> The power of the imagination is not apt soon to find another champion of such vigor. . . . He takes with him the secret of an undiscourageable creativity, he leaves behind a resplendent oeuvre.

Updike's admiration of Nabokov's work is one shared by many readers. Although he is best known for *Lolita*, his 1955 novel about the perverse Humbert Humbert's love for a twelve-year-old girl, Nabokov wrote seventeen other novels, dozens of poems, essays, lectures on literature, and over fifty short stories. He stands today among the ranks of Joseph Conrad, James Joyce, and Virginia Woolf as one of the twentieth-century's foremost literary stylists.

''That in Aleppo Once . . .'' first appeared in the *Atlantic Monthly* in 1943. It was included in the 1958 collection *Nabokov's Dozen*. The story's title is an allusion to Shakespeare's *Othello,* in which the title character, through the machinations of the villainous Iago, becomes so jealous of his innocent wife that he eventually strangles her and kills himself. Like *Othello,* Nabokov's story explores the issues of jealousy, marital fidelity, and the ways that a credulous mind is affected by one more crafty.

The story is like many other works by Nabokov, which demand careful reading (and rereading) to

understand. Upon first glance, the story seems to be one of an innocent man whose wanton wife makes a fool of him through her adulterous affairs. However, the story, like the narrator's wife, proves more elusive and the events of its plot more difficult to pin down upon closer examination. Nabokov demanded readers tolerate ambiguity and examine the ways in which ambiguity affects the narrator.

Author Biography

Vladimir Vladimirovich Nabokov was born on April 23, 1899, in St. Petersburg, Russia to an upper-class family. As a child, he and his brother enjoyed long walks at Vyra, his grandfather's estate, as well as the attention of private tutors. He learned to read English and French before Russian. All of the passions that marked Nabokov's adulthood (languages, literature, chess, lepidoptera—which is the study of insects such as butterflies and moths) were born in his happy childhood, which he describes in his 1951 memoir, *Speak, Memory*.

Nabokov's father was a lecturer on criminal law and the editor of a liberal law journal. After becoming a member of the St. Petersburg City Duma (council) and urging the adoption of such reforms as a written constitution and the guarantee of civil rights, his father was forced to resign from teaching. He served a three-month jail sentence in 1908 for signing a manifesto urging the public to disobey the Tsar, and subsequently became more involved in government reform, rising through the liberal ranks. In 1922, while attempting to save the life of a fellow official, he was killed by an assassin's bullet. Nabokov, by then a student at Cambridge, graduated the year his father died. His detestation of tyranny is apparent in many of his works.

Like many of his compatriots, Nabokov spent the early twenties in Berlin, where a large number of Russians had fled the turbulence of their native land. While in Berlin, he wrote poetry, concocted crossword puzzles, and translated *Alice's Adventures in Wonderland* into Russian. In 1925, he married Vera Slonim, who would become his life-long assistant and secretary. In fact, he dedicated all of his books to her. During 1925, he composed *Mashen'ka* (translated as *Mary*), his first novel, and a number of short stories. Important works from this

Vladmir Nabokov

period include *Chelovek iz SSSR* (his first play, title meaning "The Man from the USSR," 1926), *Korol', dama, valet* (translated as *King, Queen, Knave*, 1928), *Zashchita Luzhina* (translated as *The Defense*, 1929) and *Kamera obskura* (translated as *Laughter in the Dark*, 1931). In 1934, his only son, Dmitri, was born.

As his literary reputation grew, Nabokov traveled extensively throughout Europe, visiting his siblings and giving readings of his work. In 1937, he obtained permission for his family to relocate to France, where he wrote his first novel in English, *The Real Life of Sebastian Knight* (1938). With the rise of Hitler, however, the Nabokovs' time in France was short; they fled the Nazis in 1940 and sailed to the United States, where Nabokov wrote reviews, collected butterflies, and taught Russian Literature at Stanford University in California and Wellesley College in Massachusetts. His first short story in English, "The Assistant Producer," was written in 1943. "That in Aleppo Once . . .," his second short story in English, was composed the same year. In 1945, he and Vera became American citizens.

Nabokov continued teaching, translating, and writing throughout the 1940s, but in 1955 his greatest period of fame began with the publication of

Lolita in Paris. Fearing its scandalous subject (a middle-aged man's love for a twelve-year-old girl), the novel was rejected by a number of American publishers. It broke onto the international scene when, in the London *Sunday Times,* the English novelist Graham Greene named it one of the three best books of 1955. After long legal struggles and the seizure of foreign copies by U.S. Customs officers, *Lolita* was finally published in the United States in 1958, selling 100,000 copies in three weeks and adding the word ''nymphet'' to the English language. Nabokov was now free from financial concerns and able to wholly devote the rest of his life to his art, which he did mostly in Switzerland. Although some of his later works, such as 1962's *Pale Fire* and 1969's *Ada,* met with equal critical praise, no single work of his ever saw the attention devoted to *Lolita.* His last complete work, *Details of a Sunset and Other Stories* was published in 1976. In 1977 Nabokov died of a lung ailment, with Vera and Dmitri at his hospital bedside. *The Stories of Vladimir Nabokov*, edited by Dmitri, was published in 1995.

Plot Summary

Nabokov's story is written in the form of a letter from an unnamed narrator to V., his Russian expatriate friend living as a novelist in the United States. The narrator begins by telling V. that he has arrived in America. While in New York City, he fortuitously met a mutual friend of theirs (Gleb Alexandrovich Gekko), who provided V.'s address.

After fondly recalling their days as young, eager poets, the narrator begins telling the story of his doomed marriage—the real subject of his letter. He was married ''a few weeks before the gentle Germans roared into Paris,'' which occurred in 1940. However, the narrator claims that he is ''positive'' that his wife ''never existed.'' Her name is ''the name of an illusion'' and he is therefore able to speak of her with ''as much detachment'' as he would a character in a story. When he first met her, he felt no great emotions, but one night she said something ''quaint'' on a walk and he kissed her on the hair. Despite his recollection of this scene, she remains ''nebulous'' to him; he tells V. that he has great difficulty trying to imagine her face. She was younger than the narrator and the reader learns that she was initially attracted to his verse, although the narrator assumes that once she had penetrated the mysteries of his poetry, she found herself stuck with ''a stranger's unlovable face''—his own.

The narrator reveals he had been planning to follow V.'s lead and move to the United States. His wife informs him that she has an uncle living in New York City. The couple writes a ''passionate'' letter that receives no reply. Meanwhile, the narrator has received an invitation to come to the United States from a fellow Russian living in Chicago. Although he has done little to secure the papers he needs to leave France, he knows that he has to begin the process, since the Germans have just invaded and he has written in one of his books that ''Germany was bound to remain for ever and ever the laughing stock of the world.'' Fearing that the German commanders will be shown the book by ''some helpful compatriot,'' the narrator and his wife begin their journey out of France on a series of ''unscheduled trains'' bound for ''unknown destinations.''

During one of their many railroad rides, his wife begins to sob about a dog they left at their flat. Although the narrator is ''struck'' by her grief, he is puzzled, since they never owned a dog. When he makes this point, she says that she tried to imagine that they *had* bought a setter they had previously discussed, although the narrator contends they never discussed buying a setter.

At Faugeres, a stop on the way to Nice, the narrator leaves the train for ten minutes to buy food. When he returns, the train is gone. Several attempts at finding his wife by telephone and telegraph fail, so he decides to continue, hoping to discover that she has continued the journey on her own. A week after his arrival in Nice, a detective informs him that he has located the narrator's wife. He takes the narrator to a seedy hotel where he says the narrator's wife is living. When they arrive, the narrator finds that the woman identified by the detective is not, in fact, his wife.

The narrator leaves the hotel and, on the way back to his lodgings, sees his wife standing in a line outside a food store. She tells him that she had returned to Faugeres, where she met a party of refugees and stayed with them, sleeping in a bicycle shop. When she realized that she did not have enough money to reach Nice (since he had both of their tickets), she borrowed some from one of the refugees. She then boarded the wrong train, arrived in a town whose name she had forgotten, and only made it to Nice two days before he found her. However, she later tells him that this story is a lie and that she had spent several days in Montpellier with a man she had met on the train. Stunned, the narrator grills her for information about her adultery as his anger and jealousy increases to unbearable intensity. During these days of interrogation, the narrator and his wife are also trying to secure the necessary papers permitting them to go to the United States—a formidable task.

At some point during this trying time, the narrator breaks down and begins weeping. Inexplicably, his wife then tells him that she did not commit adultery and that her whole story of the man on the train is a lie. Eventually, with great struggle, the narrator believes her. He also obtains the necessary visas allowing them to travel to the United States. After obtaining them at an office, he returns to their flat to find her and all of her things gone. Distraught, the narrator asks a number of acquaintances if they have seen her but no one provides any information. An old woman, Anna Vladimirovna, accuses him of being "a bully and a cad"; the narrator's wife had apparently told Anna a story about falling in love with a Frenchman and the narrator's refusal to grant a divorce. Anna also rebukes him for hanging his wife's dog before leaving Paris, another story told to her by his wife. Frustrated and indignant, the narrator leaves Anna to sail to the United States alone.

During his sea voyage, the narrator meets a doctor on the ship whom he knows from Paris. The doctor tells him that he saw the narrator's wife in Marseille two days before boarding the ship. The wife had apparently told the doctor that the narrator would be joining her soon with their bags and tickets. "It was at that moment," the narrator explains, "that I suddenly knew for certain that she had never existed at all." When he arrives in New York City, he checks her uncle's address but finds it to be "an anonymous gap" between two buildings. Gekko informs him that the uncle had moved to San Francisco after the death of his daughter.

The narrator concludes his letter by asking V. to tell this story in order to "clarify" it "through the prism" of his art. He is no longer certain if his wife is an adulteress or a pathological liar. He adds that he fears she is walking along the beaches of Marseille, waiting for him to arrive. Fearing that his guilt over leaving her may cause him to replicate the actions of Shakespeare's Othello, who killed himself after

realizing he had murdered his innocent wife, he asks V. not to allude to the play in the story's title. Of course, this is exactly what V. does.

Characters

Gleb Alexandrovich Gekko

An acquaintance of both the narrator and V. who has also emigrated to the United States, Gekko supplies the narrator with V.'s address.

Holmes

Holmes is the "plain-clothes man" from the Nice police who assists the narrator in the search for his wife. Unlike his namesake, the infallible detective Sherlock Holmes, he fails in his attempt to solve the mystery at hand and leads the narrator to a seedy hotel, where he insists that a stranger he produces is the narrator's wife.

The Narrator

"That in Aleppo Once . . ." takes the form of a letter written by an unnamed narrator to V., a fellow Russian expatriate living in New York City. A harmless, earnest, and innocent man, the narrator is reduced to despair over his wife's probable infidelity. Her seeming naiveté is what first attracted him to her. He met her several times "without experiencing any special emotions" and only kissed her on her hair (rather than, for example, her mouth or neck) when she said "something quaint." He cannot imagine her as a potential adulteress. During a railway stop in Faugeres, he kindly steps off the train to buy some food for himself and his new bride. When he discovers that the train has left, he feels he is facing an "atrocious void" and takes great pains to find his missing wife. His concern for her is both believable and commendable. Clearly, he suspects nothing. When he finds her in Nice, he believes her "hazy" yet "perfectly banal" story of how she met up with a band of refugees and friends at a Russian church. The fact that he is admiring her beauty ("she was combing her soft hair and tossing her head back with every stroke") while she delivers the terrible news of her betrayal suggests just how unsuspecting of her he is at that moment.

As if this is not sufficient torture for any husband to bear, his wife then tells him that she did not commit adultery. Her excuse—"Perhaps I live several lives at once. Perhaps I wanted to test you.''—is unconvincing to the reader, yet somewhat sufficient for him, since he yearns to live again in the world of quaint remarks and kisses on the head. Although he grows to accept her excuse, he cannot rid himself of the nagging doubts that her presumed ''test'' of him have engendered: the ''happier'' they become after this rift, the stronger he feels ''an undercurrent of poignant sadness.'' The narrator's telling himself that such a feeling of sadness is ''an intrinsic feature of all true bliss'' is an attempt by him to impose order on the chaos that has infected his mind.

Such an attempt to make sense out of his wife's disappearances and reappearances is what fuels the narrator's letter. He hopes that V. will be able to use his talent by making sense out of disparate pieces of data and ''clarifying things'' through his art. By the letter's end, however, the narrator appears a hopeless man whose doubts about his wife cause her to seem ''an illusion.''

The Narrator's Wife

As the narrator tells the entire story from his point of view, the reader is never allowed to view events through the lens of the story's presumed adulteress. There are different possibilities for her behavior, however, room for all of which Nabokov allows. The first is that, as the reader most likely suspects, she is an unfaithful wife who attempts to retract her confession with a lame excuse and eventually spreads rumors about her husband amongst their expatriate friends. This seems the most likely scenario. After an incident when she cries about leaving an imaginary dog in their home, the narrator says, ''There had never been any talk of buying a setter,'' and the reader has little reason to doubt him. In addition, the narrator hardly seems like the kind of man who would kill such an animal in cold blood, as his wife tells Anna Vladimirovna he did. His wife's reappearance on the embankment, telling the doctor that the narrator ''would presently join her with bag and tickets,'' causes the reader to regard her as an adulteress who assumes that her credulous husband will always receive her into his arms.

However, the possibility remains that she is *not* the strumpet she appears to be in the narrator's account of their marriage. Such a reading would imply that she suffers from some mental disease that prompts her to create stories and tell them to other people (like the narrator, her Russian friends, Anna Vladimirovna, and the doctor). While this possibility may seem unlikely, or even ludicrous, the narrator's guilt in leaving her at the end of the story

suggests that he has certainly entertained this idea. Either she is an adulteress and he has, in his mind, rightfully forsaken her—or he has abandoned a sick woman to the Nazi menace in France. Both possibilities haunt the narrator.

V.

Very little is known of V., the narrator's friend who left France for the United States several weeks before the Germans entered Paris. The fact that he is a novelist, however, suggests to the narrator that V. is capable of making sense of his story. The narrator tells V. that he ''can hardly be expected to puzzle out my misfortunes in terms of human communion, but you may clarify things for me through the prism of your art.'' The narrator seeks a kind of literary third-party to arbitrate the disputing versions of his wife's actions. Regardless of V.'s chosen interpretation of the facts, his naming the story what he does is a suggestion to the narrator that the narrator, like Othello, should take his own life.

Anna Vladimirovna

Anna Vladimirovna is a busybody of a woman who knows the gossip and rumors concerning her fellow émigrés. When the narrator asks her if she has seen his wife, Anna Vladimirovna calls him ''a bully and a cad'' and scolds him for not granting his wife a divorce. She never suspects (like the narrator and the reader) that the narrator's wife invented her tale of a ''young Frenchman who could give her a turreted home and a crested name.'' She also berates the narrator for hanging his wife's dog, another story told by his wife that Anna Vladimirovna, like the other refugees, wholly believes.

Themes

Communication and Miscommunication

Nabokov's France is a place where attempts at communication routinely break down. For example, when the narrator and his wife write to her uncle in New York, they receive no reply. After finding his wife (and the train) gone at Faugeres, the narrator engages in a ''nightmare struggle with the telephone'' trying to find her, and sends ''two or three telegrams which are probably on their way only now.'' These examples of bureaucratic miscommunication serve to underscore the more subtle examples of miscommunication that occur throughout the story. For example, the narrator's wife is initially attracted to his ''obscure'' verse, only to eventually find behind it ''a stranger's unlovable face.'' She had thought the man would be as mysterious as his poetry, but was mistaken. Similarly, before his wife tells him that she has been unfaithful, her body language communicates to him tenderness (he ''held her by her slender young hips'') and beauty (''she was combing her soft hair and tossing her head back with every stroke''), not the horrifying and jarring news she is about to impart. The narrator's visit to Anna Vladimirovna also raises this issue for Vladimirovna accuses him of hanging his wife's dog, despite the fact that he and his wife never even owned one. Apparently, his wife's lies about her marriage are more believable than his truths.

The story's primary communication occurs at the very end, when the narrator tells V., ''It may all end in *Aleppo* if I am not careful.'' With this remark, he is telling his friend (in a literary and roundabout way) that he is considering suicide. When V. titles the story as he does, he is implying to the narrator that he *should* ''end in *Aleppo*'' and take his own life.

Jealousy

In *Othello,* the evil Iago offers his famous warning to Othello:

O, beware, my lord, of jealousy!
It is the green-eyed monster, which doth mock
The meat it feeds on.

Of course, Iago knows that a mind infected with jealousy is almost impossible to set right again. As his own wife remarks, jealous men ''are not ever jealous for the cause, / But jealous for they are jealous.'' The meat that feeds a jealous mind is never in short supply.

Like Othello, the narrator becomes obsessed by the tormenting thoughts of his wife sleeping with another man. When his wife tells him that she spent ''several nights in Montpellier with a brute of a man'' she met on the train, the narrator struggles to extract every shred of information he can about the affair. As Othello becomes wracked with a seizure after imagining his wife making love with Cassio (her supposed lover), the narrator spends his days ''crushing and crushing'' his ''mad molar'' until his jaw ''almost burst with pain.'' Also like Othello,

Topics for Further Study

- Research the events that immediately led to the German invasion of France during World War II, and the plight of those who tried to escape. Compare your findings with the presentation of such events in Nabokov's story.

- Like the narrator, Nabokov also left France once the Germans invaded. Consult a biography of Nabokov and explain how he may have used experiences from his own life while creating the plot of the story.

- Rewrite the story from the narrator's wife's point-of-view, giving clarity to the events that puzzle the narrator and the reader. Decide whether she is innocent, mentally disturbed, or as licentious as the narrator suspects.

- Find another piece of literature whose title alludes to another work and explore how the author in question appropriates the alluded-to work as Nabokov does with *Othello*. Some possible works are Robert Frost's ''Out, Out—,'' Stephen Ambrose's *Band of Brothers,* William Styron's *Darkness Visible,* James Joyce's *Ulysses,* or Ernest Hemingway's *For Whom the Bell Tolls.*

nothing the narrator does to dispel his jealousy has any effect. Although he says that he eventually believed his wife when she later said she was not unfaithful, he still ''felt an undercurrent of poignant sadness.'' While he tries to console himself with the lame excuse that this sadness ''was an intrinsic feature in all true bliss,'' he cannot cleanse his mind of the jealousy and mistrust that has taken root there.

Unlike Othello, however, who learns that his jealousy was the result of Iago's malice, the narrator never knows if his jealousy is grounded in fact. His not knowing the truth concerning his wife's activities proves just as torturous as having a definitive answer. As Iago tells Othello,

That cuckold lives in bliss
Who, certain of his fate, loves not his wronger;

But O, what damned minutes tells he o'er
Who dotes, yet doubts; suspects, yet strongly loves!

These last lines perfectly describe the narrator, who still feels very strongly for his wife (he is considering suicide over leaving her) yet cannot shake the suspicion that she has betrayed him. This inability to ever know the truth is what leads him to seek the assistance of V., whom he hopes will be able to tell him whether he is a cuckold or a callous man.

Style

Setting

Nabokov presents the narrator's struggles with his wife against the background of the German occupation of France during World War II. Thus, domestic horror is likened to national horror; the bureaucratic problems the narrator has with the "consuls and *commissaires*" in obtaining the necessary papers to leave France are likened to the marital problems he faces upon learning of his wife's possible infidelity. The narrator is married in 1940, the same year when the "gentle Germans roared into Paris." As the Nazis bring suffering to everyone in their path, the narrator's wife inflicts tremendous emotional and mental pain upon her husband.

While describing their flight from France, the narrator explains,

> the farther we fled, the clearer it became that what was driving us on was something more than a booted and buckled fool with his assortment of variously propelled junk—something of which he was a mere symbol, something monstrous and impalpable, a timeless and faceless mass of immemorial horror that still keeps coming at me from behind even here, in the green vacuum of Central Park.

Here, Hitler (the "booted and buckled fool") is a symbol of death. All humans are conscious of their inevitable ends, but many are able to keep this thought at bay during their day-to-day lives. Death, however, haunts the narrator even in the pastoral setting of Central Park, which is supposed to be, as he calls it, a vacuum where such thoughts of destruction never occur. Because the narrator is fearful of his own death by suicide, the Nazis are presented as a force whose power extends beyond the reach of both space and time. While the narrator once penned

that Germany would "remain for ever and ever the laughing stock of the world," he is now the laughing stock, humiliated by his wife's possible infidelity.

Allusion

The story's title is an allusion to Shakespeare's *Othello*. Othello's wife, Desdemona, is free from corruption, yet Othello, provoked by the words of Iago, comes to believe that she has been unfaithful to him. At the end of the play, Othello murders Desdemona, learns that Iago has duped him, and then kills himself out of grief and shame. Before killing himself, however, Othello addresses the nobles who have rushed to the chamber where Desdemona lays strangled by his own hands:

> Set you down this;
> And say besides that in Aleppo once,
> Where a malignant and a turbaned Turk
> Beat a Venetian and traduced the state,
> I took by the throat the circumcised dog
> And smote him—thus. *He stabs himself.*

Like the narrator, Othello asks others to tell his story; also like the narrator, he has felt the burden of immeasurable jealousy. Unlike Desdemona, however, the narrator's wife is, perhaps, not wholly innocent. Othello's story about the "malignant" and "turbaned Turk" is a metaphor for himself: a man who hurt a Venetian (Desdemona) and "traduced the state." By killing himself, Othello seeks the punishment he deserves for behaving like a "circumcised dog." At the end of his letter, the narrator writes, "It may all end in *Aleppo* if I am not careful." He fears that he, too, will kill himself out of remorse, if his wife is innocent and he left her to her fate with the Germans. Although the narrator begs V. not to allude to *Othello* in his title, Nabokov's doing so implies that the narrator will meet the same fate as Shakespeare's tragic hero. As Stephen Jan Parker writes in *Understanding Vladimir Nabokov* (1987), "The serious point of these games of parody and allusion" is that they set Nabokov's works "within a line of literary antecedents" which add depth to the works at hand. Thus, "That in Aleppo Once . . ." is enriched greatly by a reader's understanding of *Othello*.

Nabokov also has his narrator allude to the marriage of the Russian poet Alexander Pushkin: "She was much younger than I—not as much younger as was Natalie of the lovely bare shoulders and long ear-rings in relation to swarthy Pushkin," but young enough to allow "a sufficient margin for that kind of retrospective romanticism which finds pleasure in imitating the destiny of a unique genius.'' Like Pushkin, the narrator is a Russian poet with a younger wife. More significant is the fact that Pushkin was betrayed by his wife as the narrator fears he has been. The narrator states that Natalie ''yawned'' whenever Pushkin's verse ''happened to exceed the length of a sonnet,'' but that his own wife was ''attracted by the obscurity'' of his poetry. The narrator's wife's fascination with his verse, however, proves ephemeral, since she eventually ''tore a hole through its veil and saw a stranger's unlovable face.''

The narrator makes another allusion when he tells V., ''I come to you like that gushing lady in Chekhov who was dying to be described.'' The lady in question here is the title character of Anton Chekhov's story, ''The Lady with the Pet Dog'' (1899). Chekhov's story concerns Anna Sergeyevna, a young woman in an unhappy marriage who eventually betrays her husband with Dmitry Dmitrich Gurov, a married man whom she meets while on holiday. The narrator's comparison of himself to Anna Sergeyevna is significant, for in Chekhov's story she is a confused person who cannot reconcile her desires with her duty, just as the narrator cannot reconcile his love for his wife with what he thought was his duty to himself in forsaking her.

Symbolism

While describing to V. the first time he kissed his wife, the narrator compares the moment to ''that blinding blast'' caused when a soldier picks up ''a small doll from the floor of a carefully abandoned house.'' In the context of World War II, the doll is meant to be viewed as a booby-trap containing an explosive detonated by the unwitting soldier; in the context of their marriage, the soldier and the doll symbolize the narrator and his wife. Like a doll, the narrator's wife seems innocent and harmless, but, like *this* particular doll, she is capable of destruction. Like the soldier, the narrator is attracted to the doll but fails to realize that the house has been ''carefully abandoned'': the doll is part of a larger set-up meant to destroy such unsuspecting fools. Death lurks in unlikely places, such as the abandoned house or the ''vacuum'' of Central Park, where the narrator composes the letter intimating his suicidal thoughts.

A second symbol is the dog mentioned by the narrator's wife to him at the train station and to Anna Vladimirovna in Nice. Although the dog does not exist, the narrator's wife becomes distraught at the mere thought of such an animal being abandoned and ''whining behind a locked door.'' Simi-

larly, at the end of the story, the narrator feels remorse for abandoning his wife to the Germans in Marseilles.

Historical Context

World War II and Occupied France

On May 10, 1940, German forces attacked the Netherlands, Belgium, and France. By June 9, the Germans had crossed the Somme River and effectively destroyed any hopes of French retaliation. In an attempt to appease the Germans and end the destruction they caused, Henri Philippe Petain (an eighty-four-year-old Marshal who had become the French premiere on June 16) asked the Germans for an armistice, which they formally granted on June 22. Petain offered the Germans the control of northern France (at France's expense) and asked if the French could establish a government in the southern city of Vichy. The Germans agreed and on July 2 the Vichy government was established. At this time the Nazis held approximately two-thirds of France.

Petain was named chief of state of the Vichy government on July 10, 1940. As many suspected during its formation, the Vichy government proved to be a puppet regime for the Nazis. With his prime minister, Pierre Laval, Petain ruled the unoccupied area of France as a totalitarian dictator and operated in complete collusion with Hitler. Although Petain dismissed Laval for fear of his growing power, the Germans reinstated him in 1942.

Occupied France was essentially a war zone. French citizens were routinely interrogated, arrested by secret police, and forced into labor. Many Jews found in France were sent to concentration camps—a fate that Nabokov's wife, Vera, escaped. During this period of occupation, however, the French general Charles de Gaulle, who had once been an aide to Petain and had escaped to London shortly after the fall of his country, drummed up Allied support for his besieged people and formed the Free French. The Free French was a committee established in London on June 28, 1940, which sought to continue the fight against Germany until France was freed from Nazi terror. Eventually, the Allies invaded Normandy on June 6, 1944 (D-Day), and France was liberated shortly thereafter. The Free French troops, with de Gaulle at their head, were the

Compare & Contrast

- **1940s:** A number of authors naturally turn to World War II for their subject matter. Books such as Ilya Eherenberg's *The Fall of Paris,* Ernie Pyle's *Here Is Your War,* and Ted Lawson's *Thirty Seconds over Tokyo* brought the complexities of the war into the libraries of millions.

   Today: World War II is still a widely-discussed era that has inspired a number of important works of fiction and nonfiction, including Thomas Pynchon's *Gravity's Rainbow,* Stephen Ambrose's *Citizen Soldiers,* and Tom Brokaw's *The Greatest Generation.*

- **1940s:** After World War II ends, the East German Social Democrats merge with the Communists, eventually leading to the division of Germany into East and West, and the construction of the Berlin Wall in 1961.

   Today: Largely due to the actions of U.S. President Ronald Reagan and Soviet President Mikhail Gorbachev, the Berlin wall has been destroyed (1989) and the two Germanys have been reunited under a reformist government.

- **1940s:** Technology grows exponentially. This decade sees the splitting of the atom, the development of the first automated computers, and the first uses of magnetic recording tape.

   Today: The rate of technological growth has increased. Atomic energy is in use at many sites around the world, computers continue to become smaller and faster, and the recordable compact disc drive had become a standard computer feature.

---

first to enter liberated Paris on August 25, 1944. Petain and Laval were tried for treason and collaborating with the enemy. Laval was executed and Petain died in prison, after having his death sentence commuted.

The events of "That in Aleppo Once ..." reflect the nightmarish sense of life under the Vichy government. Any author who criticized the Germans in his or her work was arrested and punished, which explains why the narrator feared that "some helpful compatriot" of his would point out to "the interested party" the passages in his books where he argues that Germany will be "for ever and ever the laughing stock of the world." On his long journey by rail, the narrator speaks to some fellow Russians in Nice, remarking that he "heard those among them who chanced to have Jewish blood talk of their doomed kinsmen crammed into hell-bound trains." The narrator's discovery of his wife at the end of a long line at a food store reflects the short supply of things as common as oranges during the occupation. Finally, the criss-crossing of trains and confusion endured by the narrator reflects the difficulties

many refugees had in escaping the German menace. At the time Nabokov wrote this story (1943) in the city of Boston, Massachusetts, that menace was still very powerful.

Critical Overview

While generally overshadowed by towering works such as *Lolita*, *Pale Fire*, and *Ada*, "That in Aleppo Once ..." has piqued the curiosity of several Nabokov scholars. In his 1995 study *The Magician's Doubts: Nabokov and the Risks of Fiction,* Michael Wood places the story in the context of several Nabokov works featuring "ordered but unsympathetic" worlds "run by a heavy-handed deity"—in this case, V., who is certainly unsympathetic when he uses the title, "That in Aleppo Once ..." as he does. While Wood explains that "[t]his is not the way the world is, for Nabokov or for us," he does state that this is "the way it may feel" to people in times of crisis. Writing in *The Garland*

Companion to Vladimir Nabokov (1995), Gennady Barabtarlo praises the story as "a concentrated study of jealousy on a severe scale, jealousy that is capable of quaking and deforming reality." Barabtarlo also examines the ways in which the narrator's inability to know exactly what sins his wife has committed leads to his implied suicide. His "suffering is real" even if it is based upon events that did not actually occur, and it is reasonable to conclude "when his suffering becomes unbearable, the hero takes his life." Unlike Barabtarlo, the biographer and critic Andrew Field argues in his 1967 work *Nabokov: His Life in Art* that the narrator's wife acts "with a morbid and sadistic self-consciousness." However, Field allows for the possibility that the narrator has made some fatal error in abandoning her in Marseilles; mistakes lead to "our phantoms, our losses, and, in the end, madness." Field also explains that the story fits into Nabokov's overall negative attitude towards Germany and quotes Nabokov's German translator as bemoaning the fact that Nabokov never acknowledged the existence of "another Germany, a country consisting of art, culture, and humanism."

Two critics who have examined "That in Aleppo Once . . ." at some length are L. L. Lee and Geoffrey Green. Writing in 1965 in *Studies in Short Fiction*, Lee examines the ways in which the story uses dialectically opposed images and characters to ultimately "make the reader aware of his own ambiguity, of his possession or lack of self." In his 1988 book *Freud and Nabokov*, Green examines the events of the story in light of the works of Sigmund Freud, the founder of psychoanalysis. As Green acknowledges, "Nabokov hated Freud and psychoanalysis with a passion" and "sustained the grandest and most extravagant contempt for psychoanalysis known in modern literature." Still, Green manages to find interesting connections between the story and Freud's *Beyond the Pleasure Principle* and *Civilization and Its Discontents,* ultimately arguing that the story dramatizes a number of Freudian "drives" that lead the narrator to his suicide.

Criticism

Daniel Moran

Moran is a teacher of English and American literature. In this essay, Moran examines Nabokov's use of ambiguity and how he draws upon the reader's understanding of Othello.

In his opening paragraph to V., the narrator of "That in Aleppo Once . . ." explains that he learned V.'s address from a mutual acquaintance who "seemed to think somehow or other" that V. "was betraying our national literature." While the opinions of "good old Gleb Alexandrovich Gekko" matter little to V. or the narrator (who even slightly mocks him), this easily forgotten character raises the issue of betrayal in the story's first paragraph. The different types of betrayal dramatized in the story are dizzying: the narrator may have been betrayed by his wife; the narrator may have betrayed his wife by leaving her to the Nazis in France; the Germans betray humanity; and V. betrays the narrator by giving his letter the title he does.

In light of this title, the narrator is linked to his Shakespearian counterpart, who betrays his wife and is betrayed by "honest" Iago. Betrayal is certainly one of Shakespeare's predominant themes: works such as *Hamlet, King Lear, Henry IV Part 1, Richard III, Coriolanus,* and, of course, *Othello* all explore the ways in which a character betrays his or her love, family, or country—and is sometimes betrayed by them as well. However, in Nabokov's story, the distinctions between betrayer and betrayed are blurred and confused, perplexing the first-time reader who searches for clues concerning the "truth" of the events described by the narrator. Did his wife cuckold him? Was she really "testing" him with her story of the salesman? Does she really believe that she lives "several lives at once?" Or is the narrator the guilty party, who, like a character from the tales of Edgar Allan Poe, tells his story with the most honest of intentions while simultaneously revealing his own perceptual limitations? These questions are deliberately left unanswered by Nabokov, who invites the reader to assume the role of judge yet never allows him or her the relief of hearing the gavel sound its note of finality. The issue facing a re-reader, therefore, becomes one not of facts (what really happened) but feelings (how it *feels* to betray or be betrayed). Despite his foolishness, King Lear can justly state, "I am a man / More sinned against than sinning," but Nabokov's narrator can never stand on such terra firma, nor can the reader, for whom all the story's evidence remains inconclusive. Only V. passes judgment and whether he does so after a careful weighing of the evidence *or* simply as an act of cruelty to his desperate friend

The Germans invade Paris during WWII

is never explained, although an understanding of *Othello* suggests the latter possibility as more probable.

The incident involving the uncle of the narrator's wife can be read as a representative example of the kind of ambiguity that haunts the narrator and perplexes the first-time reader. His wife tells the narrator that she has an uncle living in New York. After she and the narrator compose a "dramatic letter" to him, however, they receive no reply. At this point, the reader assumes that the uncle is, like the narrator's wife's imaginary dog, "whining behind a locked door." After his arrival in the United States, the narrator investigates the address his wife had given for her uncle and finds it to be "an anonymous gap between two office buildings." The uncle's name does not appear in the directory, which adds to the narrator's (and the reader's) suspicion of his wife and makes her adultery much more likely—she seems a very untrustworthy figure. However, immediately after these conclusions are drawn, Gekko (who significantly "knows everything") tells the narrator that "the man and his horsey wife existed all right, but had moved to San Francisco after their little deaf girl died." Now the reader is back where he or she started; nothing concerning the uncle can be said with any defini-

tiveness other than that he existed. The narrator's wife may have been lying about the address *or* she may have simply made a mistake. This ambiguity unsettles the reader but traumatizes the narrator, who can think of nothing concerning his wife to have any definitiveness. "Viewing the past graphically," he explains, "I see our mangled romance engulfed in a deep valley of mist between the crags of two matter-of-fact mountains." Mountains are likened here to immovable and unalterable truth, which is what the narrator seeks from V.: a "mountainous" explanation of what happened with his "misty" wife.

The narrator, like many people when faced with painful doubts, hopes to turn his mists into mountains and writes to V. for assistance in this endeavor. Early in his letter, the narrator fondly recalls his days as a poet composing his first "udder-warm bubbling verse." Although he states "just now I am not a poet," his artistic vocation deserves to be examined against V.'s vocation. The reader learns that V. has become a writer of fiction; he has moved from an art form often concerned with the impressions of things to one that (in its traditional sense) offers its readers a series of events possessing clarity and definitiveness. This clarity is missing from the story of the narrator's wife, which is why

What Do I Read Next?

- Shakespeare's tragedy *Othello* (1604) lends Nabokov's story its title and is widely regarded as one of the playwright's greatest works. Like "That in Aleppo Once . . . ," *Othello* concerns the effects of jealousy on a married man's mind.

- *The Winter's Tale* (1610), one of Shakespeare's late romances, concerns Leontes, a king whose jealousy of his innocent wife almost destroys her and her daughter. Unlike *Othello,* however, Leontes is saved from his own passions before they destroy himself and his family.

- Nabokov's most famous novel, *Lolita* (1955), follows the exploits of Humbert Humbert, a pervert whose love for the "nymphet" Dolores Haze provokes great jealousy, confusion, and death.

- Nabokov's 1947 novel *Bend Sinister* is a dark, satirical portrait of a totalitarian state (in some ways like the Nazis) that, in the name of equality and progress, destroys free thinking.

- *Speak, Memory* (1951; revised 1966), Nabokov's autobiography, traces his development as an artist against the backdrop of his Russian childhood. The action of the book ends in 1940, when Nabokov and his wife emigrate to the United States.

- Like "That in Aleppo Once . . . ," the plot of Nabokov's comic play *The Waltz Invention* (1938) is ambiguous. In the play's case, the ambiguity lies in whether or not the play's hero has invented a machine capable of destroying the entire world.

- *Lectures on Literature* (1980) contains the lectures Nabokov delivered while teaching at Cornell. These lectures treat such writers as Joyce, Stevenson, and Kafka while simultaneously revealing Nabokov's own literary tastes and opinions.

- Anton Chekhov's story "The Lady with the Pet Dog" (1899) is alluded to in "That in Aleppo Once . . . ." Like Nabokov, Chekhov's story concerns marital infidelity and its ramifications.

---

she seems so unreal to him and why he asks V. to transform his miserable set of impressions into a narrative with a beginning, middle, and end. While the narrator knows that V. "can hardly be expected to puzzle out" his "misfortune in terms of human communion," he does ask V. to "clarify things for me through the prism of your art." In effect, he is asking V. to impose the order of fiction on the chaos of experience.

But what does V. do? He does not write a story about the narrator. He *reprints* the narrator's letter, with all its pathetic pleas and confusion. No one who wrote such a letter would want anyone other than its recipient to read it, but this obviously does not affect V. Rather than offering his friend an artistic version of his suffering at the hands of a deceptive wife (which would vindicate him and excuse his jealousy) or one in which his friend is portrayed as a horrible man who abandoned his wife (which would be devastating but would at least ease his doubts), V. changes nothing in the letter. Since the narrator advises V. that he should not make the doctor he met on the ship a doctor in the story, "as that kind of thing has been overdone," and the doctor remains, the reader can assume that V. has changed nothing else in the letter itself. V. also titles the story with the very phrase the narrator begs him to forsake: "Spare me, V.: you would load your dice with an unbearable implication if you took that for a title." But V. does not spare the narrator and tacks the phrase from *Othello* before the text of the letter.

Why V. employs the accursed title can be understood by comparing the characters of the story to those of *Othello*. The narrator is obviously the Othello-figure, who moves from obsessive jealousy ("I must find out every detail, reconstruct every

> " ... in Nabokov's story, the Iago-figure is V., who takes a collection of events and ... gives them a meaning he knows will drive his 'friend' to suicide."

minute'') to remorse at destroying the woman he loved by leaving her in occupied France (''Somewhere, somehow, I have made some fatal mistake''). His wife is the Desdemona-figure, who uses a smile to ''wriggle into the semi-security of irrelevant commentaries'' when interrogated. While the audience never questions Desdemona's innocence, it is questioned by Othello, just as the narrator's wife falls under suspicion here. The hair-lotion salesman with whom the narrator's wife may or may not have slept is like Cassio, the dashing and, as Bianca's presence in the play suggests, licentious young soldier. The remaining major character in *Othello* is Iago, the villain whose enthusiasm for cruelty and skill with language convinces Othello that Desdemona is false—and in Nabokov's story, the Iago-figure is V., who takes a collection of events and deliberately (and coldly) gives them a meaning he knows will drive his ''friend'' to suicide.

To understand how V. betrays the narrator in his own Iago-like way, consider the manner in which Iago works on Othello. In the middle of the play, after Cassio has disgraced himself with public drunkenness, Iago and Othello approach Emilia (Iago's wife), Desdemona, and Cassio, who have been discussing the way in which Desdemona will beg her husband to reinstate the dismissed Cassio. Upon seeing his superior, Cassio leaves in shame and Iago makes a seemingly nonchalant observation to Othello:

Iago. Ha! I like not that.
Othello. What dost thou say?
Iago. Nothing, my lord; or if—I know not what.
Othello. Was that not Cassio parted from my wife?
Iago. Cassio, my lord? No, sure, I cannot think it,
That he would steal away so guilty-like,
Seeing you coming.
Othello. I do believe 'twas he.

Everything Iago says here is designed to take a neutral, matter-of-fact event (Cassio's exit) and fill it with significance. If Iago had said nothing, Cassio's exit would have appeared to Othello as simply a man hurriedly leaving a room. Iago, however, transforms the exit into something suspicious (''I like not that''), unpleasant to discuss (''Nothing my lord; or if—I know not what''), and bordering on criminal behavior (''steal away so guilty-like''). This ability to turn, in the narrator's terms, mists into mountains in so short a time is what makes Iago so dangerous. Later in the play, he performs the same trick with Desdemona's handkerchief (given to her by Othello while they were courting): after planting it on Cassio and then telling Othello he saw Cassio wipe his beard with it, Othello's suspicions are aroused. He asks his wife, who has already expressed to Emilia her pain at having lost it, for the handkerchief. Desdemona tries to stall her husband's relentless questions, for fear of hurting his feelings, but Othello is too far away from her by then:

Desdemona. Why do you speak so startlingly and rash?
Othello. Is't lost? Is't gone? Speak, is it out o' th' way?
Desdemona. Heaven bless us!
Othello. Say you?
Desdemona. It is not lost. But what an if it were?
Othello. How?
Desdemona. I say it is not lost.
Othello. Fetch't, let me see it!
Desdemona. Why, so I can, sir; but I will not now.
This is a trick to put me from my suit.
Pray you let Cassio be received again.
Othello. Fetch me the handkerchief! My mind misgives.

By this point, Iago has shown Othello his wife through the prism of *his* art and by the time Othello sees her without the artistic embellishments offered by Iago, she will be dead.

V. and Iago are both artists who offer their readers (the narrator and Othello) logical and definitive explanations for events. The falsity of Iago's explanations and the potential falsity of V.'s explanations are irrelevant; what is important is that these explanations are taken as truth by Othello and the narrator. As the narrator asks V. to ''clarify things'' through the ''prism'' of his art, Iago *pretends* to clarify such things as Cassio's exit and the missing handkerchief for Othello. Had V. titled the story ''A Deranged Wife'' or ''Pity the Poor Cuckold,'' he would have communicated to the narrator his opinion that he did the right thing by abandoning her in Marseilles, but like Iago, he frames the data before him in such a way that the confused narrator must assume that V. finds him guilty of having made "some fatal mistake."

When he learns of Iago's villainy at the end of the play, Othello asks him why he "hath thus ensnared" his "soul and body." Iago's short reply ("Demand me nothing") and refusal to speak confound the other characters. Similarly, V. offers the narrator an "unbearable implication" by titling the story as he does without offering any rationale or afterward explaining why he did so. However, while the motives of these artist-villains may seem inscrutable, there is one possibility for why each man acts as he does: each man enjoys, and employs, his creative powers as a means by which he asserts his superiority over weaker men. As artists can, in their work, create life, they can also destroy it. In *Othello,* a man kills himself because of the convincing lies (i.e., fictions) offered to him by his "friend," as in Nabokov's story a man will kill himself because of *his* "friend's" artistic use of an allusion.

In his *Lectures 1808–1819 on Literature,* the English Romantic poet Samuel Taylor Coleridge describes Iago as "A being next to Devil—only *not* quite Devil." Coleridge's reason for this assessment of "*not* quite" has to do with the fact that, at times, Iago himself searches for his own motives, such as when he speaks of Othello's rumored liaisons with Emilia or when he remarks of Roderigo, "Thus do I ever make my fool my purse," as if money is the reason why Iago does the terrible things he does (Coleridge's often-misunderstood phrase "motiveless malignity" applies in this context). In other words, Iago is evil yet still retains, to a small degree, the human desire to find motives for his own inexplicable cruelty. Nabokov, however, offers no such motive-hunting in V., who offers no apologies or motives for his betrayal other than the betrayal itself which, with Shakespeare's assistance, raises betrayal to an art form: specifically, a story entitled, "That in Aleppo Once . . ."

Source: Daniel Moran, Critical Essay on "That in Aleppo Once . . .," in *Short Stories for Students,* The Gale Group, 2002.

Jennifer Bussey

Bussey holds a master's degree in interdisciplinary studies and a bachelor's degree in English Literature. She is an independent writer specializing in literature. In the following essay, Bussey demonstrates that the narrator's identity as a poet is his defining characteristic, and discusses the significance this has for the story as a whole.

Vladimir Nabokov's "That in Aleppo Once . . ." is in the form of a letter from the narrator, a poet, to a friend named V., who is a fiction writer. In this letter, the narrator tells the story of his strange, brief marriage, and does so in a way that reveals the poetic nature of his thinking and writing about life. Clearly, being a poet is much more than a hobby or occupation for this man; it is his identity and it defines the way he perceives and relates to the world. His love is not the wife of whom he writes but rather poetry, writing, and words. In his letter, this love is expressed directly, indirectly, and in literary references, and the sum of these expressions makes clear that the narrator casts himself, above all, in the role of the poet.

The narrator makes direct references to himself as a poet. He recalls wistfully when he and V. were young and "wrote our first udder-warm bubbling verse, and all things, a rose, a puddle, a lighted window, cried out to us: 'I'm a rhyme!'" From his youth, the narrator has regarded the world as a source of art and inspiration. As an adult, he compares his wife to one of his poems and reveals that in response to his crumbling marriage, he composed poetry. He admires the poetry of Aleksandr Pushkin, who is widely considered Russia's premier poet and whose verse he feels he can never match.

The narrator writes poetically even when he is writing a letter to a friend. Indirectly, he reveals his identity as a poet in the way he describes the world and his feelings. As early as the second paragraph, the narrator's poetic impulse is evident in his word choice and use of literary devices. He writes:

> And the sonorous souls [alliteration] of Russian verbs [personification] lend a meaning to the wild gesticulation of trees [personification] or to some discarded newspaper sliding and pausing, and shuffling again, with abortive flaps and apterous jerks along an endless [exaggeration] windswept embankment. But just now I am not a poet [irony].

The narrator introduces vivid imagery when he describes the sky as "a chaos of black and flesh-colored clouds with an ugly sunburst beyond a hooded hill." The poet's eye for contrast is evident as he describes seeing "coal dust glittering in the heat between naked indifferent rails, and a lone piece of orange peel." Examples of literary devices occur throughout the letter, as when he employs both alliteration and oxymoron in the comment, "the gentle Germans roared into Paris." Later in the same paragraph, he writes of his wife, "I am able to speak of her with as much detachment as I would of a character in a story (one of your stories, to be

> Nabokov makes a strong statement that literature is a means by which to interpret, embellish, and transform reality. At the same time, however, he seems to say that literature must be rooted in real people, experiences, and events."

precise)." This comment is significant because he compares his wife to a literary figure (a character in a story). The narrator also describes his wife as being "as nebulous as my best poem," a simile with a literary element. The metaphor he chooses for his honeymoon is the theater, writing that he and his wife were "walking through the stale stage setting of abstract towns." Again, notice the use of alliteration. Although Nabokov was born in Russia, he produced an impressive body of work in English, including this story. This is an important observation because it demonstrates that Nabokov himself— not a translator—crafted all of the story's alliterative phrases.

The narrator is apparently a well-read man— not only a writer of poetry but also a student of literature. He makes literary references that are intended to make a point, not to show off his knowledge. That he makes these references in a letter to V. reveals that the two share literature as a frame of reference. At one point, for example, the narrator likens his relationship with his wife to Pushkin's relationship with his love, Nathalie. He is thrilled to have something in common with such a great literary mind. When his wife leaves, he comes upon a garden with a "blue Arabian Nights jar," a reference to the classic tales *One Thousand and One Arabian Nights.*

During the course of the letter, the narrator casts himself in many roles, but that of the poet undergirds them all. He presents himself as a friend to V., a bridegroom and lover to his wife, and a soldier in Paris. What is significant is that the poet inhabits all the other roles. For example, the narra-

tor's description of himself as a soldier coming upon an abandoned house is imagistic as well as poignant and insightful. The reader hears the poet's voice in the soldier's description: "We all know of that blinding blast which is caused by merely picking up a small doll from the floor of a carefully abandoned house: the soldier involved hears nothing." He also relates with poetic images and figurative language a moment shared with his wife. He recalls that "her dim smile changed all at once into an odd quiver and she placed one hand on my shoulder, staring down at me as if I were a reflection on a pool, which she had noticed for the first time."

To the narrator, the roles of friend, groom, and soldier are like clothes he puts on; the self who wears the clothes is the poet. It is the poet who makes up the core of his identity, who perceives and interprets the world and his experiences in it. If his friendship with V. were to end or had never begun, if he had not served in the military, or if he had not been briefly married, he would still be a poet. The poet functions independently of the other roles, although the poet draws on the experiences they provide. Yet if he found himself alone on a desert island, he would still find inspiration to write poetry.

That this short story portrays one writer addressing another is important to understanding one of Nabokov's major themes of the story: the interdependent relationship between life and literature. First, the narrator comments that his life became fiction when his broken marriage made the rounds among the gossips. He is amazed at the dramatic rumors he has heard about what went wrong in his marriage and where his wife has gone. His life quickly became literature, although in a debased form—"popular literature" in the most literal sense. Then, the fiction writer, V., takes his poet friend's story, as revealed to him in the letter, and crafts it into a short story—a "higher" form of literature. Interestingly, when V. turns the letter into a short story, the narrator is not surprised; to the contrary, the narrator anticipates this and even comments in his letter about the title V. may choose for his fictionalized version of the tale. The narrator is a poet with an ever-present muse, so he understands completely that his friend will draw on the letter for fictional material. Life is supposed to give rise to literature, Nabokov seems to say, and hopefully it will be well-made and thoughtful literature.

To add a final layer to Nabokov's interweaving of life and literature, the story itself is a work of literature presented in the form of a letter, as if it were a piece of a man's life. Nabokov makes a strong statement that literature is a means by which to interpret, embellish, and transform reality. At the same time, however, he seems to say that literature must be rooted in real people, experiences, and events. He underscores these points by making his characters a poet, who interprets life poetically, and a fiction writer, who turns this poetic reality into fiction.

Source: Jennifer Bussey, Critical Essay on ''That in Aleppo Once . . . ,'' in *Short Stories for Students,* The Gale Group, 2002.

Sources

Barabtarlo, Gennady, ''English Short Stories,'' in *The Garland Companion to Vladimir Nabokov,* edited by Vladimir E. Alexandrov, Garland Publishing, Inc., 1995, pp. 101–17.

Coleridge, Samuel Taylor, *Lectures 1808–1819 on Literature,* Princeton University Press, 1987, p. 315.

Field, Andrew, *Nabokov: His Life in Art,* Little, Brown and Company, 1967, pp. 150–51, 206.

Green, Geoffrey, *Freud and Nabokov,* University of Nebraska Press, 1988, pp. 65–70.

Lee, L. L., ''Duplexity in V. Nabokov's Short Stories,'' in *Studies in Short Fiction,* Vol. II, No. 4, Summer 1965, pp. 307–15.

Parker, Stephen Jan, *Understanding Vladimir Nabokov,* University of South Carolina Press, 1987, p. 19.

Shakespeare, William, *The Tragedy of King Lear,* in *The Complete Signet Classic Shakespeare,* Harcourt Brace Jovanovich, 1972, pp. 1174–1226.

———, *The Tragedy of Othello, the Moor of Venice,* in *The Complete Signet Classic Shakespeare,* Harcourt Brace Jovanovich, 1972, pp. 1090–1136.

Updike, John, ''Notes and Comment,'' in *Critical Essays on Vladimir Nabokov,* edited by Phyllis A. Roth, G. K. Hall & Co., 1984, pp. 39–40.

Wood, Michael, *The Magician's Doubts: Nabokov and the Risks of Fiction,* Princeton University Press, 1995, p. 74.

Further Reading

Boyd, Brian, *Vladimir Nabokov: The American Years,* Princeton University Press, 1991.

    This critically acclaimed and exhaustive critical biography is the follow-up to Boyd's *Vladimir Nabokov: The Russian Years. Vladimir Nabokov: The American Years* begins in 1940, when Nabokov and his wife left France for the United States.

Nabokov, Vladimir, *The Stories of Vladimir Nabokov,* Alfred A. Knopf, 1995.

    This mammoth volume contains all of Nabokov's stories as well as an introduction by his son, Dmitri.

Naumann, Maria Turkevich, *Blue Evenings in Berlin: Nabokov's Short Stories of the 1920s,* New York University Press, 1978.

    While this book does not specifically treat ''That in Aleppo Once . . . ,'' Naumann does offer many ideas about Nabokov's expatriation and how it is treated in his early short stories.

Schiff, Stacy, *Vera (Mrs. Vladimir Nabokov),* Random House, 1999.

    This biography of Nabokov's wife explores the depths to which she was involved in her husband's creative and business affairs.

Werth, Alexander, *France 1940–1945,* Henry Holt and Company, 1956.

    The opening chapters of Werth's book offer in-depth examinations of the Vichy government, the trial of Henri Petain, and the French Resistance.

To Da-duh, in Memoriam

Paule Marshall

1967

Paule Marshall's "To Da-duh, in Memoriam," first published in 1967 and reissued in *Reena, and Other Stories* in 1983, is a story imbued with thematic resonance. The story focuses on a rivalry between grandmother and granddaughter; this conflict is based on several opposing forces, particularly the rural world versus the urban world, tradition versus modernity, and age versus youth. Marshall skillfully draws these disparate elements together, thus illustrating the cycles of time and the enduring nature of family. These multifaceted themes, along with Marshall's subtle evocation of Barbadian history and her rich symbolism and metaphor, have made "To Da-duh, in Memoriam" one of the author's most interesting and discussed works of short fiction.

The story also introduces Da-duh, who appears in different forms throughout Marshall's work. Marshall openly notes the autobiographical nature of the piece, which she wrote many years after a childhood visit to her grandmother in Barbados. Understanding Da-duh's influence on Marshall is an important tool for achieving critical understanding of the author's body of work and her continuing themes. As Marshall describes her grandmother in an introduction to the story published in her 1983, "She's an ancestor figure, symbolic for me of the long line of black women and men . . . who made my being possible, and whose spirit I believe continues to animate my life and work."

Author Biography

Marshall was born on April 9, 1929, in Brooklyn, New York, the child of Barbadian immigrants who were among the first wave of Caribbean islanders to relocate to the United States. Her early life was suffused with Caribbean culture; she spoke its language and followed many of its traditions. Marshall made her first visit to the Caribbean when she was nine years old, which inspired her to write poetry.

After graduating from high school in 1949, she attended Brooklyn College (now part of the City University of New York). She graduated with a bachelor of arts degree in English literature in 1953 and became a Phi Beta Kappa member.

From 1953 to 1956, Marshall worked as a researcher and journalist for the African-American magazine *Our World*. Her job required her to travel to Brazil and the Caribbean. While attending graduate school at Hunter College, which she entered in 1955, she started writing her first novel, the autobiographical *Brown Girl, Brownstones* (1959), in her spare evening hours. She completed it on a visit to Barbados.

This novel introduced many of the themes that Marshall would further develop throughout her literary career, particularly the importance of her relationship to her family in the Caribbean. She dedicated the novel to her grandmother, who inspired her to write ''To Da-duh, in Memoriam.''

In 1960, Marshall won a Guggenheim Fellowship, which she used to complete the book of novellas *Soul Clap Hands and Sing* (1961). In this work, Marshall expands her Barbadian community to include other members of the African diaspora. In the years until her next publication, the novel *The Chosen Place, The Timeless People* (1969), Marshall worked for a Caribbean magazine, *New World,* and as a librarian for the New York Public Library.

She followed up the novel the following year with *Reena and Other Stories*, which included the previously published ''To Da-duh, in Memoriam.'' Marshall also became involved in the civil rights movement during the 1960s, joining the American Youth for Democracy and Artists for Freedom; the latter groups included other important African-American writers such as James Baldwin.

Throughout the 1970s, after marrying her second husband, a Haitian, Marshall divided her time between New York and the West Indies. She also taught creative writing and literature at several

Paule Marshall

colleges and universities. Although she did not publish any fiction in the 1970s, her work began to draw greater critical attention and was even being taught in college classes.

She published the novel *Praisesong for the Widow* in 1983. It shares with *Brown Girl, Brownstones* the theme of the search for identity. The novel *Daughters* was published in 1991. In the 1990s, Marshall also became sought after as a keynote speaker and lecturer. She also won a prestigious MacArthur Fellowship in 1992. Toward the end of the decade, she retired from a teaching position at Virginia Commonwealth University, a position that she had held for ten years, to devote herself full-time to writing.

Plot Summary

''To Da-duh, in Memoriam'' is an autobiographical story told from the point of view of an adult looking back on a childhood memory. The story opens as the nine-year-old narrator, along with her mother and sister, disembarks from a boat that has brought them to Bridgetown, Barbados. It is 1937, and the family has come to visit from their home in Brooklyn, leaving behind the father, who believed it was a waste of money to take the trip. The narrator's mother first left Barbados fifteen years ago, and the narrator has never met her grandmother, Da-duh.

Although an old woman, the narrator's grandmother is lively and sharp. When she meets her grandchildren, Da-duh examines them. She calls the narrator's older sister ''lucky,'' but she silently looks at the narrator, calling the child ''fierce.'' She takes the narrator by the hand and leads the family outside where the rest of the relatives are waiting. The family gets in the truck that takes them through Bridgetown and back to Da-duh's home in St. Thomas.

The next day, Da-duh takes the narrator out to show her the land covered with fruit orchards and sugar cane. Da-duh asks the narrator if there is anything as nice in Brooklyn, and the narrator says no. Da-duh says that she has heard that there are no trees in New York, but then asks the narrator to describe snow. The narrator takes advantage of this opportunity to impress Da-duh with all the things that New York does have, and she describes the snow as falling higher than Da-duh's house and cold enough to freeze a person. Then the narrator decides to show her grandmother popular dances from America and sing popular songs. When the performance ends, Da-duh stares at the narrator as if she came from another planet, but then smiles and gives her a penny to buy candy.

For the remainder of the visit, the narrator spends most of her time with her grandmother. They walk among the sugar cane, and the narrator tells Da-duh all about New York, describing the world of the city with its buildings, machines, and modern appliances. The narrator can sense her grandmother's fear at hearing about all of these signs of urbanity. The narrator even tells Da-duh that in New York she beats up white girls, a remark which leaves Da-duh speechless.

Toward the end of the visit, Da-duh takes her granddaughter to see a very tall palm tree. She asks the child if they have anything as tall in New York. The narrator almost wishes that she could say no, but she tells her about the Empire State building, the tallest building in the world and over one hundred stories high. Da-duh gets angry and accuses her granddaughter of lying. The narrator says that she will send a postcard of the Empire State building when she gets home. Da-duh realizes that she has been defeated. They return to the house, Da-duh looking uncertain and the narrator feeling triumphant but sad.

The next morning, Da-duh doesn't feel well. The narrator sings for her until breakfast. Then the two take their customary walk, but it is short and dispirited. At home again, Da-duh spends the rest of the afternoon napping. This pattern continues until the family returns to Brooklyn. On the day of their departure, Da-duh reminds her granddaughter to send the postcard.

However, by the time the narrator mails the postcard, Da-duh has died. Shortly after the family left, riots in Bridgetown took place. To quell the protest, the British sent planes to fly over the island and scare the people. Everyone in the village fled into the cane fields for safety, with the exception of Da-duh; she stayed in the house and watched the plans swoop down. The narrator imagines that, to her grandmother, it must have seemed that the planes were going to come right at her, in her house. When the planes withdraw and the villagers return, they find Da-duh dead in her chair by the window.

The narrator recalls how she always remembered her Da-duh. As an adult, she does penance for how she treated her grandmother, living in a downtown loft in New York and painting pictures of the sugar cane while the machines downstairs thunder noisily.

Characters

Da-duh

Da-duh is the narrator's eighty-year-old grandmother. She has lived her whole life on Barbados and is confident and proud of her lifestyle, surroundings, and ways of looking at the world. She dislikes the trappings of the modern world, such as any form of machinery, and is uncomfortable in the city of Bridgetown. When Da-duh first meets the narrator, the narrator imagines that she saw ''something in me which for some reason she found disturbing.'' However, Da-duh also feels connected to her granddaughter, as evidenced when she clasps her hand.

Da-duh is completely at home in the countryside of St. Thomas where she lives. She takes her granddaughter on daily walks on the land surrounding her house. She shows off the glories of the natural world, and listens with an air of fear to her granddaughter's descriptions of life in New York. She is not accustomed to having her life challenged, as her granddaughter does, and she attempts to assert authority through the royal palm tree, which is the tallest thing she has ever seen. When her granddaughter tells her about the Empire State building, Da-duh is finally defeated.

The small instances of surrender that the narrator had seen throughout the visit now pervades Da-duh's person. Instead of eagerly going on walks, she spends mornings staring out the window and spends her afternoons napping; grandmother and granddaughter take only brief, dispirited walks.

She dies shortly after her family leaves, and her death suggests both her stubbornness and her defeat. When Britain sends planes to fly low over the island in retaliations for riots and strikes, Da-duh, alone among her community, refuses to take cover in the cane fields. She stays in the house and watches the planes. The narrator imagines that it must have seemed to Da-duh that the planes were going to destroy her house and the whole island. When the rest of the village returns to their homes after the planes have departed, Da-duh is dead, still sitting in her chair at the window.

Narrator

The narrator is nine years old when she visits Barbados and meets her grandmother, Da-duh, for the first time. The narrator is a strong-willed, unique child. Her stubbornness matches Da-duh's, and both of them immediately recognize this similarity. Sensing this, the two lock gazes upon first meeting, and the narrator revels in her triumph when her grandmother looks away first.

Their likeness draws them together. On the day after their arrival, the pattern of their relationship emerges when Da-duh takes her granddaughter on a walk through the countryside. Da-duh shows off her world, and when prodded by her grandmother, the narrator agrees that they have no natural, healthy environments like this in Brooklyn. Da-duh's comments make the girl realize what her world is missing. At the same time, however, the natural world discomfits the girl. She sees the sugar canes as ''giant weeds'' and thinks they have taken over the island. The narrator brings into her grandmother's world songs, dances, ideas, and descriptions of the city, which her grandmother listens to, with a sense of disbelief. Throughout the course of the visit, grandmother and granddaughter battle over whose world is more grand.

Toward the end of the trip, however, the narrator wins the battle with finality when she tells Da-duh about the Empire State building, which would tower over the royal palm tree, the tallest thing that Da-duh has ever seen. However, the narrator is able to take little delight in her victory. For the rest of the trip, she tries to perk her grandmother up by performing songs.

After leaving the island, the narrator never sees her grandmother again because Da-duh dies soon thereafter. The memory of Da-duh, and the way she belittled her, remains with the narrator for the rest of her life. She also learns a valuable lesson from her grandmother: that in its unique way, the rural, natural world is as important as the urban, technological world and has something of value to offer her.

Themes

Rivalry

The story pits an aging Barbadian grandmother against her youthful American granddaughter. Upon their first meeting, the two sense a similarity in each other that far outweighs the differences presented by the seventy years between them. Most importantly, each has a stubborn strength of will and a confidence that her way of regarding the world is the right way.

The characters knowingly participate in this rivalry. Da-duh has the knowledge that comes with age and experience, but the narrator has the brash confidence of youth. Da-duh has her pride of place, showing off her land with its lush plants, trees, and cane fields. The narrator has the technological superiority of the modern world, which she uses to goad her grandmother into silent submission; Da-duh is not impressed by technology, but it is so foreign to her that she cannot even conceive of her granddaughter's descriptions of life in New York. The story ends with the narrator's victory in this rivalry, which makes her feel somewhat sad because she knows that her success only comes as a result of her grandmother's concession.

Time

As the oldest and youngest characters presented in the story, Da-duh and the narrator represent the span of time and its cyclical nature. Marshall writes in the last paragraph, ''She died and I lived''; in a sense, the role that Da-duh occupied in

Topics for Further Study

- Find out more about Barbados in the 1930s, including the riots of 1937. Does the story seem an accurate reflection of Barbados and its culture during that time?

- Marshall wrote ''To Da-duh, in Memoriam'' about thirty years after her own experience in Barbados. How do you think this lapse of time might have affected her perception of these past events and relationships?

- Read one of Marshall's works that features a Da-duh character. Compare and contrast the portrayal of the grandmother character in these works.

- Find a work of art that represents the story's setting for you. Write a response to this piece of art.

- Research Barbadian history. Describe how slavery and colonialism affected the island's development.

- Examine Da-duh's role as an ''ancestor figure.''

- Comment on Marshall's statement in the introduction: ''I had come into the world not only to love her and to continue her line but to take her very life in order that I might live.''

- Write a short scene that might have taken place if Da-duh had visited her granddaughter in New York.

the family has passed on to the narrator. She dies to make way for her granddaughter and the world, period, and change that she symbolizes.

The grandmother and granddaughter also represent how the passing of time changes the world, forcing its older members to be left behind. The granddaughter's triumph at the end of her visit illustrates that in many ways the world truly belongs to the new generation. This theme is further reinforced by Da-duh's death soon thereafter. There is no place for Da-duh in the modern world, therefore she must leave.

Rural and Urban Worlds

Because of their stubbornness, grandmother and granddaughter participate in a rivalry in which each tries to prove that her world is superior. Da-duh has the wonder and beauty of the natural world on her side, but her granddaughter has all the technological wonders of the urban world. Da-duh is frightened of the trappings of the modern world; in the truck, driving through Bridgetown, she clutches the narrator's hand tightly. Once back in the country, among the sugar cane fields, she feels safe and comfortable again. The granddaughter, a child of one of the most vibrant cities in the world, is

unimpressed by these sights, however. To her, the sugar canes—which have sustained the Barbadian economy for hundreds of years—are only giant weeds.

Da-duh and the narrator spend most of their days together walking around the land. Da-duh points out all the amazing sites of the island—the fruit-bearing trees and plants, the tropical woods, the tall royal palm. Each of these objects that are so precious to Da-duh come from the natural, rural world and represent the agricultural tradition of Barbados. In response to Da-duh, the narrator shows off the dances she learns from the movies and the songs that play on the radio. She brags about all the machines and technology New York offers—kitchen appliances, trolleys and subways, electricity—technology of the urban, modern world. She finally wins the rivalry by telling Da-duh about the Empire State building, which was the tallest building in the world at that time and hailed as a great wonder of architecture.

Slavery and Colonization

Barbados was a British colony for hundreds of years. Historically, the lands of Barbados belonged to the privileged white minority, while enslaved

Africans worked the land that made them wealthy. Emancipation came to Barbados in 1838, but the whites still held the power. Conditions for Africans on the island essentially remained the same.

Many elements in ''To Da-duh, in Memoriam'' reflect this heritage. As Martin Japtok writes in *African American Review,* in this story ''Marshall shows the inescapability of history by inscribing it into the very landscape.'' The plants that Da-duh so proudly shows off to her granddaughter, whose names Da-duh intones ''as they were those of her gods,'' are not indigenous to the island, instead originating from other British colonies. Indeed, sugar cane, which brings Da-duh so much happiness, was the fundamental cause of long-lasting African exploitation. The planes that bring about Da-duh's death also represent colonial oppression; Britain ordered these flyovers in response to a 1937 strike and riot.

Style

Point of View

''To Da-duh, in Memoriam'' is written from the first-person point of view. The majority of the story is viewed through the child narrator's eyes. She recalls when she first met Da-duh, her first impression of the sugar cane fields, and the rivalry that exists between the two family members. Hers is the only voice the reader hears, and hers are the only eyes through which the reader sees Barbados and Da-duh. Thus the rivalry—and both participants' reaction to it—is only explained as a nine-year-old child might have seen, or an adult looking back at the nine-year-old child that she was. At the end of the story, the narrator pulls back even further from the events that form the bulk of the story. Her narration of what happens after she and her family leave Barbados—the riots, the planes flying over the island, and her grandmother's death—are told from the point of view of an adult looking back at something that has happened a great distance and time away. The point of view is also less personal, more factual. The story's final paragraph, though still firmly within the narrator's point of view, shows the narrator's close ties to the past and the story she has related. She reveals the lasting guilt she has felt about showing up her grandmother and making her feel inferior. She also reveals the ties she feels to her past and to her ancestry, of which Da-duh remains the most potent symbol.

Autobiography

In her introduction to ''To Da-duh, in Memoriam'' when it was collected in *Reena, and Other Stories,* Marshall writes, ''This is the most autobiographical of the stories, a reminiscence largely of a visit I paid to my grandmother (whose nickname was Da-duh) on the island of Barbados.'' She goes on to explore the feelings that she and Da-duh experienced that year, as she recalls them from a distance. However, Marshall also acknowledges that later she tried to give a ''wider meaning'' to their rivalrous but affectionate relationship. ''I wanted the basic theme of youth and old age to suggest rivalries, dichotomies of a cultural and political nature, having to do with the relationship of western civilization and the Third World,'' she writes. Marshall also states that her grandmother is ''an ancestor figure'' for her, thus it is clear that Marshall's remembrances of her grandmother can never be wholly objective or representative of the truth. Rather, ''To Da-duh, in Memoriam'' is Marshall's recollection of the truth as she perceives it from a distance and as she has chosen to shape it. Marshall's introduction reminds the reader that the story cannot be perceived as pure autobiography and that, as the author, she has striven to create a specific world and a specific message.

Symbolism and Metaphor

Marshall infuses ''To Da-duh, in Memoriam'' with rich symbolism and metaphor. Many elements take on great significance as seen through either Da-duh's or the narrator's eyes. The narrator believes the royal palm is as proud as Da-duh in its ''flaunting its dark crown of fronds right in the blinding white face of the late morning sun.'' The planes that Britain sends over the island do not look or act like objects of the machine age, but like ''swooping and screaming . . . monstrous birds'' or ''the hardback beetles which hurled themselves with suicidal force against the walls of the house at night''; this use of metaphor shows that despite hearing about New York and the modern world, Da-duh cannot even fathom its existence. The story's most important symbol is sugar cane. To Da-duh, this plant represents a source of beauty and pride, but the narrator sees the cane fields as threatening. She walks among them feeling that the canes are ''clashing like swords above my cowering head''; the narrator's reaction to the canes reflects their history as an impetus for the slave trade and the ensuing exploitation of countless Africans. Through all this, the Empire State building, representative of one of the greatest countries of the world and the home of the narrator, symbolically towers over Barbados, a tiny colonial island.

Historical Context

Colonial Barbados

By the 1930s, Barbados had been under British colonial rule for over three hundred years. Always a poor country ruled by a white, propertied minority, Barbados suffered throughout the 1930s. The rapidly growing population, rising cost of living, and fixed wage scale was exacerbated by the worldwide Great Depression. Riots broke out throughout British holdings in the Caribbean in the late 1930s. Protests in Barbados in 1937 resulted in the deaths of fourteen people.

The British rulers created a commission to look into the cause of these riots, and Grantley Adams, a Barbadian educated in England, rose to prominence after testifying that they resulted from economic distress. He formed the Barbados Labour Party (BLP) in 1938. In 1940, he was elected to the House of Assembly. Over the next few years, he led a reform movement that protected union leaders, increased direct taxation, and created a worker's compensation program. Adams's also led the fight to broaden voting rights and, as a result, women were allowed to vote—and the cost of qualifying to vote was reduced, allowing more people to vote. Eventually, Adams became the leader of the government.

Striving toward Independence

British officials had been devising a plan for a federation of the Caribbean islands since 1953. Adams's became prime minister of the short-lived West Indies Federation, while a political rival, Errol Barrow, founder of the Democratic Labour Party, became Premier in 1961 and led the government for the next ten years. Barrow's party increased worker's benefits, supported higher wages for sugar cane workers, instituted a program of industrialization, and expanded free education. The government also pushed for completed independence from Britain, and on November 30, 1966, Barbados became an independent country within the British Commonwealth of Nations; Barrow became Barbados's first prime minister.

Sugar Cane Economy

In the 1930s, as it had done for the past three hundred years, Barbados's sugar cane industry continued to be the dominant economic force. The vast majority of the land was given over to the production of sugar cane. The few crops that were grown locally were too expensive for the average worker, and most Barbadians relied on the purchase of imported food. Not until the 1970s did the sugar cane industry relinquish its dominance over the Barbadian economy.

Barbadian Emigration

From the mid-1940s through the late 1960s, unemployed Barbadians left the country to find work elsewhere. In the 1950s, Britain was the primary destination of most Barbadian emigrants, but in the 1960s, as Britain placed restrictions on West Indian immigration, more Barbadians moved to the United States. Such emigration led to a substantial diminishment in population growth.

Critical Overview

"To Da-duh, in Memoriam" was originally published in 1967. Although it drew the attention of a few early literary scholars, at that time Marshall had a relatively small audience. Lloyd W. Brown wrote in a 1974 article for *Novel: A Forum on Fiction* that such neglect is "unfortunate, because Paule Marshall's major themes are both significant and timely" and help to define the contemporary African American identity. In 1983, "To Da-duh, in Memoriam" was reissued and published in Marshall's collection *Reena, and Other Stories*. The story was often singled out, drawing much favorable attention from readers and critics. Writing in the *Dictionary of Literary Biography*, Carole Boyce Davies called it "one of the most skillful stories" in the collection.

Over the years, critics have written about many different elements of this rich story. Brown has suggested that the musical and machine rhythms with which Marshall infuses "To Da-duh, in Memoriam" symbolize the strength of her characters and the life-death themes explored through the relationship created by grandmother and granddaughter. Similarly, in her essay included in *Black Women Writers,* Eugenia Collier suggests that Marshall "uses the ritual of dance to underscore the great contrast between the child's world and Da-duh's." According to Collier, the story ends in the

Compare & Contrast

- **1940s:** Barbados is a colony of Britain.

  1960s: Barbados gains independence from Britain in 1966, but remains a member of the British Commonwealth of Nations. The British monarch, represented by an appointed governor general, is the head of state and holds executive authority along with the prime minister and the cabinet.

  Today: In 1998, a constitutional commission recommends that Barbados become a republic and replace the British monarch with an elected head of state. However, Barbados remains a sovereign nation within the Commonwealth.

- **1940s:** The mainstay of Barbados's economy is the sugar cane industry.

  1960s: Toward the end of the 1960s, tourism becomes an important industry in Barbados, and in the following decade it surpasses the production of sugar cane as the nation's leading source of revenue.

  Today: Tourism remains the top industry of Barbados, accounting for nearly 50 percent of the island's gross national product. Tourism employs more than 10 percent of the Barbadian workforce. Sugar cane, however, is still the island's main cash crop.

---

child's discovery of a "vital dimension of her self" as she realizes that the natural, traditional world of Barbados has value as well.

As Marshall has increasingly grown in stature as an important African-American writer, critics continue to explore the many themes of the story, which include the conflict between older and younger people, Western civilization and the Third World, the urban world and the rural world, and modernity and tradition. The story also reflects the history of Barbados, with its heritage of slavery, colonialism, and a reliance on sugar cane.

Other critics have also studied "To Da-duh, in Memoriam" with regard to its place within the Marshall cannon, a point which Marshall previously raised. Barbara T. Christian, writing in the *Dictionary of Literary Biography,* suggests that the story's narrator could be the younger sister of Selina Boyce, the heroine of *Brown Girl, Brownstones*, Marshall's first novel. Christian also points out that Da-duh "seems to be Marshall's sketch of a more fully developed character in *The Chosen Place, the Timeless People*, which is Marshall's second novel. Read together, Marshall's works show the development of a writer. "To Da-duh, in Memoriam" further defines the themes that have been important to Marshall throughout her literary career, as well as

the people who have shaped her life. As Marshall writes in her introductory comments to the story when it was reprinted in *Reena, and Other Stories*, "Da-duh turns up everywhere."

Criticism

Rena Korb

Korb has a master's degree in English literature and creative writing and has written for a wide variety of educational publishers. In the following essay, Korb explores the contrasts that Marshall presents in the story.

Marshall's short story "To Da-duh, in Memoriam," revolving around a rivalry between a grandmother and a granddaughter, functions within a series of contrasts as each female tries to prove that her world is superior. "I tried giving the contests I had sensed between us a wider meaning," Marshall notes in her introduction to the story when it was included in *Reena, and Other Stories*. "I wanted the basic theme of youth and old age to suggest rivalries, dichotomies of a cultural and political nature, having to do with the relationship of western civiliza-

Barbados sugar cane plantation in 1934

tion and the Third World.'' Marshall infuses ''To Da-duh, in Memoriam'' with small, careful details as well as large thematic concepts that explore those opposing forces, all of which contribute to the complex link between the vigorous American child and the aging island woman. Indeed, as Adam Gussow points out in *The Village Voice,* the love shared by grandmother and granddaughter is ''fed by a mixture of love and fear.''

In the opening paragraph of the story, the narrator introduces the contrasts that will form the basis of the relationship between herself and her grandmother. Inside the embarkation shed, the narrator stands on the threshold of entering a new world. She is not quite in Bridgetown proper, yet she is no longer connected to the boat that transported her from New York. This in-between point is characteristically indistinct; it is ''dark . . . in spite of the daylight flooding in from outside.'' In failing to illuminate the interior, the sunlight is unable to carry out one of its primary functions, thus hinting at upcoming island inadequacies. The sunlight also blinds the narrator, thus illustrating its dual, opposing nature; it can provide clarity of sight, but it can also be so strong that it obscures vision. The sunlight thus represents both the granddaughter and the grandmother, who are so positive what they believe

is right that they have difficulty seeing the other's point of view. Indeed, the light symbolism applies to the narrator's entire trip to the island; although Barbados is a land of sunshine, the narrator brings darkness to her grandmother's world.

Details throughout the story strengthen this idea of contrast, many of which come at the beginning of the story and rest within the family. For example, Da-duh prefers boys to girls and ''white'' grandchildren—fair-skinned grandchildren of mixed race—to those with dark coloring. Da-duh, who lives in St. Thomas, considers her relatives from St. Andrews to be unsophisticated and awkward. Comparing the reactions of the New York relatives to her own, she is ''ashamed at their wonder'' and ''embarrassed for them.'' The words with which the Barbadians greet the American relatives also show the material and sociocultural differences between the two family groups: ''And see the nice things they wearing, wrist watch and all!'' they exclaim.

Bridgetown offers Marshall another opportunity to explore the idea of opposites. Though Bridgetown is Barbados's largest city, its third-world atmosphere makes it hard to conceive of it in the same category as a modern city such as New York. The narrator notices the donkey carts on the streets and the woman's feet that ''slurred the dust''

What Do I Read Next?

- Marshall's *"Reena" and Other Stories* (1983) collects several of the author's short fiction from the 1950s and 1960s, as well her personal comments on each.

- Michelle Cliff's *No Telephone to Heaven* (1996) explores the intermingled histories of Africans and Europeans in the Caribbean. This nonlinear novel focuses on the dual nature of culture, as a uniting and a destructive force.

- George Lamming's *In the Castle of My Skin,* written in the 1950s, recounts growing up in the 1930s in a small Barbados community. G, from a poor, black family, provides an eyewitness account to the social, racial, and political struggles that beset the island.

- Nobel Prize–winner Derek Walcott has represented the many faces of the Caribbean—its society, cultural identity, history, and development—through his rich and imagistic poetry. *Collected Poems, 1948–1981* (1987) includes some of his best poems and provides a good introduction to this unique writer.

- Cecil Foster's *No Man in the House* (1992) takes place in 1963, as Barbadians begin their bid for independence. Eight-year-old Howard is left with his brother in the care of their grandmother as his parents go to Britain to find work. Howard blossoms at school under the tutelage of a new headmaster and vows to make his way out of poverty.

- Caribbean poet Kamau Braithwaite explores multiple aspects of the Barbadian experience in the poems collected in *Ancestors.* His poems also reflect the spoken aspects of the text, such as dialect and diction.

- The semi-autobiographical *Go Tell It on the Mountain* (1953) is James Baldwin's first novel. The classic of contemporary African-American literature is based on the author's experiences as a teenage preacher in a small revivalist church.

---

of the unpaved roads. The family's journey through Bridgetown should be celebratory reunion, but it is described as "part of a funereal procession" moving toward a "grave ceremony." The reactions of the family members to the ride in the lorry further reinforce the differences between New York and Barbados. Da-duh, so confident at the embarkation shed, now holds tight to her granddaughter's hand because she is afraid of machinery. However, as soon as the truck leaves Bridgetown, surrounded again by her beloved sugar canes, Da-duh is able to relax. The narrator, in contrast, now feels overwhelmed. Looking at the tall canes lining the road,

> I suddenly feared that we were journeying . . . toward some dangerous place where the canes, grown as high and thick as a forest, would close in on us and run us through with their stiletto blades.

Nowhere, however, are the forces of opposition more apparent than in the granddaughter's and grandmother's evocations of their communities and backgrounds. To prove the superiority of her world, Da-duh introduces her granddaughter to the land. She points out the plants, the breadfruit, papaw, guava, and mango, and elicits that the only tree on the narrator's block is a chestnut tree that produces no fruit. She takes the narrator to a small topical forest that is at once a place of beauty, violence, and peace. She owns sugar cane fields, while the narrator only has processed sugar, an insubstantial, potentially harmful substance derived, as Da-duh tells her, by "squeez[ing] all the little life in them." Da-duh's words serve as a reminder that she possesses the real item—the canes—while her granddaughter only has a cheap imitation.

In response to Da-duh's boasting about the natural glory of Barbados, the narrator tells her all of the things that New York *does* have. If Barbados is a "perennial summer kingdom," New York

---

"These two females, one young and one old, can be perceived as two halves of one whole."

offers dramatically cold winters. The narrator exaggerates in telling Da-duh how the snow in New York covers the treetops. The canes, too, would be "buried under tons of snow. The snow would be higher than your head, higher than your house." She highlights Da-duh's inadequacy by pointing out that if she dressed in New York as she did in Barbados, she would "freeze to death." The narrator adds insult to injury by telling her grandmother that she has a coat "with fur on the collar."

This pattern, set on the first day of the narrator's visit, continues to develop. Da-duh shows off the natural world, while the narrator responds by "recreating my towering world of steel and concrete and machines for her." Eventually, Da-duh turns to her crowning glory, her greatest source of island pride, "an incredibly tall royal palm which rose cleanly out of the ground . . . [and] soared high above the trees around it into the sky." Da-duh challenges her granddaughter, "All right now, tell me if you've got anything this tall in that place you're from." The narrator responds with news of the Empire State building, at the time the world's tallest building, which is located in New York. Thus, with finality, she wins the competition. Not surprisingly in a story so reliant on opposition, this victory leaves her feeling "triumphant yet strangely saddened."

While "To Da-duh, in Memoriam" rests on this series of contrasts, there are also many instances in which these opposites meet in one entity. For example, when the narrator's mother is reunited with Da-duh for the first time in fifteen years, the narrator is surprised how her mother, "who was such a formidable figure in my eyes, had suddenly . . . been reduced to my status." At one time, the narrator's mother occupies the dual roles of child and mother.

This concept of merging disparate factors most aptly applies to Da-duh, however. This suggestion, raised at the narrator's first sight of her grandmother, grows increasingly stronger throughout the story. The narrator's initial impression of Da-duh is that of a woman who is both young and old, one whose vibrant force of will stubbornly fights against her weakening body. As Da-duh makes her way through the embarkation shed, her body strains not to give in to the physical debilities that wrack an eighty-year-old woman. Her posture is bent "ever so slightly" but the "rest of her . . . sought to deny those years and hold that back straight." Also significant is Da-duh's ability to transcend time periods, as evidenced by the "long severe old-fashioned white dress she wore which brought the sense of a past that was still alive into our bustling present." Indeed, when the narrator looks into her grandmother's face, she wonders if Da-duh might be "both child and woman, darkness and light, past and present, life and death," for "all the opposites [are] contained and reconciled in her."

Because Da-duh possesses youthful elements within her, she can form a close connection with her granddaughter. Similarly, the narrator is equally drawn to this relationship. In certain ways, the narrator is both child and adult, for example, in her "fierce look," her "small strength," her pride in taking after "no one but myself," and her ability to alert her grandmother to some "disturbing, even threatening" characteristic. These two females, one young and one old, can be perceived as two halves of one whole. However, they are unable to coexist as such; the old woman cannot sustain the pressure of the child's vitality, and the child, with the backing of the changing world, overpowers the old woman. Da-duh is eventually unwilling to accept the modernity that her granddaughter presents to her and instead accepts her defeat—and chooses death. In accordance with all that has come before it, the story's ending further raises the specter of opposites. As Lloyd W. Brown observes in *Novel: A Forum on Fiction,* "The opening statement [of the last paragraph] ('She died and I lived') presents the life-death antithesis." Indeed, this idea is so important to Marshall, who wrote in her introduction that she felt that she and her grandmother, upon their first meeting

both knew, at a level beyond words, that I had come into the world not only to love her and to continue her line but to take her very life in order that I might live.

Despite—or perhaps *because of*—these conflicting feelings, the narrator continues to honor her grandmother, and in doing this creates her own environment of contrasts. For a period, she lives as an artist in a loft above a New York factory. Within this stark, urban, technologically advanced world, the narrator chooses to embrace those natural elements that her grandmother so dearly loved. The story closes on an image of the narrator's pictures of "seas of sugar-cane and huge swirling Van Gogh suns and palm trees [in] a tropical landscape . . . while the thunderous tread of the machines downstairs jarred the floor beneath my easel."

Source: Rena Korb, Critical Essay on "To Da-duh, in Memoriam," in *Short Stories for Students,* The Gale Group, 2002.

Martin Japtok

In the following essay, Japtok explores "the intertwining of the forces of nature with the forces of human-shaped time" present in "To Da-Duh, in Memoriam."

There might not be a region of the world that reflects the history of colonialism in its various phases in a more direct way than does the Caribbean. Its very population is a direct result of the African slave trade, European migration, and later immigration from various parts of mostly the British empire, while little is left of the indigenous Arawaks or Caribs. The Caribbean ecology has been forever changed by the plants, animals, and agricultural methods imposed by Europe; in addition, the soil depletion characteristic of a number of West Indian islands directly results from the monocultural economy of the plantation system. The multi-lingualism of the West Indies mirrors the various participants in and stages of European colonialism—Spanish, Portuguese, Dutch, Danish, French, British—while the fractured nature of West Indian politics grows out of European and North American rivalries over the fate of the Caribbean. In her 1967 short story "To Da-Duh, in Memoriam," Paule Marshall shows the inescapability of this history by inscribing it into the very landscape. In Marshall's story, in her later work, and in works by a number of Caribbean authors, even "nature" does not offer a retreat from the political realities of the West Indies.

By focusing on the role of "nature" in Marshall's story, I wish not so much to offer an analysis concerned with representations or ideologies of "nature" in and of itself but rather an interpretation from the point of view of environmental history; that is, to quote Peter Coats, "looking at the impact of economic and political systems, ideologies and technologies on the non-human world." Much attention has been paid to the importance of landscape in Caribbean literature. One might think here of

> As descendant of the surviving Africans, the protagonist appears to intuit the historical meaning of sugar production and seems incapable of perceiving canes merely as green fields swaying in the wind, the picture the tourist industry conveys of cane fields."

Wilfred Cartey's study *Whispers from the Caribbean,* of Eduard Glissant's *Caribbean Discourse,* or of Moira Ferguson's work on Jamaica Kincaid, as well as of the importance of geography—both as metaphor and "site"—in postcolonial literary criticism. Michael Dash, in his preface to *Caribbean Discourse,* has commented that

> the relationship with the land . . . becomes so fundamental in [Caribbean discourse] that landscape . . . stops being merely decorative or supportive and emerges as a full character. Describing the landscape is not enough. The individual, the community, the land are inextricable in the process of creating history. Landscape is a character in this process.

I wish to "literalize" that attention and focus on the actual flora as flora in Marshall's story—and, later in the essay, in the work of other Caribbean authors—in order to unlock the history found in Caribbean plant life, approaching its symbolic import in the wake of migrating plants.

Wilfred Cartey's wonderful term landscaped history may best describe what I am after here: the intertwining of the forces of nature with the forces of human-shaped time. How does this process play itself out in Marshall's short story, the story of a little girl's first visit to Barbados and her encounter with her grandmother and with island culture? As is characteristic of her fiction in general, Paule Marshall works here with a set of oppositions which interplay with one another in complex ways. "In this case, the asphalt jungle of New York City is fixed against the dense vegetation of a Caribbean isle." The story juxtaposes a Barbados representing nature with a West representing technology in a sort of competition. After introducing the child protagonist to some of the Barbadian plant life, her grandmother Da-Duh triumphs, "'I know you don't have anything this nice where you come from,'" repeating the statement after not receiving an answer, to which the protagonist replies, "'No,'" and observes, "and my world did seem suddenly lacking." Barbados wins this contest through its rich, fertile, natural world. New York, as representative of the West, appears sterile and barren. When Da-Duh claims to have heard that New York is "'a place where you can walk till you near drop and never see a tree,'" all the protagonist has to offer in reply is "'a chestnut tree in front of our house.'" But even here Da-Duh—and Barbados—remains victorious: "'Does it bear?' She waited. 'I ask you, does it bear?' 'Not anymore,' I muttered. 'It used to, but not anymore.'" The only natural thing the protagonist is finally able to connect with New York—snow—only heightens the impression of sterility and death clinging to the Western metropolis. The child describes with delight the effects snow would have on Barbadian plant life, unwittingly providing a metaphor of the relations between the Third World and the West that the story further develops later on:" '. . . you see all these trees you got here,' I s aid. 'Well, they'd be bare. No leaves, no fruit, nothing. They'd be covered in snow. You see your canes. They'd be buried under tons of snow.'" But since the West becomes associated with barrenness and death here, and the island appears lush and green, full of cane fields, trees, and tropical fruits, it may at first seem that "at the time of the narrator's visit . . ., the full effects of Western 'progress' and its accompanying materialistic values have not spoiled Da-Duh's Eden," as Dorothy Hamer Denniston claims. Upon closer examination of the plant life depicted in the story, however, and especially of the descriptions of sugarcane, it appears that the West has already left an indelible physical mark on Barbados, even before the arrival of concrete and steel. A closer examination of sugarcane in a Barbadian text is a legitimate undertaking since" 'Crop,' as sugar cane harvesting is still known, defined Barbadian life," and its "idea, its permeation of all aspects of island culture was as important a s its economic fact. Every plane of Barbadian life was touched by sugar."

What did Caribbean plant life consist of before Europeans arrived? One answer is that it is difficult to know. Even in the earliest decades after the arrival of the Spanish, the Caribbean flora underwent irreversible processes. Already "Bartolome de las Casas told of large herds of cattle and other European animals in the West Indies eating native plants down to the roots in the first half of the sixteenth century, followed by the spread of ferns, thistles, plantain, nettles, nightshade, sedge, and so forth, which he identified as Castilian." With the conquistadores came conquering plants. The most fateful of these imported plants was sugarcane. After sugar plantations had been economically successful in various Mediterranean islands, and, in the fifteenth century, phenomenally so in the Atlantic islands off the African coast, such as the Canary Islands and Madeira, "Columbus, who lived for over a decade in Madeira, had the foresight to take sugar plants from the Canary Islands on his voyages to the 'Indies.'"

Seen in this context, the child protagonist's perception of Barbados' cane fields proves to be more than apt:

> They the sugarcanes] were too much for me. I thought of them as giant weeds that had overrun the island, leaving scarcely any room for the small tottering houses of sun-bleached pine we passed or the people, dark streaks as our lorry hurtled by. I suddenly feared that we were journeying, unaware that we were, toward some dangerous place where the canes, grown as high and thick as a forest, would close in on us and run us through with their stiletto blades.

The oppressive presence of the canes, the mortal danger they metaphorically pose here, points, of course, to the way in which sugarcane was cultivated in Barbados, and in the Americas in general, during much of its agricultural history—with the brutal exploitation of African slave labor, an exploitation so relentless that it necessitated a constant influx of new slaves merely to outmatch death rates. As descendant of the surviving Africans, the protagonist appears to intuit the historical meaning of sugar production and seems incapable of perceiving canes merely as green fields swaying in the wind, the picture the tourist industry conveys of cane fields. A second description of canes is even more explicit: In her first walk through her grandmother's plot of land, the protagonist refers to "the canes [as] clashing like swords above my cowering head," thus making sugarcane directly reminiscent of the swords of conquistadores and the whips of overseers—aptly so, since "sugar and slavery traveled together for nearly four centuries in the New World."

That the story envisions sugarcane as the symbolic source of oppression is emphasized even more by a passage following the quotation above, as it implies that liberation from the practices of oppression associated with sugarcane only becomes imaginable outside the cane fields. After the child protagonist and Da-Duh leave the cane fields, they go to a small forest:

> Following her apprehensively down the incline amid a stand of banana plants whose leaves flapped like elephant's ears in the wind, I found myself in the middle of a small tropical wood. . . . It was a violent place, the tangled foliage fighting each other for a chance at the sunlight, the branches of the trees locked in what seemed an immemorial struggle, one both necessary and inevitable. But despite the violence, it was pleasant, almost peaceful in the gully, and beneath the thick undergrowth the earth smelled like spring.

On leaving the cane, the protagonist encounters this place of violence, which is not a violence of whips and swords but of resistance, revolt, and struggle—all preconditions for peace, as Marshall implies. The spring-like smell of the earth suggests a new beginning, one apparently resulting from struggle. And this struggle takes place in an area not cultivated by plantation owners—and thus outside their immediate purview—but dominated by what might be indigenous woods and by plants pointing to either India or Africa. Elephants exist on both of these landmasses; the origin of bananas is uncertain—some species may have been indigenous to the East Indies, others to Madagascar. However, the English name for the plant seems to have originated from Wolof or Malinke (according to *Webster's New Universal Unabridged Dictionary*), both West African languages, or from the Congo (according to the *Oxford English Dictionary*), from which it came to English through Portuguese or Spanish. Given the trajectory of the story as a whole, one may safely assume Africa as the intended symbolic echo in this passage invoking liberation, not least because of an early uprising in Barbados—to be followed by others—by Africans intending ''to make themselves master of the island''; India and the East Indies, though, remain important points of reference in the (ecological) story.

When Da-Duh shows her grandchild the various trees growing on her plot of land, she names them with proprietary pride: '''This here is bread fruit,' she said. 'That yonder is papaw. Here's a guava. This is a mango. I know you don't have anything like these in New York. Here's a sugar apple. . . . This one bears limies. . . . ' She went on for some time, intoning the names of the trees as though they were those of her gods.'' Some of the

gods she reveres are foreign gods, however, if one takes their origin into account. Papayas come from India, both breadfruit and mango from the East Indies, which leaves only sugar apple and guava as indigenous plants, with limes and citrus fruits most likely coming to the Caribbean from the Mediterranean. Da-Duh's dietary choices are indelibly marked by British colonialism and its links to Southeast Asia. India and the East Indies are connected to the Caribbean not only through their common fate as British colonies and sugar plantations but also through a British colonial policy encouraging the importation of East Indian laborers to the Caribbean from the middle of the nineteenth century onward. Southeast Asia and India are also the home of sugarcane; in India, ''its cultivation was commonplace by the fourth century B.C.,'' and it was from there that it started its slow but fateful journey westward, a journey that speeded up once it reached the Caribbean.

Thus, the protagonist's description of the cane as ''giant weeds that had overrun the island'' is historically appropriate in two respects: For one, plants introduced by Europeans tended to thrive on Caribbean soil and spread with incredible speed, even when disregarded by their importers; secondly, the British, though only settling Barbados in 1627, expanded sugar production so rapidly that, by the early 1650s, the island ran short of timber and of land available for food crops, so that food supplies had to be imported from either England or North America. These last two, significantly, also figure in the short story as external threats. The U.S. symbolically looms over the island through its towering buildings that, in Da-Duh's eyes, threaten to obliterate the natural splendor of Barbados. Great Britain figures as a direct physical menace through the jets it sends flying over the island at the end of the story in response to a 1937 strike that was an expression of solidarity with an oil strike in Trinidad. Both of these external powers are directly linked to Barbados through sugarcane production, and the representation of sugarcane in the story is resonant with these historical linkages. The threatening and foreboding quality cane fields assume in the text is not merely an echo of the past but also of the present of the short story, the 1930s.

In 1697, ''Barbados was,'' as Eric Williams has noted in his masterly history of the Caribbean *From Columbus to Castro,* ''the most important single colony in the British Empire, worth almost as much, in its total trade, as the two tobacco colonies of Virginia and Maryland combined, and nearly three times as valuable as Jamaica. The tiny sugar island was more valuable to Britain than Carolina, New England, New York, and Pennsylvania together.'' Though Barbados' importance to Great Britain greatly declined in the eighteenth century, the sugar industry remained dominant in Barbados, as in the French and British Caribbean in general. In 1848, Sir Robert Schomburgk, when publishing his *History of Barbados,* remained well aware of the importance of sugarcane for the British empire, as evidenced by what he gives as one of his main justifications for writing that history: ''It was here [in Barbados] that the first sugar-cane was planted upon the soil of British dominions.'' In 1928, 20 percent of the population was still employed in the sugar industry, and a British commission estimated that 67 percent of the population of Barbados would be adversely affected should sugar production be abandoned. In the 1930s, most land continued to be given over to sugar production, making the importation of food a continuing necessity. Hence the protagonist's view of the canes as ''leaving scarcely any room for the small tottering houses of sunbleached pine we passed or the people.'' Locally grown food, due to a shrinking indigenous food production, was often simply too expensive for average workers, who thus often subsisted in part on imported goods—imported, to an overwhelming extent, from the United States.

This, among other things, explains a U.S. interest in the region that continues to this day, as does the necessity for Barbados to import food in significant quantities. As a military historian approvingly noted in *American History* in February 1995, U.S. troops have been deployed in the Caribbean thirty times to protect what the U.S. views as its strategic interests. ''Eons ago,'' the historian writes, preparing to introduce an unsettling simile, ''the accidental formation of land and sea masses shaped the North American continent into a colossus that—like a giant meat axe poised overhead—dominates its Central American and Caribbean neighbors.'' The threatening presence of Western powers, whether imagined as ''canes clashing like swords'' or as a ''giant meat axe,'' hovers over the island and is, in both metaphors, directly linked to food production. Indeed, the use of food metaphors in conjunction with imperial interests goes back to an earlier period of U.S. interest in the Caribbean. Listen to the n-foreign minister John Quincy Adams, commenting on Cuba's future in 1823: ''There are laws of political as well as physical gravitation[,] and if an apple severed by the tempest from its native tree, cannot choose but fall to the ground, Cuba, forcibly

disjoined from its unnatural connection with Spain and incapable of self-support, can gravitate only toward the North American Union, which, by the same law of nature, cannot cast her off from its bosom.'' Such sentiments were expanded in the same year into the Monroe Doctrine, which declared the entire Western Hemisphere as the sphere of U.S. interest and influence.

In the short story, Da-Duh explains the connection between food production and imperialism in a symbolically resonant way when teaching her grandchild about sugarcane, indirectly commenting on the inordinate consumption of sugar—first by English settlers in the New World and then by American—that, after all, is the basis for Barbados' economic position: '''I bet you don't even know that these canes here and the sugar you eat is one and the same thing. That they does throw these canes into some damn machine at the factory and squeeze out all the little life in them to make sugar for you all so in New York to eat.''' The canes in Marshall's story, historically linked to exploitation, death, and economic dependency, are plant representatives of historical forces, are ''landscaped history.''

Thus, the role they play toward the end of the story must be read in that context. Marshall's protagonist returns to New York and therefore only learns of the death of her grandmother shortly after her visit:

> On the day of her death England sent planes flying low over the island in a show of force—so low, according to my aunt's letter, that the downdraft from them shook the ripened mangoes from the trees in Da-Duh's orchard. Frightened, everyone in the village fled into the canes. Except Da-Duh. She remained in the house at the window, so my aunt said, watching as the planes came swooping and screaming like monstrous birds down over the village, over her house, rattling the trees and flattening the young canes in the field.

What the story has suggested before becomes clear here as well in a metaphorically urgent manner: The impact of imperialism and its accompanying technology on the Third World, on nature, on human beings, is that it kills. For the purposes of this analysis, it is important to note how the inhabitants of the island attempt to escape this impact: They flee from the planes into the canes, fleeing from technology into nature. But that nature is a nature already compromised by history, not a pre-colonial haven or shelter, and as such, it proves unreliable. Having served imperialist interests for hundreds of years, the sugarcanes do not harbor Barbadians in this moment of conflict but, almost as if in collusion with the metropolis, leave them exposed to the British fighter planes overhead by being flattened.

In what position does this leave the protagonist, the descendant of Da-Duh living in New York? A very ambiguous one, as she herself realizes in the last lines of the story:

> She [Da-Duh] died and I lived, but always, to this day even, within the shadow of her death. For a brief period after I was grown I went to live alone, like one doing penance, in a loft above a noisy factory in downtown New York and there painted seas of sugarcane and huge swirling Van Gogh suns and palm trees striding like brightly plumed Tutsi warriors across a tropical landscape, while the thunderous tread of the machines downstairs jarred the floor beneath my easel, mocking my efforts.

She imagines the island, tries to ''recollect it in tranquility,'' to use a Wordsworthian phrase, but even that memory is jarred by the impact of technology, the very thing the act of recollection attempts to escape. The machines ''mock'' the narrator's efforts so that even her attempt at artistic recreation is compromised. Indeed, one can see that: While one imaginary trajectory in her painting leads back to Africa, to ''Tutsi warriors,'' another one leads to Europe again, making her see a tropical sun through a European painter's eyes. The Caribbean present connects to an African past but cannot escape the present-day impact of the West. The Caribbean cannot be simply the Caribbean—even its nature always evokes reminiscences of other places.

Paradoxically, even the protagonist's paintings erase and reconstruct Barbados as much as the non-indigenous flora has. Rather than seeing the Caribbean landscape for itself, she sees a contest again, one between Europe and Africa. An earlier passage illuminates her paintings: When Da-Duh leads her grandchild on one of her tours of the island, she shows her ''an incredibly tall royal palm which rose cleanly out of the ground and, drawing the eye up with it, soared high above the trees around it into the sky. It appeared to be touching the blue dome of the sky, to be flaunting its dark crown of fronds right in the blinding white face of the late morning sun.'' Da-Duh's tall royal palm appears to symbolize Afro-Caribbean resistance against a ''white'' sun apparently representing the colonial powers, and the story's final paragraph becomes resonant with this struggle, with palm (reminiscent of Tutsi warriors) and sun (connected to Europe through Van Gogh) as antagonists in an almost mythical, timeless conflict. As Beverly Horton has said in a discussion of Michelle Cliff's *No Telephone to Heaven,* ''Buried under the surface of the island, and the sea surrounding it[,] are the intermingled histories of colonization and colonial resistance, the histories of contact between African and European peoples in the Caribbean.'' Marshall's vision here is more pessimistic than in her later fiction. Especially *The Chosen Place, the Timeless People* envisions possibilities for overcoming colonialist domination, but even there, the place the protagonist has to start from is Africa, not the Caribbean itself.

Sugarcane's role as a mirror of a tortured history is not confined to ''To Da-Duh.'' *The Chosen Place, the Timeless People* represents cane fields in similar ways; canes appear ''ranked like an opposing army . . . their long pointed leaves bristling like spears in the wind,'' the passage echoing, in its militaristic imagery, the history of conquest alluded to before. In Barbadian author Cecil Foster's novel *No Man in the House,* the grandmother of the protagonist also associates a sense of danger and threat with sugarcane plantations, and she uses this threat as a pedagogical tool to keep children at home at nighttime:

> ''That is why I keep telling you young children to stay close to the house at night. You can never tell when some man looking for a young person's heart might pass through this village and grab one of you off the streets. An the next thing we know, one of you will turn up dead in some cane field.''

It is not surprising, then, when the protagonist internalizes this outlook on sugarcane fields, so different from the one offered in tourist brochures and commercials disseminated for Western consumption: ''The houses in the villages along the highway had suddenly given way to endless fields of sugar cane. . . . I didn't want to be caught in such a desolate, frightening part of the island.'' In Michelle Cliff's *No Telephone to Heaven,* canes have a similarly threatening quality and are linked to exploitation and death. The novel's protagonist remembers walking through cane fields as a painful experience: ''She did not get far; her bare legs soon stung and bled,'' or were'' 'sliced fine,' ''as her friend says, '''by the blades of the cane . . . sharp, sharp.''' Moments later, when talking to the protagonist about a slave hospital, her friend explains,'' 'Tek a lot of smaddy fe grow cane, missis. Cyaan have smaddy dying off—not when dem cost so','' thus connecting the objectification and enslavement of Africans with the cultivation of sugarcane.

George Lamming, too, personifies canes and hints at ominous meanings when describing ''fields of sugar cane [creeping] like an open secret across the land.'' Haitian-American author Edwidge Danticat's novel *Breath, Eyes, Memory* continues this tradition of associating cane with danger. The protagonist's mother is raped in a cane field, and in a parallel to *No Man in the House,* the protagonist's grandmother tells children begging her for another story'' 'to go home before the werewolf on the sugarcane cart came out, the one who could smell you from miles away and would come and kill you.''' Indeed, Barbadian folklore has also memorialized the threat symbolically inherent in sugarcane: The ''outman,'' a spooky figure said to haunt and chase children, has sugarcane fields as his hiding place, thus imbuing them with a sense of danger.

Sugarcane and the Middle Passage that sugarcane brought in its wake haunt Marshall's Barbados and the Caribbean of other authors. It appears that landscape in ''To Da-Duh'' is never merely landscape but always the mirror of human history, bearing record through proliferating the seeds humans have planted.

Source: Martin Japtok, ''Sugarcane as History in Paule Marshall's 'To Da-Duh, in Memoriam,''' in *African American Review,* Vol. 34, No. 3, Fall 2000, pp. 475–82.

Sources

Brown, Lloyd W., ''The Rhythms of Power in Paule Marshall's Fiction,'' in *Novel: A Forum on Fiction,* Vol. 7, No. 2, Winter 1974, pp. 159–67.

Christian, Barbara T., ''Paule Marshall,'' in *Dictionary of Literary Biography,* Vol. 33: *Afro-American Fiction Writers After 1955,* edited by Thadious M. Davis, Gale Research, 1996, pp. 161–70.

Collier, Eugenia, ''The Closing of the Circle: Movement from Division to Wholeness in Paule Marshall's Fiction,'' in *Black Women Writers (1950–1980): A Critical Evaluation,* edited by Mari Evans, Anchor Books, 1984, pp. 295–315.

Davies, Carole Boyce, ''Paule Marshall,'' in *Dictionary of Literary Biography,* Vol. 157: *Twentieth-Century Caribbean and Black African Writers,* edited by Bernth Lindfors, Gale Research, 1996, pp. 192–202.

Gussow, Adam, Review of *''Reena'' and Other Stories,* in *Village Voice,* Vol. XXIX, No. 20, May 15, 1984, p. 47.

Japtok, Martin, ''Sugarcane as History in Paule Marshall's 'To Da-Duh, in Memoriam,''' in *African American Review,* Vol. 34, Issue 3, Fall 2000, p. 475.

Further Reading

Beckles, Hilary McDonald, *A History of Barbados: From Amerindian Settlement to Nation-State,* Cambridge University Press, 1990.
  Beckle's comprehensive history emphasizes the struggle for social equality, civil rights, and economic improvement that have marked the island's past.

Chamberlain, Mary, *Narratives of Exile and Return,* Palgrave, 1997.
  Chamberlain bases her social history of emigration from Barbados on interviews across multiple generations of Barbadian families.

Coser, Stalamaris, *Bridging the Americas: The Literature of Paule Marshall, Toni Morrison, and Gayl Jones,* Temple University Press, 1995.
  Coser's work evaluates the similarities between these three important African-American writers.

Denniston, Dorothy Hamer, *The Fiction of Paule Marshall: Reconstructions of History, Culture, and Gender,* University of Tennessee Press, 1995.
  Hamer's study examines Marshall's writings as they represent the author's background and experiences.

Labrucherie, Roger A., *Barbados, A World Apart,* Imagenes Press, 1995.
  Photojournalist Labrucherie presents the world of Barbados, including its history, culture, people, and wildlife, through his photographs and essays.

Pettis, Joyce, ''A MELUS Interview: Paule Marshall,'' in *MELUS,* Vol. 17, Issue 4, Winter 1991–1992, p. 117.
  The interview focuses on the role of the Caribbean in Marshall's writing and examines characters who appear in her books.

Winter Dreams

F. Scott Fitzgerald
1922

F. Scott Fitzgerald's "Winter Dreams" was first published in *Metropolitan Magazine* in December 1922 and collected in *All The Sad Young Men* in 1926. The story has come to be regarded as one of Fitzgerald's finest and most eloquent statements on the destructive nature of the American dream.

"Winter Dreams" chronicles the rise of Dexter Green, a hardworking, confident young man who becomes caught up in the pursuit of wealth and status. When he meets Judy Jones, a beautiful, vibrant young woman, he sees in her an embodiment of a glittering world of excitement and promise. Judy represents for him the epitome of what he considers to be the intense and passionate life of the American elite. Through her, Dexter hopes to experience all the benefits that he believes this lifestyle can afford him. At the beginning of their relationship, he feels ecstatic. His senses become fine-tuned to the rarefied world with which he has come in contact. As a result, he becomes filled with an overwhelming consciousness and appreciation of this new life, though at the same time he recognizes the ephemeral quality of this moment in time, admitting that he will probably never again experience such happiness. Yet he fails to see the hollowness beneath Judy's surface, a hollowness that is also at the core of her world. By the end of the story, when Dexter watches his beautiful vision crumble, he is forced to admit the illusory nature of his winter dreams.

Author Biography

F. Scott Fitzgerald was born on September 24, 1896, in St. Paul, Minnesota, to Edward and Mary McQuillan Fitzgerald. From his father, a businessman, he inherited his predisposition for alcoholism and his romantic imagination; from his mother, an heiress, he developed an attraction to wealth, all of which would become major themes in his work. At a young age, Fitzgerald expressed an interest and a talent in writing as he began to write stories that echoed ones from popular magazines. The school magazines at St. Paul Academy and Newman School, where he attended school, published several of his short stories. Every summer from 1911 to 1914 he wrote plays that neighborhood children performed for charity groups.

He entered Princeton in 1913, where he wrote short stories, poetry, plays, and book reviews for the *Nassau Literary Magazine* and the *Princeton Tiger,* and wrote plays for the school's shows. His concentration on writing took him away from his studies, and as a result, he left in January, 1916. He returned a year later but never finished his degree. When World War I broke out, he was appointed second lieutenant in the army, although he never served overseas. During his stint in the army, he completed a draft of a novel, *The Romantic Egotist.* Scribner's publishers did not accept the manuscript, but they suggested that he continue working on it.

While stationed in Montgomery, Alabama, he met Zelda Sayre, daughter of an Alabama Supreme Court judge. He soon fell in love with the beautiful but troubled Zelda and married her. Their life together would come to epitomize the excitement and tragedy of the Jazz Age, as often fictionalized in his work.

After his discharge in 1919, he returned to St. Paul determined to be, as he told a friend, one of the greatest writers who has ever lived. He began his literary career with a rewrite of *The Romantic Egotist*, renaming it as *This Side of Paradise*, which was accepted by Scribner's. The novel was well received by critics and the public, who applauded its accurate portrait of American society in the 1920s. In December 1922, *Metropolitan Magazine* published ''Winter Dreams,'' which was later included in his collection of short stories, *All The Sad Young Men* in 1926. The collection was a popular and critical success, cementing Fitzgerald's reputation as a chronicler of the destructive nature of the American dream.

Fitzgerald's subsequent novels and short stories were well received, but his and Zelda's extravagant lifestyle kept him constantly in debt. Eventually, Zelda would be hospitalized for mental illness and Fitzgerald would suffer a breakdown. At the end of his career, with few copies of his works being sold, he turned to script writing in Hollywood, where he worked on, among others, the script for *Gone with the Wind.* He died there of a heart attack, probably brought on by his alcoholism, on December 21, 1940.

Plot Summary

Part I

At the beginning of the story, fourteen-year-old Dexter Green is a caddy at Sherry Island Golf Club. He works there only for pocket money, since his father owns ''the second best grocery-store in Black Bear.'' In the winter, Dexter frequently skis over the snow-covered fairways, a landscape that fills him with melancholy. During his days there, he frequently daydreams about becoming a golf champion and defeating the wealthy members of the club. One morning he abruptly quits when Judy Jones, a beautiful, eleven-year-old girl comes to play golf and treats him as an inferior.

Several years later he decides against attending the state university his father would have paid for and instead goes to a prestigious school in the East, although he has trouble affording it. The narrator makes it clear that he was more concerned with obtaining wealth than just associating with the wealthy.

After he graduates from college, he borrows a sum of money, and that and his confidence buy him a partnership in a laundry. He works hard at the business, catering to wealthy customers as he learns how to properly clean fine clothes. As a result, by the time he is twenty-seven, he is a successful businessman, who owns an entire chain of laundries.

Part II

One day, when he is twenty-three, one of the men he had caddied for invites him to play at the Sherry Island Golf Club. As he is playing, Judy Jones accidentally hits one of his foursome in the stomach with her ball. Later that afternoon, he goes swimming and runs into Judy, who asks him to go boating with her. When she invites him to dinner the next night, ''his heart turned over like the fly-wheel of the boat, and, for the second time, her casual whim gave a new direction to his life.'' After spending a romantic evening with her, Dexter decides ''that he had wanted Judy Jones ever since he was a proud, desirous little boy.''

During the next few weeks, they see each other regularly, but Judy frequently flirts and goes off with other men, which, he discovers, is typical behavior for her. A year and a half later, Dexter grows tired of Judy's inability to commit herself to him, and finally convinces himself that she will not marry him. He then becomes engaged to ''sweet and honorable'' Irene Scheerer. The following spring, just before his engagement to Irene is to be announced, he plans one night to take her to the University Club, but since she is ill, he goes by himself. There he sees Judy, and is ''filled with a sudden excitement.'' While he tries to be casual and composed, she tells him how much she has missed him and loves him and so insists that he should marry her. She soon persuades him to break off his engagement with Irene and restart his relationship with her.

Judy's attentions toward him last for only one month. Yet, Dexter does not ''bear any malice toward her.'' Soon after they part, he moves East, intending to settle in New York. However, when World War II breaks out, he returns home and enlists, ''welcoming the liberation from webs of tangled emotion.''

Part III

The story picks up in New York seven years later, where Dexter has relocated after the war. At thirty-two, he is more successful than he had been before the war. One day, a man named Devlin comes to see him about business and tells him that his best friend is married to Judy. Devlin admits that her husband ''treats her like the devil'' while she stays home and takes care of their children. He also reveals that ''she was a pretty girl when she first came to Detroit,'' but that ''lots of women fade just like that.''

Dexter becomes extremely upset at the thought of Judy losing her beauty and allure, admitting that his ''dream was gone.'' He cries, not for her but for himself, knowing that his youthful illusions of per-

F. Scott Fitzgerald

fection have vanished. Despondent, he concludes that ''now that thing is gone. . . , I cannot cry. I cannot care. That thing will come back no more.''

Characters

Devlin

Devlin is a business associate of Dexter's. He tells Dexter that Judy's beauty has faded and she has become a passive housewife to an alcoholic and abusive husband.

Dexter Green

The story follows its main character, Dexter Green, over several years of his life. Fourteen at the beginning of the story, he is confident and full of ''winter dreams'' of a golden future. He feels superior to the other caddies, who are ''poor as sin,'' since he works only for pocket-money. He continually daydreams in ''the fairways of his imagination'' about gloriously besting the men for whom he caddies or dazzling them with fancy diving exhibitions.

The enterprising and resourceful young Dexter performs his duties expertly and so becomes the caddy most in demand at the club. As Mr. Jones notes, he never loses a ball, and he is a hard worker. Yet his desire to become a part of the glittering world of wealth he has only glimpsed compels him to abruptly quit his job when Judy Jones makes him feel that he is her inferior. The narrator explains, ''as so frequently would be the case in the future, Dexter was unconsciously dictated to by his winter dreams.''

Dexter's ambition prompts him to attend a prestigious university in the East, and then upon graduation, to work hard to master the cleaning trade and so become a successful businessman. He works diligently to improve his manners and dress so that he can become a part of the world he so admires. Besides adopting the mannerisms of those who attend a top university, he finds the best tailors to dress him.

Many who meet him, impressed with his success, like to say: ''Now *there's* a boy.'' The narrator makes it clear, however, that Dexter is not a snob; he does not want ''association with glittering things and glittering people, he wanted the glittering things themselves.'' Yet Dexter does not appear to covet glittering things for their monetary value. He instead seems to need them to fulfill his vision of a perfect life, which includes gaining the love of Judy Jones.

He does not always, however, wear his success easily. When he returns to his hometown and is invited out by the men for whom he used to caddy, he tries to close the gap between the present and the past. He notes that he fluctuates from feeling as if he is an impostor to a sense that he is clearly superior to the men he used to work for.

He shows his emotional strength when he accepts Judy's treatment of him, which causes him a great deal of pain, and does not feel any malice toward her. Yet when he learns that her beauty and vitality have faded, he breaks. Judy has been at the center of his vision of a golden world of wealth and opportunity. When she fades, so does his dream. As a result, he feels an overwhelming emptiness.

T. A. Hedrick

Dexter caddies for Hedrick, one of the wealthy patrons of the Sherry Island Golf Club. Judy Jones hits him accidentally in the stomach one day with her golf ball. Hedrick has definite ideas about a woman's place, as he reveals in his criticism of

Judy's actions. He claims that ''all she needs is to be turned up and spanked for six months and then to be married off to an old-fashioned cavalry captain.''

Judy Jones

Judy is Dexter's ideal woman, beautiful, confident, and wealthy. When she is young, she is ''inexpressibly lovely'' and full of vitality, with a ''continual impression of flux, of intense life.'' She embodies everything that Dexter wants in life. However, she is shallow and coldhearted as she toys with the emotions of Dexter and other men who become enamored with her.

When Dexter sees her at the beginning of the story, she is imperious, barking orders at him and arguing with her nurse, whom she soon begins to attack with her golf club. Later, when she accidentally hits Mr. Hedrick in the stomach with her ball, she does not show much concern, telling her partner that she has been delayed because she has hit ''something.'' Dexter, however, appreciates her manner and becomes envious of it.

She becomes an extremely fickle young woman, favoring one man over another only for a brief time. When her suitors appear to lose interest, she reels them back to her. Yet, the narrator insists, her actions are considerably innocent; she treats men in such a manner not because she holds any malice toward them, but because she truly does not realize the consequences of her actions.

Her tenacity emerges as she goes after whatever she wanted ''with the full pressure of her charm'' and her beauty. As she turns her back on Dexter and the other men who pursue her, she is confident that she will be able to win them back if she so desires. She plays the mating game by her own rules, ''entertained only by the gratification of her desires and by the direct exercise of her own charm.'' Yet, at her core is a hollowness, which she notes when she declares, ''I'm more beautiful than anybody else. . . . Why can't I be happy?''

Irene Scheerer

Dexter becomes engaged to Irene after he decides that he will never be able to convince Judy to marry him. Irene is a ''sweet and honorable,'' popular young woman, who gives him a sense of ''solidity.'' She does not, however, have Judy's vitality and beauty. Dexter ''knew that Irene would be no more than a curtain spread behind him, a hand moving among gleaming tea-cups, a voice calling to children.'' When Judy renews her interest in him, Dexter breaks his engagement with Irene.

Themes

Success

Dexter's vision of success involves a pursuit of the American dream of wealth and status. As Fitzgerald traces Dexter's movement toward this goal, he becomes, in essence, a social historian of his generation, chronicling the dreams of the men and women of the 1920s who saw unlimited opportunities in the new century. Even as a teenager, Dexter dreams of success. While working at a local golf course, he fantasizes about becoming a golf champion and winning matches against the wealthy men for whom he caddies, or dazzling them with his expert diving exhibitions. Later, his dreams involve his movement up into the wealthy class where he would be rich enough to marry Judy Jones. She becomes the embodiment of his ''winter dreams'' of a glittering world with endless glamour and promise.

Dexter eventually gains wealth and status due to two qualities that are inherent in the American character: hard work and confidence. Even as a young man in his first job, Dexter strives to be the best. At the Sherry Island Golf Club, he is the favorite caddy, due to his devotion to learning and helping others excel at the game. He is such a success in his position that one of the men at the club, ''with tears in his eyes,'' begs him not to quit. But Dexter is too confident in his abilities to stay in a service position, especially when Judy treats him as her inferior.

Later, he turns his confidence and drive to his education, choosing a prestigious Eastern college over a state school that would have been easier to afford. After college, he dives into the business world, where he learns all he can about running a successful laundry. Soon Dexter achieves his goal: he becomes a wealthy businessman and as such, catches the eye of Judy Jones. Yet, eventually, he discovers the hollowness that exists at the core of his winter dreams.

Hollowness

Dexter soon confronts the reality of the glittering world of which he has become a part. That

Topics for Further Study

- Read over the passage where Dexter skis on the snow-covered fairways and feels a sense of melancholy. Write a poem or a short sketch describing a scene in nature and your—or a character's—emotional response to it.

- Read one of the other stories in Fitzgerald's collection *All the Sad Young Men* and compare its style and themes to that of ''Winter Dreams.''

- If you were going to make a film version of the story, how would you cinematically represent Dexter's ''winter dreams?''

- Investigate the consequences the Depression had on the lives of Americans who had been wealthy during the 1920s. How many lost their fortunes? How did they survive?

reality is embodied in the character of Judy Jones, who has become the focus of his dreams of success and happiness. Underneath the beauty and vibrancy, however, Judy's shallowness and destructive character emerge.

Judy's ultimate goal is the gratification of her own desires, without any concern for those she destroys along the way. As she quickly becomes bored with one suitor, she replaces him with another, yet saves the first for future use. When she decides one of her admirers is beginning to lose interest, she pulls him back into her orbit with promises of fidelity, only to discard him again later. Dexter becomes caught up in this destructive game after he decides she has caused him to be ''magnificently attune[d] to life,'' to envision her world ''radiating a brightness and a glamour he might never know again.'' After he enters her world, he and the woman to whom he briefly becomes engaged suffer great pain and disillusionment.

Failure

At one point, Judy glimpses the hollowness of her existence when she admits, ''I'm more beautiful than anybody else. . . . Why can't I be happy?'' Her and Dexter's failure to achieve happiness illustrates Fitzgerald's fundamental criticism of the American dream. At the heart of the dream is an illusory world of glitter and glamour that ultimately contains no substance. While Dexter could have found happiness through a satisfying relationship with Judy, she does not have the strength of character to commit herself to him.

By the end of ''Winter Dreams,'' Dexter has accepted the failure of his relationship with Judy because he still believes in the glittering dream of her and her world. However, when a business acquaintance tells him that she has lost her youthful beauty and has become a passive housewife to an alcoholic, abusive man, his illusions are shattered. As a result, he concludes, ''the gates were closed, the sun was gone down, and there was no beauty but the gray beauty of steel that withstands all time.'' Ultimately, he grieves not for Judy, but for his lost golden world, ''the country of illusion, of youth, of the richness of life, where his winter dreams had flourished.''

Style

Narration

Fitzgerald employs a third person omniscient narrator in ''Winter Dreams,'' but with an innovative twist. The narrator almost becomes a separate persona in the story, as he occasionally steps back from the plot and speaks directly to the reader, giving his critical perspective on the characters or on the action. Fitzgerald borrows this technique from Joseph Conrad, who, in works like *Heart of Darkness* and *Lord Jim,* creates the character Marlow, a seasoned sailor who narrates the story of the main characters through his sometimes subjective perspective. Fitzgerald perfected this technique in *The Great Gatsby* in the character of Nick Carraway, the naïve Midwesterner whose task it is to pin down the enigmatic Gatsby for his audience.

In ''Winter Dreams,'' Fitzgerald does not name his character, but his presence is felt nevertheless. The first time his voice emerges is at the opening of Part II, where he tells readers, ''of course the quality and the seasonability of [Dexter's] winter dreams varied.'' The inclusion of ''of course'' adds an almost conspiratorial note, as if the narrator is communicating a hidden detail of Dexter's character, one of which Dexter is not aware.

Later, in Part IV, he speaks more directly to the reader just before he tells them about what happens after Dexter gets engaged to Irene Scheerer. Here he warns readers to remember Dexter's illusion of Judy's desirability, ''for only in the light of it can what he did for her be understood.'' Fitzgerald's chatty and perceptive narrator becomes an appropriate vehicle for an analysis of a character who has trouble separating illusion from reality.

Setting

Fitzgerald uses setting as a symbol of Dexter's changing state of mind during the course of his relationship with Judy. Initially, his restlessness in his position as caddy to the wealthy residents of his home town fills him with sadness, which Fitzgerald expresses through the landscape: as Dexter skis over the snow-covered fairways, he notes that ''at these times the country gave him a feeling of profound melancholy'' as he is ''haunted by ragged sparrows'' and ''desolate sand-boxes knee-deep in crusted ice.'' It is during these times that Dexter has his ''winter dreams'' of success, as represented by the ''gorgeous'' fall, which ''filled him with hope.'' After he returns from college and sees Judy again at the golf course, he takes a swim in the lake, which, due to his vision of his limitless future, becomes ''a clear pool, pale and quiet,'' turning ''silver molasses under the harvest moon.''

Historical Context

The Jazz Age

In the aftermath of World War I, American society went through a period of dramatic change. Traditional beliefs in God, country, and humanity were shaken as Americans faced the devastation of a war of this magnitude. The feelings of confusion and dislocation that resulted led to a questioning and often a rejection of conventional morality and beliefs. In the 1920s, Americans recognized that an old order had been replaced by a new, freer society, one that adopted innovative fashions in clothing, behavior, and the arts. Fitzgerald called this decade the ''Jazz Age,'' which along with the ''roaring twenties'' came to express the cultural revolution that was then taking place.

Compare
&
Contrast

- **1920s:** The Flapper, who presents a new, freer female image, becomes the model for young American women.

  Today: Women model themselves after a wide-range of role models, from popular cultural icons to political, historical or international figures.

- **1920s:** As a result of the decade's spirit of experimentation, sexual mores loosen and young men and women begin to engage in premarital sex.

  Today: The epidemics of AIDS and unwanted pregnancies prompt schools to augment sex edu-cation in the classroom, where one of the options stressed is abstinence.

- **1920s:** After the devastation of World War I, Americans turn to a pursuit of happiness through the acquisition of wealth. Their extravagant and unchecked spending habits contribute to the economic crisis America experiences at the end of the decade.

  Today: After a decade of unprecedented and unrealistic spikes in the stock market, the Dow has dropped considerably. As a result, many lose their jobs in corporate downsizing and restructuring.

During this era of Prohibition, Americans experimented with expressions of personal and social freedom in dress, sexuality, and lifestyle. Women cut their hair and wore shapeless ''flapper'' dresses that gave then an androgynous look. Premarital sex began to lose its stigma, and exciting developments in musical styles pulled whites into predominantly black neighborhoods. The pursuit of pleasure, especially as related to the accumulation of wealth, became a primary goal, overturning traditional notions of hard work, social conformity, and respectability. Literary historian Margot Norris in her essay ''Modernist Eruptions'' notes that during this age, ''the aesthetics of glamour produced by material and social extravagance'' were ''simulated and stimulated by the celluloid images of the burgeoning movie industry.''

The Lost Generation

This term became associated with a group of American writers during this period that felt a growing sense of disillusionment after World War I. As a result, many left America for Europe. T. S. Eliot and Ezra Pound initially relocated to London, while Fitzgerald and Ernest Hemingway traveled to Paris, which appeared to offer them a much freer society than America or England did. During this period, Paris became a mecca for these expatriates, who congregated in literary salons, restaurants, and bars to discuss their work in the context of the new age. One such salon was dominated by Gertrude Stein, who at one gathering, insisted ''you are all a lost generation.'' Stein, an author herself, supported and publicized artists and writers in this movement. Ernest Hemingway immortalized her quote in *For Whom the Bell Tolls,* which like Fitzgerald's *The Great Gatsby*, has become a penetrating portrait of this lost generation.

W. R. Anderson, in his article on Fitzgerald for *Dictionary of Literary Biography,* explains that the author never quite felt as comfortable in Paris as did his compatriots. Even though he lived there for over six years, during a most productive period in his literary career, ''an air of transience'' emerges in his writing. Yet, he notes, Paris, and his association with the other writers of the lost generation, had a major impact on his work.

The characters in works by these authors reflected their growing sense of disillusionment along with the new ideas in psychology, anthropology, and philosophy that had become popular in the early part of the century. Freudian psychology, for example, which had caused a loosening of sexual morality during the Jazz Age, began to be studied by these writers, as they explored the psyche of their characters, and recorded their often subjective points of view of themselves and their world. Hemingway's men and women faced a meaningless world with courage and dignity, exhibiting "grace under pressure," while Fitzgerald's sought the redemptive power of love in a world driven by materialism.

This age of confusion, redefinition, and experimentation produced one of the most fruitful periods in American letters. These writers helped create a new form of literature, later called modernism, which repudiated traditional literary conventions. Prior to the twentieth century, writers structured their works to reflect their belief in the stability of character and the intelligibility of experience. Traditionally, novels and stories ended with a clear sense of closure as conflicts were resolved and characters gained knowledge about themselves and their world. The authors of the Lost Generation challenged these assumptions as they expanded the genre's traditional form to accommodate their characters' questions about the individual's place in the world.

Critical Overview

"Winter Dreams," first published in *Metropolitan Magazine* in 1922 and later collected in *All The Sad Young Men* in 1926, earned accolades for its thematic import and its style. Ruth Prigozy, in her article on Fitzgerald for the *Dictionary of Literary Biography* concludes, "The story is richly evocative, containing some of Fitzgerald 's best writing." In an overview of "Winter Dreams," Joseph Flibbert praises Fitzgerald's skillful structuring of the story to highlight its themes.

All The Sad Young Men became Fitzgerald's most popular collection of stories to date. In a review of the collection for *Bookman,* a reviewer concluded that the stories prove Fitzgerald to be "head and shoulders better than any writer of his generation." Furthermore, the stories exhibit "compelling fineness, along with more conventional pieces of story telling that are sufficiently amusing with the old Fitzgerald talent."

Ironically, today Fitzgerald's works have become more popular than they were when they were published. None of his works became bestsellers in his lifetime and toward the end of his career, he was regarded as dated in his portraits of young men and women caught up in the Jazz Age. In the last few decades, however, he has come to be recognized as one of America's most important writers. Few freshman survey courses do not include a reading of *The Great Gatsby*, and "Winter Dreams" is now considered to be one of his finest short stories.

Criticism

Wendy Perkins

Perkins is an instructor of English and American literature and film. In this essay, Perkins considers Fitzgerald's short story in relation to his novel The Great Gatsby.

Fitzgerald wrote his short story "Winter Dreams" while he was drafting *The Great Gatsby*, which became one of the most celebrated novels of all time. The two works share several thematic and stylistic elements as they each center on a young man from a modest background who strives to be a part of the exclusive world inhabited by the woman he loves. A close comparison of the two works will reveal that while *The Great Gatsby* becomes a more complex and penetrating critique of the pursuit of the wealth and status, the short story stands on its own as a compelling portrait of a man who is forced to face the illusory nature of his "winter dreams."

There are strong similarities between Jay Gatsby and Dexter Green. Although Dexter, unlike Gatsby, came from a middle-class background, (his father owned the "second-best" grocery-store in his town), he subscribes to the same American dream as does Gatsby, who grew up in poverty. Both spent their childhood in the Midwest, and from an early age, were determined to gain entry into the glittering and glamorous world of the rich. Through a combination of ambition and hard work, they achieve their goal and become successful businessmen who are accepted into this exclusive world.

The process by which they rise to the top, however, is quite different. Fitzgerald clearly outlines the steps Dexter takes to become successful: he attends a prestigious Eastern university and upon graduation learns everything he can about the laundry business. The knowledge he gains, coupled with his confidence and a small financial investment, guarantees his prosperity. Fitzgerald is not as straightforward about Gatsby's rise. There are suggestions that he may have been involved in a cheating

What Do I Read Next?

- Fitzgerald's highly celebrated novel, *The Great Gatsby* (1925), shares many of the same themes as ''Winter Dreams.''

- Fitzgerald's ''Rich Boy'' presents a different view of a young man enamored with the world of the rich.

- *The Sun Also Rises* (1926), by Ernest Heming-way, one of Fitzgerald's ''lost generation'' compatriots, focuses on a group of disillusioned Americans living in Paris after World War I.

- *Discontented America: The United States in the 1920s (The American Moment)* (1989), by David J. Goldberg, presents an overview of this fascinating decade and focuses specifically on how World War I affected American society.

---

scandal and a bootlegging operation with some shady New York entrepreneurs. Fitzgerald's inclusion of the possibility that Gatsby may have prospered by his involvement in illegal activities highlights the sense of corruption he finds at the heart of American materialism, a theme he develops more completely in his searing portrait of Tom Buchanan, Daisy's fabulously rich and morally corrupt husband.

While both of Fitzgerald's protagonists start out wanting only the status and power that wealth will afford, they shift their focus to a beautiful woman who embodies their dream and with whom they fall in love. Eventually, each finds little satisfaction in purely materialistic gain. Initially Dexter, like Gatsby, is not a snob; he does not want ''association with glittering things and glittering people,'' but he does want ''the glittering things themselves.'' Both men amass fortunes, but their wealth ultimately does not fulfill their dream, which focuses on gaining the love of a beautiful woman who expresses the glamour and promise of that exclusive world. At Gatsby's extravagant parties, for example, the host retreats to the study, waiting for Daisy to appear, refusing to participate in the hedonistic atmosphere of the gathering. Likewise, Dexter has no social aspirations and ''rather despised the dancing men who were always on tap for the Thursday or Saturday parties and who filled in at dinners with the younger married set.'' Neither man is affected by the attitudes of others in his pursuit of his dreams, nor does either bear any malice toward the women who repeatedly scorn them.

Daisy and Judy also are quite similar in character. Each is a shallow, ultimately cold-hearted woman who is entertained, as Fitzgerald describes Judy, ''only by the gratification of her desires and by the direct exercise of her own charm.'' Like Judy, Daisy enjoys ''the mystery that wealth imprisons and preserves, of the freshness of many clothes . . . gleaming like silver, safe and proud above the hot struggles of the poor.'' The two male characters have their hearts broken by these lovely women who exhibit ''a continual impression of flux, of intense life.'' Daisy and Judy are ''careless people'' who ''smashed up things and creatures and then retreated back into their money or their vast carelessness . . . and let other people clean up the mess they had made.''

Daisy appears to be the crueler of the two, as she allows Gatsby to take the full responsibility for her accidentally running down Myrtle, Tom's mistress, which results in Gatsby's murder by Myrtle's husband. Judy's only crime is breaking hearts. Readers feel a bit sorry for her when she wonders to Dexter, in a broken voice, ''I'm more beautiful than anybody else. . . . Why can't I be happy?'' But ultimately, Fitzgerald creates a fuller, more sympathetic character in Daisy.

Through his manipulation of the narrative's chronology, readers are privy to a demonstration of the intense love Daisy had at one point for Gatsby, revealed when she breaks down in the shower, immediately before her marriage to Tom. Jordan notes how Daisy had to be forced into her wedding

> "Through Dexter Green, Fitzgerald has chronicled the journey of a realist, who forces himself to shatter the illusions he has held for so long."

dress by her parents, who were determined that their daughter marry so well. Readers also see how she suffers in her relationship with her brutish husband. Fitzgerald portrays Daisy as someone who had the potential for happiness, but was not strong enough to achieve that goal. By the end of the novel, she retreats with Tom into the only world she knows.

Fitzgerald does not develop Judy into a complete character. Readers never know how she became so callous and shallow, and as a result, they have little sympathy for her, even when they discover at the end of the story that her beauty has faded. Like Daisy, Judy has become a passive wife to an abusive husband, but because readers do not see how that process occurred, as they do with Daisy, her character remains undeveloped and not as interesting as her counterpart.

The settings of the two works reveal Fitzgerald's rhetorical brilliance in his poetic descriptions of the landscape. He paints detailed portraits of the landscape that artfully reflect each work's themes. Throughout much of *The Great Gatsby*, Fitzgerald concentrates on images that illustrate the corruption at the heart of the American dream. His landscapes become the wastelands of garbage heaps and burned out valleys of ashes. The eyes of Dr. T. J. Eckelberg, a symbol of crass materialism and loss of spirituality, peer down from billboards along the highway. At the end of the novel, however, Fitzgerald presents perhaps the most lyrical passage in literature when he describes Daisy's green light, representing to Gatsby the possibility of an "orgastic future" with Daisy.

Fitzgerald's descriptions in "Winter Dreams" are equally lyrical and resonant. They also reflect the dual nature of the main character's experience. At the beginning of the story, when Dexter can only fantasize about a golden future, the landscape re-

flects his depression: the long winter "shut down like the white lid of a box" as he skis over the golf course's snow-covered fairways. The narrator notes Dexter's identification with his surroundings when he describes his melancholic response to the links' "enforced fallowness, haunted by ragged sparrows for the long season" and "desolate sand-boxes knee-deep in crusted ice." At that period of his life "the wind blew cold as misery" and the sun cast a "hard dimensionless glare."

At the beginning of his relationship with Judy, however, when the world is filled with excitement and promise, the landscape dramatically changes. One afternoon, soon after he has run into Judy on the golf course, the sun sets "with a riotous swirl of gold and varying blues and scarlets" and the water turns "silver molasses under the harvest-moon."

While Fitzgerald ends the two works with each main character losing the woman he loves, he leads the two in different directions, and as a result, creates two distinct and compelling commentaries on the pursuit of the American dream. As each story draws to a close, Fitzgerald delineates important differences between Dexter and Gatsby.

At the end of "Winter Dreams," Dexter accepts the fact that he has lost Judy, and accepts also "the deep pain that is reserved only for the strong" since he had also, "tasted for a little while the deep happiness." He does, however, receive a shock at the end that alters his vision of the golden world he experienced for a time. When a business associate tells him that Judy has lost her beauty and her vitality, his dream shatters and he breaks down, overcome by a profound sense of loss. Joseph Flibbert, in his critique of the story in the *Reference Guide to Short Fiction,* argues "As long as he could maintain a vision of Judy as the embodiment of genteel youth and beauty, he could continue to believe in an attainable ideal of power, freedom, and beauty." The world now becomes cold and gray with no point to the accumulation of material objects.

Struggling desperately to regain that vision, Dexter tries to picture "the waters lapping on Sherry Island and the moonlit veranda, and gingham on the golf-links and the dry sun and the gold color of her neck's soft down," but cannot, insisting, "these things were no longer in the world! They had existed and they existed no longer." He finally understands that he can never follow the same vision that had compelled him to travel in one direction all of his life. All he is left with now is a sense of emptiness, for "even the grief he could have borne was left behind in the country of illusion, of youth, of the richness of life, where his winter dreams had flourished.''

Gatsby, however, dies with his vision of Daisy and the promise of a life with her in tact. He never sees Daisy's beauty fade, nor does he realize that she has returned to the safety of her relationship with Tom. His inability to give up his dream earns Nick's respect and his conclusion that Gatsby was ''worth the whole damn bunch put together.'' Gatsby becomes a mythic figure in the novel, the tireless pursuer of the American dream—the ''fresh green breast of the New World.'' Fitzgerald's closing lines reinforce this mythic dimension when Nick notes Gatsby's inability to see through the illusion and so remain devoted to his vision of Daisy. Nick echoes this enduring sense of hope in the novel's last lines as he insists that although happiness eludes people, ''tomorrow we will run faster, stretch out our arms farther. . . . So we beat on, boats against the current, bourne back ceaselessly into the past.''

Fitzgerald's exquisite crafting of these two works has created enduring portraits of characters whose fate expresses a deep resonance of the American experience. Through Dexter Green, Fitzgerald has chronicled the journey of a realist, who forces himself to shatter the illusions he has held for so long. In his creation of Gatsby, Fitzgerald presents the romantic, who refuses to give up his pursuit of the woman he loves, who represents to him, all that is possible in America.

Source: Wendy Perkins, Critical Essay on ''Winter Dreams,'' in *Short Stories for Students,* The Gale Group, 2002.

Clinton S. Burhans, Jr.

In the following essay excerpt, Burhans focuses on the character of Dexter and the loss of his idealized view of Judy.

Men like Dexter Green do not cry easily; his tears and the language explaining them therefore point either to melodrama or to a complex significance. The difficulty lies in understanding precisely what Dexter has lost and whether its loss justifies the prostration of so strong and hard-minded a man. It seems clear that he is not mourning a new loss of Judy herself, the final extinction of lingering hopes; he had long ago accepted as irrevocable the fact that he could never have her. Nor has he lost the ability to feel deeply, at least not in any general sense: Fitzgerald makes it clear that Dexter has lost only the single and specific ability to respond deeply to images of Judy and of their moments together; and he is certainly able to feel deeply the loss of this response. Similarly, he is not crying over the loss of any illusions of eternal youth or beauty. Given his character, the nature of his dreams, and the history of his striving to achieve them, Dexter is simply not the kind of man to have such illusions. And in the unlikely event that he could somehow entertain them, he is even less the kind of man to weep over the loss of abstractions. Hardly more plausible are the views that he is shocked by a sudden awareness of the destructiveness of time or of the impossibility of repeating the past. Again, it seems unlikely that this man, especially at thirty-two, could have missed the reality of time and the finality of the past.

What is it, then, that Devlin's description of Mrs. Lud Simms has destroyed in Dexter Green? To begin with, Devlin has taken from Dexter's image of Judy the same things he would have lost if he had married her and seen her suddenly ''fade away before his eyes'': the specific features and qualities that comprised her unparalleled beauty and desirability, her appeal to him as one of the ''glittering things,'' one of the ''best.'' These had been the basis of his love for her—not her reflection of eternal youth or beauty but their physical and perishable realities. Once before, in turning from Judy to Irene Scheerer, he had found almost unendurable the loss of these tangible and emotional qualities: ''fire and loveliness were gone, the magic of nights and the wonder of the varying hours and seasons . . . slender lips, down-turning, dropping to his lips and bearing him up into a heaven of eyes. . . . The thing was deep in him. He was too strong and alive for it to die lightly.'' At first glance, *thing* may seem a strange and imprecise word for Dexter's profound and encompassing love, but it is more consistent and apt than it might appear. His love for Judy is no more Platonic than his other winter dreams; it is sensuous and emotional, and ''thing'' suggests this tangible reality as well as the nature of what he has lost. Moreover, Fitzgerald's conscious use of the term for these purposes is reflected in his repetition of it nine times in the final passage of the story.

Paradoxically, in finally giving up all hope of Judy and in going to New York, Dexter is able to have her in a way he never could had they married. With the real Judy out of his life, the girl he had dreamed of having can remain alive in his imagination, unchanging in the images of her youthful beauty and desirability. More importantly, these images keep alive in Dexter the ''thing'' they had

> When his images of Judy Jones no longer create an imaginative present, he loses not only his ability to go on loving her but also something else equally and perhaps even more shattering. Gone, too, is a part of himself."

originally so deeply stirred in him—his love for Judy and his dream of having her. It is all this that Devlin kills in Dexter by forcing on him a new and intolerable image of Judy.

In Devlin's description of her as Mrs. Lud Simms, Fitzgerald carefully strips away every feature and every quality of the Judy Jones Dexter had known and still loves in his images of her. His "'great beauty'" becomes an ordinarily pretty woman; the unique and imperious paragon courted by worshippers becomes a conventional and submissively put-upon housewife; the queen of his love and dreams becomes a rather mousy commoner he could not conceivably love. No wonder Dexter is devastated. Having accepted the loss of the real Judy Jones, he had thought himself safe from further hurt; now, with every word of Devlin's, he finds himself not only losing her again but what is worse losing the ability to go on loving her.

As long as Dexter knows little or nothing new about Judy, she can stay alive and immediate in his imagination; thus, the real past continues unchanged as the imaginative present. Responding to these images of Judy Jones, Dexter can continue to love her as he had in the beginning, when the dream of having this "glittering thing" and the striving for her could still be part of that love. But Devlin destroys the time-suspending equation. When he tells Dexter what has happened to Judy, when he forces him to imagine her as the older and fading Mrs. Lud Simms, then the young and vibrant girl Dexter had loved disappears into the wax museum of the irredeemable past. The real present supplants the imaginative present and forces the past to become only the past.

For Dexter, "the dream was gone"; when he tries to recall his images of the earlier Judy, they come to him not as a continuing present but as a completed past, as "things . . . no longer in the world," things that "had existed and . . . existed no longer." Now they are only memories of a girl he had known and loved who has unaccountably become Mrs. Lud Simms, and they no longer have the power to stir his love or his dreams. "He did not care about mouth and eyes and moving hands. He wanted to care, and he could not care." Dexter wants desperately to care because these images have been the source of his love for Judy Jones and the means of keeping it alive. The end of their power to stir him is therefore the end of that love, and his tears are a bitter mourning for a second and this time total loss of Judy Jones. "'Long ago,' he said, 'long ago, there was something in me, but now that thing is gone. . . . That thing will come back no more.'"

Dexter cries with good reason, then, but he has even more reason to cry. When his images of Judy Jones no longer create an imaginative present, he loses not only his ability to go on loving her but also something else equally and perhaps even more shattering. Gone, too, is a part of himself also deeply associated with and still alive in these images: the fragile moment in time when youth and his winter dreams were making his life richer and sweeter than it would ever be again.

Fitzgerald makes it clear that the story centers on this moment in time and its significance. The story is not Dexter's "biography . . . although things creep into it which have nothing to do with those dreams he had when he was young." Specifically, Fitzgerald writes, "the part of his story that concerns us goes back to the days when he was making his first big success." These are the years between twenty-three and twenty-five, the years just after college and just before New York. "When he was only twenty-three . . . there were already people who liked to say: 'Now *there's* a boy—.'" Already Dexter is making a large amount of money and receiving guest cards to the Sherry Island Golf Club, where he had been a caddy and had indulged his winter dreams. At twenty-four he finds "himself increasingly in a position to do as he wished," and at twenty-five he is "beginning to be master of his own time" as "the young and already fabulously successful Dexter Green. . . ."

This progress towards making his winter dreams come true is not, however, unqualified. Almost from the beginning, disillusion casts strange shadows on Dexter's bright successes. He had dreamed of being a golf champion and defeating Mr. T. A. Hedrick ''in a marvellous match played a hundred times over the fairways of his imagination''; now, as a guest playing in a foursome on the real fairways of the Sherry Island Golf Club, Dexter is ''impressed by the tremendous superiority he felt toward Mr. T. A. Hedrick, who was a bore and not even a good golfer any more.'' A year later, ''he joined two clubs in the city and lived at one of them. . . . He could have gone out socially as much as he liked—he was an eligible young man, now, and popular with the down-town fathers . . . But he had no social aspirations and rather despised the dancing men who were always on tap for Thursday or Saturday parties and who filled in at dinners with the younger married set.'' The farther he moves into the world of his winter dreams, the more he is disillusioned with it.

Significantly, and again reflecting Fitzgerald's central concern with the relationship between reality and the imagination, the only one of Dexter's winter dreams with which he is not ultimately disillusioned is the only one he cannot have in the real world and time—Judy Jones. After quitting his job rather than caddy for her, he doesn't see her again until she plays through his foursome on the afternoon when he is a guest at the Sherry Island Golf Club. That evening they meet again and Fitzgerald carefully creates a scene in which Judy becomes identified with this particular moment in Dexter's life. ''There was a fish jumping and a star shining and the lights around the lake were gleaming.'' Lying on a raft, Dexter is listening to a piano across the lake playing a popular song, a song he had heard ''at a prom once when he could not afford the luxury of proms, and he had stood outside the gymnasium and listened. The sound of the tune precipitated in him a sort of ecstasy and it was with that ecstasy he viewed what happened to him now. It was a mood of intense appreciation, a sense that, for once, he was magnificently attune to life and that everything about him was radiating a brightness and a glamour he might never know again.''

For Dexter, the melody drifting over the water fuses the past and the present, the years of struggle just behind and the fulfillment just beginning. This is the magic moment when dreaming and striving reach out to grasp realization, the time of rapture before the fullness of achievement brings its seemingly inevitable disillusion. Suddenly, a motor-boat appears beside the raft, ''drowning out the hot tinkle of the piano in the drone of its spray,'' and Judy

Jones becomes part of this moment in which Dexter is ''magnificently attune to life'' as he will never be again. She asks him to take her surf-boarding; and highlighting her association with Dexter's ''mood of intense appreciation,'' Fitzgerald repeats the line with which he had begun the scene. As Dexter joins Judy in the boat, ''there was a fish jumping and a star shining and the lights around the lake were gleaming.'' When she invites him to dinner on the following night, ''his heart turned over like the fly-wheel of the boat, and, for the second time, her casual whim gave a new direction to his life.''

This is the night Dexter realizes he is in love with Judy, and her identification with his sense of being ''magnificently attune to life'' deepens. '''Who are you, anyhow?''' she asks him. '''I'm nobody,' he announced. 'My career is largely a matter of futures.''' He is '''probably making more money than any man my age in the Northwest'''; and with all the ''glittering things'' shining just ahead of him, Dexter realizes that he has wanted Judy since boyhood. She ''communicated her excitement to him,'' and her youthful beauty thus becomes both a part of his dreams as well as the embodiment of his ''intense appreciation'' of life at the beginning of their fulfillment.

As the next two years bring him increasing success and his first disillusion with its products, Dexter's love for Judy remains constant. ''No disillusion as to the world in which she had grown up could cure his illusion as to her desirability.'' Not even her roller-coaster inconstancy can diminish his love for her or disillusion him with her. In Judy, he continues to find the excitement and anticipation that had made the striving for his winter dreams and the threshold of their fulfillment somehow better than their realization was proving to be. When he first loses her and becomes engaged to Irene, he wonders ''that so soon, with so little done, so much of ecstasy had gone from him.'' And when Judy returns to him, ''all mysterious happenings, all fresh and quickening hopes, had gone away with her, come back with her now.'' In finally giving up all hope of having her, Dexter is thereafter safe from being disillusioned with Judy and thus can keep imaginatively alive the excitement and anticipation she represents for him not only in herself but also in her identification with his youthful winter dreams.

Against this background, Dexter's tears are even more comprehensible. At thirty-two, he finds that all his winter dreams, except for Judy Jones, have come true, and there are ''no barriers too high for him." But the world he has won has lost the brightness it had had in his dreams; realizing them has cost him the illusions that were their most precious dimension. Now, having long ago accepted the loss of Judy and with his illusions gone, he thinks he has "nothing else to lose" and is therefore "invulnerable at last." Devlin's detailed picture of Judy as Mrs. Simms strips away this last illusion.

Because Judy Jones and his love for her had become so closely associated with the untarnished richness of his youthful winter dreams, the imaginative present in which she remains alive for Dexter also preserves that youthful richness. When Devlin destroys this imaginative present, Dexter finally and forever loses not only Judy and his love for her but also his ability to keep alive in his imagination the best part of his youth and its winter dreams. He has "gone away and he could never go back any more." Devlin has wrought a kind of death in Dexter's imagination, and "even the grief he could have borne was left behind in the country of illusion, of youth, of the richness of life, where his winter dreams had flourished." Dexter's tears are justifiably for himself, then: he has lost even more than his love for Judy Jones. In realizing his winter dreams, he has discovered that their greatest value was in the dreaming; and now he has lost the only way left to preserve that priceless capacity.

In this complex and moving conclusion, "Winter Dreams" becomes a story with many values. In itself, it is an interesting and often profound treatment of the ironic winner-take-nothing theme, the story of a man who gets nearly everything he wants at the cost of nearly everything that made it worth wanting. In its relationship to Fitzgerald's other writing, "Winter Dreams" makes a valuable prologue to *The Great Gatsby* and reflects several of the themes that characterize Fitzgerald's view of the human condition.

Because of Fitzgerald's explicit linking of the two works, it is common to parallel Dexter Green and Jay Gatsby, but the difference between them are even more instructive than the similarities. Both men have generally similar economic and social backgrounds: Dexter's family is higher on the socioeconomic scale than Jimmy Gatz's shiftless parents, but neither boy starts out anywhere near the wealthy upper class or social elite. Both boys are bright and ambitious, dream of wealth and position, and associate their dreams with a rich and beautiful young girl. Both achieve wealth at an early age, only to find its products strangely disillusioning; each loses the girl he loves and thereafter makes her the center of his imaginative life.

Nevertheless, the differences between Dexter Green and Jay Gatsby are essential and revealing: they not only point up the separate interest of the story but also illuminate by contrast many of the complexities of the novel. Dexter, for example, is from beginning to end Dexter Green; he wants not a different self but a richer life, and his dreams are mundane and specific. Jimmy Gatz, however, rejects Jimmy Gatz in favor of a "Platonic conception of himself"; he is "a son of God," and he dreams of "a universe of ineffable gaudiness." Similarly, Judy Jones is *part* of Dexter's dreams, one of the "glittering things" he dreams of having who also embodies his reasons for wanting them. But Daisy is the *incarnation* of Gatsby's dreams, the ineffable made flesh and therefore no longer ineffable.

Dexter gains his wealth by conventional and respectable means entirely consistent with his dreams and, indeed, largely indistinguishable from them. Gatsby's means are apparently corrupt; but, even if they weren't, no earthly means could be any more consistent with the nature of his dreams than is his incarnation of them in a mortal form. Dexter keeps alive his love for Judy Jones and the brightness of his youthful winter dreams in the only way the past can remain alive—by fixing its images out of time and the real world in an imaginative present. Gatsby tries to recapture the past by regaining the real Daisy and through her repeating in the real world the actual moment in time and the actual situation in which his dreams started to become "confused and disordered."

In effect, then, Dexter Green succeeds in recapturing the past only to lose it when new images from the real world and the real present destroy his imaginative present. Gatsby fails to repeat the past and therefore never loses the illusion that he can; his failure is only a temporary setback making even more necessary and stronger his resolve to regain and thereby reshape the past. In his tears, Dexter realizes what Gatsby never learns—that his dreams are forever "behind him, somewhere back in that vast obscurity beyond the city, where the dark fields of the republic rolled on under the night," back in "the country of illusion, of youth," where dreaming was still untouched by the bruising fall of coming true. Dexter survives with most of his limited dreams realized but having lost twice and forever the richest dimension of those dreams; primarily, he symbolizes the power and also the tragic fragility of the imaginative present. Gatsby is killed, but he dies with his illimitable dreams apparently intact; ultimately, he symbolizes man's unquenchable and tragic capacity for imagining a perfection he not only can never achieve but also inevitably destroys in pursuing.

Beyond its useful relationship to Fitzgerald's masterpiece, ''Winter Dreams'' is also valuable in its early reflection of the themes that characterize most of his significant writing. The dream- and-disillusion motif in the story appears in varying forms and degrees from its intermittent emergence in *This Side of Paradise* to its central exploration in *The Last Tycoon*; it is Fitzgerald's major theme. Dexter Green's painful recognition that the richest part of dreams is not their fulfillment but the dreaming of and striving for them appears implicitly or explicitly in many other works; related to this theme and even more important in Fitzgerald's thought and art is the central stress of the story on the power and value of imaginative life and time. Taken together, these themes reflect the essentially tragic vision of the human condition working at the core of Fitzgerald's serious writing: his increasing concern with man as a creature whose imagination creates dreams and goals his nature and circumstances combine to doom. For any reader, then, ''Winter Dreams'' can be a fertile and challenging story; for a student of Fitzgerald, its careful analysis is a rewarding necessity.

Source: Clinton S. Burhans, Jr., '''Magnificently Attune to Life': The Value of 'Winter Dreams,''' in *Studies in Short Fiction*, Vol. 6, No. 4, Summer 2000, pp. 401–12.

Quentin E. Martin

In the following essay excerpt, Martin examines the contradictory, yet equally unrealistic, ways in which men react to Judy Jones in ''Winter Dreams.''

In her first appearance, Judy is a ''beautifully ugly'' eleven-year-old whose behavior is unpredictable and outrageous (ordering people around, raising a golf club against her nurse). Also in this first scene she is described as ''passionate'' and ''radiant,'' and as having ''vitality.'' When she's next seen, at age twenty, she is again described as having ''passionate vitality'' (the word ''passionate'' is used three times in these first two descriptions, and later her ''passionate energy'' is noted); she gives an impression of ''intense life.''

> " To accuse him of being sexist or misogynist because he portrays male characters as bewildered by and at times antagonistic toward unconventional women and because he portrays female characters as oftentimes confused and crippled by this society is the logical equivalent of shooting the messenger."

And how do the men in the story react to her passionate vitality? ''All she needs,'' says Mr. T. A. Hedrick, ''is to be turned up and spanked for six months and then to be married off to an old-fashioned cavalry captain.'' Hedrick echoes the attitude of many other fictional characters, and those in society, who want to tame this New Woman. Dr. Ledsmar in *The Damnation of Theron Ware* believes that the outspoken and independent Celia Madden should be ''whipped.'' In *The Awakening*, Edna Pontellier's father, ''the Colonel,'' counsels Edna's husband that ''authority, coercion are what is needed'' to tame the wayward Edna; ''Put your foot down good and hard,'' the Colonel says; that's ''the only way to manage a wife.'' And, to cite one more example, a character in *Main Street* tells Carol's husband, Dr. Kennicott, that ''the way to handle wives, like the fellow says, is to catch 'em early, treat 'em rough, and tell 'em nothing.''

Vitality and passion, though attractive, threaten the ability of men to contain women, so men like Hedrick want to beat those qualities out of them and render them childish (''spanked'') in their subservience and docility. In short, they want to tame these new creatures. Women, according to Hedrick, should be passive and silent (and, incidentally, not allowed on golf courses), active only in their service to men and children. Hedrick is perhaps most offended because Judy is a fiery young woman and not a wife-and-mother-in-waiting. ''Contemptuously,'' he points out her propensity for "turning those big cow-eyes on every calf in town!" And the narrator says that "it was doubtful if Mr. Hedrick intended a reference to the maternal instinct." Dexter has similar thoughts: while trying to convince himself that Judy is unworthy, "he enumerated her glaring deficiencies as a wife." The irony is that Judy does turn out to be a loyal wife and mother; she loves her husband even though "he drinks and runs around," and she "stays at home with her kids." Her married life is admittedly not developed in the story, but it can be tentatively cited as making another point: that vitality and individuality in a woman do not necessarily negate her ability to be a good wife and mother, as Mr. Hedrick and Dexter believe.

But men not only try to tame and control women like Judy; they also, paradoxically, idealize them. On the night that Judy and Dexter go motorboating, Judy introduces herself and explains why she's riding alone on the lake: "I live in a house over there on the Island, and in that house there is a man waiting for me. When he drove up at the door I drove out of the dock because he says I'm his ideal." This is the most explicit reference to the tendency of men to idealize Judy, but other attempts occur throughout the story and they, along with the attempts to tame Judy, create an intractable dilemma for her. She desperately wants to be treated fairly, not trampled over by "an old-fashioned cavalry captain" and not absurdly idealized, as by the man waiting in her house. But these are the only ways men know how to react to her—either to tame or to idealize.

Olive Chancellor in James's *The Bostonians* feels a similar frustration, believing that most men can be divided into two groups, "palterers and bullies." This Scylla-and-Charybdis dilemma also exists for Daisy Buchanan, whose "choices," as Fetterley writes, "amount in reality to no more than the choice of which form she wishes her oppression to take." Just as Daisy is trapped between the tamer (Buchanan) and the idealizer (Gatsby), so Judy is caught between the cavalry captain (Hedrick) and the idealizers (the man at her house and others). Therefore, she fights back with the only weapon she has—her beauty. Since "she was not a girl who could be 'won'" like some trophy, she fights off these men by "immediately resolv[ing] the affair to a physical basis." She forces them to play "*her game and not their own*" (emphasis added), and as a result they become frustrated, confused, bitter, and angry. To call her behavior selfish, spoiled, dishonest, irresponsible, or flirtatious is to confuse a counterpunch for a punch. She reacts to the "youthful lovers" and "youthful" love affairs. As the narrator surmises: "Perhaps from so much youthful love, so many youthful lovers, she had come, in *self-defense,* to nourish herself wholly from within" (emphasis added).

All Judy wants is to find one man who is not "youthful" or immature—she calls men "children" later—and who does not have the urge to tame or idealize her. This explains why "when a new man came to town every one dropped out" and why she has in her young life stepped into so many cars, sat in so many leather seats, rested her elbow on so many doors—"waiting" for a man who will not view her and treat her as all previous men have. In addition, it's made clear that she is not just waiting for a rich man. A story she tells Dexter seems to indicate that she is a gold digger (it's the type of label that might be turned against her). She says that her relations with "a man I cared about" ended when "he told me out of a clear sky that he was poor as a church-mouse. He'd never even hinted it before." But she did not end the relationship because of his poverty—"I've been mad about loads of poor men," she says—but because he tried to conceal it, tried to be something he was not. In short, he was not able to provide what Judy is looking for: a fair, honest, forthright, and mature man who will not try to tame or idealize her, someone with whom she can develop "individual camaraderie [*sic*]." By lying, this man without money "didn't start right."

It's Dexter's apparent lack of artificiality, especially about his money, that first attracts Judy to him. When Dexter finishes telling her how rich he is, "There was a pause. Then she smiled." She smiles not for the money but for the frankness. And soon after that the "unpredictable compound" of her lips—not the presumably predictable compound of a tamed or idealized woman's lips—initiates the affair.

The manner in which Judy then seems to "toy with Dexter," as Cross says, convinces Dexter and most readers that Judy is a heartless flirt (another label that might be used to categorize her). The narrator's comments about Judy seem to support that reading: she has "the most direct and unprincipled personality with which [Dexter] had ever come in contact"; "there was a very little mental side to any of her affairs"; "she was entertained only by the gratification of her desires"; "she had beckoned . . . and yawned at [Dexter]." Within a week she is running off with another man, and Dexter soon discovers that a dozen men ''circulated about her.'' Dexter's ''first exhilaration'' turns into ''restlessness and dissatisfaction.'' It seems that the sole cause of this dissatisfaction is Judy's inconstant behavior, but again Judy's behavior is being misread; again a counterpunch is seen as a punch, self-defense as attack. For Dexter has, subtly, played the same game that other men have played with Judy. His apparent lack of artificiality is just that—apparent. His frank start had given Judy hope that he would be different, and when he turned out not to be different, her treatment of him is ''revenge for having ever cared for him at all.''

How is Dexter like all the other men? First, he has the same urge to tame Judy. On that first night of those kisses, the night after the motorboat ride, he feels ''that for the moment he controlled and owned'' that ''exquisite excitability'' of Judy. With this feeling, this attempt to own and control a woman who could not be ''won,'' he too does not start right. He also commits the other sin, namely that of idealizing her. On this first date, he sees that Judy is wearing a casual dress, which makes him ''disappointed at first that she had not put on something more elaborate. This feeling was accentuated when, after a brief greeting, she went to the door of a butler's pantry and pushing it open called: 'You can serve dinner, Martha.' He had rather expected that a butler would announce dinner, that there would be a cocktail.'' Already, in what she wears and how she acts, Dexter senses a gap between what she is and what—as a pretty rich girl from an important family—she should be. And this gap, this failure to be the girl he wants her to be, makes him ''disappointed.'' While they eat, he grows more disappointed because she does not act like a predictable and tamed beauty. She slips into ''a moody depression,'' smiles at unconnected things—''at him, at a chicken liver, at nothing''—and speaks petulantly. And Dexter's reaction is not an increased interest or attraction; rather, he feels an ''uneasiness'' and becomes ''worried'' and ''disturbed.'' She is untamed and does not match Dexter's idealized picture of her; hence he is ''disturbed.''

Dexter cannot deal with Judy's individuality, unpredictability, and unconventional behavior. Such behavior makes him disappointed, uneasy, worried— all on their first date. And though it is not explicitly stated that Judy senses and reacts to Dexter's ideas and feelings, it is certainly not implausible that she feels Dexter's unease, his idealization and attempt to tame (if not own) her, since she has seen such behavior in every other man she's met. In this light, her subsequent treatment of him is at least partially understandable.

Dexter's unnaturalness, his attempt to be what he is not, is brought up throughout the story and is a trait that Judy might also have perceived. Dexter, like Gatsby, is embarrassed about his past: his mother's name and her origins as ''a Bohemian of the peasant class'' bother him; he insists on calling his hometown Keble and not Black Bear Village because Keble is not a ''footstool'' for a fashionable lake. As a successful businessman, he becomes interested in music and books because ''he had a rather priggish notion that he—the young and already fabulously successful Dexter Green—should know more about such things.'' Since he idealizes himself, tries to fit the complications of his past into a neat contemporary portrait, and even refers to himself in the third person, it is no surprise that he similarly idealizes and compartmentalizes—and hence misunderstands—Judy.

That Judy reacts against Dexter's behavior is revealed at a later meeting when, ''for almost the first time since they had met,'' he acts naturally with her, does not parrot the things all the men usually say to her: ''he did not ask her to sit out with him or tell her that she was lovely.'' And she, significantly, ''did not miss these things.'' She is tired of conventional behavior and words. At a later meeting, furthermore, he will ''find no casual word with which to profane the hour,'' and this, in part, leads to a resumption of their affair.

The male characters, to repeat, are bewildered and made miserable by Judy because she cannot be tamed and because she resists idealization; yet, almost unconsciously, they are enormously attracted to her. Her passion and vitality, her ''unpredictable compound,'' set her off from other women. Her smile is so radiant that ''at least a dozen men were to carry [the memory of it] into middle age''; her inexpressible loveliness brings ''no end of misery to a great number of men.'' Men are enraptured by her because the women of their creation—tamed, protected, idealized—are pallid in comparison. Indeed, ''light-haired'' Irene, the woman Dexter becomes engaged to, is literally pallid.

But though men help to create women like Irene, they don't like them because they're boring, as Dexter's feelings about Irene show. Just four months into his engagement to Irene, he marvels ''that so soon, with so little done, so much of ecstasy had gone from him.'' Imagining his future with her, he "knew that Irene would be no more than a curtain spread behind him, a hand moving among gleaming teacups, a voice calling to children." Here is the angel in the house, yet what is the result: "fire and loveliness were gone, the magic of nights and the wonder of the varying hours and seasons." The engagement is to be announced soon, one that "no one would be surprised at." Dexter is doing the expected thing, following the standard pattern, marrying the "right" girl; there will be no more surprises in his life, no more distracting "fire" and "magic." In a late scene in the story, while looking at some people dance (he is no longer dancing himself) and thinking of this future, "he leaned against the door-post, nodded at a man or two—yawned." Then he hears, "Hello, darling."

At the moment that Dexter is yawning into a solid, predictable life of no surprises, Judy appears, slender and golden, and "he could have wept at the wonder of her return" when all weeping and wonder seemed lost from his life. For when Judy left, "all mysterious happenings, all fresh and quickening hopes, had gone away with her." It is Judy and women like her who provide the compound that make life a mysterious happening, and make Dexter "magnificently attune to life." Yet the men in the story do all they can to deny and eliminate that mystery, that unpredictable compound, by taming it or making it unreal by idealizing it.

The second act between Dexter and Judy lasts only a month, and once more Fitzgerald implies that Dexter's urge to control and own Judy—and not Judy's mere toying and mindless flirtation—is what dooms the affair. Dexter again starts off wrong by thinking "this was his girl who was speaking, his own, his beautiful, his pride"; significantly, the word "his" is used four times in this one sentence. Moreover, during this affair or after (the story does not make this clear), Dexter realizes that "he did not possess in himself the power to move fundamentally or to hold Judy Jones," implying again that Dexter has tried to control and own a person who refuses to be owned. Other taming and idealizing behavior may also have resurfaced during this monthlong second affair, behavior that Judy reacted to. And when this affair ends and he does not "bear any malice toward her," it's left unsaid whether Judy might have borne any malice toward him for trying again to control and own her, for falling into a predictable pattern of male behavior, for hinting at but not fulfilling the possibility of creating "a deep and spontaneous mutual attraction," for disappointing *her*.

Eventually, however, Judy gives up her search. Though it's not told, since this is ostensibly the story of Dexter's lost dreams and not Judy's, it can be deduced that Judy kept looking, kept trying any new man in town (and in her trips to Florida and Hot Springs), and finally discarded *her* dreams. "I'm awfully tired of everything," she says late in the story. She's tired of those youthful love affairs and youthful lovers and of those "idiotic dance[s]" filled "with those children." She's worn out from fighting men who try to tame and idealize her. Dexter at this late point sees her cry for the first time; something, too, has perhaps broken in her. She asks, "why can't I be happy?." So she marries Lud Simms—his name alone indicates a lack of grace, if not a cavalry captain—who "drinks and runs around," who can be "particularly outrageous," and who "treats [Judy] like the devil." Yet, apparently resigned to not realizing her own dreams, she forgives and perhaps even loves him, and stays home with her children. She never finds a life that is not dominated by children.

Thus, at the end of the story, one can say, as the narrator says about Dexter, that Judy Jones—like many other women in Fitzgerald's fiction and in American society at the time (her name has an Everywoman aspect to it)—also had something in her long ago, a desire for mature camaraderie, for a man who would not try to tame or idealize her, for a life where her passion and vitality would not be resented and curbed, but that thing is gone, and it will come back no more.

Fitzgerald, as McCay has argued, was a "chronicler and critic of the world in which he lived," a world "not entirely of Fitzgerald's fictional making." He was committed, almost to the point of obsession, to transcribing the reality of his times. "More than any other writer," Malcolm Cowley argues, "Fitzgerald had the sense of living in history. He tried hard to catch the color of every passing year: its distinctive slang, its dance steps, its songs (he kept making lists of them in his notebooks), its favorite quarterbacks, and the sort of clothes and emotions its people wore. He felt in the beginning that his own life was not merely typical but representative of a new generation."

The characterization of Judy Jones, then, is a part of Fitzgerald's attempt to bring a representative figure of his generation into literature, a woman, like many women, caught between contradictory forces. To accuse him of being sexist or misogynist because he portrays male characters as bewildered by and at times antagonistic toward unconventional women and because he portrays female characters as oftentimes confused and crippled by this society is the logical equivalent of shooting the messenger. Yet this is the thought process of many critics of Fitzgerald (and of other writers of the time) and one that blinds them to the complexity of Fitzgerald's views of women and his sympathy for their plight.

The failure to understand Fitzgerald's view of Judy Jones is linked to the mistaken impression that Fitzgerald is somehow a part of the reactionary forces that were intent on putting down the New Woman, as the *Norton* editors argue. Fitzgerald has become as misunderstood as Judy Jones herself, and this intellectual sloppiness has resulted in a grievous cheapening and trivialization of one of this country's greatest writers.

Source: Quentin E. Martin, "Tamed or Idealized: Judy Jones's Dilemma in 'Winter Dreams,'" in *F. Scott Fitzgerald: New Perspectives,* edited by Jackson R. Bryer, Alan Margolies, and Ruth Prigozy, University of Georgia Press, 2000, pp. 159–72.

Sources

Anderson, W. R., "F. Scott Fitzgerald," in *Dictionary of Literary Biography,* Vol. 4: *American Writers in Paris, 1920–1939,* Gale Research, 1980, pp. 132–50.

Flibbert, Joseph, "'Winter Dreams': Overview," in *Reference Guide to Short Fiction, 1st ed.,* St. James Press, 1994.

Norris, Margot, "Modernist Eruptions," in *The Columbia History of the American Novel,* edited by Emory Elliot, Gale Research, 1989, 311–30.

Prigozy, Ruth, "F. Scott Fitzgerald," in *Dictionary of Literary Biography,* Vol. 86: *American Short-Story Writers, 1910–1945, First Series,* Gale Research, 1989, 99–123.

Review, in *Bookman,* May 1926.

Further Reading

Berman, Ronald, *Fitzgerald, Hemingway, and the Twenties,* University of Alabama Press, 2001.
    Berman presents a penetrating analysis of the literary world in the 1920s.

Bruccoli, Matthew J., and Mary Jo Tate, *F. Scott Fitzgerald A to Z: The Essential Reference to His Life and Work,* Facts on File, 1998.
    Bruccoli and Tate focus on the life and literary works of Fitzgerald and his wife.

Donaldson, Scott, *Hemingway vs. Fitzgerald: The Rise and Fall of a Literary Friendship,* Overlook Connection Press, 1999.
    This work explores the friendship and rivalry between these two lost generation authors.

Fitzgerald, F. Scott, *A Life in Letters,* edited by Matthew J. Bruccoli and Judith S. Baughman, Scribner, 1994.
    Bruccoli, a renowned Fitzgerald scholar, has amassed a fascinating collection of Fitzgerald's letters that reveal his artistry and humanity.

The Wives of the Dead

Nathaniel Hawthorne

1832

Nathaniel Hawthorne's short story "The Wives of the Dead" was first published in 1832 in *The Token*, an annual, along with three other stories, "My Kinsman, Major Molineux," "The Gentle Boy," and "Roger Malvin's Burial." Hawthorne had tried, unsuccessfully, to publish the stories as a group in 1829. "The Wives of the Dead" was subsequently republished in other magazines such as *Democratic Review* under the title "The Two Widows." Hawthorne included the story in his 1852 collection *The Snow-Image, and Other Twice-Told Tales*. He named them "twice-told" because each tale was first told in a periodical or gift-book. Set in the eighteenth century in a Bay Province, Massachusetts, seaport, the story concerns two sisters-in-law, who have just been informed that their husbands have died—one drowned in the Atlantic when his ship capsized, the other killed in a "skirmish" in Canada. The story details the women's responses to news of their husbands' deaths and, later, to news that they are, in fact, still alive. Although it has not received the degree of critical attention that some of Hawthorne's other stories have such as "The Birthmark," "Rappaccini's Daughter," and "Ethan Brand," "The Wives of the Dead" is considered important because it is an early work that embodies the kind of dream world for which Hawthorne's stories have become known. In fact, one of the controversies surrounding the story is whether the events portrayed are actually dreams of the main characters. Critics often point to the story's last sentence as

proof of this interpretation and to illustrate Hawthorne's characteristic use of ambiguity. In addition to exploring the borders between appearance and reality, the story delves into themes such as the relationship between thinking and feeling, responses to loss, and familial guilt.

Author Biography

The son of a ship captain, Nathaniel Hathorne, and Elizabeth Clarke Manning, Nathaniel Hawthorne was born on Independence Day in 1804 in Salem, Massachusetts. His paternal ancestors came over from England in 1630, and his maternal ancestors in 1679. Hawthorne's father died in 1808, and his mother and her sisters raised him in Salem and at his maternal uncle's house in Raymond, Maine. There, Hawthorne spent time roaming the woods and taking long meditative walks around Lake Sebago, developing what he called his "cursed habits of solitude." After graduating from Samuel Archer's School in Salem, Hawthorne attended Bowdoin College, graduating in 1825. At Bowdoin, Hawthorne made connections and friends that would prove influential throughout his life, including future President Franklin Pierce; Horatio Bridge, his lifelong best friend; Congressman Jonathan Cilley; and poet Henry Wadsworth Longfellow. While in college, Hawthorne added a *w* to his name; read widely, both in and outside of the curriculum; and began writing fiction. In 1828, he self-published a romance, *Fanshawe*, influenced by his reading of Gothic novels and the adventure stories of Sir Walter Scott. However, he soon grew embarrassed of the work, withdrawing and burning all remaining copies.

A few years later, Hawthorne began publishing short stories. Called by some critics the father of American fiction, Hawthorne plumbed family and local history for ideas and characters. Obsessed by the ways in which the Puritans shaped New England culture, Hawthorne drew on the lives of his own ancestors for his writing. His first American ancestor, William Hathorne (circa 1606–1681), was involved in a version of events depicted in "The Gentle Boy." The story of Hathorne's son John (1641–1717), a magistrate during the Salem witch trials of 1692, influenced a spate of Hawthorne works including "Young Goodman Brown" and *The Scarlet Letter*. His first published story, "The Hollow of the Three Hills," (1830) addresses themes that would occupy Hawthorne throughout his life,

including the concept of sin, religious persecution, and the effects of guilt on the human heart and mind. Other early stories include "The Gentle Boy," "The Wives of the Dead," "My Kinsman, Major Molineux," and "Roger Malvin's Burial." The latter three stories are published in *The Snow-Image, and Other Twice-Told Tales* (1852).

Today Hawthorne is perhaps best known for his novel *The Scarlet Letter* (1850), a tale of witchcraft, adultery, and illicit love. Other novels include *The House of the Seven Gables: A Romance* (1851), *The Blithedale Romance* (1852), and *The Marble Faun* (1860). Dedicated to writing, Hawthorne struggled to make a living with his pen, though at various points in his life he also worked as an editor, a weigher and gagger at the Boston Customs House, surveyor for the Salem Customs House, and U.S. Consul in Liverpool, England. In May 1864, while visiting former President Franklin Pierce in Plymouth, New Hampshire, Hawthorne died in his sleep.

Plot Summary

Part One

In the first part of "The Wives of the Dead," the narrator assures readers his tale is "scarcely worth relating," then proceeds to tell it in detail. A hundred years ago, in the early eighteenth century, two "young and comely" (attractive) women in a Massachusetts seaport town married brothers and set up house together. In "two successive" days, they learn of their husbands' deaths: one is lost at sea, while the other is killed fighting the French and Indians in Canada. The British battled with the French for control of North America at this time, and colonists from the Bay colonies often fought on the Canadian frontier. Though many townspeople turn out to offer their sympathy, the women want to be left alone to console each other.

After the mourners leave, Mary, the more practical and disciplined of the pair, prepares dinner, but Margaret, distraught and bitter, cannot eat. The two go to bed, and although Mary falls asleep easily, temporarily forgetting her loss, Margaret remains awake, in a "feverish" state, gazing at the living room both couples had shared and grieving the past. Hawthorne uses imagery of light, in terms of the hearth and the lamp, to suggest the warmth of the past and the coldness of the present.

Part Two

While trying to sleep, Margaret hears a knock at the door and, reluctantly, answers it, taking the lamp from the hearth with her. Goodman Parker, a neighbor and innkeeper, brings news that Margaret's husband is, in fact, still alive. Speaking of a messenger who recently stopped at Parker's house on his ride through town with news of the frontier, Parker tells Margaret, "He tells me we had the better in the skirmish you wot of, and that thirteen men reported slain are well and sound, and your husband among them." (The phrase "wot of" means "know of." "Goodman" was a common name in the American colonies and appeared in other Hawthorne stories (e.g., "Young Goodman Brown"). Margaret is elated, but decides not to wake Mary and tell her because it might change the way Mary feels towards her. She returns to bed and to "delightful thoughts," which sleep transforms into "visions."

Part Three

Mary awakens from a "vivid dream," hearing "eager knocking on the street-door." Like Margaret, she takes the lamp from the hearth and opens the window, which had been left unhasped. A former suitor of Mary's named Stephen, a sailor, tells her that her husband survived the shipwreck and is alive and well. Hawthorne uses irony when he names the capsized ship *Blessing*. Initially thinking he had come to win her back, Margaret is appalled, and the narrator writes that she "was no wit inclined to imitate the first wife of Zadig," who is a wealthy man in Voltaire's story, "Zadig's Nose." (A day after Zadig fakes his death, his wife takes up with another man.) But Mary, like her sister-in-law, is overjoyed when she hears the news that her husband is alive. However, she resists waking Margaret, fearing the news would only compound her own sorrow. The last line of the story is ambiguous. That is, it is unclear whether Margaret suddenly awoke when Mary touched her, or whether Mary awoke to her own tears, and Stephen's visit was a dream.

Characters

Margaret

Along with her sister-in-law, Mary, Margaret is one of the wives referred to in the title. Both are "recent brides," and still "young and comely"; that is, attractive. She has a "lively and irritable

temperament," and is bitter, virtually inconsolable, about her husband's death. She declines eating the meal Mary offers her, saying, in reference to God, "Would it were His will that I might never taste food more." She cannot sleep and stays up listening to the rain, looking at the hearth and the furniture in the living room the two couples shared, grieving her loss. When she hears a knock on the door, she answers it with apprehension, saying to herself, "I have nothing left to fear, and methinks I am ten times more a coward than ever." Agitated, she screams at Goodman Parker, asking him what he wants. When Parker tells her that her husband, in fact, was never killed in the skirmish in Canada, and is alive and well, Margaret can scarcely contain her joy. However, she does not wake Mary, feeling that "her own better fortune had rendered her involuntarily unfaithful." Benjamin Friedlander, in his essay "Hawthorne's "Waking Reality," writes, "This guilt, Margaret's feeling of unfaithfulness, pierces the story's dreamy surface, allowing a revelation of hidden desires—perhaps even a revelation of adultery." Margaret returns to sleep, her dreams now happy "visions," deciding to tell Mary the news in the morning.

Mary

Mary is the more pious and more practical of the two sisters-in-law, level headed, with an even temperament, and the character with whom Hawthorne begins and ends the story. After the other mourners have left the house of the sisters-in-law, Mary prepares a meal, encouraging Margaret to be grateful for what they still do have. She sleeps peacefully until she is woken in the middle of the night by the knocking of a former suitor, Stephen, a sailor who brings her the news that he saw her husband on a ship the day before, alive and well. At first she thinks that Stephen is taking advantage of the situation and has come to seduce her, but when she hears his news, she is happy. As Stephen leaves, Mary watches him "with a doubt of waking reality." In his essay, "Hawthorne's 'The Wives of the Dead,'" John McDermott interprets this line as meaning that Mary's meeting with Stephen is a dream, and John Selzer, in "Psychological Romance in Hawthorne's 'Wives of the Dead,'" notes that Mary "simply means to substitute for her lost husband. . . . Her dream appears, then, as a wish-fulfillment to fill the void in her heart." Mary cannot bring herself to tell Margaret about her good news, for she fears Margaret would "awake to thoughts of death and woe," which would only be compounded by Mary's happiness. Mary is unaware that Margaret herself had received news earlier in the night that her own husband was also still alive. Before going back to bed, Mary straightens Margaret's blankets to protect her from the cold. As she does, "her hand trembled against Margaret's neck, a tear also fell upon her cheek, and she suddenly awoke." The meaning of the story rests on this last line of the story. It is left unclear whether Mary awakens Margaret or wakes herself up with her own crying.

Goodman Parker

Goodman Parker is "a friendly innkeeper of the town" and the man who brings news to Margaret that her husband, whom she thought had died fighting the French and Indians in Canada, is still alive. The narrator describes him as "a man in a broad brimmed hat and blanket-coat" and as an "honest man."

Stephen

Stephen, Mary's former suitor, whom the narrator describes as a "rejected lover," brings her the news that her husband is still alive. He is described as "a young man in a sailor's dress, wet as if he had come out of the depths of the sea." After he comes home from a voyage, his mother tells him the bad news about Mary's husband. Stephen rushes to assure Mary that her husband is still alive, saying that he saw him on a brig the day before, and that same brig will be in port by daylight. The narrator describes him as a "generous seaman."

Themes

Loss

Hawthorne's story illustrates how a person's response to death and loss reveals true character. Both women mourn the loss of their husbands. However, Mary's "mild, quiet, yet not feeble character" and her faith enable her to endure the emotional torment of her husband's death with more equanimity than Margaret. She prepares a meal and sets the table soon after the mourners leave, and tries to help her sister-in-law calm down. Margaret, on the other hand, of a "lively and irritable temperament," cannot accept the loss and remains bitter, dwelling on the past and taking no comfort in her faith. Later, Mary drifts into sleep with relative ease, while Margaret stays awake "groan[ing] in bitterness." The motivation of each in not waking

Media Adaptations

- Blackstone Audiobooks has released a 450-minute audiocassette of Walter Covell and others reading Hawthorne's *Tanglewood Tales.*

- Dick Hill reads Hawthorne's *The Scarlet Letter* on a CD released by Brilliance in 2001.

- Durkin-Hayes Audio publishes an audiocassette of Winifred Phillips reading Hawthorne's short story masterpiece, "The Birthmark."

- Turner Classic Movies now has the rights to the 1926 silent film of *The Scarlet Letter,* based on Hawthorne's classic novel. The film, shown occasionally on cable television, stars Lillian Gish, Lisa Anne Miller, and Mark Northam. *The Scarlet Letter* has been adapted for film a number of times since then. The most recent adaptation, available on video, is Hollywood Pictures' 1995 *The Scarlet Letter,* starring Demi Moore and Gary Oldman.

the other after hearing their respective news reflects their characters. Margaret is more worried about how Mary's response would diminish her own joy, saying to herself, "Shall I waken her, to feel her sorrow sharpened by my happiness?" Mary, on the other hand, is more concerned with the pain that Margaret would feel if Mary told her about Stephen's news. "My poor sister!" she thinks to herself as she looks at Margaret, "you will waken too soon from that happy dream."

Reality and Appearance

"The Wives of the Dead" is both a story about two widows and a meditation on the nature of reality, asking readers to question the dreamlike quality of their waking life and the reality of their dreams. Hawthorne's setting creates a world in which things are never as they appear because appearance itself rests upon the volatile emotional state of the two primary characters, through whose eyes the story is told, and upon the trustworthiness

Topics for Further Study

- Keep a diary of your dreams for two weeks, then write an essay exploring some of the common elements of the dreams. What, if anything, does this tell you about your waking life?

- Both Margaret and Mary are visited by men who bring them news about their husbands' fate. What if they learned this news in another way? Put yourself in 1730 and write a story for the local newspaper conveying the information the women learn about their husbands. Feel free to embellish where appropriate.

- Imagine how your friends and family would respond if they learned that you had died. Write a description of the scene. Is this different than how you would like them to respond?

- Research the average life expectancy of early eighteenth-century Americans. At what age did they marry? What was the most common cause of death for men? For women?

- Mary was initially told that her husband drowned in a shipwreck in the Atlantic. Research the history of shipwrecks in the early eighteenth century. How common were they? What was the primary cause?

- A major Hollywood studio has hired you to direct a film adaptation of ''The Wives of the Dead.'' Who would you cast in the lead roles and why? If the tale were made contemporary, describe the changes you would make (e.g., characters, setting, dialogue, plot changes, etc.) and the reasons why you would make them.

- ''The Wives of the Dead'' was originally published in a ''gift-book'' of literature and illustrations, along with three other Hawthorne stories. Research the names of these stories and then read them. Write an essay ranking them according to their literary appeal. What criteria did you use, and why?

- Compare the theme of guilt as it appears in ''The Wives of the Dead'' with the theme of guilt as it appears in Hawthorne's story ''Roger Malvin's Burial.'' Discuss the similarities and differences.

---

of the narrator, whose honesty is in doubt. The bulk of the events take place at night, and the narrator repeatedly emphasizes what the characters can and cannot see. In bed, Margaret, agitated and unnerved, sees the lamp throw ''the shadows of the furniture up against the wall, stamping them immovably there, except when they were shaken by a sudden flicker of the flame.'' This image calls to mind Plato's *Allegory of the Cave,* a dialogue in which the Greek philosopher argues for the existence of a higher reality than the one human beings experience with their senses. Hawthorne employs other visual symbolic imagery such as the lantern, the hearth, morning mist, and windows to emphasize the relationship between truth and seeing, sight and insight. For example, after Goodman Parker reports to Margaret that her husband is still alive, the narrator says that Parker's lantern ''gleamed along the street,

bringing to view indistinct shapes of things, and the fragments of a world, like order glimmering through chaos.'' Such a description embodies Margaret's response to the good news.

Style

Romance

''The Wives of the Dead'' is an American romance. The term ''romance'' emerged during the Middle Ages and often referred to stories with far-fetched plots and exotic settings, involving knights and their quests, and chivalric behavior. In the eighteenth and nineteenth centuries, the term became synonymous with stories emphasizing emotion and subjective experience. Classical romance includes intricate plots, mistaken identity, random events, and separated lovers, most of which Hawthorne's story contains. American romantics, especially Hawthorne, occasionally digressed from the traditional formula and incorporated Gothic features such as ghosts and the supernatural into their writing. The romance, however, should not be confused with the romantic movement, which literary historians date from the late eighteenth century to the middle of the nineteenth century. In their treatment of original subjects, their focus on the psychology of the individual, and their use of symbol to point to a reality beyond the physical world, American writers such as Hawthorne, Herman Melville, Margaret Fuller, Emily Dickinson, Edgar Allan Poe, and Ralph Waldo Emerson all shaped the American romantic period.

Ambiguity

Ambiguity is a literary device, often a word or phrase signifying multiple meanings. Poets and fiction writers use it to create possibility and mystery. The ambiguity of Hawthorne's story rests on the final sentence and the meaning of the words ''her'' and ''she.'' Depending on which woman the pronoun refers to determines, in large part, what part of Hawthorne's story can be read as a dream.

Imagery

Undergirding the ambiguous ending is the story's symbolic imagery. Imagery is symbolic when it suggests or stands for something other than what it is. For example, Hawthorne's image patterns of light versus darkness echo the degree of separation or togetherness the sisters feel toward each other, and also their changing emotional complexions. Of particular significance is the lamp, a conventional symbolic image used to suggest insight and understanding, and the hearth, a symbol of home and domesticity.

Structure

The story is organized symmetrically around pairs. Two sisters-in-law of two brothers learn in two successive days about the deaths of their husbands. They then have almost identical experiences during the night, each awakened by a messenger bearing good news about her (supposedly dead) husband. Each takes a lamp from the hearth to address her visitor at the window while the other is asleep, and each declines to wake the other, though for different reasons. This symmetrical structure

allows Hawthorne to contrast the women's characters, showing how each responds differently to a similar experience.

Historical Context

Eighteenth-Century Newspapers

Hawthorne sets his story in the early eighteenth century in Massachusetts' Bay Province, and his two principle characters, Margaret and Mary, learn of their husbands' fate through men who visit them at their home. As one can imagine, news traveled slowly more than three hundred and fifty years ago. British censors kept a tight grip on what could be printed, and attempts to disseminate information that was not sponsored by the British government was forbidden. In 1690, for example, the governor of Massachusetts shut down Benjamin Harris's independent newsletter, *Publick Occurrences, Both Foreign and Domestick,* almost immediately because of its perceived threat to power. The first successful newspaper publisher in the colonies was William Campbell, postmaster of Boston, whose *News-Letter* was launched in 1704 to keep people in the Bay Colony apprised of world events. This changed to the *Boston Gazette* in 1719. Benjamin Franklin's older brother, James, who printed the *Boston Gazette,* founded Boston's *New England Courant* in 1724. By the middle of the century, two dozen newspapers flourished in the colonies including the *Philadelphia American Weekly Mercury,* the *Pennsylvania Gazette,* the *Maryland Gazette,* the *Charlestown South Carolina Gazette,* and the *New-York Gazette.* As newspapers spread, the colonies began to assert their freedoms and separate themselves from Britain. In 1735, John Peter Zenger, the publisher of the *New-York Weekly Journal,* was acquitted of criminal libel, something virtually unheard of in England. ''Freedom of speech or of the press'' was to become part of the First Amendment to the U.S. Constitution, ratified in 1791.

French and Indian War

The ''Canadian warfare'' in which Margaret's husband supposedly dies refers to the numerous conflicts and wars between the British and the French for control of North America. Both allied themselves with different Indian tribes, among them the Iroquois and the Algonquin. In the early eight-

Compare & Contrast

- **1721:** Benjamin Franklin's older brother, James, launches the first independent American newspaper, the *New-England Courant,* in Boston.

  1835: Samuel Morse invents the telegraph.

  Today: The Internet makes news gathering and reporting almost instantaneous and open to individuals as well as to news organizations.

- **1754–1760:** The French and Indian War is fought between the French and British over North American territory, specifically whether the Ohio River valley is a part of the British Empire and therefore open for trade and settlement to British colonists. Ultimately the war spreads to every part of the world where either of the two nations have territorial interests.

  1846: The United States and Britain sign the Oregon Treaty, a compromise by which British navigation rights on the Columbia River are guaranteed and the land boundary is drawn along latitude 49° N. In 1859, Oregon enters the Union as a free state.

  Today: The United States is no longer involved in expanding its land holdings. However, conflicts over what some countries see as American cultural imperialism are common.

- **1713:** The Treaty of Utrecht affirms possession of Hudson's Bay, Newfoundland, and Acadia by the British. Cape Breton is still French.

  1843: Fort Victoria is built by Britain to establish claim to Vancouver Island.

  1995: Reflecting the continuing conflict between French and British culture, the Canadian province of Quebec holds a referendum on whether it should become a sovereign state. The referendum is barely defeated by a small majority.

---

eenth century, France held claim to most of what is now Canada and the land along the Mississippi River, extending all the way down to Louisiana. The British, seeking to wrest control from the French, often staked claim to the same land. English and French hostilities led to the outbreak of Queen Anne's War, which lasted from 1702 until 1713. Hostilities erupted again with the outbreak of King George's War (1744–1748), and then the French and Indian War (1754–1760). Much of the fighting in Canada took place in Nova Scotia and Cape Breton, parts of New France that had been ceded to England by a previous treaty. A few years after King George's War, the French began building forts in the Ohio River Valley and positioning troops in Canada, and the British sent expeditions against them. As colonists from Pennsylvania southward battled in the Appalachian region, colonists from New York and New England fought the French and Indians in Canada. Driving the French from Canada became crucial if Britain was to continue its expansion in North America.

Nineteenth-Century Literary Culture

"The Wives of the Dead" was initially published in *The Token,* a publication known as a gift-book. Gift-books flourished in nineteenth-century America and England from the 1820s through the 1850s. They contained poetry, prose, and illustrations, and were elegantly produced, often with colored plates. *The Token* came out in the fall but had the coming year on its cover, so shoppers could buy it for either Christmas or the New Year season. In addition to Hawthorne, writers such as Edgar Allan Poe and Ralph Waldo Emerson published in gift-books, often anonymously. Women edited many gift-books. For example, Lydia Maria Child edited *Looking Towards Sunset* (1865) and *The Oasis* (1834); Sarah Josepha Hale, who penned the children's poem "Mary Had a Little Lamb," edited *The Opal* in 1845, 1848, and 1849; and Lydia Sigourney edited the *Religious Souvenir* in 1839 and 1840. Though these books were popular, their authors were often poorly paid. Hawthorne himself struggled throughout his life to make money at his writing, while writers of sermons, sentimental novels, and patriotic essays often fared much better. Hawthorne vented his anger and expressed his envy of the success of women writers such as Maria Susanna Cummins in the 1850s when he wrote to his publisher complaining of the ''damned mob of scribbling women.'' Ironically, literary historians and critics mark the span 1828–1865 as the American Renaissance in literature, as writers such as Henry David Thoreau, Margaret Fuller, Harriet Wilson, Ralph Waldo Emerson, Herman Melville, Hawthorne, and Edgar Allan Poe helped to carve out a distinctly American body of work.

Critical Overview

When ''The Wives of the Dead'' first appeared in 1832, it was published anonymously. Terrence Martin in his book *Nathaniel Hawthone* writes that Samuel G. Goodrich, the publisher of *The Token,* the annual in which the story appeared, included ''The Wives of the Dead'' along with ''The Gentle Boy,'' ''Roger Malvin's Burial,'' and ''My Kinsman, Major Molineux'' because they were the best he had received and no one could object to so many stories from the same author if the stories were published anonymously. Though virtually ignored when first published in 1832, ''The Wives of the Dead'' has gained in critical attention since then, primarily because it is one of Hawthorne's earliest published stories. Writing in 1918, George Edward Woodberry, in his study *Nathaniel Hawthorne: How to Know Him,* argues that the story is ''drenched with Hawthorne's temperament. No other pen could have written it.'' Mark Van Doren is more specific in his assessment, noting in his book *Nathaniel Hawthorne,* Hawthorne's characteristic use of light and darkness to describe the setting: ''No reader . . . will forget the speed with which its interior lights up and stays lit with a significance almost too delicate to name.'' Edward Stephenson does name it, arguing in his essay for the *Explicator* that the story is Hawthorne's attempt to ''demonstrate the real nature of human experience.'' Offering a crafty reading of the story's symbolic imagery, Stephenson's 1967 essay argues against critics who interpret the widows' experiences as dreams, contending that Margaret is the only one truly asleep. John McDermott, however, also in an essay for the *Explicator,* argues just the opposite, that it is Mary who is asleep: ''When we read the story's final sentence, we may be assured that it is Mary who

suddenly awakens from her dream and, in crying, realizes her dream was simply that—a dream.'' Offering yet another view, Neal Frank Doubleday, in *Hawthorne's Early Tales: A Critical Study,* claims that both brothers are alive, to believe anything else would be to question the truthfulness of the narrator. Doubleday also suggests that Hawthorne ''did not much value this tale,'' because he passed it over for inclusion in two other short story collections. More recent interpretations have not sought to argue for the story taking place in either a dream or the physical world but to show how Hawthorne's language creates a netherworld that resists interpretation. Calling the final lines of the story ''the most inexplicable in all of Hawthorne's work, a body of writing well noted for its purposeful ambiguity,'' Benjamin Friedlander, in his 1999 essay ''Hawthorne's 'Waking Reality,''' claims '''The Wives of the Dead' demands a style of reading that remains open to possibilities of meaning, not certainties.''

Criticism

Chris Semansky

Semansky is an instructor of literature and composition and publishes regularly in literary journals and magazines. In this essay, Semansky considers the function of the narrator in Hawthorne's story.

Although ''The Wives of the Dead'' is a story about events surrounding two widows in early eighteenth century colonial America, it is the narrator who sets the tone of the story and filters information in such a way as to shape the reader's understanding of events. The narrator is not Hawthorne but a persona created to tell the story. Think of a persona as a mask. Hawthorne puts on a mask and tells the story from behind it. Readers must suspend their own doubt and believe the mask is a real person. The persona that Hawthorne uses as his narrator to tell the story of Mary and Margaret is one of a wise, gentle man who is nonetheless intrusive. This means that he not only reports on the action but also comments on it, evaluating events and the motives of the characters. By doing so, the narrator becomes a character himself, effectively helping to shape the tale's meaning.

The narrator introduces himself in the opening paragraph, telling readers, ''The following story, the simple and domestic incidents of which may be

What Do I Read Next?

- Hawthorne's first collection of stories, *Twice-Told Tales,* was originally published in 1837, then reprinted in 1841 and 1851. The best text of Hawthorne's *Twice-Told Tales* is that published as Volume IX of the *Centenary Edition of the Complete Works of Nathaniel Hawthorne,* edited by J. Donald Crowley, 1974.

- Hawthorne's 1852 collection, *"The Snow Image" and Other Twice-Told Tales,* contains some of his best-known short stories, including "My Kinsman, Major Molineux," "Ethan Brand," and "The Wives of the Dead."

- Harry Levin's acclaimed 1967 study, *The Power of Blackness: Hawthorne, Poe, Melville,* argues that the tradition of American fiction lay not in the realistic novel of man in society but in the romance, a form which uses methods and materials of folklore, fable, myth, and allegory to explore what Hawthorne called the "truth of the human heart."

- James C. Wilson's *The Hawthorne and Melville Friendship: An Annotated Bibliography, Biographical and Critical Essays, and Correspondence Between the Two* (1991) is a veritable casebook on the friendship and professional relationship between two of the nineteenth century's most revered writers.

- Hawthorne had an often frustrating time with his publishers, one of whom was Ticknor and Fields. Michael Winship's 1995 study of the publishing industry, *American Literary Publishing in the Mid-Nineteenth Century America: The Business of Ticknor and Fields,* analyzes the records and publications of Boston-based Ticknor and Fields, revealing how its books were produced, marketed and distributed, and the extent of its expenses and profits.

---

deemed scarcely worth relating, after such a lapse of time, awakened some degree of interest, a hundred years ago, in a principal seaport of the Bay Province." This introduction suggests that the teller of the tale is modest, yet has the reader's best interest at heart. His assumption is that because the story had interest to those in the seaport town a hundred years ago, it has interest for Hawthorne's readers in 1830. His modesty and the fact that he is drawing from an (allegedly) historical account help him to establish credibility with readers. But he doesn't just disappear after that. Rather, he both tells the story *and* he interprets it.

The first time the narrator visibly intrudes into the story is after he describes Margaret's tossing and turning in her bed, the night she learns of her husband's death. Feverish and bitter, she tries to decide whether or not to answer the knock at the door. It is here that the narrator interjects, "It is difficult to be convinced of the death of one whom we have deemed another self." This puts the narrator on the outside looking in and temporarily jars the reader's involvement in the story's action. He explains Margaret's feelings by universalizing them, not just showing her behavior or thoughts and letting readers do with them as they will. Hawthorne sprinkles this story with such observations. These comments have the effect of telling the reader how to respond. However, they also carry with them a kind of authority, as they help to establish the value system in which characters act, as well as establishing those of the narrator.

Hawthorne's narrator again intrudes when Margaret decides to wake Mary and tell her of Goodman Parker's visit. He does this subtly, and then more overtly, as he first describes Mary's sleep and then comments on it:

> Her face was turned partly inward to the pillow, and had been hidden there to weep; but a look of motionless contentment was now visible upon it, as if her heart, like a deep lake, had grown calm because its dead had sunk down so far within. Happy it is, and

strange, that the lighter sorrows are those from which dreams are chiefly fabricated.

These are the narrator's eyes upon Mary, not Margaret's, and the "happy it is" comment is the narrator's, not one of the characters. This "editorial" does two things: it tells readers that Mary's sorrow is genuine and that it is deep; secondly, it alerts readers to consider the idea that Margaret's sorrow is perhaps not so deep or genuine. In his study of Hawthorne's fiction, *Nathaniel Hawthorne,* Mark Van Doren sees such narrative intrusion not only as benign but also as a virtue. He writes,

> [Hawthorne] is moved to create, and then to contemplate with characteristic tenderness—a tenderness unique in the story—the love of two girls not only for each other but for their husbands whom we never see.

What Van Doren doesn't contemplate, however, is the relationship between what readers think of the narrator and how they understand the events of the story. For example, the ambiguous ending asks to be read one way if readers believe that the narrator's motivation is to relate a true story. They must believe that the visitations by Stephen and Goodman Parker actually occurred and that the husbands are, indeed, alive and well. If, however, the events are read as either a pair of dreams or as one or the other sister dreaming her episode, the narrator's own truthfulness must be questioned, and hence any universalizing messages as well. Such questioning, rather than invalidating the tale for some critics, adds to its emotional richness. Benjamin Friedlander, for example, argues in his essay "Hawthorne's 'Waking Reality,' that the uncertainty of the narrator's character adds to the texture and emotional complexity of the story:

> However misleading Hawthorne's initial historicizing gesture, however unsatisfying the ambiguity of his ending, Hawthorne's handling of the sisters' inner lives and of the shared interiority of their dwelling stands beyond reproach, a marvelous depiction of hidden household dynamics brought to light by intense grief and extreme shifts of fortune.

Other critics, such as Neal Frank Doubleday, writing in his *Hawthorne's Early Tales: A Critical Study,* argue that to read the episodes as being dreams would be to question the narrator's honesty. After claiming that the "narrative point of view has a subtlety which for the most part eludes analysis," Doubleday claims that to read the ending as suggesting that one or both episodes were dreams would be to "assume an entirely dishonest narrator, a narrator who . . . distinctly tells us that, although Mary has been dreaming, she awakes and realizes

> "If, however, the events are read as either a pair of dreams or as one or the other sister dreaming her episode, the narrator's own truthfulness must be questioned, and hence any of his universalizing messages as well."

the knocking on the door." But what's wrong with assuming a dishonest or naïve narrator? Fiction, especially eighteenth- and nineteenth-century fiction, has a rich history of unreliable and intrusive narrators, including narrators who may or may not be aware of contradictions within their own stories. Hawthorne presents the tale as if his narrator had physically been present. He not only has access to the minds and hearts of the characters but also to the setting in the absence of his characters. For instance, after Parker has given his message to Margaret, the narrator describes him walking away:

> His lantern gleamed along the street, bringing to view indistinct shapes of things, and the fragments of a world, like order glimmering through chaos, or memory roaming over the past. But Margaret stayed not to watch these picturesque effects.

In this way, Hawthorne shifts from a focus of narrator to a focus of character. These shifts in point of view contribute to the story's mysterious atmosphere, which Hawthorne has already worked to develop through his use of symbolic imagery, particularly that relating to light and darkness. This "gray zone," where readers are never sure what is dream and what is reality, where the characters' perceptions are not clearly attributed, creates a dream-like world which prepares the reader for the ambiguity of the story's final sentence. However, in his essay "The Wives of the Living?: Absence of Dreams in Hawthorne's '"The Wives of the Dead,'" Mark Harris claims Hawthorne's dream-like setting is not meant to lure readers in, but is designed instead to warn them against confusing dreams and reality. Harris writes, "'The Wives of the Dead'" turns out to be not a darkly ironic treatise on the hopelessness of the wives' dreams, but simply a caution against ignorance of the distinction between dreams and reality.''

But what is to be gained by offering such a caution, and such a banal one at that? Hawthorne, by employing an intrusive and possibly unreliable narrator, who may or may not be aware of the contradictions in his own story, manages artfully to create a landscape in which dream and waking life are fused. If readers are confused by the ending and feel a need to resolve it as either a dream or reality, they have missed the point (and the art) of Hawthorne's story.

Source: Chris Semansky, Critical Essay on ''The Wives of the Dead,'' in *Short Stories for Students,* The Gale Group, 2002.

Mark Harris

In the following essay, Harris examines dream and reality in ''The Wives of the Dead,'' and the importance of distinguishing between the two.

The few Hawthorne commentators who have given any attention to the undeservedly neglected ''The Wives of the Dead'' have either ignored the question of whether it deals with dreams or reality, or acknowledged the question and then dismissed it in one or two cryptic statements. Even those who have looked at the details of the story in any depth have evaded the mystery that asks for solution, or have arrived at erroneous conclusions that contradict the details the story presents.

H. J. Lang, who devotes over two pages to the story (which is, relatively, a lot), summarizes the first two types of criticism I have mentioned:

> Arlin Turner summarizes the ''slight'' story as showing the response of each [sister] when she receives her own good news while believing her sister remains bereaved. Mark Van Doren finds it ''one of Hawthorne's most attractive tales. Its atmosphere is the atmosphere of sadness and death, but its outcome—though the full effect of it upon the principals is withheld from us at the end—is in some rich, strange way happy and reassuring.'' For these and other critics the story is slight, plain, realistic and uncomplicated.

Unfortunately, Lang then goes on to applaud Harry Levin for the passing, unexplained remark that ''The Wives of the Dead'' ''dream vainly of their husbands' return.'' Although Lang avers that ''the story . . . must be read as a dream of the widows,'' he dismisses the primary question of the story—*do* the wives really dream?—with a simplistic ''the title . . . alone should be sufficient.'' Having revealed to us (without explanation) that the husbands' ''happy return was only a dream; reality is as terrible as it is,'' Lang leaves the dream/reality question of the story and tells us that the light and the dark in the story are the key elements, with ''the center of the story's symbolism [being] the lamp''—again, without explaining why.

Michael Colacurcio treats the tale in some depth, but like other critics he makes erroneous statements about the plot (e.g., that both husbands die ''on a single day'' and that ''Both women, we are told, do eventually fall asleep'' and devotes most of his discussion to the sisters' individuality. Thomas Friedmann follows Lang in support of Levin's contention that the wives dream. However, Friedmann goes too far to the other extreme, presenting an overly imaginative thesis that alternately ignores and distorts the story's details. A close analysis of the story simply does not support the contention that ''each [wife] dreams a scenario in which the other's husband survives.'' Richard Poirier, though otherwise reticent about the story, identifies one of its integral aims: ''Hawthorne . . . is trying to suspend us . . . between actuality and dream.''

''The Wives of the Dead'' is written by a man about whose writing Poe says, ''Every word tells, and there is not a word which does not tell.'' We should look closely at the details of this tale that is obviously meant to raise (and evoke answers to) the question of whether the events it relates are dreams or reality.

From the start, the narrator tries to deceive us as to what is dream and what is reality by making us move too quickly over the story's details. Why, for example, does he say that the incidents of the story related in ''The Wives of the Dead'' ''may be deemed scarcely worth relating?'' Because, as he immediately goes on to say, his relating of the incidents takes place ''after such a lapse of time.'' The *story,* he goes on to say—perhaps by way of explaining what he is going to tell us in spite of what he has just said—''awakened some degree of interest, a hundred years ago.'' The narrator then launches us into the story, himself fading into the background, and we may fall too quickly and deeply into the story without paying adequate attention to the few preceding lines and the caution they imply. For example, the narrator does not tell us that the *incidents* of the story *happened* a hundred years ago; he says that the *story* awakened . . . interest'' at that time, which puts into question whether the story is or ever was supposed to be based on fact. Thus, a key element of the story is introduced: the difficulty of distinguishing between reality and unreality. At times the narrator will try to mislead us, burying reality beneath what may appear to be dreams, and we must distinguish dream from reality by the clues he provides.

Margaret is the first of the two sisters to receive a visitor who tells her that her husband is not dead as reported. To find out whether the visitor is right, we first need to determine whether Margaret dreams her visit or whether it actually occurs. This is rather easily determined, in spite of the narrator's misleading clues; Margaret does not dream her visit because she does not fall asleep before it happens. Her "mind" may have come "nearer to the situation of" the calmer Mary's, but nothing in the story suggests that the same is true of her heart. Margaret does not fall asleep before her visit because she cannot; unlike Mary, she is still greatly disturbed by her grief. This is shown through the description of Margaret's state right up through the point when she hears "a knock at the street door":

> Margaret became more disturbed and feverish, in proportion as the night advanced with its deepest and stillest hours. She lay listening to the drops of rain, that came down in monotonous succession, unswayed by a breath of wind; and a nervous impulse continually caused her to lift her head from the pillow, and gaze into Mary's chamber and the intermediate apartment . . . While Margaret groaned in bitterness, she heard a knock at the street-door.

The passage includes nothing that suggests Margaret has slept. Unlike Mary, who is clearly emerging from sleep when her visitor knocks the first time, Margaret hears and understands her summons the first time, even though it is "apparently given with the soft end of a doubled fist, . . . through several thicknesses of wall." She expresses thoughts immediately, she "breath[es] hurriedly, . . . straining her ears to catch a repetition of the summons," and she gets out of bed lucid and alert. Clearly, Margaret is awake when her visitation occurs.

As is true also of Mary's visit, however, establishing Margaret's wakefulness and the reality of her visit do not necessarily insure that the visitor's report is true. Examining Margaret's visit, however, we find nothing suggesting that the visitor and his information are unbelievable, notwithstanding the wonderful use the storyteller makes of light, dark, and color in his description of the outside of the house. The visitor, Goodman Parker, is known by

> "'The Wives of the Dead' clearly presents to the reader 'realities' shrouded in—but not necessarily made less real by—an atmosphere of unreality, exuding mystery and suggesting dreams without actually presenting them."

Margaret "as a friendly innkeeper of the town" and is called "honest" by the narrator. Nothing seems disputable or ambiguous in his account of having received from "an express" the "tidings on the frontiers" that include news of Margaret's husband and 12 other soldiers' being alive. Parker's report to Margaret is straight-forward and simple. And although it is true that, unlike Mary's visitor, Goodman Parker brings secondhand information, the narrator says nothing to cast doubt on Parker's source, who has been traveling from the eastern jurisdiction."

As Goodman Parker leaves, the narrator tells us that "his lantern gleamed along the street, bringing to view indistinct shapes of things, and the fragments of a world, like order glimmering through chaos, or memory roaming over the past." Is the narrator telling us that there is something unreal about what has just happened? No: unlike the "doubt of waking reality" that follows Mary's visit, which is clearly attributed to Mary's thoughts, we are told that Margaret "stayed not to watch these picturesque effects," much less created them out of her own alternately doubting and hopeful thoughts, as Mary perhaps does. Since we have seen that Margaret's visit does occur, and since there likewise seems no doubt that her visitor is sincere and his report accurate, the only thing that may seem "unreal" to Margaret is the welcomed shock, still sinking in, that her husband is alive after all.

After her visit, Margaret runs to tell Mary, but, realizing that doing so might make Mary feel worse, she "turned away. . . Her mind was thronged with delightful thoughts, till sleep stole on." Speeding the reader on, the narrator now turns to detailing Mary's experience.

He tells us that even before going to bed, Mary,

> all of whose emotions were influenced by her mild, quiet, yet not feeble character, began to recollect the precepts of resignation and endurance, which piety had taught her . . . Her misfortune, besides, as earliest known, should earliest cease to interfere with her regular course of duties.

The slightly ironic tone of parts of this passage is reminiscent of the narrator's earlier subtle criticism of the superficially sympathetic mourners who had left "one by one, whispering many comfortable passages of Scripture, that were answered by more abundant tears." However, the narrator may also be subtly chiding Mary for yielding too quickly to those "precepts of resignation and endurance." Margaret, obviously still very upset by her loss, is "given" back her husband, perhaps via the actual facts of the incident, but perhaps only via the narrator's story. Will Mary, then, since she seems much more accepting of her loss, remain without her husband? Mary fixes a meal, begging Margaret to join her in both her meal and her resignation. "Arise, I pray you, and let us ask a blessing on that which is provided for us." Margaret protests that "There is no blessing left for me"—further evidence that Margaret's visit will not be a creation of wishful thinking—but Mary feels that life must go on and that other blessings can still befall her. Does she, then, dream her visit, out of wishful thinking? Or is she thinking of other blessings?

When Margaret, after her visit, enters Mary's room to tell Mary what has happened, she notices that upon Mary's face

> a look of motionless contentment was now visible, as if her heart, like a deep lake, had grown calm because its dead had sunk down so far within. Happy is it, and strange, that the lighter sorrows are those from which dreams are chiefly fabricated.

The reader who moves too quickly over this passage might later assume that Mary looked happy here because she was dreaming that her husband was alive. However, the passage does not say that Mary looked happy. The narrator describes her look as one of "contentment," which echoes the "resignation" to her husband's death more than it suggests the elation a grief-stricken wife would feel on finding her beloved alive after all. The rest of the passage also supports this: Mary's heart "had grown calm"—again evoking an image of peaceful resignation, acceptance of the situation—"because its dead had sunk so far within." If the narrator had said "deadness," we might take that as the sorrow

Mary was feeling. But the nominative use of "dead" here may just as likely mean Mary's dead husband, and thus it would be he who, in Margaret's view, has "sunk so far within" Mary's heart that it has "grown calm." In either case, the entire passage, especially in conjunction with Mary's actions before going to bed, suggests that Mary is practically over her loss—at the least, resigned, and at most, content. Then we come to the final sentence of the passage, which, in light of our analysis of the sentences before it, now makes perfect sense: "Happy is it, and strange, that the lighter sorrows are those from which dreams are chiefly fabricated." We find out in the next paragraph that Mary has in fact been dreaming, and her sorrows, relative to Margaret's, are "the lighter" sort, because she no longer fights them. We must read further to see how this information can help us determine the truth or unreality of Mary's visit.

Though "a vivid dream had latterly involved her in its unreal life" and although the description of Mary's coming to recognize a knock on the door is clearly that of a person who has been asleep, the narrator also adds unequivocally that "Mary awoke." She does not answer her summons—that is, the actual meeting with her visitor does not begin—until, clearly, she is wide awake: "The pall of sleep was thrown back from the face of grief . . . she unclosed her eyes . . . [She] hastened to the window. By some accident, it had been left unhasped, and yielded easily to her hand." As with Margaret, however, that Mary is awake when her visit occurs does not necessarily mean that her visitor's report is true. And upon examining Mary's visitor and his story, we find many suggestions that neither is a reliable source of information, but rather that Stephen is either lying or mistaken.

A few brief but important details in the first paragraph describing Stephen can help us. We are told that "the storm was over, and the moon was up," and that Stephen's "livelihood was gained by short voyages along the coast." How and why, then, is Stephen "wet as if he had come out of the depths of the sea?" The phrase suggests that Stephen is not merely rain-soaked or wet from shallow coastal waters; if this is so, then a possible explanation is that Stephen has drowned—whether Mary's husband has also or not—and, as a ghost, has come to tell Mary either the truth (to do penance?) or a lie (to seek revenge). All of this information about Stephen may just be the narrator's misleading us, but it certainly serves to cast doubts on Stephen, which further information from the narrator increases.

First, we are told that Stephen, "previous to [Mary's] marriage . . . had been an unsuccessful wooer of her own," and the narrator refers to him as "the rejected lover." Mary herself is at first suspicious of Stephen's intentions, and we might well be also. It does seem odd that a "rejected lover" who "got home not ten minutes ago" would rush to tell the woman who had spurned him that his rival for her affections was in fact alive rather than dead as reported. That is exactly the opposite of what one would expect Mary's "unsuccessful wooer" to do. Since we have established that Mary is awake and that, therefore, her visit occurs, what we must ask is not whether Stephen has "run" to tell Mary, but *why* he has. The most likely answer in light of Stephen's being a "rejected lover" is that he is lying, either to give Mary false hope in revenge on her for having rejected him—or perhaps to resurrect his chances for winning her affections by seeming to do her a kind deed. The narrator refers to Stephen as "the generous seaman" midway through Stephen's account, and this label may also suggest that, if Stephen is not intentionally lying, he may still be mistaken, exaggerating what he has seen or heard in order to please Mary.

The status of Mary's husband is ultimately harder to prove than that of Margaret's, but the evidence seems to cast doubts on Stephen and his story's legitimacy. After the visit, Mary watches Stephen

> with a doubt of waking reality, that seemed stronger or weaker as he alternately entered the shade of the houses, or emerged into the broad streaks of moonlight. Gradually, however, a blessed flood of conviction swelled into her heart, in strength enough to overwhelm her had its increase been more abrupt.

Instead of the unquestioning conviction with which Margaret leaves her visitor, even Mary's positive feelings seem just that, feelings—a rush of emotion that may be as inconsistent as Stephen seems to be. And if, as may well be the case, the narrator is giving us more than a straight retelling of the story he came across, Mary may be getting the false report he feels she deserves for too quickly getting over her loss.

Finally, the "she" in the story's last sentence is purposely ambiguous, but it necessarily refers to Margaret. Mary is definitely awake already, and the grammar and syntax of the surrounding sentence make it appropriate for the "she" to refer to Margaret. "The Wives of the Dead" clearly presents to the reader "realities" shrouded in—but not necessarily made less real by—an atmosphere of unreality, exuding mystery and suggesting dreams without actually presenting them. If we succumb to false assumptions, such as that the wives must be dreaming because (1) the story is written by Hawthorne, or (2) what transpires in the story is exactly what the wives would be likely to dream, or (3) the mood and setting of the story suggest dreaminess, with the "rainy twilight of an autumn day" and the use of light and dark imagery throughout—we miss the point, and the narrator has succeeded in deceiving us. His deception is that a story by Hawthorne the dreamer, which is seemingly full of dreams, and the interpretation of which seems to hinge on the interpretation of those dreams, in fact contains only one dream, which is not described and which is of no direct importance to interpreting the story. Thus, "The Wives of the Dead" turns out to be not a darkly ironic treatise on the hopelessness of the wives' dreams, but simply a caution against ignorance of the distinction between dreams and reality.

Source: Mark Harris, "The Wives of the Living?: Absence of Dreams in Hawthorne's 'The Wives of the Dead,'" in *Studies in Short Fiction,* Vol. 29, No. 3, Summer 1992, pp. 323–29.

Bill Christophersen

In the following essay, Christophersen explores how Hawthorne "challenges conventional moral assumptions" in "The Wives of the Dead."

In 1832, the year Hawthorne wrote "Roger Malvin's Burial" and "My Kinsman, Major Molineux," he also wrote a less remembered, but no less exquisite story entitled "The Wives of the Dead." In it Margaret and Mary, the "young and comely" brides of two brothers, discover within a day of each other that their husbands have been killed. Grief draws them together. But during the night, each unknown to the other receives word her "dead" husband is alive and on his way home. A drama of mixed emotions ensues: neither woman can bring herself to break her news to the other, for fear of accentuating the other's sorrow.

The few critics who have addressed this tale have underlined the ambiguity of what happens that night: Do the women only dream their husbands' return, or are they really so blessed? Critics have also stressed that "the 'core of meaning' lies with the difference of the two women's response" to their husbands' death. Such differences are usually viewed along traditional Christian lines: "Margaret is rebellious and bitter; Mary is resigned and tolerant."

> At its outermost bourne, 'The Wives of the Dead,' as subversive as it is tender, is an ironic parable of self-salvation posing as a fairy tale of divine grace."

But perhaps the point is not that the women's experiences during the night elude easy definition (they do), but that, whether or not their husbands live, their lives have been permanently changed by the fatal news and by their subsequent adaptations. And perhaps the point is not that the women differ (they do), but that the traditional Christian norms by which we tend to judge these differences belie their complexity. In short, perhaps Hawthorne's story not only eschews transparent plot and characterization, but also challenges conventional moral assumptions; perhaps the story we think we see—a story of faith rewarded—is only one of several shadows cast by Hawthorne's lamp.

To begin with, I submit that Hawthorne's two "sisters" (as he terms them) derive, at least in part, from the New Testament sisters, Mary and Martha, whose brother, Lazarus, Jesus raised from the dead, according to John 11. This account of miraculous resurrection and the triumph of faith over despair adumbrates Hawthorne's plot, since Mary and Margaret's men are, as it were, raised from the dead and returned to them. Hawthorne's sisters, moreover, resemble their Biblical counterparts in more than name. The Biblical Mary personifies piety, faith, submission, and an unswerving sense of spiritual priorities; Martha, though devoted to Jesus, has a "weaker" faith, a more human nature. Martha, for instance, is at first unable to believe Christ intends to raise her dead brother. (Christ rebukes her doubt before accomplishing his miracle.) On another occasion Jesus, while visiting Mary and Martha, rebukes Martha for complaining that her sister, who is listening at Jesus' feet, has left her to do all the chores. "One thing is needful," says Jesus, "and Mary has chosen that better part, which shall not be taken from her." So when we read, in Hawthorne's tale, of Margaret's recalcitrance and Mary's pious

resignation in the face of death, the image of their Biblical counterparts recurs, however subconsciously or fleetingly.

But with it recurs a familiar moral grid against which we can scarcely help viewing the wives' acts and attitudes—a moral grid Hawthorne's story questions. His setting alone, stark as it is, hints at an ambiguous moral universe. The widows' house is "plainly furnished . . . yet decorated with little curiosities from beyond the sea and a few delicate specimens of Indian manufacture." We need only recall the dubious connotations of sea and forest in Hawthorne's fiction—the mutually pagan pirates and Indians Pearl romps with in *The Scarlet Letter*, for example—to doubt this otherwise innocent setting. Moreover, though the tale enacts a resurrection of sorts, and reinstates, at last, a "daylight" universe, it begins on "The rainy twilight of an autumn day," and takes place almost entirely at night. Daylight and the order it represents have been banished from the story. The sisters, despite their Bible-quoting well-wishers, are suddenly immersed in a dark and seemingly godless world. How the two adapt to such a world is, in fact, the central drama of the piece. And while the two sisters indeed cope differently—Mary, seemingly, better than Margaret—Hawthorne plays something of a Devil's advocate, querying Mary's reaction at least as much as Margaret's.

Both sisters at first resist their lot and the prescriptions of Christian duty; their visitors' Scriptural condolences, we are told, only elicit "more abundant tears." But Mary, after outpouring her grief, resigns herself to her husband's death and to the Lord's will. Margaret, on the other hand, rebels—not just against her bad fortune, but against God. "Come, dearest sister," says Mary, "Arise, I pray you, and let us ask a blessing on that which is provided for us." But Margaret responds, "There is no blessing left for me, neither will I ask it." Now there *is,* in fact, a blessing—albeit an ironic one—left for both women, but more of that later. Margaret's retort mirrors her outspoken and contentious stance toward experience in general. Like her husband, the Indian fighter, Margaret grapples with her fate—as she does with her emotions. When Goodman Parker rouses her during the night, claiming news of her husband, Margaret "screams" for him to fill her in—while Mary, under the same circumstances a short while later, falls "speechless."

If Margaret, meanwhile, takes after her husband, the "landsman" and Indian fighter, Mary, like her husband, is aptly identified with the sea, whose surface conceals what lies below. While Margaret, like the land, blows hot and cold, Mary, like the sea, submerges her sorrows. This style of coping seems, on the surface, mature, laudable, and eminently Christian: we watch approvingly as Mary reins in her grief and begins to pick up the pieces, all the while supporting Margaret and encouraging her to do likewise. Yet the same mechanism that allows Mary to recover so admirably also leads her to submerge essential feelings, to court ''temporary forgetfulness''—and perhaps even to dissemble in matters of the heart.

For the crux of the story is the way the sisters adjust to their husbands' death *by cleaving to each other.* It's easy to miss this almost-too-obvious point. But Hawthorne's message, if not explicit, is certainly implicit: The two sisters ''join their hearts''—remarry, as it were—during their hours of grief. The story pivots on this transfer of affections that the sisters themselves only gradually acknowledge.

Neither woman—understandably—seems fully aware of the emotions at work in her breast following her bereavement. Margaret, however, unlike Mary, is openly troubled—unable to sleep; a vague anxiety, Hawthorne notes, impels her to gaze repeatedly into Mary's chamber. Over and above grief for her husband, can an awareness of her deepening attachment to Mary figure in her insomnia? Whatever Hawthorne may wish to imply by this contrast, Margaret is certainly the first to realize the nature of her dawning emotion. This becomes clear after Goodman Parker informs Margaret that her husband lives—at the moment she turns to tell Mary the news. Margaret's husband's imminent return, however wonderful, dooms the ''marriage'' grief and love has forged between her and Mary, and Margaret, acknowledging the dilemma, resists the reinstated order to the extent it threatens the new bond. Margaret, that is, refuses to awaken Mary—and not merely out of delicacy:

> Margaret shrunk from disturbing her sister-in-law, and felt as if her own better fortune *had rendered her involuntarily unfaithful,* and as if altered and diminished affection must be the consequence of the disclosure she had to make. With a sudden step she turned away (my italics).

Later that evening Mary receives word that her own husband is alive, and on his way home. She too is overjoyed. But her affections too, we sense, have been in flux—though she, unlike Margaret, seems blind to the fact until the story's close. It isn't until she sets about arranging the bed clothes over Margaret's sleeping form that Mary's heart betrays how deeply she feels toward Margaret. Hawthorne doesn't paraphrase Mary's thoughts as he did Margaret's; we can only guess what's on her mind as she approaches Margaret's bed. But unlike Margaret, who acknowledged and refused to sever their tie, Mary seems disposed, however reluctantly, to submerge her inchoate love for Margaret under the guise of a sister's solicitousness (hence her unnecessary fussing with Mary's bedclothes)—and to the extent, however slight, that she does so, she betrays her own heart.

Perhaps it is to dramatize Mary's equivocation that Hawthorne includes the seemingly gratuitous scene in which Mary mistakes Stephen's motives for visiting her. Stephen, the sailor who goes out of his way on a rainy night to inform Mary that her husband lives, had courted Mary, we are told, before she married. Seeing him at her window and hearing his obscure preamble, Mary jumps to the conclusion that he seeks selfish advantage from her tragedy. Mary, that is, thinks he is making advances, and is appalled that he should think her capable of entertaining new affections so soon after being widowed. Now, ironically, this is precisely what she has already done, as I have suggested—and perhaps no more than what steals across anyone's mind in the lonely and desperate hours after losing a loved one. In fact, as if to stress the point, Hawthorne limns Stephen as a virtual projection of Mary's own heart. (Her heart, we are told, was ''a deep lake . . . grown calm because its dead had sunk so far within.'' Stephen, meanwhile—one of Mary's figurative dead—looks ''wet as if he had come out of the depths of the sea.'') Mary, in any case, rebukes his seeming effrontery and moves (characteristically) to close the window, never for a moment admitting any such ambiguous emotions herself. But moments later, when she finds herself lingering over Margaret's sleeping form, the news of her husband's rescue still ringing in her ears, her tears overflow. Hysteria notwithstanding, perhaps her tears stem as much from self-realization as from emotional release or a sister's sorrow. Perhaps Mary glimpses her humanity peeking out from beneath the robes of Charity and Christian duty she all-too-resolutely draws about herself.

Hawthorne, though, is finally less concerned with psychoanalyzing Mary and Margaret's differences for their own sake than for the sake of the larger universal drama they attest to; less concerned with spotlighting the individual psyche's sleight-of-hand than with querying the modern (Christian) community's. For Hawthorne's story vibrates with the theological implications of its New Testament iconography. I have already suggested in part its relation to the Mary-Martha-Lazarus story—the story of *a* resurrection that anticipates *the* Resurrection. So too Hawthorne's tale of imminently returning bridegrooms recalls the parable of the Returning Bridegroom—i.e., Christ—and the anxieties of those who wait. Bereavement, in other words, becomes a spiritual metaphor—one which, even if we interpret Hawthorne's story optimistically, poses grave questions.

In "The Wives of the Dead," God ostensibly rewards the sisters' faith by returning their husbands. But by focusing on the loss accompanying this dispensation, Hawthorne radically qualifies the sisters' renewed state of grace—renders it (to borrow Hawthorne's own conceit) something of an inverted blessing.

For "The Wives of the Dead" is finally a tale about surviving in the modern world. Two women, awash in a "deluge of darkness," evolve a hybrid love that, however unorthodox, offers solace appropriate to the void that has overwhelmed them. Figuratively speaking, the women adapt to the dark; finding "whatever consolation . . . grief admits . . . in the bosom of the other," they accommodate themselves to a moral night in which there may be no Father to appeal to for a blessing. Their love, a lamp fashioned in isolation, glows tentatively, perhaps even promisingly—until the curtain is, as it were, withdrawn to reveal a prank: daylight without . . . Given the circumstances as Hawthorne presents them, and the New Testament context in which he steeps them, we are left to wonder whether Dawn, with its prospect of the Returning Bridegroom, isn't as much an imposition as a comfort.

Do the wives' husbands really live? Are they indeed returning? We can't say for sure. The hardest evidence we have is hearsay. Moreover, the possibility that all or part of what seems to transpire may be no more than an overwrought widow's dream qualifies still further any conclusions we may be tempted to draw, and neither Hawthorne's lamp imagery nor the text in general seems likely to clarify the issue. Hawthorne's tale, as tactful and ambiguous a masterpiece as he ever wrote, at last resists explication.

This ambiguity informs even the story's minor motifs. The Biblical ironies proposed earlier, for instance, resonate against other potentially reassuring Biblical images of subsiding waters, blessed mourners, faithful virgins and well-trimmed lamps. The "deluge of darkness" finds its counterpart in the "blessed flood of conviction" that fills Mary's heart after she accepts the news that her husband lives. The dire images of night and storm and sea and season also suggest a larger, cyclical world in which good and evil, pain and pleasure, despair and promise balance out. Dark implications about the relativity and complexity of our most idealized emotions fall back in perspective alongside the simple, apparently selfless love Stephen displays in visiting Mary. Divine goodness seems, miraculously, to prevail over the most compelling doubts.

But what if the husbands don't live—except in their wives' frantic dreams? At its outermost bourne, "The Wives of the Dead," as subversive as it is tender, is an ironic parable of self-salvation posing as a fairy tale of divine grace. Like Margaret's husband and his twelve fellow Indian-fighters—frontier apostles who grapple with their fate rather than submit to it; like Mary's husband and his mates, who "saved themselves on a spar, when the Blessing turned bottom upward," Hawthorne's two women, by joining their hearts in inverted matrimony, *save themselves* in the most anti-Christian sense after their bright, blessed world capsizes. And given a moral night whose darkness, in the Bridegroom's absence, threatens to suffocate, Margaret's Promethean mode rather than Mary's mode of resigned submission may well prove "the better part."

Source: Bill Christophersen, "Hawthorne's 'The Wives of the Dead': Bereavement and the 'Better Part,'" in *Studies in Short Fiction,* Vol. 20, No. 1, Winter 1983, pp. 1–6.

Sources

Doubleday, Neal Frank, *Hawthorne's Early Tales: A Critical Study,* Duke University Press, 1972, pp. 2147–3018.

Friedlander, Benjamin, "Hawthorne's 'Waking Reality,'" in *American Transcendental Quarterly,* March 1999.

Harris, Mark, "The Wives of the Living?: Absence of Dreams in Hawthorne's 'The Wives of the Dead,'" in *Studies in Short Fiction,* No. 29, 1992, pp. 323–29.

Lang, H. J., "How Ambiguous Is Hawthorne?" in *Hawthorne: A Collection of Critical Essays,* edited by A. N. Kaul, Prentice-Hall, 1966, pp. 86–98.

Martin, Terrence, *Nathaniel Hawthorne,* Twayne Publishers, 1965, pp. 24–26.

McDermott, John V., ''Hawthorne's 'The Wives of the Dead,''' in *Explicator,* Vol. 54, No. 3, Spring 1996, pp. 145–47.

Selzer, John L., ''Psychological Romance in Hawthorne's 'Wives of the Dead,''' in *Studies in Short Fiction,* Vol. 16, 1979, pp. 311–15.

Stephenson, Edward, ''Hawthorne's 'Wives of the Dead,''' in *Explicator,* Vol. XXV, No. 8, item 63, April 1967.

Van Doren, Mark, *Nathaniel Hawthorne,* Sloane Associates, 1949, pp. 82–84.

Waggoner, Hyatt H., *Hawthorne: A Critical Study,* Harvard University Press, 1967.

Woodberry, George Edward, *Nathaniel Hawthorne: How to Know Him,* Bobbs-Merrill, 1918, pp. 68–69.

Further Reading

Erlich, Gloria C., *Family Themes and Hawthorne's Fiction: The Tenacious Web,* Rutgers University Press, 1984.
  Erlich believes it is Margaret's husband who lives, and Mary's who dies.

Gale, Robert L., *A Nathaniel Hawthorne Encyclopedia,* Greenwood, 1991.
  Gale's exhaustive reference work includes entries on every story, sketch, and novel that Hawthorne wrote. This is an indispensable reference book.

Mellow, James R., *Nathaniel Hawthorne in His Times,* Johns Hopkins University Press, 1998.
  This is a reprint of the 1983 edition, which won the 1983 National Book Award. Mellow's biography places Hawthorne in the midst of the literary and cultural turmoil of the early republic. The biography traces Hawthorne's literary concerns to the events of his life.

Pickard, Samuel T., ed., *Hawthorne's First Diary,* 1972.
  Though the authenticity of this book has been questioned, it contains a wealth of information on Hawthorne's personality, his living situation, and his literary opinions.

Thompson, G. R., *The Art of Authorial Presence: Hawthorne's Provincial Tales,* Duke University Press, 1993, pp. 66–76.
  Thompson provides a useful review of the scant critical literature on Hawthorne's story.

Young, Philip, *Hawthorne's Secret,* David R. Godine, 1984.
  Young's biography draws on Hawthorne's fiction, letters, and diaries to argue that Hawthorne, who shared a passionate attachment with his sister, Elizabeth (Ebe), discovered that an ancestor on his mother's side had committed incest in the seventeenth century. Young claims that this conjunction filled Hawthorne with revulsion and the fear that he had been cursed to repeat the sins of the past.

Glossary of Literary Terms

A

Aestheticism: A literary and artistic movement of the nineteenth century. Followers of the movement believed that art should not be mixed with social, political, or moral teaching. The statement ''art for art's sake'' is a good summary of aestheticism. The movement had its roots in France, but it gained widespread importance in England in the last half of the nineteenth century, where it helped change the Victorian practice of including moral lessons in literature. Edgar Allan Poe is one of the best-known American ''aesthetes.''

Allegory: A narrative technique in which characters representing things or abstract ideas are used to convey a message or teach a lesson. Allegory is typically used to teach moral, ethical, or religious lessons but is sometimes used for satiric or political purposes. Many fairy tales are allegories.

Allusion: A reference to a familiar literary or historical person or event, used to make an idea more easily understood. Joyce Carol Oates's story ''Where Are You Going, Where Have You Been?'' exhibits several allusions to popular music.

Analogy: A comparison of two things made to explain something unfamiliar through its similarities to something familiar, or to prove one point based on the acceptance of another. Similes and metaphors are types of analogies.

Antagonist: The major character in a narrative or drama who works against the hero or protagonist. The Misfit in Flannery O'Connor's story ''A Good Man Is Hard to Find'' serves as the antagonist for the Grandmother.

Anthology: A collection of similar works of literature, art, or music. Zora Neale Hurston's ''The Eatonville Anthology'' is a collection of stories that take place in the same town.

Anthropomorphism: The presentation of animals or objects in human shape or with human characteristics. The term is derived from the Greek word for ''human form.'' The fur necklet in Katherine Mansfield's story ''Miss Brill'' has anthropomorphic characteristics.

Anti-hero: A central character in a work of literature who lacks traditional heroic qualities such as courage, physical prowess, and fortitude. Anti-heroes typically distrust conventional values and are unable to commit themselves to any ideals. They generally feel helpless in a world over which they have no control. Anti-heroes usually accept, and often celebrate, their positions as social outcasts. A well-known anti-hero is Walter Mitty in James Thurber's story ''The Secret Life of Walter Mitty.''

Archetype: The word archetype is commonly used to describe an original pattern or model from which all other things of the same kind are made. Archetypes are the literary images that grow out of the ''collective unconscious,'' a theory proposed by psychologist Carl Jung. They appear in literature as incidents and plots that repeat basic patterns of life. They may also appear as stereotyped characters. The ''schlemiel'' of Yiddish literature is an archetype.

Autobiography: A narrative in which an individual tells his or her life story. Examples include Benjamin Franklin's *Autobiography* and Amy Hempel's story ''In the Cemetery Where Al Jolson Is Buried,'' which has autobiographical characteristics even though it is a work of fiction.

Avant-garde: A literary term that describes new writing that rejects traditional approaches to literature in favor of innovations in style or content. Twentieth-century examples of the literary *avant-garde* include the modernists and the minimalists.

B

Belles-lettres: A French term meaning ''fine letters'' or ''beautiful writing.'' It is often used as a synonym for literature, typically referring to imaginative and artistic rather than scientific or expository writing. Current usage sometimes restricts the meaning to light or humorous writing and appreciative essays about literature. Lewis Carroll's *Alice in Wonderland* epitomizes the realm of belles-lettres.

Bildungsroman: A German word meaning ''novel of development.'' The *bildungsroman* is a study of the maturation of a youthful character, typically brought about through a series of social or sexual encounters that lead to self-awareness. J. D. Salinger's *Catcher in the Rye* is a *bildungsroman*, and Doris Lessing's story ''Through the Tunnel'' exhibits characteristics of a *bildungsroman* as well.

Black Aesthetic Movement: A period of artistic and literary development among African Americans in the 1960s and early 1970s. This was the first major African-American artistic movement since the Harlem Renaissance and was closely paralleled by the civil rights and black power movements. The black aesthetic writers attempted to produce works of art that would be meaningful to the black masses. Key figures in black aesthetics included one of its founders, poet and playwright Amiri Baraka, formerly known as LeRoi Jones; poet and essayist Haki R. Madhubuti, formerly Don L. Lee; poet and playwright Sonia Sanchez; and dramatist Ed Bullins. Works representative of the Black Aesthetic Movement include Amiri Baraka's play *Dutchman,* a 1964 Obie award-winner.

Black Humor: Writing that places grotesque elements side by side with humorous ones in an attempt to shock the reader, forcing him or her to laugh at the horrifying reality of a disordered world. ''Lamb to the Slaughter,'' by Roald Dahl, in which a placid housewife murders her husband and serves the murder weapon to the investigating policemen, is an example of black humor.

C

Catharsis: The release or purging of unwanted emotions—specifically fear and pity—brought about by exposure to art. The term was first used by the Greek philosopher Aristotle in his *Poetics* to refer to the desired effect of tragedy on spectators.

Character: Broadly speaking, a person in a literary work. The actions of characters are what constitute the plot of a story, novel, or poem. There are numerous types of characters, ranging from simple, stereotypical figures to intricate, multifaceted ones. ''Characterization'' is the process by which an author creates vivid, believable characters in a work of art. This may be done in a variety of ways, including (1) direct description of the character by the narrator; (2) the direct presentation of the speech, thoughts, or actions of the character; and (3) the responses of other characters to the character. The term ''character'' also refers to a form originated by the ancient Greek writer Theophrastus that later became popular in the seventeenth and eighteenth centuries. It is a short essay or sketch of a person who prominently displays a specific attribute or quality, such as miserliness or ambition. ''Miss Brill,'' a story by Katherine Mansfield, is an example of a character sketch.

Classical: In its strictest definition in literary criticism, classicism refers to works of ancient Greek or Roman literature. The term may also be used to describe a literary work of recognized importance (a ''classic'') from any time period or literature that exhibits the traits of classicism. Examples of later works and authors now described as classical include French literature of the seventeenth century, Western novels of the nineteenth century, and American fiction of the mid-nineteenth century such as that written by James Fenimore Cooper and Mark Twain.

Climax: The turning point in a narrative, the moment when the conflict is at its most intense. Typically, the structure of stories, novels, and plays is one of rising action, in which tension builds to the climax, followed by falling action, in which tension lessens as the story moves to its conclusion.

Comedy: One of two major types of drama, the other being tragedy. Its aim is to amuse, and it typically ends happily. Comedy assumes many forms, such as farce and burlesque, and uses a variety of techniques, from parody to satire. In a restricted sense the term comedy refers only to dramatic presentations, but in general usage it is commonly applied to nondramatic works as well.

Comic Relief: The use of humor to lighten the mood of a serious or tragic story, especially in plays. The technique is very common in Elizabethan works, and can be an integral part of the plot or simply a brief event designed to break the tension of the scene.

Conflict: The conflict in a work of fiction is the issue to be resolved in the story. It usually occurs between two characters, the protagonist and the antagonist, or between the protagonist and society or the protagonist and himself or herself. The conflict in Washington Irving's story ''The Devil and Tom Walker'' is that the Devil wants Tom Walker's soul but Tom does not want to go to hell.

Criticism: The systematic study and evaluation of literary works, usually based on a specific method or set of principles. An important part of literary studies since ancient times, the practice of criticism has given rise to numerous theories, methods, and ''schools,'' sometimes producing conflicting, even contradictory, interpretations of literature in general as well as of individual works. Even such basic issues as what constitutes a poem or a novel have been the subject of much criticism over the centuries. Seminal texts of literary criticism include Plato's *Republic,* Aristotle's *Poetics,* Sir Philip Sidney's *The Defence of Poesie,* and John Dryden's *Of Dramatic Poesie.* Contemporary schools of criticism include deconstruction, feminist, psychoanalytic, poststructuralist, new historicist, postcolonialist, and reader-response.

D

Deconstruction: A method of literary criticism characterized by multiple conflicting interpretations of a given work. Deconstructionists consider the impact of the language of a work and suggest that the true meaning of the work is not necessarily the meaning that the author intended.

Deduction: The process of reaching a conclusion through reasoning from general premises to a specific premise. Arthur Conan Doyle's character Sherlock Holmes often used deductive reasoning to solve mysteries.

Denotation: The definition of a word, apart from the impressions or feelings it creates in the reader. The word ''apartheid'' denotes a political and economic policy of segregation by race, but its connotations—oppression, slavery, inequality—are numerous.

Denouement: A French word meaning ''the unknotting.'' In literature, it denotes the resolution of conflict in fiction or drama. The *denouement* follows the climax and provides an outcome to the primary plot situation as well as an explanation of secondary plot complications. A well-known example of *denouement* is the last scene of the play *As You Like It* by William Shakespeare, in which couples are married, an evildoer repents, the identities of two disguised characters are revealed, and a ruler is restored to power. Also known as ''falling action.''

Detective Story: A narrative about the solution of a mystery or the identification of a criminal. The conventions of the detective story include the detective's scrupulous use of logic in solving the mystery; incompetent or ineffectual police; a suspect who appears guilty at first but is later proved innocent; and the detective's friend or confidant—often the narrator—whose slowness in interpreting clues emphasizes by contrast the detective's brilliance. Edgar Allan Poe's ''Murders in the Rue Morgue'' is commonly regarded as the earliest example of this type of story. Other practitioners are Arthur Conan Doyle, Dashiell Hammett, and Agatha Christie.

Dialogue: Dialogue is conversation between people in a literary work. In its most restricted sense, it refers specifically to the speech of characters in a drama. As a specific literary genre, a ''dialogue'' is a composition in which characters debate an issue or idea.

Didactic: A term used to describe works of literature that aim to teach a moral, religious, political, or practical lesson. Although didactic elements are often found in artistically pleasing works, the term ''didactic'' usually refers to literature in which the message is more important than the form. The term may also be used to criticize a work that the critic finds ''overly didactic,'' that is, heavy-handed in its delivery of a lesson. An example of didactic literature is John Bunyan's *Pilgrim's Progress.*

Dramatic Irony: Occurs when the reader of a work of literature knows something that a character in the work itself does not know. The irony is in the contrast between the intended meaning of the statements or actions of a character and the additional information understood by the audience.

Dystopia: An imaginary place in a work of fiction where the characters lead dehumanized, fearful lives. George Orwell's *Nineteen Eighty-four,* and Margaret Atwood's *Handmaid's Tale* portray versions of dystopia.

E

Edwardian: Describes cultural conventions identified with the period of the reign of Edward VII of England (1901–1910). Writers of the Edwardian Age typically displayed a strong reaction against the propriety and conservatism of the Victorian Age. Their work often exhibits distrust of authority in religion, politics, and art and expresses strong doubts about the soundness of conventional values. Writers of this era include E. M. Forster, H. G. Wells, and Joseph Conrad.

Empathy: A sense of shared experience, including emotional and physical feelings, with someone or something other than oneself. Empathy is often used to describe the response of a reader to a literary character.

Epilogue: A concluding statement or section of a literary work. In dramas, particularly those of the seventeenth and eighteenth centuries, the epilogue is a closing speech, often in verse, delivered by an actor at the end of a play and spoken directly to the audience.

Epiphany: A sudden revelation of truth inspired by a seemingly trivial incident. The term was widely used by James Joyce in his critical writings, and the stories in Joyce's *Dubliners* are commonly called ''epiphanies.''

Epistolary Novel: A novel in the form of letters. The form was particularly popular in the eighteenth century. The form can also be applied to short stories, as in Edwidge Danticat's ''Children of the Sea.''

Epithet: A word or phrase, often disparaging or abusive, that expresses a character trait of someone or something. ''The Napoleon of crime'' is an

epithet applied to Professor Moriarty, arch-rival of Sherlock Holmes in Arthur Conan Doyle's series of detective stories.

Existentialism: A predominantly twentieth-century philosophy concerned with the nature and perception of human existence. There are two major strains of existentialist thought: atheistic and Christian. Followers of atheistic existentialism believe that the individual is alone in a godless universe and that the basic human condition is one of suffering and loneliness. Nevertheless, because there are no fixed values, individuals can create their own characters—indeed, they can shape themselves—through the exercise of free will. The atheistic strain culminates in and is popularly associated with the works of Jean-Paul Sartre. The Christian existentialists, on the other hand, believe that only in God may people find freedom from life's anguish. The two strains hold certain beliefs in common: that existence cannot be fully understood or described through empirical effort; that anguish is a universal element of life; that individuals must bear responsibility for their actions; and that there is no common standard of behavior or perception for religious and ethical matters. Existentialist thought figures prominently in the works of such authors as Franz Kafka, Fyodor Dostoyevsky, and Albert Camus.

Expatriatism: The practice of leaving one's country to live for an extended period in another country. Literary expatriates include Irish author James Joyce who moved to Italy and France, American writers James Baldwin, Ernest Hemingway, Gertrude Stein, and F. Scott Fitzgerald who lived and wrote in Paris, and Polish novelist Joseph Conrad in England.

Exposition: Writing intended to explain the nature of an idea, thing, or theme. Expository writing is often combined with description, narration, or argument.

Expressionism: An indistinct literary term, originally used to describe an early twentieth-century school of German painting. The term applies to almost any mode of unconventional, highly subjective writing that distorts reality in some way. Advocates of Expressionism include Federico Garcia Lorca, Eugene O'Neill, Franz Kafka, and James Joyce.

F

Fable: A prose or verse narrative intended to convey a moral. Animals or inanimate objects with human characteristics often serve as characters in fables. A famous fable is Aesop's "The Tortoise and the Hare."

Fantasy: A literary form related to mythology and folklore. Fantasy literature is typically set in non-existent realms and features supernatural beings. Notable examples of literature with elements of fantasy are Gabriel Garcia Marquez's story "The Handsomest Drowned Man in the World" and Ursula K. LeGuin's "The Ones Who Walk Away from Omelas."

Farce: A type of comedy characterized by broad humor, outlandish incidents, and often vulgar subject matter. Much of the comedy in film and television could more accurately be described as farce.

Fiction: Any story that is the product of imagination rather than a documentation of fact. Characters and events in such narratives may be based in real life but their ultimate form and configuration is a creation of the author.

Figurative Language: A technique in which an author uses figures of speech such as hyperbole, irony, metaphor, or simile for a particular effect. Figurative language is the opposite of literal language, in which every word is truthful, accurate, and free of exaggeration or embellishment.

Flashback: A device used in literature to present action that occurred before the beginning of the story. Flashbacks are often introduced as the dreams or recollections of one or more characters.

Foil: A character in a work of literature whose physical or psychological qualities contrast strongly with, and therefore highlight, the corresponding qualities of another character. In his Sherlock Holmes stories, Arthur Conan Doyle portrayed Dr. Watson as a man of normal habits and intelligence, making him a foil for the eccentric and unusually perceptive Sherlock Holmes.

Folklore: Traditions and myths preserved in a culture or group of people. Typically, these are passed on by word of mouth in various forms—such as legends, songs, and proverbs—or preserved in customs and ceremonies. Washington Irving, in "The Devil and Tom Walker" and many of his other stories, incorporates many elements of the folklore of New England and Germany.

Folktale: A story originating in oral tradition. Folktales fall into a variety of categories, including legends, ghost stories, fairy tales, fables, and anecdotes based on historical figures and events.

Foreshadowing: A device used in literature to create expectation or to set up an explanation of later developments. Edgar Allan Poe uses foreshadowing to create suspense in "The Fall of the House of Usher" when the narrator comments on the crumbling state of disrepair in which he finds the house.

G

Genre: A category of literary work. Genre may refer to both the content of a given work—tragedy, comedy, horror, science fiction—and to its form, such as poetry, novel, or drama.

Gilded Age: A period in American history during the 1870s and after characterized by political corruption and materialism. A number of important novels of social and political criticism were written during this time. Henry James and Kate Chopin are two writers who were prominent during the Gilded Age.

Gothicism: In literature, works characterized by a taste for medieval or morbid characters and situations. A gothic novel prominently features elements of horror, the supernatural, gloom, and violence: clanking chains, terror, ghosts, medieval castles, and unexplained phenomena. The term "gothic novel" is also applied to novels that lack elements of the traditional Gothic setting but that create a similar atmosphere of terror or dread. The term can also be applied to stories, plays, and poems. Mary Shelley's *Frankenstein* and Joyce Carol Oates's *Bellefleur* are both gothic novels.

Grotesque: In literature, a work that is characterized by exaggeration, deformity, freakishness, and disorder. The grotesque often includes an element of comic absurdity. Examples of the grotesque can be found in the works of Edgar Allan Poe, Flannery O'Connor, Joseph Heller, and Shirley Jackson.

H

Harlem Renaissance: The Harlem Renaissance of the 1920s is generally considered the first significant movement of black writers and artists in the United States. During this period, new and established black writers, many of whom lived in the region of New York City known as Harlem, published more fiction and poetry than ever before, the first influential black literary journals were established, and black authors and artists received their first widespread recognition and serious critical appraisal. Among the major writers associated with this period are Countee Cullen, Langston Hughes, Arna Bontemps, and Zora Neale Hurston.

Hero/Heroine: The principal sympathetic character in a literary work. Heroes and heroines typically exhibit admirable traits: idealism, courage, and integrity, for example. Famous heroes and heroines of literature include Charles Dickens's Oliver Twist, Margaret Mitchell's Scarlett O'Hara, and the anonymous narrator in Ralph Ellison's *Invisible Man*.

Hyperbole: Deliberate exaggeration used to achieve an effect. In William Shakespeare's *Macbeth,* Lady Macbeth hyperbolizes when she says, ''All the perfumes of Arabia could not sweeten this little hand.''

I

Image: A concrete representation of an object or sensory experience. Typically, such a representation helps evoke the feelings associated with the object or experience itself. Images are either ''literal'' or ''figurative.'' Literal images are especially concrete and involve little or no extension of the obvious meaning of the words used to express them. Figurative images do not follow the literal meaning of the words exactly. Images in literature are usually visual, but the term ''image'' can also refer to the representation of any sensory experience.

Imagery: The array of images in a literary work. Also used to convey the author's overall use of figurative language in a work.

In medias res: A Latin term meaning ''in the middle of things.'' It refers to the technique of beginning a story at its midpoint and then using various flashback devices to reveal previous action. This technique originated in such epics as Virgil's *Aeneid.*

Interior Monologue: A narrative technique in which characters' thoughts are revealed in a way that appears to be uncontrolled by the author. The interior monologue typically aims to reveal the inner self of a character. It portrays emotional experiences as they occur at both a conscious and unconscious level. One of the best-known interior monologues in English is the Molly Bloom section at the close of James Joyce's *Ulysses.* Katherine Anne Porter's ''The Jilting of Granny Weatherall'' is also told in the form of an interior monologue.

Irony: In literary criticism, the effect of language in which the intended meaning is the opposite of what

is stated. The title of Jonathan Swift's ''A Modest Proposal'' is ironic because what Swift proposes in this essay is cannibalism—hardly ''modest.''

J

Jargon: Language that is used or understood only by a select group of people. Jargon may refer to terminology used in a certain profession, such as computer jargon, or it may refer to any nonsensical language that is not understood by most people. Anthony Burgess's *A Clockwork Orange* and James Thurber's ''The Secret Life of Walter Mitty'' both use jargon.

K

Knickerbocker Group: An indistinct group of New York writers of the first half of the nineteenth century. Members of the group were linked only by location and a common theme: New York life. Two famous members of the Knickerbocker Group were Washington Irving and William Cullen Bryant. The group's name derives from Irving's *Knickerbocker's History of New York.*

L

Literal Language: An author uses literal language when he or she writes without exaggerating or embellishing the subject matter and without any tools of figurative language. To say ''He ran very quickly down the street'' is to use literal language, whereas to say ''He ran like a hare down the street'' would be using figurative language.

Literature: Literature is broadly defined as any written or spoken material, but the term most often refers to creative works. Literature includes poetry, drama, fiction, and many kinds of nonfiction writing, as well as oral, dramatic, and broadcast compositions not necessarily preserved in a written format, such as films and television programs.

Lost Generation: A term first used by Gertrude Stein to describe the post-World War I generation of American writers: men and women haunted by a sense of betrayal and emptiness brought about by the destructiveness of the war. The term is commonly applied to Hart Crane, Ernest Hemingway, F. Scott Fitzgerald, and others.

M

Magic Realism: A form of literature that incorporates fantasy elements or supernatural occurrences into the narrative and accepts them as truth. Gabriel Garcia Marquez and Laura Esquivel are two writers known for their works of magic realism.

Metaphor: A figure of speech that expresses an idea through the image of another object. Metaphors suggest the essence of the first object by identifying it with certain qualities of the second object. An example is "But soft, what light through yonder window breaks?/ It is the east, and Juliet is the sun" in William Shakespeare's *Romeo and Juliet.* Here, Juliet, the first object, is identified with qualities of the second object, the sun.

Minimalism: A literary style characterized by spare, simple prose with few elaborations. In minimalism, the main theme of the work is often never discussed directly. Amy Hempel and Ernest Hemingway are two writers known for their works of minimalism.

Modernism: Modern literary practices. Also, the principles of a literary school that lasted from roughly the beginning of the twentieth century until the end of World War II. Modernism is defined by its rejection of the literary conventions of the nineteenth century and by its opposition to conventional morality, taste, traditions, and economic values. Many writers are associated with the concepts of modernism, including Albert Camus, D. H. Lawrence, Ernest Hemingway, William Faulkner, Eugene O'Neill, and James Joyce.

Monologue: A composition, written or oral, by a single individual. More specifically, a speech given by a single individual in a drama or other public entertainment. It has no set length, although it is usually several or more lines long. "I Stand Here Ironing" by Tillie Olsen is an example of a story written in the form of a monologue.

Mood: The prevailing emotions of a work or of the author in his or her creation of the work. The mood of a work is not always what might be expected based on its subject matter.

Motif: A theme, character type, image, metaphor, or other verbal element that recurs throughout a single work of literature or occurs in a number of different works over a period of time. For example, the color white in Herman Melville's *Moby Dick* is a "specific" *motif,* while the trials of star-crossed lovers is a "conventional" *motif* from the literature of all periods.

N

Narration: The telling of a series of events, real or invented. A narration may be either a simple narrative, in which the events are recounted chronologically, or a narrative with a plot, in which the account is given in a style reflecting the author's artistic concept of the story. Narration is sometimes used as a synonym for "storyline."

Narrative: A verse or prose accounting of an event or sequence of events, real or invented. The term is also used as an adjective in the sense "method of narration." For example, in literary criticism, the expression "narrative technique" usually refers to the way the author structures and presents his or her story. Different narrative forms include diaries, travelogues, novels, ballads, epics, short stories, and other fictional forms.

Narrator: The teller of a story. The narrator may be the author or a character in the story through whom the author speaks. Huckleberry Finn is the narrator of Mark Twain's *The Adventures of Huckleberry Finn.*

Novella: An Italian term meaning "story." This term has been especially used to describe fourteenth-century Italian tales, but it also refers to modern short novels. Modern novellas include Leo Tolstoy's *The Death of Ivan Ilich,* Fyodor Dostoyevsky's *Notes from the Underground,* and Joseph Conrad's *Heart of Darkness.*

O

Oedipus Complex: A son's romantic obsession with his mother. The phrase is derived from the story of the ancient Theban hero Oedipus, who unknowingly killed his father and married his mother, and was popularized by Sigmund Freud's theory of psychoanalysis. Literary occurrences of the Oedipus complex include Sophocles' *Oedipus Rex* and D. H. Lawrence's "The Rocking-Horse Winner."

Onomatopoeia: The use of words whose sounds express or suggest their meaning. In its simplest sense, onomatopoeia may be represented by words that mimic the sounds they denote such as "hiss" or "meow." At a more subtle level, the pattern and rhythm of sounds and rhymes of a line or poem may be onomatopoeic.

Oral Tradition: A process by which songs, ballads, folklore, and other material are transmitted by word of mouth. The tradition of oral transmission predates the written record systems of literate society.

Oral transmission preserves material sometimes over generations, although often with variations. Memory plays a large part in the recitation and preservation of orally transmitted material. Native American myths and legends, and African folktales told by plantation slaves are examples of orally transmitted literature.

P

Parable: A story intended to teach a moral lesson or answer an ethical question. Examples of parables are the stories told by Jesus Christ in the New Testament, notably "The Prodigal Son," but parables also are used in Sufism, rabbinic literature, Hasidism, and Zen Buddhism. Isaac Bashevis Singer's story "Gimpel the Fool" exhibits characteristics of a parable.

Paradox: A statement that appears illogical or contradictory at first, but may actually point to an underlying truth. A literary example of a paradox is George Orwell's statement "All animals are equal, but some animals are more equal than others" in *Animal Farm.*

Parody: In literature, this term refers to an imitation of a serious literary work or the signature style of a particular author in a ridiculous manner. A typical parody adopts the style of the original and applies it to an inappropriate subject for humorous effect. Parody is a form of satire and could be considered the literary equivalent of a caricature or cartoon. Henry Fielding's *Shamela* is a parody of Samuel Richardson's *Pamela.*

Persona: A Latin term meaning "mask." Personae are the characters in a fictional work of literature. The persona generally functions as a mask through which the author tells a story in a voice other than his or her own. A persona is usually either a character in a story who acts as a narrator or an "implied author," a voice created by the author to act as the narrator for himself or herself. The persona in Charlotte Perkins Gilman's story "The Yellow Wallpaper" is the unnamed young mother experiencing a mental breakdown.

Personification: A figure of speech that gives human qualities to abstract ideas, animals, and inanimate objects. To say that "the sun is smiling" is to personify the sun.

Plot: The pattern of events in a narrative or drama. In its simplest sense, the plot guides the author in composing the work and helps the reader follow the work. Typically, plots exhibit causality and unity and have a beginning, a middle, and an end. Sometimes, however, a plot may consist of a series of disconnected events, in which case it is known as an "episodic plot."

Poetic Justice: An outcome in a literary work, not necessarily a poem, in which the good are rewarded and the evil are punished, especially in ways that particularly fit their virtues or crimes. For example, a murderer may himself be murdered, or a thief will find himself penniless.

Poetic License: Distortions of fact and literary convention made by a writer—not always a poet—for the sake of the effect gained. Poetic license is closely related to the concept of "artistic freedom." An author exercises poetic license by saying that a pile of money "reaches as high as a mountain" when the pile is actually only a foot or two high.

Point of View: The narrative perspective from which a literary work is presented to the reader. There are four traditional points of view. The "third person omniscient" gives the reader a "godlike" perspective, unrestricted by time or place, from which to see actions and look into the minds of characters. This allows the author to comment openly on characters and events in the work. The "third person" point of view presents the events of the story from outside of any single character's perception, much like the omniscient point of view, but the reader must understand the action as it takes place and without any special insight into characters' minds or motivations. The "first person" or "personal" point of view relates events as they are perceived by a single character. The main character "tells" the story and may offer opinions about the action and characters which differ from those of the author. Much less common than omniscient, third person, and first person is the "second person" point of view, wherein the author tells the story as if it is happening to the reader. James Thurber employs the omniscient point of view in his short story "The Secret Life of Walter Mitty." Ernest Hemingway's "A Clean, Well-Lighted Place" is a short story told from the third person point of view. Mark Twain's novel *Huckleberry Finn* is presented from the first person viewpoint. Jay McInerney's *Bright Lights, Big City* is an example of a novel which uses the second person point of view.

Pornography: Writing intended to provoke feelings of lust in the reader. Such works are often condemned by critics and teachers, but those which can be shown to have literary value are viewed less harshly. Literary works that have been described as pornographic include D. H. Lawrence's *Lady Chatterley's Lover* and James Joyce's *Ulysses.*

Post-Aesthetic Movement: An artistic response made by African Americans to the black aesthetic movement of the 1960s and early 1970s. Writers since that time have adopted a somewhat different tone in their work, with less emphasis placed on the disparity between black and white in the United States. In the words of post-aesthetic authors such as Toni Morrison, John Edgar Wideman, and Kristin Hunter, African Americans are portrayed as looking inward for answers to their own questions, rather than always looking to the outside world. Two well-known examples of works produced as part of the post-aesthetic movement are the Pulitzer Prize-winning novels *The Color Purple* by Alice Walker and *Beloved* by Toni Morrison.

Postmodernism: Writing from the 1960s forward characterized by experimentation and application of modernist elements, which include existentialism and alienation. Postmodernists have gone a step further in the rejection of tradition begun with the modernists by also rejecting traditional forms, preferring the anti-novel over the novel and the anti-hero over the hero. Postmodern writers include Thomas Pynchon, Margaret Drabble, and Gabriel Garcia Marquez.

Prologue: An introductory section of a literary work. It often contains information establishing the situation of the characters or presents information about the setting, time period, or action. In drama, the prologue is spoken by a chorus or by one of the principal characters.

Prose: A literary medium that attempts to mirror the language of everyday speech. It is distinguished from poetry by its use of unmetered, unrhymed language consisting of logically related sentences. Prose is usually grouped into paragraphs that form a cohesive whole such as an essay or a novel. The term is sometimes used to mean an author's general writing.

Protagonist: The central character of a story who serves as a focus for its themes and incidents and as the principal rationale for its development. The protagonist is sometimes referred to in discussions of modern literature as the hero or anti-hero. Well-known protagonists are Hamlet in William Shakespeare's *Hamlet* and Jay Gatsby in F. Scott Fitzgerald's *The Great Gatsby.*

R

Realism: A nineteenth-century European literary movement that sought to portray familiar characters, situations, and settings in a realistic manner. This was done primarily by using an objective narrative point of view and through the buildup of accurate detail. The standard for success of any realistic work depends on how faithfully it transfers common experience into fictional forms. The realistic method may be altered or extended, as in stream of consciousness writing, to record highly subjective experience. Contemporary authors who often write in a realistic way include Nadine Gordimer and Grace Paley.

Resolution: The portion of a story following the climax, in which the conflict is resolved. The resolution of Jane Austen's *Northanger Abbey* is neatly summed up in the following sentence: "Henry and Catherine were married, the bells rang and everybody smiled."

Rising Action: The part of a drama where the plot becomes increasingly complicated. Rising action leads up to the climax, or turning point, of a drama. The final "chase scene" of an action film is generally the rising action which culminates in the film's climax.

Roman a clef: A French phrase meaning "novel with a key." It refers to a narrative in which real persons are portrayed under fictitious names. Jack Kerouac, for example, portrayed various his friends under fictitious names in the novel *On the Road.* D. H. Lawrence based "The Rocking-Horse Winner" on a family he knew.

Romanticism: This term has two widely accepted meanings. In historical criticism, it refers to a European intellectual and artistic movement of the late eighteenth and early nineteenth centuries that sought greater freedom of personal expression than that allowed by the strict rules of literary form and logic of the eighteenth-century neoclassicists. The Romantics preferred emotional and imaginative expression to rational analysis. They considered the individual to be at the center of all experience and so placed him or her at the center of their art. The Romantics believed that the creative imagination reveals nobler truths—unique feelings and attitudes—than those that could be discovered by logic or by scientific examination. "Romanticism" is also used as a general term to refer to a type of sensibility found in all periods of literary history and usually considered to be in opposition to the principles of classicism. In this sense, Romanticism signifies any work or philosophy in which the exotic or dreamlike figure strongly, or that is devoted to individualistic expression, self-analysis, or a pursuit of a higher realm of knowledge than can be discovered by human reason. Prominent Romantics include Jean-Jacques Rousseau, William Wordsworth, John Keats, Lord Byron, and Johann Wolfgang von Goethe.

S

Satire: A work that uses ridicule, humor, and wit to criticize and provoke change in human nature and institutions. Voltaire's novella *Candide* and Jonathan Swift's essay ''A Modest Proposal'' are both satires. Flannery O'Connor's portrayal of the family in ''A Good Man Is Hard to Find'' is a satire of a modern, Southern, American family.

Science Fiction: A type of narrative based upon real or imagined scientific theories and technology. Science fiction is often peopled with alien creatures and set on other planets or in different dimensions. Popular writers of science fiction are Isaac Asimov, Karel Capek, Ray Bradbury, and Ursula K. Le Guin.

Setting: The time, place, and culture in which the action of a narrative takes place. The elements of setting may include geographic location, characters's physical and mental environments, prevailing cultural attitudes, or the historical time in which the action takes place.

Short Story: A fictional prose narrative shorter and more focused than a novella. The short story usually deals with a single episode and often a single character. The ''tone,'' the author's attitude toward his or her subject and audience, is uniform throughout. The short story frequently also lacks *denouement*, ending instead at its climax.

Signifying Monkey: A popular trickster figure in black folklore, with hundreds of tales about this character documented since the 19th century. Henry Louis Gates Jr. examines the history of the signifying monkey in *The Signifying Monkey: Towards a Theory of Afro-American Literary Criticism,* published in 1988.

Simile: A comparison, usually using ''like'' or ''as,''of two essentially dissimilar things, as in ''coffee as cold as ice'' or ''He sounded like a broken record.'' The title of Ernest Hemingway's ''Hills Like White Elephants'' contains a simile.

Social Realism: The Socialist Realism school of literary theory was proposed by Maxim Gorky and established as a dogma by the first Soviet Congress of Writers. It demanded adherence to a communist worldview in works of literature. Its doctrines required an objective viewpoint comprehensible to the working classes and themes of social struggle featuring strong proletarian heroes. Gabriel Garcia Marquez's stories exhibit some characteristics of Socialist Realism.

Stereotype: A stereotype was originally the name for a duplication made during the printing process; this led to its modern definition as a person or thing that is (or is assumed to be) the same as all others of its type. Common stereotypical characters include the absent-minded professor, the nagging wife, the troublemaking teenager, and the kind-hearted grandmother.

Stream of Consciousness: A narrative technique for rendering the inward experience of a character. This technique is designed to give the impression of an ever-changing series of thoughts, emotions, images, and memories in the spontaneous and seemingly illogical order that they occur in life. The textbook example of stream of consciousness is the last section of James Joyce's *Ulysses.*

Structure: The form taken by a piece of literature. The structure may be made obvious for ease of understanding, as in nonfiction works, or may be obscured for artistic purposes, as in some poetry or seemingly ''unstructured'' prose.

Style: A writer's distinctive manner of arranging words to suit his or her ideas and purpose in writing. The unique imprint of the author's personality upon his or her writing, style is the product of an author's way of arranging ideas and his or her use of diction, different sentence structures, rhythm, figures of speech, rhetorical principles, and other elements of composition.

Suspense: A literary device in which the author maintains the audience's attention through the buildup of events, the outcome of which will soon be revealed. Suspense in William Shakespeare's *Hamlet* is sustained throughout by the question of whether or not the Prince will achieve what he has been instructed to do and of what he intends to do.

Symbol: Something that suggests or stands for something else without losing its original identity. In literature, symbols combine their literal meaning with the suggestion of an abstract concept. Literary symbols are of two types: those that carry complex associations of meaning no matter what their contexts, and those that derive their suggestive meaning from their functions in specific literary works. Examples of symbols are sunshine suggesting happiness, rain suggesting sorrow, and storm clouds suggesting despair.

T

Tale: A story told by a narrator with a simple plot and little character development. Tales are usually relatively short and often carry a simple message. Examples of tales can be found in the works of Saki, Anton Chekhov, Guy de Maupassant, and O. Henry.

Tall Tale: A humorous tale told in a straightforward, credible tone but relating absolutely impossible events or feats of the characters. Such tales were commonly told of frontier adventures during the settlement of the west in the United States. Literary use of tall tales can be found in Washington Irving's *History of New York,* Mark Twain's *Life on the Mississippi,* and in the German R. F. Raspe's *Baron Munchausen's Narratives of His Marvellous Travels and Campaigns in Russia.*

Theme: The main point of a work of literature. The term is used interchangeably with thesis. Many works have multiple themes. One of the themes of Nathaniel Hawthorne's ''Young Goodman Brown'' is loss of faith.

Tone: The author's attitude toward his or her audience may be deduced from the tone of the work. A formal tone may create distance or convey politeness, while an informal tone may encourage a friendly, intimate, or intrusive feeling in the reader. The author's attitude toward his or her subject matter may also be deduced from the tone of the words he or she uses in discussing it. The tone of John F. Kennedy's speech which included the appeal to ''ask not what your country can do for you'' was intended to instill feelings of camaraderie and national pride in listeners.

Tragedy: A drama in prose or poetry about a noble, courageous hero of excellent character who, because of some tragic character flaw, brings ruin upon him- or herself. Tragedy treats its subjects in a dignified and serious manner, using poetic language to help evoke pity and fear and bring about catharsis, a purging of these emotions. The tragic form was practiced extensively by the ancient Greeks. The classical form of tragedy was revived in the sixteenth century; it flourished especially on the Elizabethan stage. In modern times, dramatists have attempted to adapt the form to the needs of modern society by drawing their heroes from the ranks of ordinary men and women and defining the nobility of these heroes in terms of spirit rather than exalted social standing. Some contemporary works that are thought of as tragedies include *The Great Gatsby* by F. Scott Fitzgerald, and *The Sound and the Fury* by William Faulkner.

Tragic Flaw: In a tragedy, the quality within the hero or heroine which leads to his or her downfall. Examples of the tragic flaw include Othello's jealousy and Hamlet's indecisiveness, although most great tragedies defy such simple interpretation.

U

Utopia: A fictional perfect place, such as ''paradise'' or ''heaven.'' An early literary utopia was described in Plato's *Republic,* and in modern literature, Ursula K. Le Guin depicts a utopia in ''The Ones Who Walk Away from Omelas.''

V

Victorian: Refers broadly to the reign of Queen Victoria of England (1837–1901) and to anything with qualities typical of that era. For example, the qualities of smug narrow-mindedness, bourgeois materialism, faith in social progress, and priggish morality are often considered Victorian. In literature, the Victorian Period was the great age of the English novel, and the latter part of the era saw the rise of movements such as decadence and symbolism.

Cumulative Author/Title Index

Nationality/Ethnicity Index

Subject/Theme Index